Free Trade and Prosperity

How Openness Helps Developing Countries Grow Richer and Combat Poverty

ARVIND PANAGARIYA

OXFORD
UNIVERSITY PRESS

OXFORD
UNIVERSITY PRESS

Oxford University Press is a department of the University of Oxford. It furthers
the University's objective of excellence in research, scholarship, and education
by publishing worldwide. Oxford is a registered trade mark of Oxford University
Press in the UK and certain other countries.

Published in the United States of America by Oxford University Press
198 Madison Avenue, New York, NY 10016, United States of America.

© Oxford University Press 2019

Library of Congress Cataloging-in-Publication Data
Names: Panagariya, Arvind, author.
Title: Free trade and prosperity : how openness helps developing countries grow richer
and combat poverty / Arvind Panagariya.
Description: New York, NY : Oxford University Press, [2019] |
Includes bibliographical references and index.
Identifiers: LCCN 2018026679 (print) | LCCN 2018028942 (ebook) |
ISBN 9780190914509 (UPDF) | ISBN 9780190914516 (EPUB) |
ISBN 9780190914493 (hardcover : alk. paper)
Subjects: LCSH: Free trade—Developing countries. | Economic development—Developing countries.
Classification: LCC HF2580.9 (ebook) | LCC HF2580.9.P359 2019 (print) |
DDC 382/.71091724—dc23
LC record available at https://lccn.loc.gov/2018026679

1 3 5 7 9 8 6 4 2

Printed by Sheridan Books, Inc., United States of America

To
Jagdish Bhagwati,
the world's foremost living advocate of free trade,
a true intellectual,
and
a friend and mentor for life

CONTENTS

BACKGROUND AND ACKNOWLEDGMENTS

This book has been written over a period of almost a decade. I began working on it soon after the publication of *India: The Emerging Giant* in 2008, but the work on it was interrupted by two major projects. In 2010 I launched the Columbia Program on Indian Economic Policies, which occupied my attention nearly exclusively for the following three to four years. Research conducted as a part of this program was published in four volumes under the series Studies in Indian Economic Policies by Oxford University Press, New York. In addition, I wrote *Why Growth Matters* with Jagdish Bhagwati.

After the publication of this last book in 2013, I devoted much of my time to completing the present book. I made substantial progress, but in January 2015 work on the volume was interrupted yet again. Prime Minister Narendra Modi, who had come to the helm in May 2014, asked me to join his government as the vice chairman of the newly created National Institution for Transforming India, or NITI Aayog, which he had established to succeed the erstwhile Planning Commission. With the prime minister himself serving as the chairman of the institution and the position carrying the rank of a cabinet minister, this was a great honor, and I readily accepted the invitation. I joined NITI Aayog on January 13, 2015, and served there until August 31, 2017, after which I returned to Columbia. That finally permitted me to return to the book full-time. The result is in your hands.

Intellectually, my greatest debt remains to Jagdish Bhagwati, to whom I am very pleased to be able to dedicate this book. His writings have deeply influenced my thinking on nearly all important subjects but especially trade policy. Additionally, almost-daily phone conversations with him on wide-ranging subjects have been a great source of inspiration throughout my professional life.

Alan Deardorff and Douglas Irwin carefully read the manuscript and provided chapter-by-chapter comments, which I have endeavored to incorporate into this final version. I am deeply grateful to Alan and Doug for their generosity.

I also wish to thank Lee Branstetter, Judith Dean, and Mary Lovely for their valuable comments on different chapters. Exchanges with Pravin Krishna, Devashish Mitra, and Larry Westphal on some key issue were most helpful in clarifying my thinking. My thanks also go to Atisha Kumar, who provided comments on Chapter 3, on infant industry, and to Senthil Nathan for help on Chapter 13, on China.

In a somewhat unusual experience for me, David Pervin, my OUP editor, carefully read the penultimate draft of the book and offered numerous suggestions on both content and style. As a result, this final version of the volume is greatly improved.

As always, the encouragement and support of my wife, Amita, throughout the ten years that I have taken to complete the volume have been pivotal. Had she not freed me from many tasks and worries, I would still be far away from getting this volume out the door.

PREFACE

In his masterly work *Economic Sophisms* (1845), Frédéric Bastiat systematically exposes the myths surrounding free trade in his time. In the preface to the book, he points out that the "opposition to free trade rests upon errors, or, if you prefer, upon *half-truths*." He goes on to state that the task facing proponents of free trade is inherently more difficult than that of opponents because the benefits of protection concentrate in the sectors that get protected and are therefore easily identified. Costs of protection, on the other hand, are spread throughout the economy and therefore remain hidden. This gives the opponents a great deal of advantage over the proponents. In the words of Bastiat himself:

> But, it may be asked, are the benefits of freedom so well hidden that they are evident only to professional economists?
>
> Yes, we must admit that our opponents in this argument have a marked advantage over us. They need only a few words to set forth a half-truth; whereas, in order to show that it is a half-truth, we have to resort to long and arid dissertations.
>
> This situation is due to the nature of things. Protection concentrates at a single point the good that it does, while the harm that it inflicts is diffused over a wide area. The good is apparent to the outer eye; the harm reveals itself only to the inner eye of the mind.

Remarkably, 170 years after Bastiat published that work, the uneven terms of engagement between the proponents and opponents of free trade remain unchanged. Indeed, with many questions today turning empirical in nature, the asymmetry has become more pronounced. Accordingly, in assessing the impact of trade openness on growth and poverty alleviation, the subject of this volume, the proponents of free trade must provide watertight evidence of freer trade having a causal effect on growth and poverty alleviation. In contrast, the opponents have only to point out a few flaws in the underlying data and methodology to raise doubts about the evidence, thereby allowing them to deny the connection and claim victory. Whereas the proponents are held to the highest standard of proof that the latest techniques permit, opponents get away with offering fragmented evidence that free trade causes damage to production and dislocates workers, evidence that can be readily found in the liberalized sectors. When it comes to explaining success stories such as those of South Korea, Taiwan, and China, all the opponents offer is the argument that these economies have not followed the neoclassical model in its strict form, have deployed domestic policy instruments to target certain sectors, or have succeeded only because they chose to open the economy partially instead of adopting full free trade. In a nutshell, if the proponents of free trade do not provide conclusive and incontrovertible evidence that causally links free trade to increased incomes, faster growth, and low poverty ratios, victory belongs to the critics.

To appreciate the asymmetry, suppose for a moment that we were to ask the opponents to provide evidence causally linking high and rising protection to faster growth and declining poverty ratios. Will they be up to the task? Not by a long shot. Indeed, deep down, the opponents know that systematic evidence connecting high or increased protection to superior growth and poverty outcomes cannot be found, and that is the reason they have never looked for it. I know of no serious econometric study that even attempts to find such a link.

Much has been written in defense of free trade, especially since the publication of *The Wealth of Nations* by Adam Smith in 1776. Smith provided the first systematic critique of the mercantilists' case for protection and made a coherent case for free trade as the means to maximizing a nation's wealth. Subsequently, Bastiat and Henry George provided two witty book-length critiques of pro-protection arguments that continued to have currency throughout the nineteenth century. Among modern writers, Douglas Irwin has offered a comprehensive defense of free trade covering both theoretical arguments and empirical evidence.

But nearly all book-length defenses of free trade have taken developed countries as their context. While the arguments made for the developed countries generally apply to the developing countries as well, the context matters. For instance, infant industry protection is essentially relevant to the developing countries today. Catalyzing and sustaining growth at near-double-digit rates is an issue that arises largely in the context of the developing countries. And whereas the income distribution effects of trade carry greater relevance in the developed country context, it is the impact of trade openness on poverty that is of greater importance in the developing countries.

Much research has been done during the last several decades on the role of trade in determining economic outcomes in the developing countries. The issue of whether the countries that achieved near-double-digit growth during the 1960s and 1970s owed their success to outward-oriented policies or to cleverly designed industrial policies, including infant industry protection, has been widely researched and hotly debated. The question of whether the developing countries that performed poorly during the 1980s did so because they exposed themselves to the vagaries of open trade without putting proper safeguards in place has also been a subject of controversy. Nevertheless, even after the passage of seventy years since the developing countries first embarked upon their development journey, we lack a unified, coherent, and full-scale defense of pro-free-trade policies with these countries at its center. This is the glaring gap in the literature that the present volume proposes to fill.

In the 1970s and 1980s, several multivolume studies, sponsored by such institutions as the Organisation for Economic Co-operation and Development (OECD), the National Bureau of Economic Research (NBER), and the World Bank, had systematically analyzed the development experiences of many countries, with trade policy as an important focus. These studies brought leading scholars of international trade such as Bela Balassa, Jagdish Bhagwati, Anne Kruger, and Ian Little to apply their talents to the study of trade and development. They gathered the available evidence and carried out in-depth analyses to tease out the implications of outward orientation for growth and prosperity.

Subsequently, however, serious challenges to the case they made arose from economists Ha-Joon Chang, Erik Reinert, Dani Rodrik, and Joseph Stiglitz and political scientists Alice Amsden and Robert Wade. But no full-scale, focused response to these and other critics has been mounted to date. Books defending globalization, such as those by Jagdish Bhagwati and Martin Wolf, have appeared in recent times, but because their subject matter is much wider, they do not go into the detailed evidence on how free trade has helped developing countries grow faster and conquer poverty.

This absence of a systematic attempt at revisiting the case for free trade is ironic for two reasons. First, it is precisely during the decades following the publication of the OECD, NBER, and World Bank studies that a vast number of people in the developing world have reaped the benefits of more liberal trade policies. Two Asian giants—China and India—that had been autarkic during the first three decades of their development programs have gone on to adopt more liberal trade policies, with rather happy outcomes for their citizens. Equally, many other countries, including several in Africa and Latin America for which significant improvement in living standards had seemed unachievable, have come to reap the benefits of freer trade.

The second reason the absence of a full-scale defense of free trade in recent decades is ironic is that during these decades, a number of trade and development scholars have come to apply their empirical skills to large data sets to establish the causation between trade openness, on one hand, and growth and poverty alleviation, on the other. While this literature is now too vast to be covered exhaustively in this book, parts that directly bear on the issues central to it do need to be brought to the attention of a wider audience.

Two further points are worth making. First, even if we limit the scope of the book to the developing countries, liberal trade policies are criticized on far too many grounds, such as decimation of local industry, enhanced poverty, rise in inequality, environmental degradation, proliferation of child labor, running down of labor standards, gender inequality, and much more, for us to deal with here. While I have elsewhere written about some of these issues, in this volume I have restricted myself to the impact of free trade on growth, poverty, and, occasionally, inequality.

Second, while this book addresses and counters the arguments made by the opponents of free trade, I have no expectation that it will change their minds. My hope instead is that it will help those with an open mind to better assess the pros and cons of freeing up trade in the developing countries. In the end, each of us must draw our own conclusions, though such conclusions are more likely to be sound if they are informed by systematic analysis and evidence rather than based on half-truths.

Free Trade and Prosperity

Setting the Stage

No nation was ever ruined by trade, even seemingly the most
disadvantageous one.

—Benjamin Franklin, 1774

Immediately following the Second World War, there was consensus that trade liberalization would help speed up the reconstruction and recovery of war-torn European economies while also helping North America grow faster. Ironically, there was also consensus that trade would not serve well the cause of economic development in the emerging independent Third World countries. Consequently, whereas both intellectuals and policymakers rallied behind the efforts to liberalize trade among Western industrial countries under the auspices of the General Agreement on Tariffs and Trade, they simultaneously blessed without qualification indiscriminate trade barriers and import substitution in Third World countries, which today we call "developing countries."

It so happened, however, that the British had maintained their colony Hong Kong as a free port with no tariffs or other trade barriers since its acquisition in the early 1840s. Additionally, in the late 1950s and early 1960s, farsighted political leadership in three East Asian nations—Taiwan, Singapore, and South Korea—recognized that import substitution in labor-intensive products in which they enjoyed comparative advantage had been largely exhausted. Their options were to either continue with import substitution by moving into progressively more capital-intensive products or, discarding the conventional wisdom, switch to greater reliance on exports, which would permit them to expand further the production of labor-intensive products in which they enjoyed comparative advantage but had exhausted the scope for import substitution. They chose the latter.

The results of the turn to this outward-oriented strategy were spectacular. Taking advantage of the vast global markets, these three countries managed to grow at rates of 8 to 10 percent on a sustained basis, a feat never before accomplished in human history. Alongside them, Hong Kong continued to flourish under its free trade regime. The four "Asian tigers," or newly industrialized economies (NIEs), as they eventually came to be called, achieved in three decades the kind of prosperity that Western industrial economies had taken a century or longer to achieve.

By contrast, the two largest countries of the world by population, China and India, remained staunchly wedded to protectionist, even near-isolationist, trade policies. The entire effort of these countries was geared toward replacing more and more imports by domestic production, with the state playing a direct and dominant role in the production activity. Both countries performed poorly economically, with their per capita incomes becoming a small fraction of those of the four tiger economies by 1980. Lack of sustained rapid growth was also the fate of other developing countries in Asia, Africa, and Latin America that broadly followed the path of industrialization through import substitution.

The success of the East Asian tiger economies and the relatively poor performance of many other developing countries that remained wedded to import substitution led numerous economists to reassess their views. Large-scale multicountry studies conducted in the 1970s eventually replaced the existing conventional wisdom, which promoted industrialization through import substitution, with one that saw outward orientation as the key to growth and development.

Armed with this new conventional wisdom, in the 1980s the International Monetary Fund (IMF) and the World Bank aggressively used their considerable financial resources to induce debt-ridden developing countries, especially in Africa and Latin America, to rapidly drop protection against imports. In a large number of countries, the local leadership saw this liberalization as having been externally imposed under fiscal stress, and therefore they either subverted the recommendation of the IMF and the World Bank at the implementation level or eventually reversed liberalization once the crisis situation had been overcome.[1] The recommendation generally failed to produce the promised results.

Alongside these developments, influential authors began to reinterpret the success of the East Asian tigers as the result of clever industrial policies by their governments. They contended that well-calibrated interventions targeting specific sectors, infant industry protection, and coordination of interrelated investment activities by governments were behind the success of these countries. This revisionist view went some distance toward complementing the hostility to trade liberalization that had accompanied the failure of IMF- and World Bank–led trade liberalization to produce recovery in Africa and Latin America during the 1980s.

Notwithstanding the economic failures during the 1980s and the revisionist critique, during the 1990s country after country in the developing world went on to embrace outward-oriented policies. In part this happened because the Uruguay Round of trade negotiations brought the developing countries into the center of multilateral trade talks. Breaking from past practice, the developed countries insisted in this round of negotiations that the developing countries too must undertake liberalization obligations if they wished to maintain access to developed-country markets on a nondiscriminatory basis.

But this was not the only factor at work. At least three additional developments led the developing countries themselves to come to the view that trade openness was good for them. First, the Soviet Union, which once had been seen as embodying the success of autarkic policies, saw a steady decline of its economy throughout the 1980s and finally collapsed spectacularly in 1991. Second, China, which had voluntarily, rather than under pressure from the IMF and the World Bank, adopted outward-oriented policies beginning in the late 1970s, saw its economy grow at double-digit rates during the 1980s. Finally, countries such as India also came to appreciate that decades of efforts at import substitution had delivered outcomes far poorer than what the NIEs had been able to achieve through outward orientation.

This change of mind meant that developing countries' leaders came to own these policies of liberalization. Furthermore, in numerous cases liberalization was supported by complementary policies that helped translate openness into faster growth. Today the developing world is far more open to trade and foreign investment than at any other time in post–Second World War history.

Nonetheless, with the threat of protectionism constantly lurking in the background, those with a stake in greater prosperity for the developing countries can ill afford to be complacent. Left-leaning intellectuals, including many economists, staff at nongovernmental organizations (NGOs), and journalists, rarely pass up the opportunity to blame any country's economic failure on "neoliberal" prescriptions, foremost among them liberal trade. Moreover, thanks to the liberalization that has already taken place, the share of imports in gross domestic product (GDP) has risen substantially in recent decades in nearly all developing countries. As a result, the scope for import substitution is once again quite large. As the brilliant French economist Frédéric Bastiat reminded us 170 years ago, the expansion of industry that receives import protection is visible to all, but the damage from such protection, which is spread throughout the economy, is not.[2] As a result, import substitution remains a tempting target for politicians keen on demonstrating the successes of their policies to an unsuspecting electorate.

If outward-oriented policies are to be sustained in the developing countries, it is important that their benefits and the damage done by protection are exposed in ways that allow the public at large to see them. During the last two centuries, many volumes advocating the case for free trade and exposing the fallacies underlying the arguments by protectionists in the context of the developed countries have appeared.[3] But it is remarkable that despite the passage of seventy years since the former colonies began winning independence, a similar volume devoted to a systematic defense of openness in the context of the developing countries has been lacking. While vast amounts of research have been done on the importance of pro-free-trade policies in the developing countries, a full-throated and focused defense of trade openness as applied to the developing countries has not been attempted to date. It is this glaring gap that the present volume aims to fill.

During the past two decades, skeptics have written extensive critiques of outward-oriented policies and extolled the benefits of industrial policies reinforced by import substitution. I make an effort to systematically analyze their arguments and point out the logical flaws in them. Among other things, building on the seminal work of economist Robert Baldwin, published half a century ago, I pinpoint the conceptual flaws in arguments advocating infant industry protection. I also explain why a logical case for infant industry protection cannot be made, just as Baldwin concluded.[4]

I go on to argue that the one-time benefits of freeing up trade, though worthwhile, are insufficient to overcome political hurdles to the removal of protectionist policies in the developing countries. Instead, under most circumstances, the ability of economists and policy analysts to convince policymakers to adopt and sustain outward-oriented policies depends on establishing a link between these policies, on the one hand, and growth and poverty alleviation, on the other. A large part of the book is devoted to examining this link. This is done at both the aggregate level and the individual-country level. I present voluminous evidence showing that whenever countries have seen sustained rapid growth, low or declining barriers to trade and a high or rising share of trade in GDP have accompanied it. At the aggregate, cross-country level, we now have persuasive evidence causally connecting trade to per capita income. Individual country experiences reinforce this evidence.

The remainder of this chapter is organized as follows. In the first section, I briefly discuss the contrasting experiences of South Korea and India to set the tone for the book. In the second section, I explain how the study of these and other contrasting experiences led to a switch in the conventional wisdom on trade policy for the developing countries from import substitution to an outward orientation. In the third section, I briefly introduce the revisionist critique of the new conventional wisdom. In the fourth section, I address the common allegation that advocates of free trade are motivated by ideological impulses instead of by logical arguments and evidence. In the final section, I provide an outline of the book.

India and South Korea: An Elephant and a Tiger

In the 1950s, the official view in the United States was that while countries such as India would rapidly grow out of poverty, there was a big question mark about countries in the Far East. The prospect of South Korea turning into a basket case was seen as realistic. In a speech delivered on October 4, 2004, to African governors of the IMF, economist Anne O. Krueger, who at the time was the IMF's first deputy managing director, described the South Korea of the late 1950s in these terms:

> Picture a poor, largely rural peasant economy, almost wholly lacking in natural resources. So poor, in fact, that this economy is crucially dependent on foreign aid transfers—amounting to more than 10% of GDP. It is so poor and so dependent on outside help that some economists doubt it is a viable economy without those large aid inflows. It has the highest density of people on arable land anywhere in the world; the highest rate of inflation in the world; and its exports are 3% of GDP, 88% of which are primary commodities. . . . And I am not exaggerating the situation. There was genuine alarm [among South Koreans] when it became clear that the United States had decided to scale down the financial assistance it was providing Korea, on the grounds that Korea would not grow, so only providing support to maintain very low consumption levels was appropriate.[5]

In contrast, the United States had been favorably inclined toward India as it kicked off its development program in the early 1950s, largely because India was a democracy and Prime Minister Jawaharlal Nehru was a charismatic leader who commanded wide respect. The recognition that India was experimenting with economic and political ideas that were widely shared in the West led U.S. scholars throughout the 1950s and early 1960s to champion India as the model from which lessons would be gleaned for other developing countries.

Yet by the early 1970s, the tables had turned. India lost its shine, and a wide gulf in relations appeared between it and the United States. The first major failure came in agriculture, with the country's food grain production failing to keep pace with its rapidly rising population. Between 1961 and 1964, India had to import 25 million tons of food grain. Then followed two back-to-back droughts in 1965 and 1966, during which 19 million tons of food grain had to be imported. The United States provided a large part of this food grain via its aid program under Public Law 480. Seeking to leverage the aid in order to get India to change its policies, President Lyndon Johnson kept the country on what he himself called "ship-to-mouth" existence.[6] In turn, this produced outrage in India toward the United States.

As the years went on, India's general economic failure became further apparent. The country turned progressively inward, with its imports-to-GDP ratio declining from a peak of nearly 10 percent in the 1950s to below 5 percent in the early 1970s. This decline cut off Indian manufacturing firms from access to high-quality inputs and the latest technology, which is often embedded in imported machinery. That resulted in poor-quality products, for which there were few takers in the export markets. Poor export performance in turn reinforced the need for import controls. The vicious circle of import restrictions leading to poor export performance and poor export performance necessitating import controls was thus complete. Efficiency and productivity growth suffered.

Prime Minister Indira Gandhi, who came to office in 1966 and ruled until 1984, with a short break from 1977 to 1980, repeatedly called for the elimination of poverty, but little progress was achieved. In what was perhaps the first comprehensive study of poverty in the developing countries, economist Gary Fields described the state of poverty in India in the late 1970s in these stark terms:

> India is a miserably poor country. Per-capita yearly income is under $100. Of the Indian people, 45 percent receive incomes below $50 per year and 90 percent below $150. . . . India's poverty problem is so acute and her resources so limited that it is debatable whether any internal policy change short of a major administrative overhaul and radical redirection of effort might be expected to improve things substantially.[7]

In contrast to India, South Korea, which had been predicted to have no realistic prospects of economic growth in the 1950s, shot up like a rocket beginning in the early 1960s. In the 1950s and early 1960s, both India and South Korea had grown approximately 4 percent per year. In the 1950s, both had pursued import substitution. But, unlike India, South Korea began to shift toward an export-oriented policy in the late 1950s and early 1960s. Rather than go deeper into import substitution in products in which it lacked comparative advantage, it chose to expand the output of labor-intensive products in which it had comparative advantage and sell them in the export markets. This approach allowed it to benefit from scale economies, competition in the global marketplace, and access to high-quality inputs and the latest technologies. During the years that followed, its performance turned out to be dramatically different from India's.

The contrasting strategies of India and South Korea produced contrasting outcomes. Whereas India's trade expansion could barely keep pace with its abysmal growth in GDP, that of South Korea exploded. Exports of goods and services as a proportion of GDP in South Korea rose from a paltry 4.6 percent in 1963 to a hefty 28.7 percent in 1973. Over the same period, the ratio fell from

4.5 percent to just 4.0 percent in India. Import performance exhibited the same contrast. Imports of goods and services as a proportion of GDP in South Korea rose from 15.7 percent in 1960 to 31.8 percent in 1973. In India, the ratio fell from 6 percent in 1963 to 4.7 percent in 1973.

The differences in the performance in trade were mirrored in the differences in GDP growth. In the period 1963–73, South Korea registered an impressive growth rate of 9.5 percent. During the same period, India grew barely 3.4 percent annually. The proportion of the population living below the poverty line remained unchanged in India, with the absolute number of poor growing on account of increased population. In contrast, poverty fell dramatically in South Korea.

At a personal level, in 1974 I came to Princeton University to do my doctorate in economics. Studies of the success of the East Asian tigers had just begun to emerge at the time, and so there was at best limited awareness of the success of these countries in India. Indeed, even scholars and teachers who may have known about it were probably unwilling to give the countries due credit or admit that India had much to learn from their experience. Until as late as the end of the 1980s, most Indian scholars and policymakers could be heard arguing that these countries were too small to be relevant to a populous country such as India.

Therefore, my first effective introduction to the dramatic difference between the economic performances of India and South Korea took place in the supermarkets and shopping malls of the United States. On my visits to these stores, I discovered that products of daily use such as stationery, clothing, furniture, and kitchen utensils invariably came from South Korea or other Asian tiger economies. Anytime I randomly picked a product in the shops, there was a non-negligible probability that it would bear a "Made in Korea" stamp and a near-zero probability that it was imported from India. Even a careful combing of the store for items made in India yielded no results.

A Turnaround in the Conventional Wisdom

As I have already noted, South Korea was not the only developing country that broke away from the conventional wisdom of the time to achieve an unconventionally high growth rate on a sustained basis. During the years 1963–73, Taiwan and Singapore were also successful in sustaining GDP growth rates of over 10 percent. Hong Kong missed the double-digit mark by a tiny margin, growing 9.8 percent per year.[8] These countries more or less maintained this exceptional performance in the 1970s.

As more and more data on the experience of the developing countries became available, economists began to analyze these countries to better understand the sources of sustained rapid growth. The 1970s saw the publication of two large-scale cross-country studies. The first of them, conducted under the auspices of the Organisation for Economic Co-operation and Development (OECD) and summarized by project directors Ian Little, Tibor Scitovsky, and Maurice Scott, produced detailed narratives of six countries: Brazil, India, Mexico, Pakistan, Philippines, and Taiwan.[9] The second study, sponsored by the National Bureau of Economic Research (NBER) and synthesized by its co-directors, Jagdish Bhagwati and Anne Krueger, in two separate volumes, focused on the experiences of ten countries: Brazil, Chile, Colombia, Egypt, Ghana, India, Israel, Philippines, South Korea, and Turkey.[10] Complementing these large-scale studies was a study done at the World Bank. Edited by Bela Balassa, this study covered six semi-industrialized economies: Argentina, Colombia, Israel, South Korea, Singapore, and Taiwan.[11]

These studies led economists to rethink the prevailing consensus on economic development. Little, Scitovsky, and Scott noted that the conventional wisdom of the time had overemphasized industry relative to agriculture and underestimated the importance of exports as against import substitution in promoting industrialization. They reasoned that support to industry could be provided in ways that did not discourage the exports of either industrial or agricultural products. They concluded that this would "promote greater efficiency in the use of resources" and "create less unequal distribution of income and higher levels of employment in both industry and agriculture."[12]

The evidence gathered by the Bhagwati-Krueger NBER project considerably strengthened the view that outward orientation had not received the attention it deserved. The project's case study of South Korea's success, prepared by Charles Frank, Kwang Suk Kim, and Larry Westphal, offered compelling evidence in favor of the superiority of outward-oriented policies over import substitution.[13] The authors drew the following contrast between the contributions of export expansion and import substitution to South Korean growth:

> The most striking result of this analysis is the predominance of export expansion over import substitution. From 1955 to 1968, 20.2 percent of total growth was attributable directly and indirectly to export expansion, while –0.6 percent was due to import substitution. Thus, on balance, there was negative import substitution but substantial export expansion.... From 1960 to 1968, export expansion was relatively even more important, and accounted for 22.4 percent of growth compared with –1.4 percent for import substitution.
>
> Another striking conclusion to be drawn ... is that export expansion generated considerable domestic backward linkages while import substitution did not. The average contribution of export expansion for

either the 1955–68 or 1960–68 period almost doubles when indirect effects are taken into account.[14]

In parallel, reporting on the impact of inward-looking policies on growth in the NBER case study on India, Bhagwati and T. N. Srinivasan reached the conclusion that the country's "foreign trade regime led to a wasteful misallocation of investible resources among alternative industries and also accentuated the under-utilization of investment within these industries." They further found that the trade regime had undermined competition among the firms in these industries and "practically eliminated the incentive that such competition normally provides for reducing costs."[15]

The Balassa study of six semi-industrialized countries reinforced the findings of the OECD and NBER projects. It found that the incentive systems in Korea, Singapore, and Taiwan had discriminated least between nontraditional primary and manufacturing activities and between sales in export and domestic markets. The bias in favor of import substitution and against exports within the manufacturing sector was the greatest in Argentina, followed by Colombia and Israel, in that order. The first set of countries had clearly outperformed those in the second set.

By the early 1980s, the conventional wisdom among economists had shifted away from import substitution and in favor of outward orientation. This change coincided with the election of Ronald Reagan as president of the United States. Reagan, who firmly believed in free trade and markets, went on to deploy the United States' considerable influence to press the World Bank and the IMF to use their financial clout to promote free trade policies in the developing countries. Acting under U.S. pressure, these institutions considerably accelerated the use of conditionality in loans to the developing countries to coerce them into adopting liberal trade policies. They also sponsored numerous country-specific studies that broadly concluded in favor of outward-oriented policies.

With the evidence of the failure of import substitution policies accumulating, a handful of countries other than the four Asian tigers had begun to partially dismantle their protectionist policies during the second half of the 1970s. In Latin America the most notable example was Chile, which began the process in 1974, and in Asia it was China, which launched its open-door policy in December 1978.[16] Even in India, the protectionist regime had peaked by the mid-1970s, and the liberalization process got under way to a certain extent in the second half of the 1970s.[17] But the process accelerated greatly during the 1980s as the World Bank and IMF began to actively promote it. These institutions were especially successful in getting many small, crisis-ridden developing countries to liberalize.

Revisionists Strike Back

But as Paul Samuelson has famously said, fighting protectionism is like fighting a skin disease—no sooner do you cure it in one place than it appears in another. As it became increasingly accepted that outward-oriented policies promised outcomes superior to those of import substitution, critics regrouped and mounted a counterattack. Careful early work by Westphal had emphasized the importance of industrial policy and infant industry promotion in South Korea.[18] But he had always taken pains to emphasize the centrality of outward orientation to the Korean experience. In his subsequent writings, he was also cautious about drawing any sweeping lessons in favor of targeting and promoting infant industries in other developing countries.[19]

In contrast, in what were zealous attempts to resuscitate the case for protection as a means to foster rapid growth in the developing countries, political scientists Alice Amsden and Robert Wade went on to reinterpret the successful experiences of South Korea and Taiwan as the triumph of not just industrial policy but also import substitution.[20] Subsequently, economist Dani Rodrik widened the scope of those claims to include the experience of a wide spectrum of developing countries that he claimed had flourished under import substitution industrialization in the 1960s and early 1970s. He also argued that trade liberalization in Africa and Latin America in the late 1970s and beyond had met with systematic economic failure.[21] More recently, Joseph Stiglitz, Andrew Charlton, Erik Reinert, Ha-Joon Chang, and influential NGOs such as Oxfam and Christian Aid have thrown their weight against trade liberalization in the developing countries.[22]

Free Trade Advocates, Not Free Trade Ideologues

Critics of free trade policies often like to discredit proponents of free trade by labeling them as ideologues. While this characterization may fit certain individuals, the vast majority of the first-generation scholars who began to refocus attention on outward-oriented policies in preference to import substitution arrived at this position through careful study and analysis. It is often forgotten that at one time these proponents had been actually sympathetic to—even advocates of—import substitution and infant industry protection. After all, with truly rare exceptions, there were no economists prescribing pro-free-trade policies for the developing countries in the 1950s and 1960s despite the fact that most saw free trade as a worthy goal for the developed countries. Virtually all of them gave a nod to not just tariffs but also quantitative restrictions in the developing countries. This virtual consensus in favor of a positive role for protection was most likely the reason that even the General Agreement on Tariffs and Trade, signed in 1947, gave the developing countries free rein to impose quantitative restrictions and did not ask them to liberalize trade in the early negotiating rounds.

The conversion of two specific scholars, Jagdish Bhagwati and Ian Little, to a pro-free-trade view illustrates this point. After completing his studies at Cambridge and Oxford, Bhagwati returned to India in 1961. Though on-the-ground reality in India and elsewhere would gradually turn him into the world's foremost advocate of free trade, in 1961 he shared the intellectual attitudes that had shaped India's increasingly inward-looking trade policies. Motivated by those attitudes and nationalistic instincts common among Indians of his generation, upon his return to India Bhagwati was appalled by the craze for foreign products he observed among his fellow citizens. He happened to share this sentiment in a letter with Harry Johnson, his teacher and a distinguished trade economist at Cambridge who by then had moved to the University of Chicago. Johnson, a quick wit, shot back in his reply to Bhagwati that if the paper on which his letter was written was any indication of the quality of Indian products, he found the craze for foreign products by Indians quite rational.

This episode might conceivably have been a turning point in the conversion of Bhagwati into a free trade advocate. But it was not. Instead, the process was a gradual one, as illustrated by his 1970 book on India, co-authored with Padma Desai and published as a part of the OECD project mentioned earlier. For one thing, the title of the book—*India: Planning for Industrialization*—scarcely points to any ideological adherence to free trade. More substantively, a modern-day critic of free trade would likely find the trade policy recommendations in the book wholly acceptable.

The book recommends dismantling the import licensing regime and either replacing fixed exchange rates with a flexible exchange rate regime or moving to a system of competitive auctions of foreign exchange, with a small fraction of the foreign exchange reserved for high-priority sectors. The recommendations explicitly allow the use of tariffs for protection of domestic industries. In explaining what a more rational trade policy regime would have looked like, the authors note, "These arrangements [relating to the removal of import licensing and reform of the foreign exchange system] would have been consistent with protection of domestic industries, where necessary, since it would have always been open to use tariff policy for this purpose."[23] Today Bhagwati goes much further, advocating a trade policy that is significantly closer to free trade and eliminates protection aimed at import substitution.

The second example is equally dramatic. Economist Ian Little, who co-directed the OECD project, had been an active advocate of import substitution in the early 1960s. In a 1960 article on the policy choices facing India, he expressed export pessimism and a preference for import substitution in these words:

> The present pattern of exports . . . is a most unpromising basis for expansion. Any major expansion of exports could come about only if India deliberately set about producing new manufactures for exports on a large scale. This would seem to be unjustifiably risky. . . . It would be surprising if it did not turn out to be economical for her to produce something of almost everything, and surprising if international trade should ever come to more than a small fraction of national income.

In the next paragraph, he went on to explicitly defend import substitution:

> Thus, the relative attractions of import substitution are great. There is no doubt about the demand being there. One can, as it were, see what to produce. There are the obvious advantages of goodwill for domestic products, and transport costs act in favor not against them. Lower quality goods can be more easily absorbed. In short, the risks of failure are much less.[24]

As with Bhagwati, Little's thinking evolved gradually. Though his OECD study, published in 1970, questioned the old conventional wisdom, it did not entirely reject import substitution. Its main thrust was against policies that discouraged exports. From a policy perspective, it mainly advocated granting exporters a free trade regime through tariff-free availability of imported machines and raw materials. Much later, in the 1990s, he shifted to a view that favored complete free trade. In an article published five years after India launched its liberalizing reforms, he wrote:

> I believe there was in 1991, and still is, a wide consensus that the Indian Economic Model that prevailed from 1947 to 1991 did not well serve the objective of a rapid rate of growth in which all, especially the poor, would share. To put it crudely, the regime was too dirigiste and too autarkic.[25]

When he described the type of economic system toward which reforms should be directed, the first element was this: "There is virtual free trade, and freedom of foreigners to invest in India, and Indians to invest abroad."

Both Bhagwati and Little arrived at their free trade positions after long journeys through failed efforts to promote industrialization behind a protective wall.

Main Elements and the Plan of This Book

At the outset, I note that I do not claim that opening to trade will always produce prosperity. Instead, my argument throughout this book is that sustained growth and prosperity almost always require low or declining barriers to trade. To be sure, growth spurts may occur in a protected economy, but if such spurts are to translate into sustained growth, reduction in protection will be a necessary element in any policy package. To support their position, critics often point to cases when trade liberalization did not catalyze growth. But this is a non sequitur. Development is a complex process, and it is unlikely that any single policy on its own would ever suffice to produce sustained rapid growth. Careful advocates of outward-oriented policies have always recognized the importance of complementary policies.

Given the challenge to outward-oriented policies and the shortcomings of the analysis on which this challenge is based, it is important to revisit the case for trade liberalization in the developing countries. In doing so, I systematically expose the flaws underlying free trade critics' arguments for protection. I also offer the positive case for outward orientation based on the gains arising from exchange, specialization, scale economies, and technological diffusion.

I revisit in detail the empirical evidence on the impact of trade openness on growth, poverty, and inequality. I examine, for example, the common assertion by critics that the 1960s and early 1970s, which were characterized by import substitution, constituted the "golden period" of growth for the developing countries. I discuss at length the contentious issue of two-way causation between openness and growth, and the consequent difficulty of identifying the former as the cause of the latter. I further build the case that the available evidence supports the hypothesis that trade openness helps countries overcome poverty and that it has no definite relationship to inequality.

I reexamine in detail the cases of the four Asian tiger economies, especially South Korea and Taiwan, which have generated much controversy. I uncover new evidence supporting the hypothesis that trade openness was a central element in their success regardless of whether industrial policy was a positive or negative force. I offer evidence supporting the hypothesis that openness was critical to both *triggering* faster growth in these countries and *sustaining* it over substantial periods of time. And I offer a systematic critique of the arguments made by authors such as Wade, Rodrik, and Chang.

The empirical case for liberal trade policies is further reinforced by the experience of the developing countries in the years since the publication of the large-scale studies on trade openness and development and the critiques of these studies by the revisionists. Particularly important are the cases of two giant economies, China and India, where a large part of the population of the developing world resides. Because these countries have experimented with both protectionist and outward-oriented polices for substantial periods of time, they make excellent case studies. While several authors have analyzed the experiences of these countries, a thorough examination from a free trade perspective remains to be done.

Apart from these prominent cases, numerous countries spread across Asia, Africa, and Latin America provide evidence that outward-oriented policies and rapid growth go hand in hand. I provide brief case studies of these countries, which include Bangladesh, Cambodia, and Vietnam in Asia; Botswana, Uganda, Mozambique, and Tanzania in Africa; and the Dominican Republic, Peru, Chile, and Costa Rica in Latin America. There remains one intriguing case, however. Mexico liberalized trade and witnessed its trade grow rapidly in the 1990s and 2000s. Yet it has not seen this trade expansion translate into sustained rapid growth. I explain that the failure in this case can be attributed to the concentration of trade expansion in an enclave at the U.S.-Mexico border, which has at best limited interaction with the rest of the Mexican economy. This factor is reinforced by the absence of reforms of many growth-retarding domestic policies.

The book consists of fourteen chapters spread over four parts in addition to this introductory chapter. Part I is devoted to building the positive case for free trade and a critical examination of the arguments for protection offered by critics in the developing country context. Chapter 2 lays out the positive case for free trade, showing how it generates gains through efficient exchange and specialization, exploitation of economies of scale, and diffusion of technology. Chapter 3 systematically takes apart the case for infant industry protection, while Chapter 4 considers other popular arguments for protection, such as those based on coordination failure, diversification of production, and capital market imperfections.

In Part II I consider the empirical relationship of openness to growth, poverty, and inequality. I begin in Chapter 5 by critiquing a number of specious arguments questioning the importance of openness for rapid growth and poverty alleviation. In Chapter 6 I turn to a detailed examination of cross-country evidence on trade and growth. Here I bust the myth that the 1960s and early 1970s represented the golden period of growth for the developing countries. I also show that "miracles," defined as cases of sustained growth of 3 percent or more in per capita income, have nearly always occurred in an open trading environment. Symmetrically, "debacles," defined as cases of no or negative growth in per capita income, have rarely resulted from import surges. Finally, I also present econometric evidence linking trade causally to per capita income.

In Chapters 7 and 8 I address the issues of poverty and inequality, respectively, as they relate to trade. In Chapter 7 I offer an overview of the empirical evidence on the relationship between trade openness and poverty. I argue here that the bulk of the impact of trade on poverty alleviation is intermediated through growth. In Chapter 8 I turn to inequality. Here I argue that when it comes to the poor countries, the issue of poverty trumps inequality. If openness leads to a significant decline in poverty but also increases inequality in the process, it is an outcome to be welcomed over the one in which no reduction in poverty is achieved. I also summarize the empirical literature on trade and inequality. The bottom line here is that to date, no causal relationship between trade openness and inequality has been shown to exist.

Parts III and IV are devoted to detailed discussions of country case studies. Part III revisits the miracles of the 1960s and 1970s: Hong Kong and Singapore in Chapter 9, Taiwan in Chapter 10, and South Korea in Chapter 11. In Chapters 10 and 11, I challenge a number of claims made by free trade critics. For instance, I provide evidence showing that the switch to export-oriented policies was critical to catalyzing as well as sustaining rapid growth in both Taiwan and South Korea.

In Part IV I consider the more recent miracles: India in Chapter 12, China in Chapter 13, and several smaller countries in Asia, Africa, and Latin America in Chapter 14. In each success story, trade liberalization is shown to play a critical role. In Chapter 14 I also discuss the puzzling case of Mexico and explain why openness and trade expansion have not translated into sustained rapid growth in this country. In Chapter 15 I provide some concluding thoughts. Three appendixes provide technical details.

Notes

1. In this context, see Yatawara 2000.
2. Bastiat 1845.
3. Two old classics are Bastiat 1845 [1996] and George 1886 [1949]; a more recent one is Irwin 2005. In modern times, the focus has shifted to globalization, of which free trade is merely a part, albeit an important one. Several volumes on globalization have appeared during the past two decades. In particular, see the excellent volumes by Bhagwati (2004) and Wolf (2004), which also address many issues related to developing countries.
4. Baldwin 1969.
5. Krueger 2004.
6. Richard Solomon and Nigel Quinney state, "Ignoring the pleas of Agriculture Secretary Orville Freeman and Secretary of State Dean Rusk, Johnson continued to impose on India what he himself called a 'ship-to-mouth' existence" (2010, 260).
7. Fields 1980, 204.
8. Little 1979, 448–49.
9. Little, Scitovsky, and Scott 1970.
10. Bhagwati 1978; Krueger 1978.
11. Balassa 1982.
12. Little, Scitovsky, and Scott 1970, 1.
13. Frank, Kim, and Westphal 1975.

14. Frank, Kim, and Westphal 1975, 92.
15. Bhagwati and Srinivasan 1975, 191.
16. Edwards and Lederman 2002 on Chile; Panagariya 1993 for China.
17. Panagariya 2008, ch. 4.
18. Westphal 1978, 1982.
19. Westphal 1990.
20. Amsden 1989; Wade 1990.
21. Rodrik 1999.
22. Stiglitz 2002; Stiglitz and Charlton 2005; Reinert 2007; Chang 2002, 2007.
23. Bhagwati and Desai 1970, 495.
24. Little 1960, 25.
25. Little 1996a, 162.

PART I

WHY FREE TRADE MATTERS

2

The Positive Case for Trade Openness

> God did not bestow all products upon all parts of the earth, but distrib-
> uted His gifts over different regions, to the end that men might culti-
> vate a social relationship because one would have need of the help of
> another. And so He called commerce into being, that all men might be
> able to have common enjoyment of the fruits of earth, no matter where
> produced.
>
> —Libanius, fourth century

Smith provided the first systematic case for free trade in his *Wealth of Nations*, published in 1776.[1] At the time he wrote, the dominant system of political economy in Europe was what had come to be called the "mercantile system." This system occupied the center stage of policy in Europe throughout the six-teenth, seventeenth, and eighteenth centuries. It rested on the premise that the wealth of a nation was synonymous with its stock of gold. With gold as the means of payment, maximizing the difference between exports and imports maximized gold acquisition and therefore the additions to the nation's wealth. Interventionist policy prescriptions aimed at discouraging imports and encour-aging exports followed. Treating wealth as synonymous with gold stock also im-plied that international trade was a zero-sum game in which the net recipient of gold benefited while the net payer of gold lost.

In broad terms, the mercantilist system approved of policies that would discourage imports and encourage exports. Imports that were purely for con-sumption were discouraged, especially when similar goods were domestically produced. In modern terminology, this meant approval of import substitution. The mercantilist system also encouraged duty exemption on imported goods used in exports and exemption from local taxes on goods destined for foreign markets. Indeed, it went so far as to favor import subsidies on inputs used in exports, in order to encourage exports. On the export side, the mercantilist system saw export subsidies favorably and encouraged export restrictions on inputs so that the producers of final goods could buy them cheaply and generate high-value-added exports.[2]

Adam Smith's Case for Free Trade

Smith provided a unified and systematic critique of the mercantile system as he went on to expound his free trade doctrine.[3] His key innovation was to reason that a nation's wealth must be measured not by how much gold it acquires but by the value it produces annually. He then went on to build the case for free trade on the ground that the barriers to imports and stimuli to exports would lower rather than raise the value of the domestic produce. He argued that just as households specialize in what they do best and buy everything else from others, nations benefit by specializing in what they do best: "If a foreign country can supply us with a commodity cheaper than we ourselves can make it, better buy it of them with some part of the produce of our own industry employed in a way in which we have some advantage."[4]

Smith further argued that consumption was the sole goal of all production. Therefore, producer interests should be promoted only so far as they also serve the interests of consumers. This led him to further question the wisdom of import barriers: "In the restraints upon importation of all foreign commodities which can come into competition with those of our own growth or manufacture, the interest of the home consumer is evidently sacrificed to that of the producer."[5]

The focus on the interests of consumers also led Smith to take a critical view of export subsidies: "It is altogether for the benefit of the producer that bounties are granted upon the exportation of some of his production. The home consumer is obliged to pay, first, the tax which is necessary for paying the bounty, and secondly, the still greater tax which necessarily arises from the enhancement of the price of the commodity in the home market."[6]

Smith came down particularly hard on manufacturers who benefited the most from mercantilist policies of protection against imports and subsidies for exports. In view of the continued popularity of import-substitution industrialization with many free trade critics, it is instructive to quote from the final paragraph of his concluding chapter on free trade: "It cannot be very difficult to determine who have been the contrivers of this whole mercantile system; not the consumers, we may believe, whose interests have been entirely neglected; but the producers, whose interest has been so carefully attended to; and among the latter class our merchants and manufacturers have been by far the principal architects."[7]

The Gains from Specialization and Exchange

While Smith's critique administered a fatal blow to the mercantilist orthodoxy, his positive case for free trade remained incomplete. It was not clear from his discussion how a country that is able to produce every commodity at a lower cost in terms of resources (say, labor) used per unit than all its potential trading partners would gain from trade. Or, conversely, how a country with a higher per-unit resource cost of every commodity could compete with rival countries. The task of demonstrating that a country was not handicapped by benefiting from trade even when it enjoyed absolute cost advantage or suffered from absolute cost disadvantage in every single commodity fell upon David Ricardo, who pioneered the principle of comparative advantage.[8]

Ricardo provided a two-country, two-commodity example that demonstrated that the gains from trade would accrue to both countries even if one country produced both commodities at lower per-unit labor cost. He demonstrated that what mattered for trade to benefit each country was not absolute but relative cost advantage. The theory of international trade as we know it today has grown out of this demonstration by Ricardo.

The principle of comparative advantage derives from a strictly mathematical relationship between relative costs of commodities at home and abroad. As such, its validity is beyond question. Yet the logic underlying the principle is sufficiently subtle that the generations of free trade critics have fallen into the trap of arguing in contradiction of it. Paul Samuelson tells a story that illustrates the point. He writes that mathematician Stanislaw Ulam once asked him to name "one proposition in all of the social sciences which is both true and non-trivial." Samuelson notes that he could not immediately reply, but the correct response would have been the principle of comparative advantage: "That the principle is logically true need not be argued before a mathematician; that it is not trivial is attested by the thousands of important and intelligent men who have never been able to grasp the doctrine for themselves or to believe it after it was explained to them."[9]

In the interest of simplicity, consider Ricardo's argument in the context of a single country.[10] Call this country India and assume there is only one homogeneous factor of production, labor. There are two commodities, shirts and wheat, that Indian workers can potentially produce. Each worker can annually produce either one shirt or one bushel of wheat. This means that for each extra shirt the country produces, it must sacrifice one bushel of wheat, and vice versa. That is to say, the opportunity cost of a shirt is a bushel of wheat and vice versa. The question we ask is whether India should divide its workforce between the two commodities such that it produces precisely the quantities it consumes or choose to produce a different basket and then exchange it for the one it wishes to consume with the rest of the world.

As long as India has the option to buy or sell the two commodities in the world market at prices different from its opportunity costs at home—one shirt for one bushel of wheat or vice versa—it stands to benefit from specialization in one of the two commodities, selling the part of that commodity that it does not want to consume domestically to the rest of the world in return for the other commodity.

To see how, suppose one shirt exchanges (sells) for two bushels of wheat in the world market.[11] In this situation, if India shifts its production toward shirts and away from wheat, for each bushel of wheat it stops producing, it can produce one extra shirt. It can then sell this shirt for two bushels of wheat in the world market.

In effect, trade turns out to be equivalent to a technological breakthrough in the production of the import commodity, wheat. At home, India must uses two person-years of labor to produce two bushels of wheat. But with the exchange opportunities available through trade, it can use one person-year to produce one shirt and then exchange it for two bushels of wheat. It is as if the production cost of wheat fell in half from one person-year of labor per bushel to half a person-year of labor per bushel.

What if the world prices go the other way around: two shirts for one bushel of wheat? It is easy to see that India still benefits from trade, but this time by specializing in wheat and exchanging it for shirts. As it shifts production away from shirts, it obtains one extra bushel of wheat for each shirt it gives up producing domestically. It can then sell that bushel of wheat for two shirts in the world market. Domestically, India can transform each bushel of wheat into only one shirt. But internationally, it can transform it into two shirts. As long as the world price differs from one shirt for one bushel of wheat—the rate at which India can transform one product into the other domestically—strictly positive gains from trade exist. In the borderline case in which the rate of exchange in the world market coincides with the domestic rate of transformation—one bushel of wheat for one shirt—trade does not generate strictly positive gains. But it does not inflict any losses either.[12]

Gains from Factor-Endowment-Based Trade

In the Ricardian theory, the gains from trade for a country arise from differences in technology at home and abroad that give rise to differences in the rate at which one commodity can be transformed into the other in the two parts of the world. Trade allows each side to benefit by exploiting these differences in the rates of transformation.

Similar differences between the rates at which one product can be transformed into the other can arise even in the absence of international differences in technology provided the products require two or more factors of production and the relative supplies of these factors are different in the two countries. To illustrate the point, suppose there are two factors of production, labor and land, and that production technologies are such that shirts require more workers per unit of land than wheat. That is to say, the technology for shirts is labor intensive while that for wheat is land intensive. Suppose further that India has a lot more labor relative to land than the rest of the world, so it is labor abundant relative to the latter. If India and the rest of the world have the same set of technologies for shirts and wheat available to them and demand patterns between them are similar as well, India will have a cost advantage in the production of shirts, the labor-intensive commodity. It could then benefit by specializing in the production of shirts and exporting them in return for wheat.

Intuitively, with shirt production being labor intensive relative to wheat production, India being labor abundant relative to the rest of the world, and demand patterns being internationally the same, absent trade, shirts cost less in terms of wheat in India than in the rest of the world. For instance, in the absence of trade, if one shirt exchanges for one bushel of wheat in India, it would exchange for more than that—say, two bushels of wheat—in the rest of the world. India would then gain by exporting shirts for wheat to the rest of the world. That is to say, relatively labor-abundant India would benefit by exporting the labor-intensive product (shirt) in return for the land-intensive product (wheat). This is the central conclusion of the famous Heckscher-Ohlin theory of international trade: each country benefits by exporting the product that uses its relatively abundant factor more intensively and importing the product that uses its relatively scarce factor more intensively.[13]

Economies of Scale

The Ricardian and Heckscher-Ohlin theories are based on relative-cost differences between countries. In the Ricardian theory, cost differences arise from differences in technologies and in the Heckscher-Ohlin theory they result from differences in the factor endowments. In each case, relative-cost differences give rise to differences in the rates at which products exchange within regions in the absence of trade. Each country can then benefit from trade by buying abroad the product that is more expensive at home in the absence of trade.

An altogether different basis for trade arises in the presence of scale economies. When scale economies are present, per-unit costs of production decline as we expand output. This may happen either with the expansion of the individual firm or with the expansion of the industry as a whole. In the former case, indivisibilities are perhaps the most important source of declining costs. For example, the investment in machines required to produce the first aircraft is extremely large. But as the number of aircraft produced rises, machines can be used more and more fully and the cost per aircraft is progressively reduced.

Costs may also decline with the expansion of the industry instead of an individual firm. This may come about due to agglomeration economies. As the industry expands, the pool of skilled labor on which each firm can draw may grow bigger. A larger industry may also bring an increasing number of input suppliers into the area and lower the costs of input supply to each producer. A larger industry may also accelerate the pace of innovation that leads to lower per-unit costs for all producers.

Without specifying the source of scale economies, let us just focus on their implications for the gains from trade. The key point is that when production is subject to declining costs, opportunities for gainful trade arise even when there are no differences in the costs of production. Thus, for example, suppose there are two goods, automobiles and computers, both of which are produced under conditions of declining average costs. If we consider two countries that are identical in all respects, they will have the same prices and unit costs of production in both commodities in the absence of trade. Yet if we allow them to trade, each of them can specialize in one product, lower the per-unit cost of production of that product, and exchange some of it for the other product with the other country. With per-unit cost of production of each product having declined, both countries can achieve a higher living standard.

Scale economies strengthen the proposition that trade leads to beneficial outcomes. Absent trade, each country will produce each product subject to limited scale economies dictated by the size of the domestic market. This will result in high production costs of all goods subject to scale economies. Trade allows the country to exploit the larger world market.

Traditionally, this factor has been seen as particularly important for small countries such as Vietnam, Cambodia, Singapore, and Hong Kong, which can be hamstrung by the small size of the domestic market for any given commodity in the absence of trade. But the experience of China during the last two decades has shown that trade can be a powerful instrument of exploitation of scale economies even in large economies. Taking advantage of the large world market, China has successfully built massive factories for the manufacture of electronic products and office equipment. In the process, it has been able to bring down the unit costs of these products significantly. Both China and the rest of the world have benefited from this specialization. China has seen its economy grow at double-digit rates and the countries in the rest of the world have been able to purchase the products at a fraction of the cost they would have incurred had they produced them on their own.[14]

The Gains from Trade Through Increased Product and Input Variety

Traditional theories had considered the gains from trade in the context of homogeneous products. These theories saw a country exporting one type of product such as shirts and importing another type of product such as wheat. But empiricists studying the patterns of trade, especially in the post–Second World War era, observed that a significant part of the trade was in similar products. Countries exported and imported different varieties of the same product. For example, they exported one set of varieties of automobiles while importing another set of varieties of automobiles. Or they exported one set of varieties of steel in exchange for another set of varieties of steel. This came to be called two-way trade in similar products or simply trade in differentiated products. The latter terminology captures the idea that the basic product being traded is the same but has multiple varieties that are differentiated, with some varieties exported and others imported.

During the last four decades, this empirical literature has led trade economists to construct theories of trade in similar products. These new theories combine economies of scale with product variety and emphasize the gains that trade brings both by lowering costs through the exploitation of scale economies and by making a larger variety of the product available. Trade leads each country to specialize in fewer varieties than under autarky, and this specialization allows each variety to be produced on a larger scale. Further, trade makes foreign varieties available, so when both domestically supplied and foreign varieties are added, the total number of available varieties rises relative to that under autarky. Therefore, gains from trade also arise from increased product variety. Each consumer has the option to choose the variety she likes from a larger set of varieties of the product that trade makes available.[15]

When product differentiation and scale economies are combined with trade costs such as those incurred on after-sale service, the cost of even small amounts of protection can be large. This is because some of the imported varieties may be operating on small per-unit profit margins. Given that average costs depend on the scale of operation, the introduction of a tariff, which forces sales to shrink, causes the average cost to rise. With the initial per-unit profit margin small, this increase in per-unit cost leads to losses and forces the seller to withdraw entirely from the market. The withdrawal of some varieties in this manner can lead to large costs. This is in contrast to the traditional, homogeneous goods models with the usual upward-sloped supply curves in which small tariffs only lead to small reductions in imports and give rise to small deadweight losses on the margin.[16]

The variety effect can also operate through production. For example, the production of a final good may require a variety of imported inputs including machinery. This context may be particularly relevant to a small developing country, which must import the bulk of the inputs and concentrate mainly on the assembly of the final goods. If foreign suppliers of the inputs face fixed costs of marketing, even a small tariff can render the sales of some of the inputs unprofitable. This happens because there are some inputs on the margin that are barely profitable to sell in the market under consideration. The tariff reduces sales and, given scale economy, raises per-unit sales costs. For varieties with small initial profit margins, suppliers withdraw from the market altogether. Reduced variety of inputs in turn lowers productivity in the final goods production since the firms must now substitute the surviving varieties of inputs for those that disappear from the market.[17]

No country illustrates the high costs of disappearance of foreign varieties better than India during the 1960s, 1970s, and 1980s. The Ambassador and Fiat cars available in India in the 1980s were virtually identical to those introduced in the 1950s. Even bicycles available in the 1980s were of very poor quality. The same was true of garments. Apparel manufacturers had to use domestically produced fabric, and fabric manufacturers were forced to use domestically produced fiber. Unsurprisingly, Indian garments were unable to compete in the world markets, while domestic consumers were denied access to high-quality garments available elsewhere in the world. The losses in terms of both productivity and direct consumer welfare were astronomical.

Pro-Competitive Effects of Openness

We can identify three distinct channels through which pro-competitive effects work. First, we have cost reductions and quality improvements that result from "rubbing shoulders" with the best in the world and from having to satisfy the most discriminating and demanding customers. These effects have not received the attention they deserve, principally because they are empirically difficult to capture. The commonsense argument is that in the same way a country cannot produce large numbers of world-class cricket players without competing in test cricket, world-class soccer players without playing World Cup soccer, and world-class academics without being subject to competition against the best in their fields, it cannot produce world-class manufacturers without competing against world-class entrepreneurs. Having discriminating customers who demand the highest quality also forces firms to work that much harder to deliver and maintain high quality. It is simply inconceivable that China's manufacturing industry and India's information technology (IT) industry would have achieved the levels of efficiency they did without being subject to competition against the best in the world in their respective fields. In contrast, the proverbial inefficiency of Indian manufacturers three decades ago had much to do with competition being limited to domestic entrepreneurs who were all quite inefficient relative to the best in the world in their respective fields.

The second way in which pro-competitive effects obtain is when trade leads to the exit of less productive firms and paves they way for the expansion of more productive firms to fill the gap in demand. This effect has received greater attention in both the theoretical and empirical literature on international trade. The essential theoretical idea underlying these pro-competitive effects is that each industry consists of heterogeneous firms that produce different varieties of a product under scale economies and are characterized by different productivities. International trade expands the market size and allows more productive firms to expand. The expansion lowers the unit costs of production of the more productive firms due to scale economies, and forces the less productive firms to exit from the market. This outcome is consistent with a substantial body of empirical evidence showing that the firms that export exhibit higher productivity than those confined to the domestic market, and the exporters also operate on a larger scale.[18]

Finally, trade openness also serves as an antitrust policy. Due to the relatively small number of firms in many industries, markets may not be perfectly competitive in the developing countries. Freeing up trade brings foreign firms into the market and undercuts the market power of these domestic firms. The analytically simplest case of the antitrust role of free trade arises when a single firm supplies the entire market in a country that is small relative to the world market. Under autarky, this firm would behave as a monopolist, pricing the product above marginal cost and earning pure economic profits. Freeing up trade would force it to charge the world price, with its monopoly power entirely eliminated.

Technology Diffusion

New technology is often embodied in machines that a country can import. Countries that resort to import substitution in machinery by excluding imports of foreign machinery, as China and India did in the 1960s and 1970s, are left behind the technological frontier. They typically end up producing low-quality products at high costs. A closely related channel is through intermediate inputs. As previously noted, countries that allow high-quality raw materials to be imported are also able to produce high-quality final products and compete in world markets.

Both China and India failed to compete in world markets in the 1960s and 1970s partially because they were producing products such as apparel and footwear using domestically produced low-quality inputs. In contrast, the Asian tigers—Hong Kong, Singapore, South Korea, and Taiwan—allowed their exporters to freely import raw materials from abroad. It was only in the 1980s in the case of China and in the 1990s in the case of India that substantial opening up allowed them to become competitive along the quality dimension in world markets. The role played by imported inputs is most apparent in the success of India's IT industry. It is inconceivable that the software industry in India could have succeeded without delicensing and reduced duties on the imports of information technology products such as computers, peripherals, components, and software. Likewise, the telecommunications revolution in India during the 2000s would have been impossible without the imports of telecommunications equipment such as cell phones.

Trade openness also allows countries to benefit from imitation of both products and production methods innovated in the rich countries. Reverse engineering is sometimes an effective means of acquiring technology developed elsewhere. In the area of medicines, India was successful in creating a low-cost pharmaceutical industry beginning in the 1970s through reverse engineering of medicines developed elsewhere. Technology diffusion may also take place through exports. Firms that operate regularly in the export market learn from what they observe in those markets.[19]

Although econometric studies in this area remain controversial (as is usual with such studies), several authors have found a positive link between trade and technological diffusion. One study finds strong support for the hypothesis that trade leads to transfer of technology from highly industrialized countries to developing countries.[20] Another study focuses on capital goods imports by the OECD countries as the medium of technology transfer and finds the effect to be even stronger.[21] Yet another argues, however, that that the econometric evidence on technology diffusion remains inconclusive.[22]

Trade and Growth

From the viewpoint of the developing countries, a compelling case for free trade must link openness to faster growth. If openness has a detrimental effect on growth, then even if one accepts the arguments that gains can be made based on comparative advantage, scale economies, and the variety effect, few countries will be persuaded to implement free trade. If growth effects are negative, they will likely swamp the one-time, static welfare gains that result from specialization according to comparative advantage, increased product variety, and exploitation of scale economies.

At a broad, non-technical level, growth depends on two main sources: growth in inputs of production and growth in the productivity of existing inputs. Openness to trade can potentially contribute to growth through both channels. Opening to trade, which raises the return on investment, can raise savings and hence the rate of capital accumulation. Likewise, it may lead to fuller use of labor by eliminating underemployment. Finally, trade can help bring new products, new technologies, and pro-competitive effects that may raise the productivity growth rate.

Formally, growth effects of trade are most easily shown in the one-factor Harrod-Domar model. Suppose capital is the only factor of production and there is one consumption good and one investment good. The latter adds to capital stock and therefore impacts growth.

For concreteness, suppose there are 300 units of capital initially and it takes 3 units of capital to produce either 1 unit of the consumption good or 1 unit of the investment good. Investment augments capital stock, thereby increasing the future production capacity of the economy. How much investment takes place depends on how the consumers divide the total income between consumption and savings. If the savings rate (savings as a proportion of total income) was 15 percent, the economy would devote 45 units of capital to the production of the investment good and the remaining 255 units to the production of the consumption good. It will therefore produce 15 units of the investment good and 85 units of the consumption good. The total income in terms of the consumption good would be 100.

The additional 15 units of capital will augment the capital stock to 315 units, so the production capacity in terms of the consumption good would rise to 105. The economy would have grown 5 percent. If the savings rate remains 15 percent and technology is also unchanged, each year the economy would grow 5 percent. On the other hand, if the savings rate rises to 18 percent, capital stock would be augmented by 6 percent and growth rate would also rise to 6 percent. Alternatively, if productivity in the investment good rises such that 1 unit of it can be produced with 2.5 units of capital instead of 3, 45 units of capital would produce 18 units of the investment good. This would augment capital stock by 6 percent and once again translate into a growth rate of 6 percent.

Given the fixed savings rate and unchanged technology, can trade lead to a rise in the growth rate? This is certainly possible. Beginning with the same 300 units of capital and technology that allows 3 units of capital to produce either 1 unit of the consumption good or 1 unit of the investment good, suppose that the consumption good can be exchanged for 1.2 units of the investment good in the world market. The economy can then specialize completely in the consumption good and produce 100 units of it. It can retain 85 units for domestic consumption and exchange the remaining 15 units for 18 units of the investment good. Capital stock now grows 6 percent and the growth rate jumps to 6 percent as well.

While growth effects of opening to trade can thus be shown to exist, they are by no means guaranteed. Given only one factor of production in the Harrod-Domar model, the marginal product of capital is constant. This allows capital accumulation to add a fixed amount of output per unit of extra capital regardless of the level of the capital stock. But once we have more factors of production and some factors such as labor cannot increase in supply, diminishing returns to capital set in and the marginal product may eventually drop to zero. This is indeed the case in the Solow growth model—so named after its originator, the eminent growth theorist and Nobel laureate Robert Solow. In this model, there is one good produced using two factors of production, capital and labor.[23] Since labor growth is capped by the rate of population growth, attempts to accelerate the long-run growth rate by accelerating the accumulation of capital are frustrated by the diminishing marginal product of capital. In this model, neither trade nor any other policy can impact the long-run rate of growth.

Critics have seized on this insensitivity of the growth rate to free trade in the Solow growth model as a serious blow to the case for free trade.[24] But such criticisms are wholly misplaced, since the growth rate in the Solow-style neo-classical growth model is insensitive to *any* policy. As such, while this model offers a good starting point for the analysis of trade and growth, it is not a good ending point.[25]

Once we modify the features of the neoclassical model responsible for the insensitivity of the long-run growth rate to policy changes, richer outcomes follow. For example, effective labor supply can be augmented through human capital formation. Alternatively, increasing returns to scale can prevent the marginal product of capital from diminishing even when the growth in labor supply is capped by population growth.[26] These modifications allow policy changes including trade liberalization to impact the long-run growth rate.

Vent for Surplus

Our discussion of the gains from trade will be incomplete without at least a brief reference to the vent-for-surplus thesis, which points to a source of gain that is at best implicit in the modern theories of international trade. Though this thesis finds mention in the writings of classical economists including Adam Smith and John Stuart Mill, it has been essentially overshadowed by the comparative advantage and Heckscher-Ohlin theories. The thesis, expounded in detail by Hla Myint, emphasizes the gains from trade that arise from putting to use unused productive capacity. Such capacity usually exists in traditional, preindustrial societies due to a lack of domestic demand for certain resources with which they are endowed. Minerals for which traditional subsistence economies do not have much use offer the most obvious example. Trade opens the possibility of exporting these minerals in return for other goods. In modern times, oil exports by Saudi Arabia offer an even more dramatic example of this type of gain from trade.

Traditionally, the vent-for-surplus thesis has been associated with colonialism. The colonial power was often looking for minerals that it found in the colonies. It then mobilized into mining a part of the local workforce generally underemployed in subsistence agriculture, and it exported the minerals so extracted to its home market. The colony received finished products in return for the exports.[27]

In addition to minerals, unused productive land may also serve as a source of the surplus. In a traditional society, families may use land only to the extent necessary to produce subsistence levels of food grain. Prospects for exports, often opened by the advent of a colonial power, may lead to the use of this land for planting export crops. Development of plantation agriculture in many colonies provides an example of the gains from trade arising from fuller use of the available productive land.

There are two possible reasons modern trade economists have not paid attention to the vent-for-surplus thesis. First, from an analytic standpoint, the gains from trade identified by this thesis may be viewed as a special case of the gains from exchange in the modern theory: we can think of the opening to trade as raising the price of the potential export from zero to a positive number. Second, commercialization of the economy has also gone some distance toward cutting the availability of unused land and labor. Even in poor economies, unused land is a rarity and workers are typically doing something rather than sitting idle.

A Note on the Exchange Rate

The practical question many developing countries face with respect to trade policy is how best to go about liberalizing their trade regimes, which are characterized by a high degree of protection supported by both physical controls such as import licensing and price-based instruments such as tariffs. If the country is considering a broad-based liberalization whereby it plans to remove high barriers to trade within a short period of time, it cannot ignore macroeconomic effects likely to accompany the liberalization. Specifically, if the country adheres to a fixed exchange rate and does not take steps to cut either private consumption or government expenditure, by shifting demand toward foreign-sourced goods liberalization would lead to unemployment and trade deficit. A devaluation, which increases the price of foreign currency in terms of home currency, can alleviate

these problems by making imports at least temporarily more expensive and export products more attractive to foreign buyers.

In practice, devaluation of the domestic currency turns out to be an essential
part of a broad-based liberalization. Absent this complementary policy, rising
trade deficits and unemployment often force countries to reverse their liberalization. If trade liberalization is to be sustained and its benefits reaped, the exchange rate should be set at an appropriate level.[28]

Concluding Remarks

This chapter has introduced some basic principles of the theory of international
trade. The principle of comparative advantage says that countries gain from trade
even if they suffer from low productivity in all sectors relative to their trading
partners. It also tells us that high real wages resulting from high productivity
do not hamper the ability of a country to compete in its goods of comparative
advantage.

The gains from trade also arise from the exploitation of scale economies,
increased product variety, and technological diffusion. Trade allows each
country to specialize in a handful of varieties of the product and thus exploit
scale economies. Input imports allow the developing countries to produce high-
quality products. Likewise, machinery imports allow them to take advantage
of the latest technology. Products innovated in the rich countries become in-
stantly available to the developing countries through trade. For example, trade
has allowed countries such as China and India to take advantage of advances in
telecommunications technology and bring the means of communication to the
masses within a short period of time. In India, the number of telephones per
hundred individuals rose from just 3.5 at the beginning of the current century to
93 in 2017. Because the value of such benefits is difficult to measure empirically,
they often go greatly underappreciated.

Though we have expounded on various sources of the gains from trade in this
chapter, it is important to caution that development is a complex phenomenon
and no single policy on its own can deliver it. When emphasizing the importance of trade for development, economists sometimes overstate their case by
arguing that opening to trade would by itself lead the economy to achieve sustained rapid growth. Critics often seize on such claims and demolish the case for
trade by citing examples of countries that saw no perceptible improvement in
living standards even after they opened up to trade. To anticipate such criticisms,
I wish to note at the outset that the argument of this book is that trade is a necessary and important instrument of growth and development. But it is by no
means sufficient by itself. It requires several complementary conditions, with

adequate infrastructure being an obvious one to mention at this stage. If connectivity to ports is poor or harbors are full of rocks, even a policy of full free trade would result in no trade and therefore no impact on growth and development.

Notes

1. In his excellent intellectual history of free trade, Irwin (1996, 75) points out that while earlier writers extolled the virtues of free trade, Smith was the first to "present a systematic, coherent framework for thinking about economics of trade policy."
2. One might ask why the countries that ran a trade deficit and therefore lost gold did not opt for outright autarky. There are at least three possible answers to this question. First, countries did adopt autarkic policies when faced with trade deficits, but only bilaterally. They would impose a variety of restrictions on imports from a trading partner with which they had a bilateral trade deficit. They also imposed restrictions on imports of commodities they could produce at home (Smith 1776, 396). Second, as long as the countries thought that they could turn the trade deficit in a given year into a trade surplus in future years, there was the hope of net accumulation of gold in the long run. Finally, countries recognized that complete autarky would be impossible to achieve. They were aware that, despite legal restraints, goods and gold would flow into and out of the country.
3. In the *The Wealth of Nations*, which included five books, he devoted almost all of book IV to this task. Out of nine chapters in book IV, eight expound the case for free trade (chapter IX analyzes the agricultural system).
4. Smith 1776, 1:401.
5. Smith 1776, 2:155.
6. Smith 1776, 2:155.
7. Smith 1776, 2:156.
8. Ricardo 1817. There has been some controversy over whether Robert Torrens (1815) had not anticipated Ricardo and whether James Mill (1821), who gave a clearer exposition of the principle of comparative advantage than Ricardo, may have given the latter his famous example. A recent paper by Ruffin (2002) settles this controversy in favor of Ricardo.
9. Samuelson 1969, 9.
10. I outline the explanation of the full-fledged principle of comparative advantage in the standard two-country context in Appendix 1.
11. These prices can be readily stated in domestic currencies. For example, one shirt and one bushel of wheat could each be priced at 50 rupees in India and priced at $1 and $2, respectively, in the rest of the world. Setting the exchange rate at 50 rupees per dollar recasts the example in the text in terms of either rupees or dollars.
12. The examples in the text make clear that, setting aside the borderline case of identical rates of transformation in domestic and foreign markets, trade necessarily improves a country's fortunes over autarky. A different question is whether free trade is necessarily superior to restricted trade. The answer to this question depends on the size of the country. If a country is small in the sense that the world prices it faces are insensitive to how much it trades—an assumption approximately valid for most developing countries—free trade is necessarily superior to restricted trade. If the country is large in the sense that it can influence world prices by trading more or less, it will benefit from some restriction on trade. I explain how this comes about in detail in Appendix 1. Here let me just note that such gains arise at the cost of the trading partners, which would induce them to resort to similar, tit-for-tat restrictions on their own trade, making both sides worse off relative to free trade. Indeed, avoiding such restrictions is a big part of the rationale behind international cooperation in trade policy through the World Trade Organization.
13. A detailed exposition of this theory with all its technical niceties can be found in Bhagwati, Panagariya, and Srinivasan (1998, chs. 5, 6, 8–10). In the Ricardian theory, everyone derives

her income from the same factor of production, labor. Therefore, everyone benefits from trade. In the Heckscher-Ohlin theory, some derive their income from labor and others from land. This opens the possibility of trade impacting the internal distribution of income. Indeed, a key result of the theory is that trade benefits the factor used more intensively in the export good (labor in India in the above example) and hurts the factor used more intensively in the import good (land in India in the above example). The benefits to gainers are sufficiently large, however, that in principle they can potentially fully compensate the losers and still be better off relative to autarky.

14. For an early formal analysis of the gains from trade in the presence of scale economies, see Panagariya 1980.

15. This literature was pioneered by Krugman (1979), for which he won the Nobel Prize in Economics in 2008.

16. This is the key message of Romer 1994. I outline his argument more formally in Appendix 1.

17. When it comes to productivity, the harmful effect of a tariff of a given magnitude turns out to be much larger when imposed on inputs than when levied on final products. While tariffs on inputs impact productivity directly by impacting the choice of input and machinery usage, tariffs on final products impact productivity principally through scale and competition effects. For example, in a study using data from Indonesia, Amiti and Konings (2007) find that a 10 percent reduction in input tariffs increased industry productivity by 3 percent. In comparison, a 10 percent reduction in final goods tariffs increased industry productivity by less than 1 percent.

18. The key theoretical contribution modeling these pro-competitive effects is Melitz 2003. Empirical contributions showing the growth of more productive firms and downsizing of less productive firms include Aw, Chung, and Roberts 2000 for Taiwan, and Clerides, Lack, and Tybout 1998 for Colombia, Mexico, and Morocco. Aw, Chung, and Roberts also show that trade liberalization leads to the exit of inefficient firms.

19. In principle it is possible for the diffusion of technology to reduce the gains from trade to a country having a technological lead. For example, as Japan and other countries learned to make automobiles that could compete with the cars produced by the United States, the price the latter's automobiles could command in the world markets fell. This meant reduced gains from trade for the United States. Three limitations of this point may be noted. First, this potential loss from diffusion is largely relevant to the developed countries. Second, diffusion does raise world welfare. Moreover, even though the gains from trade to the technological leader may decline as a result of diffusion, they remain positive. Finally, in a dynamic world, the technological leader is continuously innovating new products and processes that produce monopoly gains for it until other countries successfully imitate them.

20. Coe, Helpman, and Hoffmaister 1997.

21. Xu and Wang 1999.

22. Keller 2004.

23. The assumption of constant returns to scale says that doubling both inputs exactly doubles output. The assumption rules out scale economies under which the doubling of inputs leads to more than a doubling of the output.

24. For example, see Wade 1990; Rodriguez and Rodrik 2000.

25. See Srinivasan and Bhagwati 2001 for a full-scale response to Rodriguez and Rodrik 2000.

26. Romer 1986; Lucas 1988.

27. Myint (1958) makes much of the *simultaneous* existence of unused productive capacity and surplus labor in the traditional agriculture due to underemployment of labor but the latter does not seem essential for the gains to arise. Even if labor is fully employed in agriculture, once the possibility of exports of minerals opens up, relocation of some labor to their exploitation would produce gains.

28. For a cogent discussion of this point, see Corden 1997, ch. 15.

3

The Mirage of Infant Industry Protection

The dominant view among economists and policymakers in the immediate aftermath of the Second World War was that the newly independent countries, which had just embarked upon their economic development, needed protection against imports of industrial products from advanced countries. Though the inspiration for this view had come partially from the success of the Soviet Union in achieving respectable levels of growth under autarkic trade polices, its true intellectual foundations can be traced to a syllogism.

The first premise in the syllogism was that the developing countries could not rely on primary products, in which they were then specialized, as the engine of growth. Instead, they needed to industrialize. The second premise was that in order to industrialize, the countries needed to provide temporary protection to industry. Absent such protection, their newly established industries would fail to withstand competition from their well-established counterparts in the developed countries. The first premise was rooted in what has been called "export pessimism" and the second in the infant industry argument for protection.

Primary products could serve as the engine of growth only if they had the potential to fetch increasing volumes of revenues in world markets over time. For in that case, the countries could endeavor to achieve progressively higher productivity in primary product production and exchange these products for larger and larger volumes of industrial products in world markets. The dominant belief of that era, however, was that primary products would fetch diminishing revenues in world markets over time.

This export pessimism derived from the empirically valid assumption that the demand for primary products had a low responsiveness to changes in both incomes and prices.[1] Low responsiveness to income meant that future increases in developed country incomes would create far less demand for primary products than for industrial products. This shift in demand with rising incomes in developed countries over time would lower the prices of primary products in terms of industrial products. As exporters of primary products, the developing countries would be hurt by this decline in the price.

In a similar vein, low responsiveness of demand to price changes meant that any increases in the demand for primary products would require proportionately large reductions in prices. Therefore, any attempts by the developing countries to expand exports of primary products through increased productivity or investments would lead to such large reductions in the prices of these products that the expanded exports by the countries would end up fetching reduced revenues. The twin conclusions implied that specialization in primary products did not offer the developing countries a winning development strategy.

Therefore, the salvation from poverty lay in industrialization. It was here that economists and policymakers made major errors of judgment. For a variety of reasons—most prominently the infant industry argument—they wound up concluding that the only road to industrialization available to the developing countries went through protection to the domestic import-competing industry.[2] Unsurprisingly, with the exception of Hong Kong, which the British had owned and maintained as a free port, virtually all developing countries chose the path of import substitution industrialization in the immediate post–Second World War era.

The key reason the old conventional wisdom fell into the trap of seeing import substitution as the only possible road to industrialization was that it conceptualized the economy as consisting of just two sectors: agriculture and industry. In this conception, the developing countries were naturally viewed as exporters of primary products and importers of industrial products. The conclusion that the only way to industrialize for such an economy was by replacing imported industrial products with similar domestically produced products was then inescapable.

The experience of the tiger economies forced economists to break out of this simplistic two-sector conceptualization of the economy. These economies demonstrated that it was possible to industrialize rapidly by exporting industrial products that used the relatively abundant labor more intensively while importing industrial products that used the relatively scarce capital more intensively. Once this fact was recognized, import substitution could no longer be defended as necessary for industrialization.[3]

Today, with rare exceptions, economists and policymakers in the vast majority of countries have come to appreciate the merits of outward-oriented policies. But this appreciation remains fragile and challenges to its wisdom remain omnipresent. Ironically, the opening up of trade during the last two to three decades, which has led to a rise in the share of imports in GDP in a majority of the developing countries, has also made these countries more vulnerable to the revival of import substitution industrialization. Politicians, often untrained in the subtleties of the economics of international trade, see great opportunity to advance industrialization by substituting domestic production for the large volume of imports they currently see around them. "Why do we have to import this or that product while we can produce it at home and expand our own industrial production?" is a common refrain.[4] The fact that restrictions on imports would also have the unintended consequence of cutting exports of products in which the country has a cost advantage and hence lead to deindustrialization on that front does not occur to them. After all, countries can only pay for the goods of their trading partners by selling their own goods to those partners.

Politicians aside, we also come across economists, political scientists, sociologists, anthropologists, and journalists who consider import protection as a more effective policy to promote industrialization. Many among them hold the view that infant industry protection makes sense and that import substitution through selective or wholesale protection of industry is the preferred road to industrialization. Therefore, in this chapter and Chapter 4, I carefully dissect the arguments for protection as the instrument of industrialization. Because the limitations of the infant industry argument remain the least well understood, I devote this entire chapter to its careful discussion. In the literature, there are three strands of this argument: protection to a specific infant industry, protection to the entire manufacturing sector in the early stages of development, and promotion of infant export industry. I examine the case for intervention in each of these situations.

Before I proceed, however, it is important to offer a word of caution. There is a strong tendency on the part of even the most sophisticated free trade critics to equate the pursuit of industrial policy with protection. When told that South Korea began growing rapidly after it turned outward, a common response of critics is, "But Korea grew rapidly as a result of industrial policy." It is important to recognize that industries can be promoted in a variety of ways, including via production and investment subsidies, without necessarily resorting to protection. The caution in this volume is against import protection as the instrument of industrialization, not against all forms of government intervention. In the context of the present chapter, we shall see that while a case for infant industry *promotion* may be defensible under certain circumstances, the case for infant industry *protection* is on thin ice. Import protection as an instrument of infant industry promotion fails to pass muster except under implausible assumptions.

The Infant Industry Argument: Historical Background

Although the infant industry argument can be traced to authors writing as far back as the seventeenth century, the two most influential early proponents

of it were Alexander Hamilton and Friedrich List.[5] As the first treasury secretary of the United States, Hamilton relied partially on that argument to
lobby the U.S. House of Representatives for increased protection to certain
industries in the country. Activist and sometime academic List deployed
the argument to advocate protection for manufacturing more generally
in temperate-zone countries that had achieved a high level of agricultural
development.

Nineteenth-century academic economists, who had largely come to sub-
scribe to the ideas of Adam Smith, remained skeptical of the argument until John
Stuart Mill blessed it.[6] In a lone paragraph in his monumental work *Principles of
Political Economy*, which became the standard text for the students of economics
for several decades, Mill accepted the argument as being theoretically valid.[7]
Objections by several contemporary writers notwithstanding, the argument as
enunciated by Mill and modified by Charles Francis Bastable remained acceptable to economists through the first half of the twentieth century.[8] In the postcolonial era, as newly independent countries began to invoke the argument, trade
economists began scrutinizing it afresh.

Influential but Incomplete Early Statements

The argument as conventionally made is that in the early phase of industrialization, a country may exhibit higher production costs in certain industries
than already industrialized countries even though it has no intrinsic cost disadvantage in those industries. Over time, infant industries are able to bring
their production costs down through "learning by doing" and compete against
their foreign counterparts. But if exposed to foreign competition in the early
phase, they fail to survive. Temporary protection is required until the infant
grows into an adult.

As noted, Hamilton was an early proponent of the argument. He argued that
the disparity in competition existed between "recent establishments of one
country" and "matured establishments of another" and that this called for "aid
and protection of the government."[9] Mill pointed out, however, that the protection to the infant industry had to be temporary.[10] Subsequently Bastable added
the important qualification that protection of infant industry would be justified
only if the immediate losses during the learning period were outweighed by
the future gains of the industry.[11] As previously noted, the argument remained
acceptable in the form expounded by Bastable until the end of the first half
of the twentieth century, though most economists remained skeptical of it in
practice.[12]

More Careful Scrutiny in the Post–Second World War Era

Following the end of the Second World War, infant industry protection returned to life as a policy issue. This revival led to another round of scrutiny of the argument by trade economists including James Meade, Harry Johnson, and Robert Baldwin.[13] The scrutiny revealed many of the limitations of the argument that had previously escaped economists.

Before considering these limitations, we note three points. First, the argument as conventionally analyzed relates to protection of specific industries rather than the entire industrial sector. A distinction needs to be drawn between this and the "infant economy" argument applied to the industrial sector as a whole and considered later in this chapter. Second, by definition, the infant industry argument calls for temporary protection. Therefore, time must enter into the analysis in an essential way, and the issue of infant industry protection must be distinguished from the argument for permanent protection, made sometimes in the context of declining average costs as an industry's output expands.[14] Finally, since the argument calls for intervention, it necessarily rests on a market failure that prevents the emergence of the optimum outcome on its own. Much of the post–Second World War dissection of the argument aims to pinpoint this market failure and assess the plausibility of protection as the instrument for correcting it.

In taking the first serious stab at the infant industry argument in the post–Second World War era, Meade pointed out that the argument required a careful distinction between learning-by-doing economies that are *internal* to the firm and those that are *external* to it. Internal economies are those that lower per-unit cost only for the firm in which learning takes place; other firms are excluded from benefiting from the learning. For example, if the firm undertakes a costly innovation that lowers future production costs and other firms cannot gain access to the innovation, the economies associated with that innovation are internal. In contrast, external economies are those that spill over to other firms. In the example just cited, if the innovation by one firm becomes available to other firms without them having to pay for it, the economies are external. Meade demonstrated that only if the economies were external, in the sense that they could spill over to other firms, could a case be made for government intervention. Baldwin demonstrated subsequently, however, that even in this case, trade protection would entirely fail to deliver the desired outcome. Intervention would have to take a different form depending on the source of the external economy.

Learning Is Internal to the Firm

Let us first assume that the benefits of any learning remain strictly within the firm. For example, the firm may invest in a cost-cutting innovation that cannot be copied by other firms. Alternatively, the firm may invest in worker training, which creates skills that are specific to it such that other firms are unable to use those skills productively. In either case, the firm is the sole beneficiary of cost reductions resulting from its investment.

To take a concrete but highly simple example, consider a market in which domestic demand is fixed at one unit and high transport costs rule out any prospects of exports. Assume that the per-unit cost of production of the product at home in the first year is higher than the import price. It follows that in the absence of protection it would be unprofitable for a domestic firm to produce the product in the first year.

Suppose further that there exists a costly innovation that can push the per-unit cost of production below the import price from the second year onward.[15] Specifically, assume that the cost per unit (including the cost of innovation) is $110 in the first year and $77 thereafter. Suppose further that the world price is $80 in all years. Given these costs and the import price, the firm incurs a loss of $30 in the first year and reaps a profit of $3 in subsequent years in perpetuity.

The first question is whether, given these initial losses and future profits, the production activity is socially beneficial. The answer to this question depends on how the society values present versus future earnings. Generally, $1 earned in the second year is valued less than $1 earned in the first year. Similarly, $1 earned in the third year is valued less than $1 earned in the second year. The precise value in the present year of $1 earned in a given future year depends on the rate at which the society discounts the future and the number of years into the future that the $1 is earned.[16]

As an example, suppose the society discounts the future at an annual rate of 10 percent. In economists' jargon, we say that the social rate of discount is 10 percent. This means that $1 received in the second year is worth $1/(1 + 0.1) \approx 0.91 received in the first year. Similarly, $1 received in the third year is worth $1/(1 + 0.1)^2 \approx 0.83 received in the first year. The value of the stream of profits earned in the above example in the first year is thus $3/(1 + 0.1) + $3/(1 + 0.1)^2 + $3/(1 + 0.1)^3 + \ldots$, and the sum of this series turns out to be exactly $30. In other words, at a 10 percent social rate of discount, the value of the future stream of profits in the first year just offsets the loss of $30 incurred in the same year. The Bastable condition is just satisfied and the production activity is socially beneficial to undertake. Recall that the Bastable condition says that an industry should only be supported if the immediate losses incurred by it during the learning phase are outweighed by the future gains reaped by it. If the social rate of discount is less than 10 percent, the Bastable condition is strictly satisfied. If it is in excess of 10 percent, the condition is violated, and it is not socially beneficial to undertake the production activity.

If we maintain that it is socially beneficial to undertake the production activity, the next question is whether the situation calls for import protection or another form of government intervention. Meade answered the question in the negative.[17] In a well-functioning capital market, savers who discount the future at 10 percent would offer loans to borrowers at 10 percent interest. The private firm or entrepreneur can then borrow the $30 at a 10 percent interest rate and annually pay $3 in interest on it out of her profits in perpetuity.[18] No intervention by the government is required.

A common way that the argument for government intervention is resurrected under internal economies is through the introduction of a capital market imperfection. For example, suppose that due to monopoly in lending, the interest rate facing the entrepreneur is 12 percent. At this interest rate, a potential entrepreneur who borrows $30 to cover the loss in the first year would have to pay $3.60 in interest each year in perpetuity. But profits at $3 would fail to cover this interest cost, and no entrepreneur would undertake the production activity even though it is socially beneficial.

In this situation, a temporary tariff that raises the price of the product in the first year to $85, thereby cutting the losses to the firm that year to $25, makes the production activity feasible. The entrepreneur can cover the loss in the first year by a loan of $25. At the 12 percent rate, the annual total interest on this amount beginning in the second year turns out to be $3 per year, which is just equal to the annual profit.[19]

The problem with this resurrection of the argument, however, is that capital market imperfections (and other similar market failures) are a separate and independent source of possible intervention on behalf of a socially beneficial activity. The presence of learning economies is not essential for intervention when these imperfections exist. For example, if a socially beneficial production activity is characterized by a large upfront investment cost and output takes a few years to come on stream, it may fail to emerge if a capital market imperfection keeps the interest rate sufficiently above the social rate of discount.

Learning Is External to the Firm

If learning is internal, then on its own it cannot form the basis for protection or any other policy intervention. Consider next whether a case for infant industry protection can be made in the presence of learning effects that are external to the firm. Because there is a widespread belief, including among many trade economists, that the presence of learning economies that are external to the firm can form a legitimate basis for protection, let us begin by outlining the conditions under which such a case can indeed be made. We then demonstrate that once we make explicit the micro-foundations of externalities, the case for import protection to promote infant industry collapses.[20]

The Act of Production in the Early Stages by Itself Lowers Future Costs

Continuing with the example considered in the context of internal learning, suppose that the cost reduction in the second and subsequent years results from the mere act of production in the first year. That is to say, learning is costless and results not from innovation or learning on the part of the worker but simply from the act of production. Therefore, the entire $110 cost in the first year represents the cost of production, with the drop in cost to $77 in the second year and subsequently being a by-product of the production activity in the first year.

With the world price at $80 each year, there is a loss of $30 in the first year and profit of $3 in all subsequent years. With the social rate of discount held at 10 percent, the production activity remains socially beneficial. The profit of $3 in perpetuity beginning with the second year offsets the extra cost of $30 in the first year at this discount rate.

Introduce now the idea that learning economies are external to the firm. What this means is that the reduction in cost to $77 from the second year onward is available not just to the incumbent firm but to any new entrant as well. Can production activity still emerge without any government intervention when loans are available at 10 percent interest?

The answer in this case turns out to be in the negative. Because future entrants can produce and sell the product at $77, the incumbent too will have to sell her product at that price from the second year onward.[21] This would deny her the ability to generate the $3 profit required to pay back the loan she must take to cover the loss of $30 in the first year. Therefore, she would choose not to enter the production activity in the first year in the first place.

This is where temporary protection could do the trick. If the government imposed a tariff of $30 per unit in the first year, the incumbent firm can cover its full cost of $110 in the first year. In subsequent years, the price drops to $77, with the benefits of learning being passed on to consumers. The socially beneficial activity becomes viable.

Sources of Learning: Skill Formation

Nearly all authors who have provided positive cases of infant industry promotion through import protection postulate that the mere act of production in the early stages leads to cost reductions in future years not just for the incumbent but for new entrants as well.[22] In their analysis, they do not account for any plausible mechanism through which future costs fall for all firms in the industry as a result of the output activity of the firms operating in the early years. They leave outside the formal analysis the mechanism through which learning by incumbent firms spills over to later entrants.

If this assumption of mechanical spillover were made purely for simplicity of analysis and the end result did not hinge on it, there would be no reason to take issue with it. But it turns out that the positive case for temporary import protection for infant industries critically hinges on this assumption. The moment we make explicit the mechanism through which the cost reduction spills over to new entrants, the case for temporary import protection of infant industries collapses. This is the key message of the pathbreaking contribution by Baldwin.[23]

To explain this, we continue with our example in the previous section but make explicit the mechanism underlying learning. In particular, assume that the high per-unit cost of $110 in the first year results from low initial productivity of workers. It so happens, however, that engaging in the production activity in the first year raises their productivity enough to lower future per-unit cost to $77 beginning with the second year. The problem the incumbent firm faces is that it can cover its first-year losses only if it can keep the skilled workers at the original wage and internalize the benefits of higher productivity from the second year onward. But with worker productivity being high enough to yield a $3 per-unit profit, new entrants can afford to pay a wage that is $3 higher than the incumbent firm can afford. Recognizing this threat, no firm would choose to engage in production activity in the first year when the cost is $110. The case for temporary protection to make entry in the first year profitable may then open up.

The key point Baldwin makes is that this case requires no intervention at all. The first entrant firm and workers know that skills acquired in the initial year have value and can be sold at a price in the market. Therefore, workers have an incentive to accept a wage that is lower than their original take (at which the firm loses $30) by an amount equal to the sum of the discounted stream of future premiums on skills they receive. The latter, of course, equals exactly $30. This then allows the incumbent firm to break even in the first year. In effect, it is able to internalize the benefits of learning.

A possible problem with this argument is that it relies on the willingness of workers to accept less than the market wage initially in return for higher wages in the future. If the workers want to maintain a certain minimum living standard that is not feasible at the lower wage in the first year, they will need to take a loan against higher future wages. But lenders may not be willing to extend a loan against future returns on an intangible asset such as skills. This brings us back to the issue of capital market imperfections mentioned in the context of internal economies of scale.

Source of Learning: Costly Innovation

Next, suppose that the reduction in cost in future years results not from skill acquisition by workers through engagement in production activity but from costly innovation. Assume that absent innovation, production cost is $90 per unit and that investment of $20 in an innovation brings future cost down to $77 per unit. Other parameters of the problem remain unchanged, so the production activity is socially beneficial.

Suppose, however, that unlike in the example of internal learning economies, innovation cannot be held secret. Through reverse engineering or other means, the innovation becomes available to all potential entrants beginning in the second year. Because future entrants do not have to invest in the innovation, competition among them would drive the product price down to $77. This would deny the incumbent firm the opportunity to recover the loss of $30 incurred in the first year. Therefore, it would choose not to enter the market. A case for government intervention that incentivizes the incumbent firm to enter and invest in the innovation opens up.

The critical question is whether import protection can incentivize the firm to invest in innovation. Baldwin explained that the answer is unequivocally in the negative. Although a temporary tariff of $30 per unit in the first year would make production activity profitable that year, it will not induce the incumbent firm to invest in the innovation. Because new entrants can still free ride on the innovation, they acquire a cost advantage over the incumbent firm. Therefore, they can prevent the latter from making any profit from the innovation in the second and subsequent years. Anticipating this fact, the firm would choose to take advantage of tariff protection without innovation. It will produce the product for $90, sell it for $110, and walk away with $20 profit in the first year. The socially beneficial innovation will fail to emerge. In practice, matters may get worse. Once entry has taken place, politics may force the government's hand and it may have to make protection permanent. Since no innovation would take place, this would cause social losses in perpetuity.

To summarize the discussion so far, we have seen that as long as learning economies are internal to the firm, a logical case for any form of government intervention cannot be made without invoking some other market failure such as capital market imperfection. Even when learning economies are external, the case for temporary protection of infant industries relies on the assumption that the mere act of production by incumbent firms in the early stages mechanically and automatically lowers the cost of production for future entrants as well. Once we identify a plausible mechanism through which spillover takes place, the case for temporary import protection as a possible remedy disappears, leading Baldwin to conclude: "If the infant-industry argument for tariff protection is worthy of its reputation as the major exception to the free-trade case, it should be possible to present a clear analytical case, based upon well-known and generally accepted empirical relationships unique to infant industries, for the general desirability and effectiveness of protective duties in these industries. The contention of this paper is that such a case cannot be made."[24]

Of course, this analysis does not suggest that the government has no role to play in the presence of learning economies that can spill over to other firms. When learning is external, markets would fail and socially beneficial activities would fail to operate at the socially desirable level. While import protection will not resolve the spillover issue in such cases, policies that directly target the source of the spillover would solve the problem. These latter may include a patent term long enough for a firm to recoup the cost of the innovation or a direct subsidy to cover the cost of innovation.

The Infant Economy Argument

The conventional infant industry argument is applied to specific industries. But some authors have advocated protecting the manufacturing sector or industry as a whole on grounds of infancy. Frederic List, one of the earliest to make such an argument, held the view that countries in the temperate zone with fully developed agriculture and dense population could progress further only by introducing manufacturing.[25] He also argued that late starters satisfying these characteristics could establish manufacturing only through protection. Though he argued that such protection must eventually be brought down and eliminated, he was prepared to allow it to last for decades.

List partially advocated protection for manufactures in pursuit of what present-day trade economists call "non-economic" objectives. He associated agriculture with despotism and manufacturing with political and personal freedom. In his view, benefits of manufacturing included greater security and independence, creation of skills, and accumulation of capital. He emphasized the importance of the power of production, arguing, "The power of creating wealth is then vastly more important than wealth itself; it secures not only the possession and the increase of property already acquired, but even the replacing of that which is lost."[26] In two key paragraphs, he articulated his philosophy of temporary protection to manufacturing:

> A nation ought to make the sacrifice and bear the privation of material riches, to acquire intellectual or social power; it might sacrifice present advantages to secure future benefits. We think it has been historically proved, that manufacturing industry, developed in all its branches, is

the characteristic of a high degree of civilization, material prosperity, and political power; if it is true, as we believe can be demonstrated, that in the actual state of the world, an infant industry, deprived of protection, is not able to sustain the competition of an industry long established, of an industry protected upon its own territory; how . . . can anyone undertake to prove that . . . the industry of a country must be left to the unaided and unsupported intelligence and enterprise of private individuals . . . ?

It is true that protective duties enhance at first the price of manufactured products; but it is equally true, as is admitted by the [Adam Smith] School itself, that in course of time, in a nation capable of large industrial development, such articles can be produced at a cheaper rate than they can be imported from abroad. If then, protecting duties at first involve some sacrifice of values, this sacrifice is amply compensated by the acquisition of a productive power, which ensures not only a larger product of wealth in future, but also a greater industrial independence in case of war or adverse commercial regulations.[27]

In analytic terms, List's argument has two components. First, there are learning effects throughout the industry: the sector is not competitive immediately, but it is so once learning has taken place. There are serious conceptual problems with protection as the corrective policy in this situation, however. If learning is internal to the firm and temporary, no intervention is required. If it is external and temporary, protection will not solve the problem.

The second component in List's argument is that even absent learning, private entrepreneurs do not take into account the benefits of manufacturing in terms of personal freedom, independence, security, and the acquisition of the power of production, and so they underestimate the social rate of return. Therefore, left to themselves, they would underinvest in manufacturing. Protection can help align the private and social rates of return.

This argument would lead to the recommendation of permanent rather than temporary protection to manufacturing. The only way to reconcile it with a recommendation of temporary protection is to further assume that once manufacturing has achieved a certain scale, even if this scale shrinks in the future, the benefits in terms of personal freedom, independence, security, and acquisition of the power of production do not reverse. This is evidently a questionable assumption. Reallocation of resources following the removal of protection will likely reduce incentives for capital formation and skill creation in manufacturing. In due course, this shrinking of manufacturing is bound to undermine the non-economic objectives associated with the production of manufactures. It is perhaps this inconsistency and lack of clarity in List's writings that led Nobel laureate economist Paul Krugman to state:

> I do, however, agree with [Clyde] Prestowitz on one point. More people should read the works of Friedrich List. If they do, they may wonder why this turgid, confused writer—whose theory led him to predict that Holland and Denmark would be condemned to permanent economic backwardness unless they sought political union with Germany—has suddenly become a favorite of [James] Fallows, Prestowitz and others. The new cult of List bears an uncanny resemblance to the right-wing supply-siders' canonization of the classical French economist Jean-Baptiste Say, who claimed that the economy as a whole could never suffer from the falls in aggregate demand that produce recessions.[28]

Before leaving the subject of protection for manufacturing as a whole, we may consider briefly a more technical contribution entitled "Helping Infant Economies Grow: Foundations of Trade Policies for Developing Countries," by economists Bruce Greenwald and Joseph Stiglitz.[29] Although this is a purely theoretical contribution, the second author is a Nobel laureate, so it has the potential to find salience with policy analysts and policymakers.

At first glance, the contribution by Greenwald and Stiglitz may appear to offer an argument for infant economy protection based on external economies. But upon closer examination, their formal model actually generates either free trade or permanent autarky as the optimal trade policy option. The authors consider an economy that can potentially produce two goods, agriculture and industry. The country's static comparative advantage is in agriculture. Industrial output generates externalities that lower per-unit costs in both industry and agriculture proportionally.

Under free trade, the country specializes in agriculture and reaps the usual gains from trade. Under autarky, it forgoes the gains from trade but stands to benefit from productivity gains brought about by the production of the industrial good. Because the rest of the world grows faster and always retains comparative advantage in the industrial good, any decision to open to trade always leads the country to specialize completely in agriculture.

There are several problems with this model, but two are worth noting. First, the conclusion that the only way to industrialize and remain industrialized is permanent protection is neither plausible nor consistent with experience. Second, by casting the problem of development in a two-sector economy, the authors repeat the mistake economists made in the 1950s. This conceptualization falsely limits the choices of the developing countries: either they specialize in and export the primary product (agriculture) or they develop industry through import substitution. By now there is enough evidence indicating that successful industrialization requires specialization in and exports of one set of industrial products and services while importing another set of industrial products and services. The choice between exporting *either* industrial *or* primary products is a false one except perhaps in the case of big oil-exporting countries. But in their case, few would suggest that the optimal solution is to forgo the gains from trade and adopt autarky to promote industrialization!

The Infant Exporter Argument

The infant exporter argument focuses on assistance to industries that are expected to be viable exporters in the long run but fail to enter the export market due to some temporary handicap. Since the argument seeks intervention with respect to sales exclusively in the foreign market, it hypothesizes an asymmetry between that market and the domestic one.

The argument may be developed in terms of internal and external economies, as in the case of the infant industry argument. Taking the former first, there are two possible sources of temporary losses on sales in the export markets despite long-run profitability of those sales: learning by the consumer and learning by the exporting firm. Foreign consumers may be poorly informed about the product and may be unwilling to try to learn about it unless offered a price below cost. Once they are convinced, they may be willing to pay a high enough price that the firm recovers the losses due to below-cost sales in the early years in net present value terms. Alternatively, the firm may face high initial costs due to learning associated with selling a product in a new market. This may result from the need to learn the local product safety standards or the need to hire and train workers in service shops that must be set up locally in the export market. In either case, intervention is unjustified since the firm should be able to borrow against future profits to cover the losses in the early years.

Turning to externalities, as long as the activity with which the externality is associated is costly, export subsidies will fail to correct the problem. For example, suppose the scale economy is associated with gathering market information that is costly. Once gathered, the information becomes freely available to future entrants. Then, despite the export subsidy, the firm will not invest in acquiring the beneficial market information for fear of later entrants gaining a cost advantage. This is because the later entrants gain information without having to incur any costs. To correct the distortion due to the externality, the government must directly subsidize the acquisition of information or collect the information and make it freely available to all potential exporters.

Wolfgang Mayer provides an argument for export subsidy based on reputation building.[30] He assumes that foreign consumers learn about the quality of a product through its consumption and that this learning automatically applies to future sales of the same product sold by other firms from the same country. The more the consumer knows about the quality, the higher the price she is willing to pay. Exporting is socially beneficial if the losses in the early phase due to the low price the consumer pays are offset by future profits in net present value terms, calculated at the social rate of discount. Given that the benefits of learning in the early phase spill over to future entrants who did not incur losses in the early phase, the price in the future drops to the marginal cost and those exporting in the early phase fail to recover their losses. Absent intervention, no firms enter the market to incur losses in the early phase. An export subsidy that covers losses until learning has taken place can solve this problem.

The problem with this analysis is that the case for export subsidy is built on the assumption that sellers have no control over product quality. When establishing reputation is the issue, a realistic analysis must allow for variable product quality, with the cost of production rising with quality. In the early phase, the choice of a high-quality product would then lead to losses because consumers still need to be convinced that the firm sells a high-quality product. These losses must be offset by profits in later phases, when the consumer is willing to pay the higher price.

But if the reputation established by early entrants spills over to later entrants from the same country that did not incur the early-phase losses, the latter will undersell the former. Therefore, the early entrants will fail to recover their early-phase losses. This would deter them from choosing a high-quality product in the first place. They would prefer to sell a low-quality product, whose cost they can recover concurrently.

Can an export subsidy alter the outcome and persuade early entrants to supply a high-quality product to establish reputation? The answer is in the negative. This is because the early entrants would anticipate being outperformed by the future entrants. They would recognize that they would not reap the benefits of reputation on future sales. Therefore, they would find it more attractive to sell the low-quality product at a lower price while collecting the export subsidy. A socially beneficial high-quality product would fail to emerge even if an export subsidy is provided to recover the losses in the learning phase.[31]

Critiquing the Claims of the Proponents of Infant Industry Protection

The absence of a sound conceptual case for import protection as the solution to infant industry promotion notwithstanding, proponents of such a case abound. Because politicians, policy analysts, and journalists, untrained in serious economic analysis, often fall victim to the claims of these proponents, it is important to subject their arguments to careful scrutiny.

Judging by the sources they cite, many of the influential proponents of infant industry protection as a means to industrialization are unaware of the post–Second World War critiques of the infant industry argument by trade economists. Among prominent names such as Alice Amsden, Ha-Joon Chang, Erik Reinert, and Robert Wade, none mention the writings of James Meade, Harry Johnson, Herbert Grubel, Robert Baldwin, and Douglas Irwin.[32] Instead, they commonly rely on Hamilton and List to make their case.[33]

In particular, Wade laments that a copy of List's book he borrowed from the Massachusetts Institute of Technology library in 1993 had been last borrowed in 1966, indicating that few academics in the United States cared about what List had to say.[34] Had Wade read Meade, Grubel, Baldwin, or Irwin, he would have known that trade economists not only had been busy reading List but also had provided compelling critiques of his defense of the infant industry argument.

A common approach to advocating protection in the writings of post–Second World War proponents of the infant industry argument is to point to one or more market failures, argue that these failures call for corrective policies by the government, and then list protection as one of those policies. The authors do not pinpoint precisely how protection is going to correct the infant-industry-specific market failure; instead, they point to it as a necessary part of the package.

The contribution by Wade to a symposium on infant industry protection in the Oxford Development Studies series provides an excellent example of this approach.[35] Defending infant industry protection on theoretical grounds, he notes, "The case for infant industry protection is *not* a case for tariffs and non-tariff barriers. It is a case for public support, of which trade protection is one kind among many others." Wade then goes on to list market failures commonly discussed in the context of learning-by-doing economies—external economies, capital market imperfections, coordination economies, and asymmetric information—but does not explain the precise mechanism by which protection is supposed to correct each of these failures. He does not recognize that protection can do little to solve the problem arising out of spillover effects of learning, nor that capital market imperfections and information asymmetries are not specific to infant industries.

Even setting aside the objections to the infant industry argument on logical and conceptual grounds, has anyone provided compelling evidence linking infant industry protection to rapid industrialization? Here once again, the proof has been by association: because interventionist policies either preceded or accompanied periods of rapid growth, they must be credited with the success achieved.

Proof by Association

The proponents of the infant industry argument have never held themselves to the same high standard of proof they demand from free trade advocates. They dismiss the findings of even the most carefully crafted studies by free trade advocates on the pretext of minor flaws that cannot be overcome given the nature of the data. Yet when it comes to building their own case, all they offer is proof by association. Even authors sympathetic to infant industry promotion can find this frustrating.

For example, Gustav Ranis, who fully embraces an expansive version of infant industry protection in the early stages of development, is highly critical of the arguments offered by some revisionists.[36] In his comments in the symposium on infant industry protection, he questions Sanjay Lall about his advocacy of selective and targeted interventions "favoring new, complex and high tech industries likely to provide externalities for others."[37] He comments that Lall's "identification of development with favored large-scale capital-intensive industry . . . is hard for me to accept in light of the record of the success cases we have witnessed to date."[38]

Ranis is equally unsparing of Wade, noting that in his book *Governing the Market*, the latter describes government interventions in Taiwan ex post but provides no primer on how to "act strategically." Referring to Wade's contribution in the symposium, he writes, "Here he urges us not to 'pick' but to 'nurture' winners; but how do you 'nurture' without first 'picking'?"

Free trade advocates take an even more critical view of defenses of infant industry protection. In a scathing review of the book *Kicking Away the Ladder: Development Strategy in Historical Perspective* by Ha-Joon Chang, Irwin takes to task the author's claim that the key to the development of today's developed countries was infant industry promotion through tariffs and other industrial policies.[39] Irwin correctly points out that just because a set of trade and industrial policies was pursued alongside rapid economic development, it does not clinch the case that those policies were responsible for the growth. Instead, the success may have resulted despite the inefficient policies because other domestic policies and institutions were favorable to rapid growth. Irwin illustrates the point with an example involving the United States: "For example, the United States started out as a very wealthy country with a high literacy rate, widely distributed land ownership, stable government and competitive political institutions that largely guaranteed the security of private property, a large internal market with free trade in goods and free labor mobility across regions, etc. Given these overwhelmingly favorable conditions, even very inefficient trade policies could not have prevented economic advances from taking place." In other words, the United States grew not because of high tariffs but despite them.

Economist Ian Little makes the same point in the context of the success of the East Asian tigers.[40]

Post-Hoc Fallacy

Chang, whom Martin Wolf of the *Financial Times* has called "probably the world's most effective critic of globalization," offers a spirited yet largely assertive defense of the infant industry argument.[41] His defense of the argument in the popular book *Bad Samaritans: Rich Nations, Poor Policies and the Threat to the Developing World* rests solely on the sequence of events, amounting to no more than *post hoc ergo propter hoc.*[42]

Early in the book, Chang begins with the story of the Japanese manufacturer Toyota, which initially produced textile machinery but moved into automobiles in 1933. At various points in time, the Japanese government provided support to car manufacturing by Toyota and protected it from foreign competition. It "kicked out General Motors and Ford in 1939," banned foreign investment in the industry, maintained high tariffs on auto imports, and even provided direct financial assistance that allowed Toyota to escape bankruptcy. Although Toyota's first attempt to export to the United States failed, the government persisted with its support for the effort.

As is well known, Toyota eventually became a success story, and Thomas Friedman went on to celebrate it in his 1999 book *The Lexus and the Olive Tree*. Referring to this fact, Chang makes his claim about the success of infant industry protection in these terms:

> However, the fact is that had the Japanese government followed the free-trade economists back in the early 1960s, there would have been no Lexus. Toyota today would, at best, be a junior partner to some western car manufacturer, or worse, have been wiped out. The same would have been true for the entire Japanese economy. . . . In other words, had they followed [Milton] Friedman's advice, the Japanese would not have been exporting the Lexus but still be fighting over who owns which mulberry tree [that feeds silkworms].[43]

In making this sweeping claim, Chang is entirely assertive, relying purely on the sequence of events: the government promoted and protected Toyota, and it succeeded some fifty years later. He provides no explanation of how exactly the ouster of General Motors and Ford in 1939 was connected to the success of Toyota some forty to fifty years later. Nor does he carry out any cost-benefit analysis to persuade the reader that the costs paid by the Japanese consumers and taxpayers were worth the benefits to the economy. Also missing is any attempt to identify the market failure that the Japanese intervention was supposed to have addressed through protection. Finally, it is not clear why Chang believes that the automobile industry would have disappeared for good, never to reappear, if Japan had not protected it in the earlier decades of its existence.

We also do not find in Chang's book any mention of the careful econometric study by economists Richard Beason and David Weinstein of the impact of the Japanese interventions on productivity and growth.[44] Beason and Weinstein analyze the impact of trade protection (tariffs and quotas), net transfers to sectors (subsidies less indirect taxes), sectoral corporate tax breaks, and government loans as targeting measures in the post–Second World War era. They find that to the extent that Japanese policies favoring certain sectors increased growth and investment rates, they did so in low-growth and declining industries. A more dramatic finding is that Japanese industrial policy had no significant impact on productivity growth in mining and manufacturing. They conclude, "The problem is that while MITI [Ministry of International Trade and Industry] White Papers often stressed the right industries, the stylized facts which describe how the policies were actually used tell a different story: a story of a government which served the interests of large and politically important, but declining, industries."[45]

In the second chapter of his book, Chang offers an even more far-fetched and assertive example of the success of infant industry protection from pre–Industrial Revolution England. Relying solely on the 1728 book by Daniel Defoe, *A Plan of the English Commerce*, he narrates how Henry VII, the ruler of England from 1485 to 1509, transformed his nation into a manufacturing powerhouse by promoting wool manufactures.[46] According to Chang's account, the king increased the export tax on wool, temporarily banned its export, and poached workers from the Low Countries. His son Henry VIII carried forward some of these policies. By 1578, in the middle of Elizabeth I's reign, Britain had created sufficient processing capacity to ban the export of raw wool. The ban ruined competing manufacturers in the Low Countries who were dependent on British raw wool.

After providing this account, Chang takes a long leap and asserts, "Defying signals from the market that his country was an efficient raw wool producer and should remain so, Henry VII introduced policies that deliberately distorted such unwelcome truths. By doing so, he started the process that eventually transformed Britain into a leading manufacturing nation."

To begin with, we have no analysis here to assess whether the losses incurred by raw wool producers for nearly a century due to export taxes and occasional export bans were more than outweighed by the benefits reaped by wool manufacturers in Britain. We also do not know what impact this policy had on the price that British customers paid for wool manufactures during this entire century. If Britain was a net importer of wool manufactures during this period, as is likely, the increased prices that wool manufacturers in the Low Countries paid for British raw wool must also have raised the prices of wool manufactures they sold to Britain.

Far more puzzling: what is the process by which Henry VII's policies "transformed Britain into a leading manufacturing nation" nearly two centuries later? Was the Industrial Revolution this easy? Does anyone believe that absent the export taxes and ban on export of raw wool by Henry VII, there would have been no Industrial Revolution in Britain?

Quite the contrary, according to the excellent detailed account provided by Ronald Findlay and Kevin O'Rourke. By the time the Industrial Revolution got under way, wool manufacturing was a declining industry in Britain.[47] It was cotton textiles that served as the leading sector. In the period 1752–54, at the beginning of industrialization, the share of cotton textiles in total English exports was 1.3 percent. In contrast, the export share of woolen textiles was 61.9 percent. By the first decade of the nineteenth century, these shares had shifted to 40 and 20 percent, respectively. Earlier, in 1700, the wool industry had sought and got protection against imports of cotton fabrics from China, India, and Persia. Rather than turning into a super-efficient and effective competitor as a result of policies adopted by Henry VII, England's wool industry actually had to resort to protectionist policies against imperfect substitute products such as cotton textiles to maintain its profitability. And even then, it lost out to that industry when the Industrial Revolution came.

A False Analogy

In the third chapter of his book, Chang returns to the infant industry argument from yet another angle. Interpreting it literally, he defends the argument by analogy with the protection parents provide their children. He reasons that just as parents protect and nurture children, sending them to school rather than forcing them to work, nations must protect infant industries against competition from foreign suppliers. But a careful examination reveals that, like his infant industry examples of Toyota of Japan and wool manufactures of Britain, this line of reasoning is deeply flawed.

As a preliminary point, strictly speaking, this analogy would imply that we should protect all firms in their initial years regardless of the source of competition. If infancy is the sole criterion, it does not matter whether competition is coming from a domestic or foreign company. But Chang does not push the infant industry argument this far. Therefore, even at a basic level, his analogy is not as apt as it may appear at first glance.

Furthermore, the case for elementary education is based on its being a public good: the gains to the society as a whole from having a literate population significantly exceed those to private individuals. The case is also partially based on the shared social goal that children must not be subjected to hardships. This shared social goal is reflected in the observation that even countries that allow child labor (because without it many families would go hungry) prohibit the employment of children in hazardous activities. These policies are applied to all children regardless of their abilities and are applied to all generations of children.

To translate the protection and nurturing of children into an argument for infant industry protection, we must demonstrate that social benefits from setting up the industries exceed their private benefits or that establishing the industries is a shared social goal even if it leads to lower private incomes than alternatives. The analogy still fails since infant industry protection is normally not applied to all industries. Moreover, the argument is about temporary protection in the early stages of development rather than in perpetuity. And finally, the desirability of import protection as the solution does not follow even if one accepts the analogy.

Conclusions

Careful analysis shows that a logical case for import protection as the instrument to promote infant industries does not exist. If the nature of costly innovation and skill formation is such that they freely spill over to future entrants, import protection will fail to induce early entrants to invest in these cost-cutting activities. Close analytic scrutiny shows that the plausible-sounding arguments of the prominent proponents of infant industry protection are in fact false. We may conclude by highlighting a number of practical points.

Competition from Established Foreign Versus Domestic Firms

One way to see the hollowness of the infant industry argument is to ask why competition from established foreign firms is special. Competition from established *domestic* firms that use conventional techniques may also pose a barrier to the entry of potentially profitable innovative infant firms. For example, new firms in the western and central provinces of China that wish to enter the market with novel techniques that lower future costs may face competition from established Chinese firms in the coastal regions. Proponents of the infant industry argument have not provided a compelling reason why infant firms facing foreign competition must be protected but not those sub-ject to domestic competition.[48]

Producer Lobbies

The ability of the government to pick true winners and provide the right level of protection is likely to be further hampered by the presence of lobbying. Even if a government merely declares its intention to provide protection to selected industries, that is likely to activate lobbies interested in seeking assistance for their favorite "infants." Moreover, producers would exaggerate the costs and the threat from foreign competition to seek the highest possible level of protection. Therefore, it is the lobbying power of interest groups rather than the social rate of return of the industries that is likely to determine the actual pattern and level of protection.

This is a point Henry George forcefully made in his masterly 1886 book *Protection or Free Trade: An Examination of the Tariff Question, with Special Reference to the Interests of Labor.* To quote him:

> All experience shows that the policy of encouragement, once begun, leads to a scramble in which it is the strong, not the weak; the unscrupulous, not the deserving, that succeed. What are really infant industries have no more chance in the struggle for govern-mental encouragement than infant pigs have with full-grown swine about a meal-tub. Not merely is the encouragement likely to go to industries that do not need it, but it is likely to go to industries that can be maintained only in this way, and thus to cause absolute loss to the community by diverting labor and capital from remunerative industries.[49]

Time Inconsistency

Even the flawed argument for infant industry protection calls for strictly tem-porary protection. But once granted, such protection is likely to become per-manent. Firms that decide to enter the market when provided protection on grounds of externalities associated with innovation and worker training do not invest in these activities. Instead, they take advantage of the higher import price to make profits using existing technologies and worker skills. Consequently, they remain uncompetitive at the world price. But once firms have entered the industry, their exit may become socially costly, making the later withdrawal of protection undesirable or policitically unacceptable.

Government's Ability to Pick Winners

In practice, the ability of the government to identify industries in which future gains outweigh the losses during the learning phase is seriously in doubt. The idea that the government is better positioned than entrepreneurs to identify potential winner industries is highly suspect. Even economist Dani Rodrik, a free trade skeptic and longtime advocate of industrial policy, concedes that governments lack the ability to pick the winners: "What I understand by 'industrial policy' is not an effort by the government to select particular sectors and subsidize them through a range of instruments (directed credit, subsidies, tax incentives, and so on). The critics of industrial policy are correct when they argue that governments do not have adequate knowledge to pick 'winners.' "[50]

A Rule of Thumb for Picking Potential Winners

If a government ignores economic logic as well as the lessons of history and feels compelled to intervene on behalf of infant industries, it is much better off supporting industries that would become exporters in the near future than industries that would substitute domestic output for imports. This approach, while still likely to inflict net losses, has three advantages over import substitution.

First, when the government bats on behalf of potential exporters, it has a much better chance of picking industries close to the margin of the country's comparative advantage. In contrast, if the government provides protection for import-substituting industries, it runs the risk of picking industries that are farthest from the margin of its comparative advantage. The force of this argument increases even more when the political process leads to the greatest sympathy for the least competitive industries.

Second, even with subsidies, exporters have to compete in global markets against the most efficient producers of the world and satisfy the most discriminating consumers. In contrast, import-substituting industries are largely protected from competing against the best in the world. They need only satisfy the home consumers, who may be far less discriminating and demanding in the early stages of development. The chances that subsidized exporters will benefit from pro-competitive effects are higher than the chances of import-competing producers internalizing similar benefits.

Finally, because subsidies attract a lot more attention from the public and are potentially subject to threats of retaliation by partner countries, it is more difficult for the government to abuse them than to abuse tariffs.

Importance of a Capable Government

A final word of caution for economists and analysts eager to advise in favor of infant industry protection is that success in promoting winners requires a highly capable government. The development history of the last seventy years is replete with episodes of governments adding their own failures to market failures while trying to correct the latter. Economist Larry Westphal, one of the earliest authors to carefully examine the Korean experience and a sympathizer of infant industry promotion, offers a set of guidelines for successful infant industry promotion. But he cautions against the mechanical replication of the Korean experience: "The relevance of these guidelines for other less developed countries is limited, mainly because following them requires an overriding commitment to meaningful economic development, a commitment that few political leaders of less developed countries appear capable of making. Taiwan is one of the few exceptions."[51]

Westphal goes on to present an episode from Korea to illustrate the kind of commitment that is necessary to achieve success: "Prior to the reform, rent seeking in relation to import licensing and tariff exemptions had provided a major source of revenue for businessmen and government officials alike. To redirect the focus of their activities, President Park [Chung-hee] had a number of preeminent businessmen arrested shortly after he came to power, and then threatened them with confiscation of their ill-gotten wealth." Leaders in most developing countries today lack the authority and political will that President Park exhibited in the 1960s and 1970s Korea. It is not surprising that the proponents of infant industry protection are rarely able to go beyond South Korea and Taiwan (and occasionally Japan) in their search for examples of successful interventions. And even then, they have not succeeded in making a persuasive case that these successes were achieved through protection in the way their icons Hamilton and List had envisaged.

Notes

1. See Bhagwati 1988a for a detailed discussion.
2. I may note here that at least in the initial years, one large developing country, India, was motivated to adopt inward-looking policies by a different consideration. Led by Prime Minister Jawaharlal Nehru, India sought self-sufficiency to avoid *any* dependence on the developed countries in general and its former colonizing power in particular. The promotion of domestic industry, both heavy and light, was seen as necessary for achieving this self-sufficiency. Panagariya 2008, ch. 2, discusses the role that this motivation played in guiding India's protectionist policy in greater detail.
3. This point is made in Krueger 2004.
4. Resorting to this argument, India recently partially reversed its trade liberalization, which had begun in earnest in 1991. In December 2017 and February 2018, it went on to raise tariffs on

a large number of products with the explicit objective of replacing imports by domestic production. Panagariya 2018 dissects this episode in greater detail.

5. Hamilton (1791) 1913, 19, and List 1856. Irwin 1996, ch. 8, provides a detailed history of the literature on the subject.

6. The historical account that follows relies on Irwin 1996, ch. 8.

7. Mill (1848) 1909.

8. Bastable 1887.

9. In the sole paragraph on the subject in his sixty-page report, Hamilton (1791) 1913, 19, wrote, "The superiority antecedently enjoyed by nations who have preoccupied and perfected a branch of industry constitutes a more formidable obstacle than either of those which have been mentioned, to the introduction of the same branch into a country, in which it did not before exist. To maintain between the recent establishments of one country and the long matured establishments of another country a competition upon equal terms, both as to quality and price, is in most cases impracticable. The disparity in the one or in the other or in both must necessarily be so considerable as to forbid a successful rivalship, without the extraordinary aid and protection of government."

10. Mill (1848) 1909, 922, wrote, "The only case in which, on mere principles of political economy, protecting duties can be defensible, is when they are imposed temporarily (espe cially in a young and rising nation) in hopes of naturalizing a foreign industry, in itself perfectly suitable to the circumstances of the country."

11. Bastable 1887, 136–37.

12. To quote Irwin 1996, 135: "Over the first half of the twentieth century, the infant industry argument remained a universally acknowledged theoretical exception to free trade, despite the continued skepticism among economists about such protection in practice."

13. Meade 1955, ch. 16; Johnson 1965; Baldwin 1969. Additional relevant contributions include Kemp 1960 and Grubel 1966.

14. Such scale economies may arise due to agglomeration. When an industry operates on a larger scale, it can support a large market for skilled labor and ancillary industries. In turn, this may bring the average costs of production down. It may be possible to make an argument for permanent protection in the presence of these agglomeration economies. See Panagariya 1980 for a formal exposition of this argument.

15. This example closely follows that provided in Corden 1997, 151.

16. In a democratic country, the government could be viewed as representing society. In that case, the social rate of discount would coincide with the rate at which the country's government discounts the future.

17. Meade 1955, 255–56.

18. In the example chosen here, the entrepreneur would never repay the loan but instead pay the interest in perpetuity.

19. Strictly speaking, the tariff creates a distortion in consumption and imposes an extra social cost. This causes the social rate of return on the investment to drop below 10 percent and thus leads to a violation of the Bastable condition. To avoid this possibility, we must assume that the demand for the product is completely inelastic, so that the price increase due to tariff protection causes no by-product consumption distortion.

20. Appendix 3 provides a concise mathematical of the arguments in this section.

21. Recall that high transport costs rule out exports. As such, the demand for the firms is confined to the domestic market.

22. For example, see Bardhan 1971; Succar 1987; Mayer 1984; Melitz 2005; Greenwald and Stiglitz 2006. Mayer 1984 presents a case for export subsidy to an infant export industry.

23. Baldwin 1969.

24. Baldwin 1969, 303. The point that specification of the transmission mechanism underlying learning, referred to as micro-foundations of learning, invalidates the case for protection also finds resonance in Grossman and Horn 1988. These authors hypothesize a situation in which consumers recognize the attributes of an established brand (for example, the iPhone) but not of new domestically supplied products (for example, generic mobile phones). In such a situation, consumers are not willing to pay the same price for the domestic product even though it may offer a service identical to that of the recognized foreign brand. The authors show that in

such situations, temporary import protection against the foreign brand makes matters worse. It encourages low-quality, fly-by-night operators who make a large profit while protection lasts and exit after it is withdrawn.

25. List 1856. Although many advocates of protection frequently invoke List to justify protection for manufacturing in the developing countries, List himself recommended specialization in agriculture and free trade for those countries. He argued that the countries in the tropical zone, which are more or less synonymous with the developing countries, are not suited for manufacturing production. List also recommended specialization in agriculture and free trade for temperate countries that had not yet fully developed agriculture.

26. List 1856, 208.

27. List 1856, 223–24.

28. Krugman 1994a, 202.

29. Greenwald and Stiglitz 2006.

30. Mayer 1984.

31. Grossman and Horn 1988 establish this result in a formal model in which firms choose product quality endogenously.

32. Amsden 1989; Chang 2007; Reinert 2007; Wade 1990, 2004; Meade 1955; Johnson 1965; Grubel 1966; Baldwin 1969; Irwin 1996.

33. The reference here is to Hamilton (1791) 1913 and List 1856. Incidentally, in a detailed analysis of Hamilton, Irwin (2004a, 800) concludes: "Hamilton's proposed tariffs were quite modest, particularly in light of later experience. This reflected his emphasis on using tariffs to generate fiscal revenue to fund the public debt; indeed, the country's finances were his top priority, not discouraging imports for the sake of domestic manufacturers. As a consequence, manufacturing interests were disappointed with Hamilton's moderate policies." Later in the paper, Irwin points out, "Despite the 'Report on Manufactures,' Hamilton was not considered a staunch friend by manufacturing interests. The import duties that he proposed were quite modest. . . . In the report, Hamilton was skeptical of high protective tariffs because they sheltered inefficient and efficient producers alike, led to higher prices for consumers, and gave rise to smuggling, which cut into government revenue."

34. Wade 2004, xlvi n. 47.

35. Wade 2003.

36. Ranis 2003.

37. The reference here is to Lall 2003.

38. Ranis 2003, 34.

39. Irwin 2004b.

40. Little 1996.

41. The endorsement by Wolf appears on the front cover of Chang 2007.

42. Literally translated, this Latin phrase means "after this, therefore because of this." It is often glossed as "the post hoc fallacy." An individual commits the fallacy when he concludes that one event causes another simply because the proposed cause preceded the proposed effect.

43. Chang 2007, 21.

44. Beason and Weinstein 1996.

45. Beason and Weinstein 1996, 286–87.

46. Daniel Defoe is better known as the author of the famous novel *Robinson Crusoe*.

47. Findlay and O'Rourke 2007, 314-18.

48. This point is due to Little, Scitovsky, and Scott 1970, 128–29.

49. George (1886) 1949, 89.

50. Rodrik 2006.

51. Westphal 1990, 58.

4

Other Common Arguments for Protection

While the infant industry argument is the one most commonly invoked to justify protection in the developing countries, it is not the only one. A number of additional arguments have found favor with pro-protection analysts. We turn to a critical examination of a select few of them in this chapter.

Diversification and Information Externalities

In the older economic development literature, industrial diversification was viewed as an important objective of development. This thinking was reflected in an active pursuit of industrial diversification in many developing countries in the 1960s and beyond. India offers the most extreme example of the pursuit of this objective. From the mid-1960s till 1990, it had the policy of automatically granting an import ban on a product that a domestic entrepreneur wanted to manufacture. In the 1980s, the government went a step further, adopting the phased manufacturing program (PMP), under which it offered a production license for one or more products to an entrepreneur provided he agreed to progressively replace the imported components with domestically sourced ones through either in-house production or purchases from other domestic suppliers. The underlying objective of PMP was to encourage production of items not previously made in the country. India's drive for diversification under draconian import controls held back its development for decades. It was only after the launch of the 1991 reforms, which finally opened the economy to foreign trade and abandoned the obsession with diversification, that India saw its growth accelerate.

During the 2000s, the diversification argument saw a comeback, though in a somewhat different guise. Economists Jean Imbs and Romain Wacziarg show that beginning at low per capita incomes, increases in per capita income up to relatively high levels are accompanied by diversification of production within sectors.[1] For example, not only does the industrial sector grow at the expense of agriculture as per capita income rises, but industry, agriculture, and services also become more diversified in terms of product and employment mix. It is only at per capita income levels comparable to those in Ireland that the diversification process reverses, with production and employment becoming more concentrated.

Building on this finding, Rodrik has revived the old industrial diversification objective, though with a twist.[2] Taking product diversification as an objective in itself, he reasons that product diversification requires the discovery of new products, variants of existing products, and new processes that allow the available products to be produced at lower costs. These discoveries do not lend themselves to patenting and are therefore subject to the usual free rider problem. This means no firms want to be the first to undertake the discovery. This situation calls for government intervention.

A moment's reflection should make clear that the diversification of production noted by Imbs and Wacziarg is largely incidental to Rodrik's argument. Even if a discovery leads to no diversification of the production basket, as long as it is subject to externality a case can be made for government intervention in its favor. For example, cut flowers, a favorite example of Rodrik's, were produced in Colombia prior to the discovery of the export markets for them. Therefore, growth in the export of cut flowers need not have led to a more diversified production basket in Colombia. The same can be said of soccer balls in Pakistan and hats in Bangladesh, two of the other examples Rodrik cites. Therefore, the central issue is not diversification but externality.

The key policy question concerns the nature of the government intervention required to correct the externality. On this score, Rodrik notes that though the first-best intervention is to subsidize investments in new, nontraditional industries, it is not a practical option: "The difficulty in monitoring the use to which the subsidy is put—an investor might as well use it for purposes that provide direct consumption benefits—renders the first best policy intervention largely of theoretical interest." Rodrik goes on to offer his preferred solution, a "carrot-and-stick strategy":

> Since self-discovery requires rents to be provided to entrepreneurs, one side of the policy has to take the form of a carrot. This can be a subsidy of some kind, trade protection, or the provision of venture capital. Note that the logic of the problem requires that the rents be provided only to the initial investor, not to copycats. To ensure that mistakes are not perpetuated and bad projects are phased out, these rents must in turn be subject either to performance requirements (for example, a

requirement to export), or to close monitoring of the uses to which they are put.[3]

There are at least four problems with this set of recommendations. First, it is not clear precisely how trade protection helps solve the externality problem. Trade protection may make entry into a product possible despite high costs, but it will not encourage costly discovery that spills over to other firms. The analysis by Baldwin shows this decisively in the context of the infant industry argument: copycat firms, which do not incur the cost of discovery, can undercut the firm undertaking the discovery and drive it out of the market, so no firm will invest in the discovery in response to trade protection.

Second, having accepted that the option to subsidize investments in new, nontraditional industries is not a practical one due to monitoring difficulties, Rodrik lays out an intervention strategy that includes subsidies and is even more demanding on the monitoring agency. Firms will have the incentive to divert government-provided venture capital to consumption in the same way as an output or investment subsidy on new products, which Rodrik rejects at the outset. It is quite unlikely that a developing country's government (with the possible exception of the Korean and Taiwanese governments of the 1960s and 1970s and the current Chinese government) will have the capacity to implement the above strategy—surely not the governments in South Asia and sub-Saharan Africa.

Third, the precise nature of performance requirements is not as simple as it may appear in Rodrik's discussion. For example, he mentions exports as a criterion for measuring performance. But it is not clear why sales abroad are a better measure of performance than sales at home. It is entirely possible that a firm could satisfy the performance criterion by exporting the product at a loss and making up for it through monopoly profits at home and a government-provided subsidy. The general point is that credible performance requirements are difficult to implement.

Finally, the success stories Rodrik cites—cut flowers in Colombia, soccer balls in Pakistan, hats and garments in Bangladesh, and software in India—did not result from a government-engineered strategy of the kind he outlines. In most of these episodes, the government had at best a limited role. On the other hand, the PMP in India employed a carrot-and-stick strategy: the carrot was a guaranteed domestic market, and the stick was the denial of import licenses for components once the deadline for diversification into them had passed. But the outcome was massive inefficiency in production and very high cost to the consumer. Rodrik can justifiably argue that the government did not subject producers to performance requirements that would promote efficiency. But that returns us to the difficulty of devising and implementing such requirements.

Coordination Externalities

More than seven decades ago, Polish economist Paul Rosenstein-Rodan offered an argument for government-engineered industrialization based on demand-side inter-industry externalities.[4] In "Problems of Industrialization of Eastern and South-Eastern Europe," he proposed that in the early stages of industrialization, production of any single item may be unviable but the production of many items simultaneously may be self-sustaining. He illustrated the point using his famous shoe factory example. He began with the observation that in a traditional, preindustrial economy, a sizable labor force is either underemployed or outright unemployed. He then proceeded to argue:

> Let us assume that 20,000 unemployed workers in Eastern and South-Eastern Europe are taken from the land and put into a large shoe factory. They receive wages substantially higher than their previous meager income *in natura*. It would be impossible to put them into industry at their previous income standard, because they need more foodstuffs than they had in their agrarian semi-unemployed existence, because these foodstuffs have to be transported to towns, and because the workers have to pay for housing accommodation. If these workers spent all their wages on shoes, a market for the products of their enterprise would arise representing an expansion which does not disturb the pre-existing market, and 90% of the problem (assuming 10% profit) would be solved. The trouble is that the workers will not spend all their wages on shoes. If, instead, one million unemployed workers were taken from the land and put, not into one industry, but into a whole series of industries which produce the bulk of the goods on which the workers would spend their wages, what was not true in the case of one shoe factory would become true in the case of a whole system of industries: it would create its own additional market, thus realizing an expansion of world output with the minimum disturbance of the world markets.[5]

It may be noted that this argument for government intervention depends crucially on indivisibilities in production. If production costs are independent of scale, an entrepreneur could readily set up a factory that produces a little bit of each product on which workers are expected to spend their income, thereby solving the coordination failure problem. In the above example, rather than employ twenty thousand workers in a factory specialized in the production of shoes, the entrepreneur could employ them in a factory with a diversified production basket including shoes, clothing, furniture, and toys. Workers could then spend their wages on these products.

It is only when the production process for each of the relevant products requires very large upfront investment and individual entrepreneurs are incapable of investing simultaneously in them that coordination failure occurs. Under scale economies, benefits from demand complementarities are multiplied since the low costs resulting from large-scale production allow each sector to pay high wages that can in turn support the production of other goods on a large scale. A "big push" strategy of development, whereby substantial investment for large-scale production is made simultaneously in a number of products, becomes optimal.[6]

A key limitation of this argument, however, is that it is valid only in a world in which the products subject to complementarities and scale economies are not internationally traded.[7] Once we recognize the possibility of exports and imports, the argument collapses. For example, a single entrepreneur employing twenty thousand workers in a shoe factory can readily kick off the process. He can export the shoes not purchased domestically. The foreign exchange so earned can then be used to import products desired by shoe factory workers receiving high wages.

An argument is sometimes made that high transport costs turn many potentially tradable goods into non-tradable goods, making coordination failure a serious issue. While this argument could have been valid fifty years ago, its significance today is highly suspect. With innovations in shipping and air transportation, transport costs are no longer a serious barrier to international trade. Even perishable goods are traded in large volumes today. Many services that were once non-traded have become tradable. High transport costs of international trade, where they exist, are the result of poor domestic infrastructure. In such circumstances, the appropriate intervention is to develop internal infrastructure rather than to artificially support a set of otherwise unviable industrial activities.

Even if we accept the assumption that there exist non-traded products subject to scale economies and demand complementarities in which investment coordination by the government can take the economy to a superior equilibrium, it does not give us a case for protection in products that are tradable. If the government intervention is itself optimally done, free trade in the tradable products continues to confer gains in the usual manner. While I am not aware of any serious scholar who claims the contrary, it is useful to explicitly recognize the point that the need for domestic intervention to correct for the coordination failure problem does not translate into a need for interference with free international trade.

Finally, it has been suggested that if the government intervenes to ensure internalization of coordination externalities, it need give no actual subsidies.[8] If the externalities have been properly identified and the activities are jointly profitable, the government can promise to absorb any losses that may accrue. Since this would lead all activities to be undertaken simultaneously, no losses would actually accrue and no subsidies will have to be given. The problem with this argument, however, is that it ignores the moral hazard that accompanies government promises to cover losses: assured of no losses, firms undertaking the activities will engage in wasteful expenditures and turn what should be socially profitable activities into socially unprofitable ones. In the end, outside of the activities such as building infrastructure that traditionally fall directly in the domain of the public sector, the government's best bet may still be to provide the necessary information to various agents and let them engage in the coordination directly, without a promise to cover any losses.

Capital Market Imperfections

We have already encountered the role the proponents of infant industry protection assign to capital market imperfections. It is useful to briefly consider the relevance of these market imperfections to industry protection more generally.

The broad argument for the correction in capital market imperfections through protection relies on a two-good conception of the economy, in which agriculture is seen as the export good and industry as the import-competing good. In this setting, if lenders are poorly informed and consistently underestimate the return on industrial projects, they underinvest in industry relative to the socially optimal level. In principle, it can be argued that entrepreneurs should be able to offer lenders a credible blueprint of their projects, thereby eliminating the information gap and thus the need for intervention. But assuming that certain institutional barriers preclude this solution, a case for intervention can be made. While the first-best intervention in this situation is an interest rate subsidy, a protective tariff may be justified as a second- or third-best policy.

Interestingly, however, even this justification for import protection remains subject to two serious reservations. First, as Krueger has argued, the two-sector conception of the economy on which the argument is based rules out the important and realistic possibility that rapid transformation may be achieved by exporting one set of industrial goods while importing another set.[9] Once we allow for this possibility by introducing two industrial goods alongside agriculture, the argument for import protection based on distortion in the capital market is considerably weakened.

To illustrate, imagine that the economy consists of two industrial sectors, which use capital and labor, and agriculture, which uses labor and land. Assume further that at any given set of factor prices, one industrial good uses more labor per unit of capital than the other. The former good, which is labor-intensive, is exported, while the latter is imported. It is then altogether possible that lenders would underestimate the return on investment in the export good because of their poor knowledge of the export market. This would lead to underinvestment in the export good rather than in the import-competing good. Protection in this situation will only exacerbate the problem by shifting capital further away from the exportable good to the import-competing good.

The second limitation of the argument, pointed out by economist Ronald McKinnon, is even more compelling.[10] He argues that land, labor, and capital markets in the developing countries are often fragmented to such a degree that it is not possible to correct the resulting distortions within the context of a simple division of the economy into broad sectors such as agriculture and industry.

McKinnon's essential argument is that fragmentation in factor markets *within* broad sectors makes it impossible to correct such fragmentation through taxes, subsidies, and tariffs that operate at those broad levels. Activities with high social returns are spread in small pockets across agriculture, industry, and services. Attempts to encourage them by protecting broad sectors will encourage not just activities with high social returns but also those with low returns. At the same time, activities with high social returns in unprotected sectors would be placed at a disadvantage compared to those with low social returns. In effect, taxes and subsidies that operate on broad sectors are a crude instrument for correcting capital market distortions, especially in the developing countries, where high- and low-return activities are spread across all sectors. To quote McKinnon:

> I hypothesize that the economic profile of underdeveloped countries is dominated by fragmentation in the markets for land, labor and capital, as well as fragmentation in the distribution of knowledge and technical opportunities. There is a wide variety of returns to be earned on existing and potential investments which cannot be easily delineated by type of product or sector. This dispersion of returns in capital markets may be classified as a "distortion," but there is no tax-subsidy arrangement by which governments can costlessly compensate for it, given the great uncertainty involved in identifying entrepreneurs with access to profitable investments.[11]

Given this fragmentation, what is required is the development of financial markets that channel savings into socially profitable activities. Applying tariffs and tax-cum-subsidy schemes at broad sectoral levels carries with it the potential to make matters worse by promoting many low-return activities in protected or subsidized sectors and neglecting many high-return activities in unprotected or unsubsidized sectors.

Unemployment

While the unemployment argument is not directly related to industrialization, it is sometimes made in the context of the developing countries considering trade liberalization. Before exploring the evidence on the link between trade liberalization and unemployment, it is useful to begin with a parable to drive home the point that often policies that appear employment friendly may turn out to be exactly the opposite and anti-development.

In the early 1980s, a U.S. civil engineer visited China. His host took him around the country to show him various construction projects in progress. One thing that struck the visitor was the use of shovels in digging the foundations everywhere. Unable to contain his curiosity, even at the risk of offending the host, he asked why the projects did not deploy bulldozers to dig the foundations. "Ah, but that would lead to massive unemployment in the economy," replied the host. "In that case, why not replace the shovels by spoons?" countered the visitor.

That mechanization or automation necessarily leads to unemployment is a common fallacy. This is because human nature is to focus attention on the point of impact: the introduction of bulldozers would necessarily render unemployed the workers performing the same activity with shovels. But we ignore the effects hidden from our eyes: cost savings in digging may lead to such a large expansion of construction activity that the total employment in it actually increases. And even if employment in construction falls, the workers so released may be absorbed in other, more productive jobs.[12]

The argument that trade liberalization causes unemployment has considerable salience in the developing countries that are predominantly labor abundant. Advocates of the argument are often fuzzy, however, about whether their claim applies to the sector subject to liberalization or the economy as a whole. If the former, the alarm is misplaced since the gains from trade arise precisely through reallocation of resources from protected sectors to the rest of the economy. Recall that in our Ricardian example, the benefits of trade accrue through reallocation of workers from the comparative-disadvantage good to the comparative-advantage good—from shirt production to wheat production in the United States and from wheat production to shirt production in India. This does not involve a decline in total employment.

A decline in employment in the import-competing sector upon liberalization, therefore, does not undermine the case for free trade. The critics must show that trade liberalization lowers total employment. This they have not done. On the contrary, there is considerable evidence that trade policy has little effect on aggregate long-run employment. South Korea opened its economy in the 1960s in a major way in terms of both trade barriers and the share of imports in GDP.

While this opening up was accompanied by a reallocation of labor from agriculture to industry and services, there is no evidence that it was accompanied by a decline in overall employment. If we go by wage movements during this period, the labor market would seem to be characterized by scarcity rather than slack.[13] The experience of India in the last two decades has been similar: real wages have shown an upward trend, with no evidence that liberalization has had an adverse impact on aggregate employment.[14]

Sometimes the proponents of this argument rest their case on the simple empirical association between trade liberalization and decline in the growth rate of employment.[15] But employment growth may fall simply due to a decline in the growth rate of the labor force: fewer additional jobs are created because fewer additional workers enter the labor force. Sometimes, declining trade barriers may be accompanied by declining growth in employment due to the presence of other rigidities (for example, a minimum wage). If so, the appropriate policy response is to remove those rigidities rather than sacrifice the gains from trade.

Theoretically, it is possible for trade liberalization to lower total employment in the presence of labor market distortions such as an economy-wide minimum wage. But the conditions for this result are more applicable to developed countries than to developing countries. With an economy-wide minimum wage within the two-sector, two-factor model, protection lowers unemployment only in countries that export the capital-intensive good.[16] Because developing countries are exporters of labor-intensive products, they actually suffer increased unemployment when subjected to increased protection.

Models with sticky urban wages exhibit a similar property.[17] In the Harris-Todaro model, the urban wage, applicable to import-competing manufacturing, is institutionally fixed above the wage in the rural, agricultural sector. The higher expected wage in the urban sector leads workers to migrate, but not all of them find employment in the cities. The equilibrium is thus characterized by urban unemployment. In this setting, a tariff that increases urban employment gives no guarantee of increased aggregate employment: increased urban employment raises the expected urban wage and leads more workers to migrate out of agriculture. In turn, the total employment may actually fall.[18]

Even when protection may give rise to increased aggregate employment in the theoretical models, there remains an important objection to its use as a policy tool. First, as the classic analysis by Bhagwati and V. K. Ramaswami demonstrates, the optimal response to a domestic distortion is not to give up free trade but to correct it at the source by neutralizing the distortion.[19] Once this correction is done, the traditional case for free trade is restored. In the minimum wage case, the first-best policy is to offer a generalized wage subsidy to the firms at a rate that eliminates the difference between the minimum wage and the competitive wage.

Freeing up trade can surely give rise to temporary unemployment as resources reallocate from declining sectors to expanding sectors. This is no different from other efficiency-enhancing policy changes that induce reallocation of resources. There are two responses to possible temporary unemployment from all policy changes. First, it is best to implement policy change gradually. This allows winning sectors to reemploy resources just as they are thrown out of employment by the declining sectors. Both India and China have gone from near autarkic to near free trade policy regimes in industrial products during the last three decades but with minimal dislocation of resources largely because they opened up gradually. Second, the governments must put in place adjustment assistance and social safety nets to soften the pain of adjustment. Admittedly, poor countries may often lack resources to finance such safety nets as well as the ability to administer them effectively. This fact points toward gradualism as the primary solution to the problem of dislocation.

Imports Are Bad, Exports Are Good

There is inherent bias among policymakers against imports and in favor of exports. A common manifestation of this bias is that when imports exceed exports, we say the trade balance is unfavorable, whereas when the opposite is true, we say that the trade balance is favorable. In a similar vein, trade policy intervention often takes the form of tax when applied to imports and subsidy when applied to exports. It is rare that countries impose taxes on exports or offer subsidies on imports, and when they do, it is to encourage the exports of higher-value-added products. In the developing countries, the tendency takes the form of industrialization through import substitution. It is commonplace that when a product is imported in large volumes, policymakers are keen to replace it with domestic production.

However intuitive the preference for exports over imports may seem, it is wholly illogical. At a basic level, as Nobel laureate Milton Friedman once graphically pointed out in one of his public lectures, we can eat imports but not exports. Imports can be directly consumed or used in the production of some other product that can then be consumed. But exports, once shipped out of the country, are no longer available to the country. Indeed, the only reason to export is as payment for imports. If other countries would give us imports for free, there would be no reason to export.

Put in a less extreme form, the less a country has to pay for its imports, the better off it is. The economics here is no different from that applicable to households. When a household wants to buy something, it wants to pay the lowest possible price for it. Or, for a given expenditure, it wants to maximize its purchases. The same goes for a nation.

As regards import substitution, which calls for restrictions on imports to replace them by domestic output, policymakers often fall into the trap of thinking that this would be a net addition to GDP. The reality, however, is that reducing imports of one set of products in order to expand domestic production leads to a reduction in exports of another set of products. One simple way to see this is to recognize that a reduction in imports reduces the demand for foreign currency and hence lowers its price in terms of the domestic currency. This in turn makes exports less attractive, leading to a reduction in them. We gain in the production of import-competing goods, in which our costs are high, and lose in the production of exportable products, which we produce more cheaply than foreigners do.

Another way to see this is to recognize that when a country reduces its imports, its trading partners have less incentive to buy its goods. It is the revenue from sales to the country that the trading partners use to buy its products. If trading partners' revenues are reduced because of a country's import restrictions, those partners will not be able to buy its products.

The reduction in trade in this manner makes both sides worse off. Trade allows each side to produce in larger volume products that it produces relatively cheaply and exchange them for products that it produces at higher cost. Restrictions on trade reverse this process. Each side ends up producing more of the higher-cost products.

A final context in which viewing imports as good and exports as bad produces harmful outcomes is in the context of bilateral trade balances. Countries want to restrict imports from trading partners with which they have a bilateral trade deficit. Once again, while politicians commonly seek to achieve bilateral trade balance, there is no economic logic behind it. A country should sell its products to partners that pay the highest prices for them. In parallel, it should buy its imports from countries that offer them at the lowest prices. There is no reason why this process should produce a pattern in which bilateral trade is balanced.

Once again, think of purchases and sales by individuals. Each individual typically sells her services to a single employer in return for a salary. She then uses these earnings to buy goods and services from different sellers. Therefore, she runs a bilateral surplus with her employer and bilateral deficits with all others from whom she buys goods and services. This leads to efficient exchange. If each individual were to instead try to achieve bilateral balance with her buyers and sellers, the outcome would be nightmarish. The idea of each nation trying to achieve bilateral trade balance with each of its trading partners is no different.

The Revenue Argument

The revenue argument is straightforward: many developing countries may lack tax instruments other than trade taxes. Strictly speaking, this is an argument for revenue, not for protection. Therefore, it does not give a country any reason to impose trade taxes to promote industrialization. If revenue is the objective, trade taxes should be so designed as to minimize the accompanying distortion. There is a vast body of literature on this subject. My own view is that given the information requirements of a theoretically optimal structure and the scope for lobbying by various interest groups, if a government wishes to collect a given amount of revenue, it is best to opt for a more or less uniform tariff on all imports.[20] It is also important that the country using tariffs as the instrument of revenue not use the absence of alternative revenue instruments as an excuse to prolong tariffs indefinitely. At some point it is important to develop more efficient instruments of revenue.

Concluding Remarks

Following on Chapter 3, which dissected the celebrated but ill-conceived argument for protection to infant industries, in this chapter I have critically examined several other arguments for protection offered in the context of the developing countries. These include inter alia the promotion of diversification, the resolution of coordination failure problems, compensation for capital market imperfections, and the elimination of bilateral trade deficits. In each case, I have offered reasons for us to take a skeptical view of protection as the corrective policy. The absence of alternative instruments for raising revenue offers a reason to resort to trade taxes, but they must be used judiciously and only temporarily until alternative revenue-raising instruments are developed.

Notes

1. Imbs and Wacziarg 2003.
2. Rodrik 2007.
3. Rodrik 2007, 106.
4. Rosenstein-Rodan 1943.
5. Rosenstein-Rodan 1943, 205–6.
6. Murphy, Shleifer, and Vishny (1989) have formalized this idea using the modern tools of analysis.
7. Rosenstein-Rodan (1943, 203) and Murphy, Shleifer, and Vishny (1989, 1006) are aware of this limitation and explicitly note it in their papers. To his credit, Rosenstein-Rodan actually considers the road to industrialization through international specialization superior: "Clearly

this way of industrialization [through international division of labor] is preferable to the autarkic one." He rejects the route, however, on the ground that "it is a tremendous task, almost without historical precedent." But today we have the examples of several developing countries successfully industrializing through international division of labor.

8. Rodrik 2007.
9. Krueger 1997.
10. McKinnon 1971, 1973.
11. McKinnon 1971, 508.
12. The idea that labor-saving innovation leads to increased unemployment is known as the Luddite fallacy. According to Easterly (2002, 53), the original Luddites were hosiery and lace workers in Nottingham, England, in 1811. When knitting machines were introduced, these workers smashed them as a protest against unemployment. The government did not buy the argument, however, and eventually hanged fourteen of the workers in 1813.
13. Panagariya 2008, ch. 6.
14. Panagariya 2008, ch. 7.
15. A debate along these lines has taken place in India, with critics arguing that India experienced joblessness growth in the 1990s. See Bhalla and Das 2005–6 for details.
16. Brecher 1974a, 110.
17. Harris and Todaro 1970; Corden and Findlay 1975. Corden 1974, ch. 6, provides an accessible discussion of these models.
18. Corden and Findlay 1975.
19. Bhagwati and Ramaswami 1963.
20. Panagariya 1994.

PART II

TRADE, GROWTH, POVERTY, AND INEQUALITY

5

Trade Openness, Growth, and Poverty

Exposing the Critics' Specious Arguments

> Those who cavalierly reject the Theory of Evolution as not being adequately supported by facts seem to forget that their own theory is supported by no facts at all.
>
> —Herbert Spencer, 1852

The static gains from trade based on differences in productivity and factor endowment between countries, economies of scale, and product variety arise from improved allocation of the existing world resources and efficient international exchange. According to available estimates, these gains can lead to one-time permanent increases in national incomes of at most 5 percent. While such gains may be significant and desirable, often they prove insufficient to persuade political leadership in the developing countries to abandon protectionist policies.

A wider political acceptance of the case for trade openness in the developing countries must be based on two related arguments: the indispensability of liberal trade policies to sustained rapid growth and the centrality of growth to combating poverty. If low or declining trade barriers can help accelerate per capita income growth by even 2 percentage points per annum for two to three decades, the accumulated increase in income can greatly contribute to the overall process of development through urbanization and building of infrastructure while also leading to substantial reductions in abject poverty. Growth helps create gainful employment, which places ever-rising wages in the hands of the poor while also generating revenue for the government that it can use to finance anti-poverty programs.

Against this background, the critical question we must address from a policy standpoint is whether low or declining barriers to trade are more conducive to faster growth and poverty alleviation than high or rising barriers. This is the central point of contention between proponents and opponents of trade openness when it comes to trade policies in the developing countries. It requires a careful study of cross-country experience over the past several decades as well as within-country experiences of countries that have followed markedly different trade policies during different time periods. This is the task we now undertake.

The question of the relationship of trade openness with growth and poverty alleviation is largely an empirical one. Unlike theory, the empirical world can be messy. In theory, free trade is the state of no trade barriers, while autarky is the state of prohibitive trade barriers. But in the real world, we are almost always somewhere between these two extremes, with some trade barriers present. Moreover, trade openness is only one of several policies that must come together to yield sustained rapid growth and poverty alleviation. Therefore, teasing out the role of trade openness empirically can be a challenge. Indeed, this factor has been at the heart of much of the confusion that prevails in the policy space on the role of trade openness. To avoid this confusion, I begin by first stating in the clearest possible terms how trade openness is to be defined and what role should be established for it in delivering growth and poverty alleviation.

Setting the Bar Right

Regrettably, when offering free trade as the key to rapid growth, some free trade advocates have fallen into the trap of setting the bar for themselves far higher than necessary. In turn, this has made the task of successfully challenging their case relatively easy for free trade critics. For example, in their otherwise well-argued and well-researched contribution to the debate, free trade advocates Deepak Lal and Sarath Rajapatirana state, "It seems to be as firm a stylized fact as any in the economics of developing countries: a sustained movement to an outward-oriented trade regime leads to faster growth of both exports and incomes."[1] The suggestion in this statement that trade openness on its own leads to sustained rapid growth is easily challenged: one does not have to look too far or too hard to find examples of countries failing to achieve either significant progress in export expansion or accelerated growth upon opening to foreign trade.

It is not my intention to defend the relationship between trade openness and growth in this strong form. Instead, the view taken in this volume is that the defense of the pro-free-trade position only requires establishing that liberal trade policies offer better prospects for sustained rapid growth than do protectionist trade policies. In a nutshell, liberal trade policies, which I identify with low or declining barriers to trade, are necessary for sustained rapid growth and poverty alleviation but not sufficient. That liberal trade policies are not sufficient for faster growth is readily seen by considering situations in which either world markets are closed or internal infrastructure linking the centers of production to ports is nonexistent. Under such circumstances, autarky would obtain even if there were no formal barriers to trade whatsoever. The removal of barriers would not hurt the country, but it would also not yield a positive benefit.

While sufficiency conditions may vary according to countries' individual circumstances, I propose to demonstrate in this volume that liberal trade policies are an integral part of nearly every policy package that has delivered sustained rapid growth and poverty alleviation. I will present empirical evidence based on cross-country experience as well as individual country experiences over time. Furthermore, I will show that an econometric analysis using cross-country data allows us to establish a causal relationship between trade openness and growth with a high degree of confidence.

Does the lack of sufficiency of trade openness for sustaining rapid growth negate the economist's case for free trade? Hardly. It still remains true that between low and high barriers, a country is better off opting for the former, since low barriers confer some immediate gains from efficient exchange and possibly specialization according to comparative advantage. And, of course, as other policies are put in place, low barriers also improve the country's prospects for sustained rapid growth. Protection offers neither advantage.

Opponents of free trade sometimes argue that if trade liberalization does not guarantee sustained rapid growth, why should a government pay its political cost? The response is that if we care enough about the country's future economic prospects, it is worth persuading its leaders to move toward a regime that promises improved economic prospects. Moreover, if done gradually and in conjunction with appropriate adjustments in the exchange rate, trade liberalization is among the least contentious reforms. Small, across-the-board tariff cuts make imports marginally more attractive relative to similar domestically produced goods. A simultaneous depreciation of the domestic currency (e.g., a change in the exchange rate from 60 rupees per dollar to 65 rupees per dollar) temporarily offsets the decline in the prices of imports and softens the blow to producers of liberalized products. Additionally, the depreciation makes the country's export goods more attractive to foreigners. This helps export sectors to expand and absorb the resources gradually released by the liberalized import-competing sectors, thus minimizing unemployment in transition.

That the political costs of broad-based trade liberalization are not as high as the critics would have us believe is evidenced by the considerable liberalization undertaken on a unilateral basis by a large number of countries in Asia, Africa, and Latin America at various points in time during the last three decades.[2] Despite continued voices of dissent, support for liberal trade policies in the developing countries today is much stronger than at any time prior to 1990.

Trade and Growth: Debunking Some Specious Arguments

In the context of the relationship between trade and growth, critics offer several arguments against freeing up trade that seem superficially plausible but turn out to be false upon careful scrutiny. Because these arguments often cloud and confuse the debate, it is best to get them out of the way at the outset.

Trade Liberalization Failed to Catalyze and Sustain Growth in Many Instances

Free trade critics frequently cite countries that opened their economies to foreign trade but failed to achieve higher growth on a sustained basis. This was true of many countries in Latin America and Africa in the 1980s. In some cases the failure is explained either by the liberalization's lack of credibility or by outright reversal. But there remain cases in which liberalization was not reversed and yet no significant jump in the growth rate was observed. At a slightly more sophisticated level, critics argue that the existing econometric evidence fails to establish a *causal* link between removal of barriers to trade and growth.[3]

A moment's reflection should convince the reader that these examples and arguments neither undermine the case for liberalization nor strengthen the case for protection. For starters, free trade advocates can cite an even larger number of examples of countries failing to stimulate growth through protectionism. They can also point out that opponents of free trade have not even *attempted* to establish a causal link between sustained rapid growth and protection. The quotation from Herbert Spencer at the beginning of this chapter is instructive in this respect.

The flaw in the argument is that a country must base its trade policy choices not on whether openness by itself will lead to higher growth but whether it will be more conducive to sustained rapid growth than protectionism would be. Few trade economists offer free trade as a cure-all. They recognize that a lack of policy credibility, macroeconomic instability, an overvalued exchange rate, structural rigidities in product or factor markets, external or internal conflicts, and poor infrastructure may block the positive growth effects of an open trade regime from being realized. What we simultaneously need to keep in mind is that beneficial internal policies will fall well below their potential without low or declining barriers to trade.

Writing as far back as 1985, Vittorio Corbo, Anne Krueger, and Fernando Ossa explicitly stated in the introduction to their book *Export-Oriented Development Strategies* that the experiences they reviewed revealed "a set of basic conditions for sustained export-led growth."[4] They went on to identify five such conditions: a stable macroeconomic framework, an appropriate real exchange rate, a free trade regime for exporters, timely financing for exporters at domestically competitive rates, and non-discrimination against savings. One can take issue with the specific elements in this list, but the essential point is that thoughtful trade economists do not claim that trade liberalization by itself will ensure sustained rapid growth.

When Countries Have Achieved Sustained Rapid Growth, the Catalyst Has Not Been Trade Liberalization

Critics also attack the case for liberal trade polices on the ground that certain successful experiences of sustained growth were actually catalyzed by alternative policies, such as land reform in the case of China, government-engineered increase in investment demand in the case of South Korea and Taiwan, and incremental domestic policy reform in the case of India.[5]

While the assertion that trade was not a catalyst to rapid growth in these countries is highly questionable, for now it suffices to note that even if this is true, open trade policies remain critical because they are necessary to *sustain* such growth.[6] Even if growth is initially stimulated by land reform, incremental domestic policy reform, or government-led expansion of investment demand, it is unlikely to be sustained if the trading environment is autarkic. A careful study of a large number of successful cases, including Hong Kong, Singapore, South Korea, and Taiwan in the 1960s and 1970s and India, China, Chile, and Vietnam in the 1980s and beyond, reveals that whatever the source of the initial stimulus, low or declining barriers to trade have almost always accompanied sustained rapid growth. Indeed, under Mao Zedong, China had tried a variety of land reforms at different points in time, but they failed to deliver rapid growth because the overall policy framework was anti-growth, with a high level of protection being a part of that framework.

High Protection Does Not Preclude Rapid Growth

Critics cite examples of countries that managed to register high growth rates behind high walls of protection to conclude that protection works. Again, high *initial* trade barriers do not preclude the *onset* of rapid growth, especially in large countries such as Brazil, China, and India. Sometimes the growth process itself may be kicked off by gradual liberalization of an initially highly protected regime. But the available evidence shows that even if protection is high and the initial stimulus comes from an alternative policy change, growth sustains and accelerates only if the country responds by undertaking liberalization that accommodates the pressures for the expansion of trade that such growth generates. Evidence pointing to the fact that a country grew rapidly while still behind a high wall of protection does not prove the efficacy of protection. The critical question for such an economy is whether it was lowering or further raising the protection during the period of rapid growth.

Import Substitution Has Preceded Outward Orientation

Free trade critics point to countries such as South Korea, Taiwan, and even Singapore, which went through a phase of import substitution before turning outward, to bolster the case for import substitution industrialization. Purely as a matter of historical record, import substitution prior to turning outward has been an integral part of the development experience of virtually all developing countries except Hong Kong. Given the conventional wisdom in the immediate postcolonial era that import substitution offered the only route to industrialization to the developing countries, this outcome was inevitable. But the key policy question is whether this phase of import substitution was a necessary condition for the success of outward-oriented policies later. For one thing, we do have the example of Hong Kong, which achieved sustained rapid growth without even a short period of import substitution. Moreover, the periods of import substitution varied greatly across countries that eventually achieved sustained rapid growth through opening up. For example, Singapore went through a very brief and mild period of import substitution, South Korea pursued it for a longer but still relatively short period, and India and China stayed with it for a very long time. The fact that each of these countries succeeded in achieving sustaining rapid growth only after turning outward suggests that import substitution was not essential to its success. The critics' argument remains a case of post hoc fallacy.

An argument can perhaps be made that the *first* stage of import substitution, during which a country replaces imports of labor-intensive non-durable consumer goods such as apparel and footwear and intermediate inputs used in them by domestic products, may not be overly costly. And if followed by a switch to outward-oriented policies, as was the case with Singapore, South Korea, and Taiwan, such import substitution may even appear to have contributed positively to sustained rapid growth. The cost is likely to be low because the country essentially encourages the production of goods in which it has a comparative advantage. But as the production structure begins to become more complex, the risks of choosing the wrong industries rise exponentially, as illustrated by the Indian experience (see Chapter 12).

In the present-day context, references to the success or otherwise of the first-stage import substitution must be seen as largely academic. Nearly every developing country is now past pursuing first-stage import substitution. As such, references to its success in the 1950s and 1960s cannot serve as the basis for continued import substitution today.

Industrial Policy Was Central to Many Growth Miracles

Some critics question the importance of outward-oriented policies on the ground that most successful countries relied on industrial policy, including targeting of certain industries. They reject the importance of reduced trade barriers by appeal to interventions in the domestic market. The efficacy of industrial policy itself constitutes a separate subject of debate among economists, but even if we accept that such policies made a positive contribution to the growth of South Korea and Taiwan, we cannot reject the contribution made by openness. Indeed, it can be argued that it is the presence of low or declining trade barriers that either minimized the damage from industrial policies or maximized their benefits. The contrasting experiences of South Korea and India during the first three decades of their development (1950–80) vividly illustrate this.

Trade Openness and Poverty: Debunking Yet More Specious Arguments

When confronted with persuasive evidence that sustained rapid growth has almost always been achieved under outward-oriented trade policies and rapidly expanding trade, anti-globalization critics often change the subject, arguing instead that the movement toward greater trade openness must still be resisted because it hurts the poor. Some scholars, most notably Robert Wade, explicitly side with the NGOs and journalists in their assault on openness as a source of increased poverty, while others, such as Ravi Kanbur, express sympathy without necessarily joining them.[7]

Before examining the arguments offered by critics, it is necessary to explain how poverty is measured. In principle, measures of poverty can be based on consumption expenditures, income, nutrition, life expectancy, infant mortality, educational attainments, and various other indicators considered relevant to human welfare. But the commonest metric is defined in terms of income or expenditure.

To measure poverty, we first define the "poverty consumption bundle" as the bundle of commodities and services necessary for a representative household, defined in terms of size and age-gender composition, to achieve a minimal acceptable living standard. We then define the poverty line as the minimum expenditure (or income) necessary to buy the poverty consumption bundle at a given set of prices. The proportion of a country's population with expenditure (or income) below this poverty line is called the country's poverty ratio or headcount ratio. Though the academic literature offers a number of additional, technically more sophisticated measures of poverty, much of the policy debate is centered on the poverty ratio.[8]

We may now examine some key claims of the critics regarding the impact of openness on poverty.

Rising Numbers of Poor Have Accompanied Rising Trade Openness

Many NGOs, international institutions, and scholars critical of openness as an instrument of promoting poverty alleviation have resorted to citing the changes in the absolute number of poor to argue that increased openness has failed the poor, even impoverished them. In the late 1990s, as part of the World Bank's effort to promote the so-called Comprehensive Development Framework, invented by its president, James Wolfensohn, the Bank played up the notion that poverty in the world had gone up during the age of globalization and economic reforms. For example, in its 1999 Annual Review of Development Effectiveness, the World Bank noted, "The number of poor people living on less than US$1 a day rose from 1,197 million in 1987 to 1,214 million in 1998. Excluding China, there are 100 million more poor people in developing countries than a decade ago." This evidence in turn served as the justification for the assertion in the foreword to the report, "Despite the potential benefits of globalization and technological change, world poverty has increased and growth prospects have dimmed for developing countries."[9] Similar statements can be found in numerous other contemporary documents from the World Bank, as well as those from the United Nations and its affiliated organizations, which traditionally have been skeptical of outward-oriented policies. In turn, anti-trade NGOs have seized on these assertions, prominently citing them on their websites.[10]

There are, of course, many problems with the assertions in that World Bank document. Counting the global poor using a common global poverty line lacks proper conceptual foundation. And if one nevertheless insists on engaging in such an exercise, there is no reason China, which made huge strides in bringing poverty down during the period 1987–98 through increased outward orientation complemented by other pragmatic reforms, should be excluded from the calculation of global poor. But above all, we must question the wisdom of using the absolute number of poor instead of the poverty ratio as the correct indicator for evaluating a policy's effectiveness in combating poverty.

To explain why the reliance on the absolute number of poor is problematic, consider the case of India. According to official estimates by the government of India, in 1983 the poverty ratio in the country was 44.5 percent and the absolute number of poor was 323 million. Between 1983 and 2004, India's population rose by 375 million to 1.1 billion. A reasonable assumption would be that absent an effective poverty alleviation strategy, 44.5 percent of the additional 375 million individuals would have been poor. That is to say, in 2004 the absolute number of poor would have risen by 166.9 million to reach 489.9 million. So if the absolute number of poor in 2004 remained unchanged at 323 million, it would imply a reduction in the number of poor by 166.9 million. The conclusion that any increase in the number of poor represents increased poverty follows only if we make the silly assumption that none of the new additions to the population were born in poverty. In reality, the number of poor in 2004 turned out to be 302 million, implying that India had successfully pulled 187.9 million people out of poverty. This substantial decline is properly captured by the poverty ratio, which fell to 27.5 percent in 2004 from 44.5 percent in 1983.

A more dramatic way to make this point is to consider the absolute number of those living above the poverty line. Suppose this number rises over time. Does this unambiguously imply that poverty has gone down? The answer is an unequivocal no. In a country with rising population, it is highly likely that the number of poor and the number of non-poor would rise simultaneously. A reasonable way to determine whether poverty has risen or fallen under such circumstances is to look at the distribution of the population between the poor and non-poor.

Rising Number of Absolute Poor Shows Openness Has Failed the Poor

All, including such critics as Wade, agree that the poverty ratio has declined globally.[11] Dissent on the efficacy of globalization in combating poverty is based on the contention that the poor rose in absolute numbers alongside the opening up of the global economy. I have already argued that the appropriate index to measure poverty when evaluating the impact of alternative policies on poverty is the poverty ratio. But even ignoring this fact, the conclusion that the rising number of poor in an era of opening up to trade represents a failure of outward-oriented policies is problematic. For one thing, as T. N. Srinivasan has cogently argued, the measurement of global poverty using a common poverty line such as $1 per day at purchasing power parity (PPP) is fraught with serious conceptual and data problems.[12] But more important from our viewpoint, the indictment of openness on the grounds that it accompanies a rise in the absolute number of the poor suffers from a serious logical problem.

I have argued that openness is a necessary condition for growth but not a sufficient one. Therefore, even if the global poverty ratio or the absolute number of poor worldwide is shown to have risen during the 1990s and beyond, it proves little against the necessity of openness to combating poverty. In countries where the absence of complementary conditions resulted in a failure to sustain growth, there is no reason to expect that openness by itself would have led to a sustained reduction in poverty. For instance, sustained rapid growth is unlikely to have been achieved in many African countries suffering from civil war during the 1990s. Indeed, the number of poor in such countries is likely to have risen on account of conflict and war. Inclusion of these countries will then bias the outcome toward an increased absolute number of poor in the world despite increased openness.

As far back as four decades ago, economist Walter Galenson offered compelling evidence demonstrating that whenever a country achieved sustained rapid growth, it also succeeded in bringing poverty down.[13] Using the data available to him at the time, he reached the conclusion that "rapid sustained growth has had positive effects on the living standards of all economic groups of those countries that experienced it." He went on to add, "Growth has not 'failed'; there has simply not been enough of it in the great majority of the less developed nations."[14]

Finally, critics do not provide evidence that protectionism has done better than openness in combating global poverty. If they are to be believed, they must show that higher or rising protection in the past has delivered better outcomes for a similar increase in population. Not only have they not done it, but even the thought that this is what is required to clinch their case has not occurred to them.

Globalization Has Bypassed the Core Poor

Sometimes critics of trade openness refer to specific groups that have not been lifted out of poverty or have even been impoverished during a period of trade liberalization accompanied by sustained rapid growth and then make the sweeping claim that openness and growth do not help the poor. They point to the continued or worsened plight of the "core poor," defined as the poorest among the poor, and proceed to conclude that openness and growth hurt the poor. This claim is reminiscent of the claim that growth does not "trickle down" to the truly poor.

Three factors make it particularly easy to focus asymmetrically on losers or non-winners rather than outright winners during periods of sustained rapid growth under increased openness. First, those lifted out of poverty are often invisible, but those still remaining poor may be highly visible. This is akin to the phenomenon in which an import-competing sector that shrinks as a result of liberalization is clearly identifiable, but sectors that expand the production of export goods to pay for increased imports are not identified in the same way, because they are not subject to direct policy action. Indeed, when these sectors expand, the credit may readily be given to alternative, directly observable factors such as the entrepreneurship of specific individuals, improved infrastructure, or even some direct government initiative.

Second, liberalization works by moving workers from less efficient sectors to more efficient ones. This means that the adverse impact on liberalized sectors in the form of workers being dislocated is immediate, whereas the impact in terms of reemployment in more productive jobs in the expanding sectors takes time.

Finally, most countries have geographically remote and hard-to-reach areas, often inhabited by groups that are among the poorest. Being physically separated, they are easily identified and are also among those usually unaffected by growth in the mainstream of the economy. Any positive impact of growth reaches them only through targeted anti-poverty programs.

Indictment of growth on the grounds that it bypasses many poverty-stricken groups, without recognition that it yields greater *aggregate* reduction in poverty than alternative policies, is not new. In his important 1980 book, economist Gary Fields cites the work of Keith Griffin, which foreshadowed the current skepticism of many toward openness and poverty. Fields summarizes Griffin's study:

> Drawing on a series of earlier studies, Griffin gives evidence of persistent poverty for *selected* groups in particular countries, even rapidly growing ones. *The indicators of poverty differ from country to country*: proportion of the rural poor below an absolute poverty line in several Asian countries; income share of the poorest 20 percent in the Philippines and 80 percent in Bangladesh; incomes of smallholders and landless workers in Malaysia and Sri Lanka; average real incomes of cocoa producers in Ghana; incomes of informal sector workers and smallholder farmers in the poorest regions of Tanzania; "pure labor share" of national income in Colombia; and so on. (Emphasis added)[15]

Two decades later, the World Bank (2000) also played up the damage done to selected groups by openness and, more generally, pro-market reforms. The following excerpt gives a flavor of the examples it cited:

Evidence from a study of six African countries highlights how different groups fared differently under reforms. Poverty was more likely to decline in countries that improved their macroeconomic balances than in those that did not. But the evidence also shows that in three countries— Kenya, Nigeria, and Tanzania—real spending by the poorest segment of the population declined, even though the incidence of poverty [poverty ratio] fell nationwide. The decline in spending was particularly marked in Tanzania, where the poorest 10 percent were worse off in 1991 than they were in 1983. In Kenya the incidence of hard core poverty increased by four percentage points. In Nigeria, where overall poverty declined markedly, the incidence of hard core poverty rose 2.5 percentage points between 1985 and 1992.[16]

Prior to enumerating examples of reforms hurting specific groups such as these, the draft report is explicit in stating that the objective of the exercise is to sensitize policymakers to the need for determining beforehand "whether the reforms (or the way in which they are implemented) can be modified to reduce the costs to the poor without sacrificing much efficiency." While this is an eminently sensible reason for analyzing in detail the impact on specific groups, the draft report winds up injecting a heavy dose of skepticism about the desirability of reforms themselves, concluding, "These examples reveal that poor people can be hurt by reforms. It is little wonder, then, that in many civil society forums one hears voices of discontent about reform."

The problem with the argument that openness and other reforms must be resisted because they have not helped specific groups or even have hurt them is that in practice there is no policy that has been shown to benefit every poor individual. Even policies designed to directly assist the poverty-stricken can and do fail to aid many of the poor. Such anti-poverty initiatives in India as above-market procurement prices for food grains, subsidized fertilizer prices, rural electrification, and publicly provided primary education have left the poorest of the poor untouched because they lack the resources necessary to access these programs. After all, who but the richer farmers with plenty of farmland can effectively access fertilizer subsidies and above-market prices for the grain they produce? Leftist parties in India resisted the Green Revolution in the 1960s because they saw it as anti-poor. The argument was that the Green Revolution would benefit well-to-do farmers by raising their productivity but leave small farmers worse off because food grain prices would decline in response to the increase in productivity.

Therefore, the critical issue is not whether openness and growth help all of the poor but whether they help more of them than protection would. To be convincing, critics must offer persuasive evidence of protectionist policies delivering better outcomes. This they have not done. In contrast, sustained rapid growth, to which openness contributes handsomely, has almost always helped reduce aggregate poverty and, given a sufficiently long period of time, eliminated it altogether, as in the cases of Taiwan and South Korea.

In the end, the overall criterion for choosing among alternative policy packages has to be the decline in aggregate poverty. Arguments such as those offered by Kanbur that "for an NGO working with street children in Accra, or for a local official coping with increased poverty among indigenous peoples in Chiapas, it is cold comfort to be told, 'but national poverty has gone down'" are misplaced.[17] In making national policy, it is aggregate poverty that should count for more than what any specific NGO seeks for the constituency it represents.

Practically speaking, only a policy that generates enough income to bring down poverty overall has the potential to then address the plight of specific groups that are otherwise left out. The policy has to target aggregate poverty, with the interests of specific, hard-to-reach groups addressed through direct anti-poverty programs and social safety nets—just as the fifteen-year plan for India prepared by Pitamber Pant of the Perspective Division of the Planning Commission recommended as far back as 1962. A policy that delivers rapid growth and helps bring down aggregate poverty also generates more revenue for the government, which it can use to finance direct anti-poverty programs aimed at assisting the "core poor."

Churning at the Bottom of the Distribution

Economist Martin Ravallion has drawn attention to the process of "churning," whereby positions get swapped between poor and non-poor over two or more time periods with no change in aggregate poverty.[18] Such churning will naturally make those falling into poverty unhappy and those escaping it happy. From a policy perspective, however, the issue is whether such churning is yet one more reason for skepticism toward openness. There are at least three reasons why the answer to this question is in the negative.

First, churning at all levels is an integral part of dynamic economies. Economist John Haltiwanger reports that in the United States between 1980 and 2009, every year 15 percent of the jobs existing in the previous year were destroyed while 17 percent of all jobs were new jobs.[19] This churning in jobs is bound to be associated with some churning in incomes as well. In contrast, economies exhibiting stability are also likely to be associated with economic stagnation. Such economies will offer very little hope of poverty alleviation.

Second, even holding the poverty ratio constant, it is not altogether clear that churning is necessarily harmful. For one thing, over time it implies a more equal distribution of income. As an example, compare two countries that are identical in all respects except that in one of them there is no churning while in the other the bottom 20 percent and the next 20 percent of the population annually exchange their positions. Then the distribution of income among the bottom 40 percent of the population over any two-year period will be more equal in the second country than in the first.

Finally, and perhaps most important, when there is no churning, fatalism is likely to afflict those experiencing poverty year in and year out. In contrast, when churning takes place, it brings hope to those at the bottom of the distribution. A family that comes out of poverty one year but falls back into it the next year is more likely to struggle to break the cycle permanently than one that stays in poverty permanently.

Concluding Remarks

In assessing the liberal trade policy framework against protectionism, the question we must ask is which of these two regimes offers better prospects for growth and poverty alleviation. Critics have often pointed to this or that deficiency of outcomes from trade liberalization without making any effort to show that protectionism yields a superior outcome on average. Critics rest their case on many specious arguments, which turn out to be false upon close examination.

They argue, for example, that trade liberalization has failed to stimulate growth in many cases; that it cannot be credited with having catalyzed many of the growth miracles; that every successful country has pursued import substitution in the early stages of development; that high protection has not been inconsistent with rapid growth; and that industrial policy has been a part of many success stories. Each of these criticisms of openness as an engine of growth distracts from the main point: there are no examples of countries having experienced sustained rapid growth without low or declining barriers to trade. Indeed, free trade critics have never even attempted to offer empirical evidence showing that high and rising protection can yield sustained raid growth.

When confronted with compelling evidence of liberal trade policies being a part of nearly all experiences of sustained rapid growth, critics switch to arguing that trade openness has failed to help the poor. For example, they argue that poverty has risen alongside opening to trade; that even if the poverty ratio has fallen, the rise in the absolute number of poor testifies to the failure of openness; that opening to trade and the accompanying growth have done precious little for the core poor; and that increased openness has been associated with churning, whereby poor come out of poverty but fall back into it after a while. A closer examination of each of these arguments reveals its hollowness. In particular, critics do not show that where trade openness has failed, protectionism has succeeded. To persuade, they must demonstrate that on average protectionism yields a superior outcome with respect to poverty alleviation. This they have not done.

Notes

1. Lal and Rajapatirana 1987, 208.
2. This is systematically documented in the excellent volume on unilateral trade liberalization edited by Bhagwati 2002.
3. For example, Rodriguez and Rodrik 2000.
4. Corbo, Krueger, and Ossa 1985.
5. For example, Rodrik 1995 on South Korea and Taiwan, and Rodrik 2003 on India and China.
6. The issue of the initial catalyst to growth in South Korea and Taiwan is analyzed in greater detail in Part III.
7. For instance, see Wade 2002 and Kanbur 2001.
8. Occasionally analysts also track the evolution of income of the bottom three or four deciles of the population to assess whether the lot of the poor is improving over time.
9. World Bank 1999, 1, ix.
10. For example, see *IFG Bulletin* 1, no. 3 (2001) by the International Forum on Globalization at http://www.thirdworldtraveler.com/Globalization/Globalization_FactsFigures.html (accessed November 26, 2017).
11. Wade 2002.
12. To quote Srinivasan from one of his many writings on this subject, "A poverty bundle common to all regions within a geographically and culturally diverse country such as India, let alone for all countries of the world, cannot be meaningfully defined. If such a bundle could be defined, then the national poverty line at any point in time would be the value of that bundle at the prices in *local currency* that households face in that nation at that point in time. There is no need for any exchange rate in such a calculation. [Angus] Deaton is absolutely right in arguing that, because such an internationally accepted bundle does not exist, it does not make sense to simply convert $1/day to local currency values using purchasing power parity (PPP) exchange rates with commodities weighted by their shares in the consumption of the poor. The reason is that doing so makes poverty lines move around with changes in PPP exchange rates arising from world market price changes that have no relevance to the poor. For example, the poverty line for one country would be shifted by a change in the world price of a commodity that is not consumed by the poor in that country but consumed by the poor in some other country, because such a price change affects the PPP exchange rate. In any case, global poverty counts are based on neither a common global poverty bundle nor conversions to local currency values using PPP exchange rates with commodity weights more relevant to the poor" (2008, 14). Additional problems characterizing global figures on poverty include non-comparability of sample surveys across countries and over time and sampling and non-sampling errors in them.
13. Galenson (1977).
14. Quoted in Fields 1980, 167. Galenson defined fast-growing economies as those exhibiting annual GDP growth rates of 7 percent or more.
15. Fields 1980, 167–68.
16. World Bank 2000, 8.14. I have suppressed a footnote from the above quotation following the expression "hard core poverty" in the context of Kenya. The footnote states, "Based on a poverty line that defines approximately 10 percent of the relevant population as poor in the base year. This line is kept constant in real terms in estimating the incidence in the terminal year."
17. Kanbur 2001, 1087.
18. Ravallion 2003.
19. Haltiwanger 2012.

6

Trade Openness and Growth

The Empirical Evidence

From the viewpoint of the developing countries, the case for trade openness depends, first and foremost, on openness being necessary to achieve sustained rapid growth. This subject has received a great deal of attention in the academic literature. Free trade critics have argued that it was during periods of high trade barriers and import substitution industrialization that the developing countries experienced the fastest growth. They also question the evidence provided by free trade advocates, claiming that at most it shows correlation, falling short of establishing causation between outward-oriented policies and growth.

The discussion of the relationship between trade and growth takes place at three levels in the literature:

1. Experience of the developing countries in aggregate over time
2. Cross-country comparisons of experience over fixed periods
3. Individual country experiences over time

In this chapter, we examine evidence for the first two: evidence based on the experience of the developing countries in aggregate over time, and evidence showing cross-country differences in policies and outcomes. We turn to detailed country case studies in Parts III and IV.

1960–73: The Golden Age of Growth?

Economist Dani Rodrik characterizes the years 1960–73 as the golden age of growth for the developing countries on the ground that this period saw per capita incomes in as many as forty-two countries grow at rates exceeding 2.5 percent.[1] In comparison, only fourteen countries grew 2.5 percent or more in per capita terms over the years 1973–84 and only fifteen did so during the period 1984–94. In a more recent contribution, Chang echoes Rodrik: "During the 1960s and 1970s, when they were pursuing the 'wrong' policies of protectionism and state intervention, *per-capita* incomes in the developing countries grew by 3.0 percent annually. . . . This growth rate is a huge improvement over what they achieved under free trade during the 'age of imperialism.' . . . It also remains the best they have ever achieved. Since the 1980s, after they implemented neo-liberal policies, they grew at only about half the speed seen in the 1960s and the 1970s (1.7 percent)."[2]

This account is at odds with the evidence I will present shortly. Rodrik rests his case principally on the observation that as many as forty-two developing countries grew at rates 2.5 percent or more in per capita terms during the period 1960–73. But these countries accounted for just 17.6 percent of the total developing country population in 1960. Using only slightly different cutoff points in terms of time periods, I will show that the population in the developing countries experiencing 3 percent or higher growth as a proportion of the total developing country population was higher during the periods 1976–94 and 1995–2013 than during the years 1961–75.[3] The period 1995–2013 turns out to be particularly significant, with the developing countries that experienced per capita income growth rates of 3 percent or more accounting for 73.4 percent of the total population in developing countries in 1995.

Therefore, if one insists on identifying the period 1960–75 as being characterized by import substitution industrialization and the subsequent ones by outward orientation, as Rodrik and Chang do, outward-oriented policies win hands down. Of course, one needs to exercise greater care in assessing individual country policies, since it is possible that policies within each period varied greatly across countries. For example, it is altogether possible that even during the first phase, the fast-growing economies pursued outward-oriented policies, as was surely the case with Taiwan, South Korea, Singapore, and Hong Kong. Symmetrically, we cannot automatically assume that all fast-growing economies in the third phase were uniformly turning away from import substitution and toward an outward orientation.

Next, let me turn to the assertion by Chang that developing countries performed far better during the 1960s and 1970s than in both the colonial era and the period following 1980. That the countries did better during the 1960s and 1970s than during the colonial period should be neither surprising nor a cause for celebration, regardless of the policy regime. Writing in a slightly different but related context, economist Deena Khatkhate provides the reason.[4] Commenting on a contribution by economist Deepak Nayyar, who defends India's pursuit of inward-looking and command-and-control policies in the 1950s and 1960s on the grounds that the country grew much faster during those decades than under the British, Khatkhate characterizes such comparisons as both "fatuous and facetious."[5] He reasons:

> During the latter [pre-independence] period there was no autonomous economic policy geared to the interests of a nation. The objective functions were different. It was a colonial policy, addressing the interests of the home country. Any policy, statist or otherwise, with India's interests at the center, would have achieved better results than under a colonial regime. The real question is whether the statist policies were superior to other alternatives, but this question can never be answered for want of counterfactual evidence.[6]

But what about Chang's claim that the performance of developing countries during the 1960s and 1970s was also superior to that since the 1980s, "after they implemented neo-liberal policies"? Here, two points may be noted. First, the very empirical basis of his claim is false: no matter how we slice the data, the best period from the viewpoint of per capita income growth turns out to be the 1990s and beyond. Second, the external environment facing the developing countries, as reflected in the growth in high-income OECD countries, was far more favorable during the 1960s and 1970s than during the 1990s and beyond.

Chang reports that per capita GDP growth rate in the developing countries since 1980 has been 1.7 percent, compared to 3 percent during the 1960s and 1970s. Unfortunately, he does not cite the source of his information. It is a fair guess, however, that the figure of 3 percent growth during the 1960s and 1970s is taken from the World Bank's 1980 *World Development Report*.[7] But regarding the 1.7 percent figure after 1980, there is no way to guess his source, since he does not mention the precise period to which it relates. An examination of the available data shows his claim to be false.

The World Development Indicators (WDI) database of the World Bank does not provide per capita GDP figures for the developing countries as a whole. But it does report real GDP in constant 2005 dollars from 1960 to 2013 for the developing Latin America and Caribbean, South Asia, East Asia and Pacific, and Sub-Saharan Africa.[8] It also gives population estimates for these regions for the years 1960 to 2013. These series can be combined to obtain real per capita GDP in 2005 dollars in developing countries excluding the Middle East and North Africa, for which information is lacking for the first half of the 1960s. In turn, per capita GDP series so obtained allow us to calculate the growth rate of per capita GDP in the developing countries for various periods. I report them in Table 6.1 alongside the growth rates in the high-income OECD countries.

Going by decades, growth rates in the 1960s and 1970s are 2.6 and 3.2 percent, respectively. These are not identical to those reported by Chang, perhaps due to a change in the base year and methodology employed to convert local currency

Table 6.1 **Average annual growth rates (in percent) of per capita GDP in the developing countries and high-income OECD countries**

Period	Developing	High-income OECD	Period	Developing	High-income OECD
1961–70	2.6	4.2	1961–75	2.9	3.6
1971–80	3.2	2.5	1976–94	2.1	2.3
1981–90	1.2	2.6	1995–2013	4.2	1.4
1991–2000	3.0	2.0			
2001–10	4.9	0.9	1961–73	2.9	4.2
2011–13	4.4	0.9	1974–90	1.9	2.3
			1991–2013	4.0	1.4
1961–80	2.9	3.4			
1981–2013	3.2	1.8			

Source: Author's calculations using the data from the World Bank WDI online.

GDP into dollar GDP, but reasonably close to them.[9] The average growth rate during the 1980s shows a dramatic fall to 1.2 percent, but it more than recovers in the following decades, jumping to 3 percent in the 1990s, 4.9 percent in the 2000s, and 4.4 percent during 2011–13.[10]

Alternatively, if we divide the years 1961 to 2013 into three periods, 1961–75, 1976–95, and 1996–2013, the growth rate during the latest period, at 4.2 percent, is significantly higher than that during the earliest period, at 2.9 percent. As expected, it is the second period, 1976–94, that is characterized by the relatively low growth rate of 2 percent per year. The last set of numbers in Table 6.1 show that growth during 1961–73, identified by Rodrik as the golden period, was 2.9 percent. This was considerably below the 4 percent achieved during 1991–2013. Here too, no matter how we slice the data, the Rodrik-Chang hypothesis of superior performance during the 1960s and 1970s does not stand up to close scrutiny.

Table 6.1 illustrates an additional important point: during the years 1961–73, the developing countries faced a much more favorable external environment in that the high-income OECD countries grew 4.2 percent per annum in per capita terms. In contrast, this growth rate was just 1.4 percent during 1991–2013. These relative rates lend support to the hypothesis that internal policy reforms in the developing countries allowed them to grow more rapidly during 1991–2013 than during 1961–73 despite the slowdown in the growth rate in high-income OECD countries.

A final point is that the fastest-growing economies even during 1961–73 were those that had turned to outward-oriented policies. The four Asian tigers, which exhibited the highest growth rates during these years, were all outward oriented. Arguably, even the fast growth in Brazil during 1961–75 took place against a backdrop of rapid expansion of imports and exports under a liberalizing trade policy regime.

Cross-Country Evidence

Sometimes critics argue that free trade leads to devastation of domestic industries and causes incomes to actually fall. According to this criticism, even if free trade is necessary for sustained rapid growth, we cannot ignore its downside: what if it leads to declining incomes?

Two Empirical Propositions

In considering cross-country evidence, our burden is twofold. We must show that when rapid growth happens, it happens in the presence of free trade, and that when incomes decline, free trade cannot be linked to it. Since countries rarely if ever embrace complete free trade, discharging these burdens requires that we posit a working definition of free trade. Keeping these considerations in view, I state below two empirical propositions that must be defended to make the case for freeing up trade.

> *Proposition 1: Low or declining barriers to trade, which frequently are reflected in a high or rising trade-to-GDP ratio, are necessary though not sufficient for sustained rapid growth.*
> *Proposition 2: Low or declining barriers to trade are not behind stagnation or declining incomes of countries.*

Several features of Proposition 1 may be noted. First, it defines openness in terms of both low and declining trade barriers. Accordingly, sustained rapid growth may be associated with either highly open economies or those that lower trade barriers despite a high initial level of protection. Hong Kong and Singapore in the 1960s and 1970s offer examples of sustained rapid growth under low trade barriers. South Korea in the 1960s and 1970s and China and India in the 1990s offer examples of sustained rapid growth under high but declining barriers. Second, it is also claimed that sustained rapid growth is associated with high or rising trade-to-GDP ratio. This feature has near universal empirical validity, as we will see below. Third, openness so defined is claimed as necessary for growth but not sufficient. This means that low or declining barriers by themselves may not result in sustained rapid growth. Finally, in the abstract, the terms "low or declining barriers" and "high trade-to-GDP ratio" are subject to interpretation. Therefore, in considering specific cases, we will need to pay special attention to explaining how these terms are defined.

Free trade critics sometimes also assert that trade liberalization plays havoc on poor countries by causing stagnation or even sustained decline in real per capita incomes. To be valid, this claim must be supported by evidence that causally links rapid import penetration to sustained reductions in per capita incomes. But consistent with Proposition 2, reality is very far from any such causal link: we do not find even an *association* between sustained reductions in per capita incomes and import penetration.

Miracles and Debacles

We now have considerable systematic evidence supporting the hypothesis that openness is a necessary condition for fast growth. Begin by considering the relationship between growth in incomes and growth in trade for all countries for which necessary data are available. The WDI database provides data on per capita incomes, goods and services exports, goods and services imports, and goods and services exports as a proportion of GDP in constant 2005 U.S. dollars for more than two hundred countries over a period of fifty-four years between 1960 and 2013.[11] Though the data series have missing values and perhaps the quality of data varies by country and year, these are the most comprehensive data available for the study of the relationship between trade and growth across countries and over time.

This database can be used to calculate growth rates for three periods: 1961–75 (fifteen years), 1976–94 (nineteen years), and 1995–2013 (nineteen years). I purposely allow for the smaller number of years in the first period because free trade critics like to think of these years as the golden period of growth for the developing countries. Extending this period further to make the division across periods even would only strengthen my conclusions.

For each period and for each country, we can calculate the average annual growth rates of per capita GDP, exports, and imports. We can then classify the countries into three groups in each period: those exhibiting per capita GDP growth of 3 percent or more, those entirely stagnant or experiencing negative growth in per capita terms, and countries with positive but less than 3 percent per annum growth in per capita GDP.

I focus on the first two of these groups, labeling the countries in the first group as "miracle" countries and those in the second group as "debacle" countries.[12] The cutoff point for the debacle countries should be uncontroversial: if we are looking for trade as a source of major blows to a country's well-being, we should look for it in the countries that have seen their per capita incomes stagnate or decline over a substantial period of time. The cutoff point for the miracle countries is more arbitrary but is based on the judgment that a significantly higher cutoff point will result in only a small number of countries making the list, while a significantly lower one will lead to the inclusion of countries whose growth experiences have been less than stellar. In any case, moving the cutoff point even 1 percentage point up or 0.5 percentage point down does not change the essential message derived below.

I note at the outset that during the entire period under consideration, more than half a century, no developed country experienced stagnant or declining per capita income on a sustained basis. Some developed countries did grow at 3 percent or more in per capita terms on a sustained basis, however. This is particularly the case during the first period. Even though the focus of my analysis is on the developing countries, I include these developed countries among miracle countries in the tables below for the sake of completeness. In the same vein, I include the successor countries of the former Soviet Union and the countries in Central and Eastern Europe, commonly called the transition economies, in the list of the miracle and debacle countries. Finally, in the tables relating to miracle countries, I list various regions such as the high-income OECD countries, East Asia and Pacific, South Asia, and Latin America regardless of whether or not they exhibit miracle-level growth rates. Growth rates of GDP and trade in these regions provide useful information on the overall growth environment regionally and globally. This information is in turn helpful in evaluating trade as a source of growth.

Tables 6.2 and 6.3 show the miracle and debacle countries, respectively, during 1961–75. For each country and region, I report the average annual growth rates of per capita GDP, exports, and imports. I also report the exports of goods and services as a proportion of GDP at the beginning and end of the period. An increase in this proportion suggests that exports grew faster than GDP during the period. In the final column, I report the population of the country at the beginning of the period. This last variable conveys information on the number of people affected by sustained rapid growth or stagnation in the country. This is useful since high growth is likely to benefit many more individuals in large countries such as India and China than in small ones such as Botswana and Gabon. Country populations can also be evaluated against the world population, which is shown at the bottom of Table 6.2.

Table 6.2 Miracles, 1961–75

Country	Growth rates (%)			Exports as % of GDP (1961)	Exports as % of GDP (1975)	Population (millions) (1961)
	Per capita GDP	Exports of goods and services	Imports of goods and services			
Developing countries other than fuel-exporting countries						
Botswana	8.5	–	–	27.2	43.6	0.5
Iran, Islamic Rep.	7.6	10.5	27.1	–	43.1	22.5
Singapore	7.1	–	–	142.5	137.1	1.7
Korea, Rep.	6.6	28.1	18.7	5.3	25.3	25.8
Georgia	5.4	–	–	–	–	3.7
Puerto Rico	5.2	1.8	0.3	45.4	48.1	2.4
Syrian Arab Republic	5.0	–	–	17.6	21.9	4.7
Israel	5.0	–	–	11.5	32.6	2.2
Brazil	4.8	8.3	10.2	7.3	7.5	75.0
Tunisia	4.6	9.8	7.3	–	31	4.3
Thailand	4.4	9.2	9.6	16.9	18.4	28.2
Barbados	4.4	–	–	45.1	50.4	0.2
New Caledonia	4.2	–	–	–	–	0.1
Dominican Republic	4.0	5.4	11.6	23.3	27.7	3.4
Togo	3.9	15.3	7	39.2	43.4	1.6

Bermuda	3.9	–	–	–	–	0.05
Malaysia	3.8	6	5	46.1	43	8.4
Panama	3.8	–	–	–	–	1.2
Hong Kong SAR, China	3.8	–	–	71.6	83.4	3.2
Papua New Guinea	3.5	15.9	11.4	16.1	40	2.0
Mexico	3.4	8.8	8.3	8.4	6.9	39.9
Belize	3.3	–	–	–	–	0.1
Lesotho	3.3	4.8	14.3	12.5	14.5	0.9
Morocco	3.2	2.2	6.3	21.8	22.5	12.7
Nicaragua	3.1	9.1	8.4	23.4	28	1.8
Pakistan	3.1	4.9	2.9	–	10.9	46.7
Turkey	3.1	–	–	5.1	4.4	28.2
Costa Rica	3.1	9.7	7.9	21.8	30.1	1.4
Paraguay	3.0	–	–	–	–	2.0
Fuel-exporting developing countries						
Oman	13.2	–	–	–	67.6	0.6
Gabon	8.7	14.8	19.7	31.2	49.5	0.5

(continued)

Table 6.2 **Continued**

Country	Growth rates (%)			Exports as % of GDP (1961)	Exports as % of GDP (1975)	Population (millions) (1961)
	Per capita GDP	Exports of goods and services	Imports of goods and services			
Developed countries						
Hungary	8.0	10.4	9.7	22.8	41.2	10
Japan	6.4	12.9	13.9	9.3	12.5	94.9
Greece	6.3	12.8	10.4	8.7	17.4	8.4
Portugal	5.8	5.7	8.5	13.5	16.2	8.9
Latvia	5.7	–	–	–	–	2.2
Spain	5.6	10.4	16.0	8.0	12.7	30.7
Italy	4.2	9.5	8.5	12.8	19.5	50.5
Finland	4.1	5.4	7.2	20.0	22.4	4.5
France	4.0	8.6	9.1	13.9	19	47.3
Belgium	4.0	6.9	6.7	39.0	49.9	9.2
Austria	3.9	7.6	7.7	23.0	29.2	7.1
Iceland	3.8	5.1	8.1	41.4	33.3	0.2
Norway	3.6	6.0	7.0	35.0	36.4	3.6
Netherlands	3.5	7.8	7.6	46.6	49.1	11.6
Canada	3.4	6.7	7.3	17.8	22.1	18.3
Sweden	3.3	6.4	5.8	22.3	27.6	7.5

Regions

Regions						
Middle East & North Africa	5.2	–	–	–	32.3	101.6
East Asia & Pacific	2.5	–	–	–	–	901.3
South Asia	1.4	5.2	0.6	5.3	6.5	585.4
Latin America & Caribbean	3.3	5.5	7.3	10.5	10.8	211.7
Sub-Saharan Africa	2.1	–	–	24.2	24.9	233.1
High-income OECD	3.6	5.8	4.3	11.4	16.1	721.1

Source: Author's calculations using the data in World Bank 2014. Due to missing data on per capita incomes, the average growth rate in a handful of the cases, including countries in the Middle East and North Africa, is calculated using annual growth rates from 1966 to 1975.

Table 6.3 **Debacles, 1961–75**

Country	Growth rates (%)			Exports as % of GDP (1961)	Exports as % of GDP (1975)	Population (millions) (1961)
	Per capita GDP	Exports of goods and services	Imports of goods and services			
Central African Rep.	0.0	–	–	26.5	21.1	1.5
Sudan	-0.2	3.0	4.3	13.3	12.1	7.7
Rwanda	-0.4	6.1	10.5	11.5	9.2	3.0
Madagascar	-0.4	7.1	2.7	14.6	15.9	5.2
Bangladesh	-0.5	3.5	-1.4	10.8	2.9	51.0
Ghana	-0.6	–	–	26.1	19.4	6.9
Senegal	-0.8	4.0	3.3	21.2	31.4	3.3
Chad	-1.1	2.2	3.9	13.9	14.4	3.1
Niger	-1.6	–	–	8.1	19.2	3.4
Kuwait	-6.2	–	–	–	80.5	0.3

Source: Author's calculations using the data in World Bank 2014.

Four points may be noted with respect to miracle countries during 1961–75. First, and most remarkable, even though free trade critics commonly identify this period as the import substitution phase in the developing countries, virtually all countries that grew rapidly in per capita terms did so while rapidly expanding their exports and imports. In the vast majority of the cases, the exports of goods and services as a proportion of GDP rose significantly. Out of a total of thirty-one developing and "transition" countries that achieved miracle status in this period, only four—Singapore, Malaysia, Mexico, and Turkey—exhibited a slight decline in their exports-to-GDP ratio. And in the case of Singapore, the *level* of openness as captured by the exports-to-GDP ratio was exceptionally high at the beginning of the period. Likewise, though Hong Kong did not experience super-high growth rates of exports and imports, it remained a very open economy throughout the period. As is well known, it had no formal barriers to trade during this and later periods. Even Brazil, which grew at the impressive rate of 4.8 percent in per capita terms, expanded its exports and imports at 8.2 and 10.3 percent, respectively. Contrary to what advocates of protection claim, it is incorrect to describe Brazil as pursuing import substitution during this period: trade barriers actually fell and the domestic currency was devalued to correct the bias against traded goods during these years.

The second point to glean from Table 6.2 is that all regions containing developing countries—Asia, Africa, and Latin America—contributed three or more miracle countries during 1961–75. This geographic spread of the miracle countries perhaps partially accounts for the impression that this period constituted the best period for the developing countries as a whole. This is quite misleading since the performance in terms of number of miracle countries was at least as good in the subsequent two periods as in this one. The last period, 1995–2013, turns out to be particularly impressive. Moreover, some of the largest developing countries—China and India—do not make the list of the miracle countries during this period.

Third, the total population in the developing countries experiencing miracle growth was 325.9 million in 1961. This figure represented 16 percent of the total developing country population at the time.[13] The figure is far smaller than in the second and third periods, both absolutely and as a proportion of the developing country population.

Finally, the first period also saw a very large number of developed countries growing at miracle rates. Notably, this period was characterized by significant opening up in the industrial countries, both through the European Economic Community (which eliminated all trade barriers among France, Germany, Italy, Belgium, Netherlands, and Luxembourg) and through multilateral negotiations (including the important Kennedy Round). Across the three periods considered, this period also turned out to have exhibited by far the highest growth in the high-income OECD countries: 3.6 percent in per capita terms. It is highly plausible that the opening up and rapid growth in these countries were partially responsible for the rapid growth in the East Asian tiger economies, which themselves opened up to take advantage of expanded opportunities to trade.

Free trade critics such as the prominent NGOs Christian Aid and Third World Network and journalist Jon Jeter contend that openness actually leads to stagnant and declining incomes.[14] To examine this claim, Table 6.3 lists all countries that experienced zero or negative growth in per capita income during 1961–75. A remarkable feature of this table is the relatively small number of debacle countries during the period. The lack of data availability in the earlier years for many poor countries perhaps exaggerates the low incidence of zero or negative growth in per capita income, but this cannot be conclusively established. Where data are available, however, we can infer that the hypothesis that import surges lead to growth debacles does not find empirical support. Out of the ten debacle cases, only Rwanda shows a high average growth rate of imports.

The same relationship between growth and trade is observed in the second and third periods. Tables 6.4 and 6.5 report growth in per capita GDP and trade, exports-to-GDP ratio, and population in the miracle and debacle countries, respectively, during 1976–94. Based on Table 6.4, three points may be noted with respect to miracle countries during this period.

First, leaving aside a handful of the cases, the miracle countries show a consistently high rate of growth in imports and exports. In the vast majority of cases, the exports-to-GDP ratio is high at the beginning of the period, rises over time, or both. The positive relationship between high growth in income and high growth in trade characterizes this period as well.

Second, in terms of the number of miracle countries and the proportion of the population exposed to such growth, the general impression that the 1980s represented a lost decade of development is not supported by data. As many as twenty-nine countries, accounting for 44.36 percent of the developing country population in 1976, experienced miracle-level growth rates during this period. The corresponding figures for the prior period, 1961–75, were thirty-one countries and 16 percent, respectively. The largest country in the world, China, joined the club of miracle-growth countries in this period, which partially accounts for the sharp rise in the population experiencing rapid growth.

Finally, per capita income growth in the high-income OECD countries fell by 1.3 percentage points to 2.3 percent during this period. The number of miracle countries in the developed world fell to five from sixteen in the previous period. During this period, the countries also had to adjust to two major oil price shocks. Considering these facts, it is not obvious that the developing countries as a group did poorly relative to the prior period in terms of miracle-level growth. Only in Latin America did a large number of countries perform poorly,

Table 6.4 **Miracles, 1976–94**

Country	Growth rates (%)			Exports as % of GDP (1976)	Exports as % of GDP (1994)	Population (millions) (1976)
	Per capita GDP	Exports of goods and services	Imports of goods and services			
Developing countries other than fuel-exporting countries						
China	7.6	11.1	13.1	–	32.1	930.7
Korea, Rep.	7.6	13.1	12.8	39.5	16.3	35.8
Bhutan	6.3	–	–	–	–	0.4
Thailand	6.2	13.9	12.4	24.1	14.3	43.4
Botswana	6.2	10.4	7.0	28.4	6.8	0.9
Hong Kong SAR, China	6.2	13.5	15.8	–	9.4	4.5
Antigua and Barbuda	6.0	–	–	–	–	0.1
Singapore	5.9	12.6	11.9	11.0	18.7	2.3
St. Kitts and Nevis	5.8	–	–	–	–	0.04
Isle of Man	4.9	–	–	–	–	0.1
St. Lucia	4.8	–	–	–	–	0.1
Cabo Verde	4.7	–	–	–	–	0.3
Malaysia	4.6	11.5	13.1	17.0	21.9	12.6

(continued)

Table 6.4 Continued

Country	Growth rates (%)			Exports as % of GDP (1976)	Exports as % of GDP (1994)	Population (millions) (1976)
	Per capita GDP	Exports of goods and services	Imports of goods and services			
St. Vincent & Grenadines	4.4	–	–	–	–	0.1
Dominica	4.1	–	–	–	–	0.1
Chile	4	9.5	10.2	24.4	11.6	10.6
Egypt, Arab Rep.	3.9	6.3	1.5	27.5	0.5	41.2
Seychelles	3.9	–	–	–	–	0.1
Belize	3.8	5.5	4.3	–	6.8	0.1
Vietnam	3.8	18.5	16.2	–	16.0	49.2
Macao SAR, China	3.7	6.7	8.6	–	5.0	0.2
Lesotho	3.5	16.7	4.7	35.5	4.1	1.2
Mauritius	3.5	7.0	6.3	–	2.9	0.9
Grenada	3.5	–	–	–	–	0.1
Sri Lanka	3.2	6.4	8.2	2.3	13.1	13.7
Paraguay	3.1	14	16.8	–	11.8	2.9
Swaziland	3.0	6.0	7.4	2.2	11.2	0.5
Puerto Rico	3.0	5.8	4.1	-0.4	2.7	3.0

Fuel-exporting developing countries

Indonesia	4.9	5.2	8.2	17.0	9.9	132.4
Developed countries						
Cyprus	6.0	12.4	9.4	65.2	8.2	0.7
Malta	5.2	6.7	5.9	16.1	7.2	0.3
Luxembourg	3.6	5.4	4.6	0.9	7.7	0.4
Japan	3.3	6.4	4.8	16.6	3.9	112.8
Ireland	3.2	9.3	7.3	8.1	15.1	3.2
Regions						
Middle East & North Africa	0.2	2.2	–0.8	9.7	4.9	150.4
East Asia & Pacific	6.2	9.3	10.2	–	21.7	1275.5
South Asia	2.4	7.5	7.6	19.1	10.3	821.3
Latin America & Caribbean	0.9	5.0	4.6	3.5	6.6	313.4
Sub-Saharan Africa	–1.2	3.0	1.9	–	3.1	341.7
High-income OECD	2.3	5.4	5.2	9.3	8.9	836.4

Source: Author's calculations using the data in World Bank 2014.

Table 6.5 **Debacles, 1976–94**

Country	Growth rates (%)			Exports as % of GDP (1976)	Exports as % of GDP (1994)	Population (millions) (1976)
	Per capita GDP	Exports of goods and services	Imports of goods and services			
Trinidad and Tobago	0.0	3.4	2.9	10.2	15.2	1.0
Gambia	-0.1	3.2	2.1	17.3	-24.5	0.5
Guyana	-0.1	–	–	–	–	0.8
Zimbabwe	-0.1	5.1	5.2	–	9.4	6.4
Mongolia	-0.2	–	–	–	–	1.5
Latvia	-0.2	-3.3	-6.3	–	-1.8	2.5
Mozambique	-0.3	0.8	-0.8	–	33.8	10.9
Ghana	-0.3	–	–	–	–	10.0
El Salvador	-0.4	1.9	5.3	-8.5	8.4	4.3
Chad	-0.4	5.6	2.2	29.7	-9.1	4.2
Comoros	-0.5	16.6	0.0	–	-5.4	0.3
Brunei Darussalam	-0.5	3.2	10.5	–	2.8	0.2
South Africa	-0.6	2.4	1.5	4.3	2.5	25.3
Somalia	-0.7	7.4	22.2	-16.3	–	4.3
Rwanda	-0.7	2.1	11.0	70.0	-61.1	4.5

Romania	-0.8	3.8	-3.7	–	19.0	21.6
Gabon	-0.8	4.1	0.4	16.6	4.5	0.7
Malawi	-0.8	–	–	–	–	5.5
Mauritania	-0.8	3.3	0.6	8.9	4.9	1.4
Bolivia	-0.9	3.1	2.3	10.8	15.1	4.9
Senegal	-0.9	3.9	2.9	16.2	48.7	5.0
Venezuela, RB	-0.9	1.6	5.3	-0.9	8.1	13.2
Peru	-0.9	4.1	2.6	3.4	19.4	15.6
Togo	-1.2	2.3	2.7	-17.0	-1.8	2.5
Slovak Republic	-1.2	7.3	-2.7	–	14.8	4.8
Suriname	-1.3	–	–	–	–	0.4
Namibia	-1.3	2.5	1.4	–	-3.2	0.9
Niger	-1.4	–	–	–	–	5.2
Andorra	-1.4	–	–	–	–	0.03
Ethiopia	-1.6	5.5	6.6	–	27.1	33.1
Sierra Leone	-1.6	-3.1	-1.8	1.8	-23.8	2.9
Albania	-1.7	38.8	72.1	–	-10.0	2.5
Iran, Islamic Rep.	-1.7	4.4	-3.0	10.9	6.5	33.9

(continued)

Table 6.5 **Continued**

Country	Growth rates (%)			Exports as % of GDP (1976)	Exports as % of GDP (1994)	Population (millions) (1976)
	Per capita GDP	Exports of goods and services	Imports of goods and services			
Central African Republic	-1.7	–	–	–	–	2.1
Nigeria	-1.8	–	–	–	–	65.4
Madagascar	-2.3	0.2	-0.6	-23.3	10.1	7.8
United Arab Emirates	-2.3	–	–	–	–	0.6
Saudi Arabia	-2.3	–	–	–	–	7.8
Zambia	-2.4	-0.8	-4.7	21.5	8.8	5.1
Kuwait	-3.2	–	–	–	–	1.1
Nicaragua	-3.8	-4.5	-1.7	4.0	-90.7	2.9
Moldova	-4.2	-10.2	-12.0	–	25.4	3.3
Georgia	-4.5	–	–	–	–	4.3
Congo, Dem. Rep.	-4.7	1.8	0.4	-6.3	-7.5	23.6
Kiribati	-5.5	–	–	–	–	0.05
Liberia	-11.0	–	–	–	–	1.7

Source: Author's calculations using the data in World Bank 2014.

with Chile and Paraguay being the only significant exceptions. This fact may partially account for the skeptical view of this period by the free trade critics, who often fall into the trap of generalizing from the experience of Latin America.

On the debacle side, the picture is more pessimistic during 1976–94 than during the earlier period. We now find as many as forty-six countries and 9.62 percent of the world population being subject to stagnant or declining per capita incomes. The corresponding figures for the prior period are ten countries and 3.4 percent, respectively. Consistent with the general impression that the second period was especially bad for Africa, the vast majority of the debacle countries during this period are located on that continent. But is there prima facie evidence for blaming these debacles on import surges? Not according to the import figures in Table 6.5. In the vast majority of the cases, import growth was sluggish in the countries with stagnant or declining incomes.

Tables 6.6 and 6.7 list growth and trade outcomes for the miracle and debacle countries, respectively, during 1995–2013. From the viewpoint of miracle growth, this is the most remarkable period. As many as fifty-eight countries, accounting for as much as 73.4 percent of the developing country population at the beginning of the period, experienced growth in per capita income at an annual rate of 3 percent or more. Countries from South Asia, East Asia, Southeast Asia, Central Asia, Africa, and Central and Eastern Europe shared in this growth. Latin America was once again the largely missing continent, with Chile and the Dominican Republic being the exceptions.

As in the previous periods, rapid growth in per capita income continues to be associated with rapid growth in trade. Out of fifty-eight miracle countries, only fourteen—Mongolia, Bhutan, Sri Lanka, Panama, the Dominican Republic, Mauritius, Chile, Botswana, Tanzania, Moldova, Nigeria, Armenia, Kazakhstan, and the Russian Federation—showed growth rates in exports below 5 percent. Even among these fourteen, Mongolia, Botswana, and Tanzania saw their exports rise at rates exceeding 4 percent. From the policy perspective, this period is generally associated with a steady opening up in most countries.

Equally remarkable, among developed nations only seven countries, with just 1.6 percent of the world population, grew at miracle rates. All other developed countries grew at less than 3 percent in per capita terms. Per capita income growth in high-income OECD countries was 1.4 percent, which is less than the corresponding rates in both prior periods. Prima facie, one can argue that it is the policy change within the miracle countries that provided the impetus for their faster growth.

The proportion of the population impacted by stagnant or declining incomes during the third period was less than those in both of the earlier periods. As in the previous periods, we find little evidence to support the view that import

Table 6.6 **Miracles, 1995–2013**

Country	Growth rates			Exports as % of GDP (1995)	Exports as % of GDP (2013)	Population (millions) (1995)
	Per capita GDP	Exports of goods and services	Imports of goods and services			
Developing countries other than fuel-exporting countries						
Liberia	11.5	6.5	9.7	–	–	2.1
China	9.2	15.4	13.7	20.2	26.4	1204.9
Myanmar	8.9	12.1	–1.5	0.8	–	45.3
Macao SAR, China	6.6	11.7	8.6	82.7	106.7	0.4
Isle of Man	6.4	–	–	–	–	0.1
Cabo Verde	5.9	–	–	17.1	–	0.4
Afghanistan	5.8	–	–	–	6.1	17.6
Rwanda	5.8	19.2	9.2	5.2	16.9	5.7
Cambodia	5.6	17.6	14.7	31.2	–	10.8
Mongolia	5.5	11.1	18.8	40.5	45.1	2.3
Bhutan	5.4	12.2	10.8	37.8	37.6	0.5
Vietnam	5.4	15.6	14.1	32.8	–	72
Kosovo	5.3	–	–	–	–	2.0
India	5.2	13.6	13.0	10.7	24.8	955.8

Lao PDR	5.1	7.4	7.7	23.2	–	4.9
Maldives	4.9	11.4	13.5	92.7	–	0.2
Timor–Leste	4.8	7.8	6.5	–	–	0.9
Ethiopia	4.8	12.6	12.8	9.8	–	57.0
Sri Lanka	4.8	4.5	5.8	35.6	22.5	18.1
Cuba	4.5	9.5	6.9	13.4	–	10.9
Mozambique	4.5	16.3	9.4	15.6	32.2	16.0
Libya	4.3	–	–	29.2	–	4.7
Slovak Republic	4.2	8.5	8.7	57.8	–	5.4
Panama	4.1	5.3	5.4	100.7	71.0	2.8
Bangladesh	4.1	11.5	9.6	10.9	22.8	119.9
Dominican Republic	4.0	4.4	4.4	35.8	26.0	8.0
Korea, Rep.	4.0	11.9	8.7	26.7	53.9	45.1
Peru	3.6	6.6	8.1	13.0	23.7	23.9
Ghana	3.5	19.4	16.7	24.5	42.3	16.8
Serbia	3.5	8.5	9.3	–	–	7.7
Uganda	3.5	14.7	10.8	11.8	22.9	20.7
Mauritius	3.4	4.8	3.4	58.7	54.3	1.1
West Bank and Gaza	3.4	8.2	6.1	15.5	–	2.5
Andorra	3.4	–	–	–	–	0.1
Burkina Faso	3.3	12.0	9.4	14.1	–	10.1

(continued)

Table 6.6 Continued

Country	Growth rates			Exports as % of GDP (1995)	Exports as % of GDP (2013)	Population (millions) (1995)
	Per capita GDP	Exports of goods and services	Imports of goods and services			
Chile	3.3	5.7	9.4	29.3	32.6	14.4
Botswana	3.2	4.3	6.9	50.8	55.1	1.6
Tanzania	3.2	13.0	13.5	24.1	28.2	29.9
Tunisia	3.1	4.2	3.5	44.9	–	9.0
Moldova	3.1	10.1	11.1	49.3	44.1	3.7
Singapore	3.1	8.1	8.0	181.2	190.5	3.5
San Marino	3.0	–	–	–	–	0.03
Fuel-exporting developing countries						
Equatorial Guinea	20.8	30.7	31.4	68.5	88.4	0.4
Angola	5.6	47.2	47.7	–	55	12.1
Trinidad and Tobago	4.3	11.1	11.5	53.8	–	1.3
Nigeria	3.9	–	–	35.8	26.7	108.4
Chad	3.7	25.6	12.8	21.9	–	7.0
Iraq	3.0	–	–	–	41.6	20.4

Transition countries other than fuel-exporting countries

Bosnia and Herzegovina	11.2	20.7	11.5	20.4	–	3.5
Armenia	7.5	6.2	3.0	23.9	27.0	3.2
Georgia	6.4	–	–	25.5	44.7	4.7
Albania	6.1	15.4	11.8	12.5	34.9	3.2
Belarus	5.9	7.1	8.3	49.7	61.2	10.2
Fuel-exporting transition countries						
Azerbaijan	8.5	16.6	17.1	27.9	48.7	7.7
Turkmenistan	5.5	16.4	5.3	84.0	–	4.2
Kazakhstan	5.3	4.6	1.8	39.0	39.5	15.8
Uzbekistan	4.2	10.4	10.4	36.7	–	22.8
Russian Federation	3.5	5.5	10.6	29.3	28.4	148.1
Developed countries						
Lithuania	5.7	9.0	9.8	47.4	–	3.6
Latvia	5.6	7.1	8.9	42.7	–	2.5
Estonia	5.3	8.4	9.3	68.1	88.0	1.4
Poland	4.3	9.4	9.7	23.2	47.8	38.6
Romania	3.4	3.9	11.8	27.6	42.0	22.7
Bulgaria	3.4	7.8	9.1	51.9	70.2	8.4
Ireland	3.3	3.7	7.7	75.3	–	3.6

(continued)

Table 6.6 **Continued**

Country	Growth rates			Exports as % of GDP (1995)	Exports as % of GDP (2013)	Population (millions) (1995)
	Per capita GDP	Exports of goods and services	Imports of goods and services			
Regions						
Middle East & North Africa	2.1	6.2	4.5	25.6	–	251.6
East Asia & Pacific	7.4	10.1	11.3	26.1	31.5	1712.8
South Asia	4.7	11.1	11.7	12.1	23.1	1259.4
Latin America & Caribbean	1.6	7.2	4.9	18.0	22.7	461.7
Sub-Saharan Africa	1.7	7.6	6.6	27.0	33.2	581.0
High-income OECD	1.4	5.2	5.0	19.8	–	950.1

Source: Author's calculations using the data in World Bank 2014.

Table 6.7 **Debacles, 1995–2013**

Country	Growth rates			Exports as % of GDP (1995)	Exports as % of GDP (2013)	Population (millions) (1995)
	Per capita GDP	Exports of goods and services	Imports of goods and services			
Bahrain	0.0	–	–	82.0	–	0.6
Congo, Dem. Rep.	0.0	12.3	18.7	28.5	–	42.0
Gabon	-0.1	-1.1	4.0	59.4	58.7	1.1
Kuwait	-0.1	2.4	4.4	52.4	–	1.6
Solomon Islands	-0.2	–	–	36.2	–	0.4
Madagascar	-0.2	6.6	9.0	24.1	–	13.5
Haiti	-0.3	9.9	10.8	9.1	–	7.8
Central African Republic	-0.3	-0.8	4.7	22.2	–	3.3
Comoros	-0.4	-12.8	0.0	19.8	–	0.5
Brunei Darussalam	-0.5	0.6	3.3	59.7	76.2	0.3
Jamaica	-0.5	-4.5	-5.2	50.5	–	2.5
Guinea-Bissau	-0.9	–	–	11.7	–	1.1
Aruba	-0.9	–	–	84.9	–	0.1
Eritrea	-0.9	14.3	-1.3	22.4	–	3.4
Burundi	-1.0	9.1	18.2	12.9	–	6.2
Zimbabwe	-1.8	-6.0	-0.3	38.2	30.1	11.6
United Arab Emirates	-3.2	11.0	15.4	–	–	2.3

Source: Author's calculations using the data in World Bank 2014.

surges were behind the growth debacles. Poor growth performance continued to be associated with slow or negative growth in imports.

Cross-Country Evidence: The Causality Issue

An obvious criticism of the analysis correlating fast growth in GDP (or per capita GDP) to fast growth in trade is that it only establishes association and does not prove causation. We cannot rule out the possibility that the causation flows from per capita GDP growth to trade rather than the other way around: countries that grow more rapidly import more and, via the trade balance condition, also export more.

There are at least four responses to this criticism. First, in the vast majority of the cases, fast growth in GDP is accompanied by a rise in the trade-to-GDP ratio. This implies faster growth in trade than in GDP. Therefore, attributing the entire growth in trade to GDP growth requires showing that GDP growth is on average biased toward trade. This is possible, but free trade critics have provided no evidence supporting it.

Second and more important, detailed country case studies show that rapid GDP growth does not merely accompany rapid growth in trade but also is characterized by either low or declining barriers to trade complemented by significant depreciation of the domestic currency to correct the bias in favor of non-traded goods relative to traded goods.[15] Low or declining barriers may not always accompany rapid growth, but rapid growth almost always accompanies low or declining barriers.

Third and perhaps most important, the relevant question from the policy perspective is: between liberal and protectionist trade policies, which one offers a safer bet? A moment's reflection would tell us that once we accept that rapid growth in trade is an integral aspect of rapid growth in GDP, liberal trade policies offer a much safer bet. The easiest way to explain the argument is by way of an analogy between the flow of trade and the flow of water from a tap. Think of GDP growth as water pressure and the degree of openness to trade as the extent to which the tap is open. The volume of water flowing out of a tap per second depends on both water pressure and the extent to which the tap is open. Analogously, growth in trade depends on GDP growth as well as the extent to which the country is open to trade. No matter how high the water pressure, if the tap is tightly closed, no water flows. Autarkic policies produce the same outcome in terms of the effect of growth on trade. India in the 1960s and 1970s offers a ready example: growth impulses produced pressures for growth in trade, but the country's near-autarkic policies prevented those impulses from translating into actual trade expansion. The policies also had a detrimental effect on GDP growth.

Finally, contrary to continued claims by critics, some recent econometric studies do offer compelling evidence connecting trade *causally* to growth. Econometric studies have generally relied on two separate measures of openness when relating it to GDP growth: trade-to-GDP ratio and policy variables such as the simple average tariff rates on different goods. Studies using the former measure consistently yield a strong and statistically significant relationship between openness and growth, while those based on policy variables lead to mixed results.

The failure of the studies using policy variables to find a robust effect of openness on growth is not surprising for at least three reasons. First, aggregating a complex structure of tariffs into a single measure for purposes of econometric applications suffers from conceptual difficulties. For example, it is natural to aggregate a 10 percent tariff on half of imports and a 20 percent tariff on the other half into an average rate of 15 percent. Yet the impact of the two tariff rates is in general different from that of a uniform tariff of 15 percent. Likewise, tariffs on inputs are likely to work differently than tariffs on final goods. For example, an economy with a 10 percent tariff on automobiles alone is more protected than one with a 10 percent tariff on both automobiles and auto parts, especially if neither economy produces any auto parts. This is because the tariff on auto parts in the latter economy counteracts the protection provided by the tariff on automobiles.

The second reason econometric studies using trade barriers as the measure of openness have produced ambiguous results is that non-tariff barriers are difficult to quantify meaningfully. As a result, when both tariff and non-tariff barriers are present, analysts often resort to using just tariffs to represent protection. But if non-tariff barriers such as import licensing are applied to hold imports at very low levels and tariffs are relatively low or moderate, tariffs would understate the degree of protection.

Finally, if some key complementary policies such as an appropriate exchange rate, political or macroeconomic stability, flexible product and factor markets, connectivity, and well-functioning ports are missing, lower trade barriers may not translate into higher volumes of trade. For example, an appreciating real exchange rate can often neutralize the incentives opened up by trade liberalization, especially in the short run. These factors make it harder to obtain a strong relationship between trade barriers and growth.

Therefore, a study by economists Jeffrey Frankel and David Romer and a follow-up study by Frankel and Andrew Rose have chosen to establish causation by separating out a component of trade that does not depend on per capita income and measuring its impact on per capita income.[16] The studies use the gravity model to identify the part of the total trade that depends solely on geographical factors. They then use this part of trade, unrelated to per-capita income, as the independent variable to measure the impact of openness on per-capita income. Their exercise reveals a strong effect of trade openness on per-capita income. For example, Frankel and Romer find that a 1 percentage point increase in the trade-to-GDP ratio raises per capita income by 2 percentage points on average.

In their critical examination of the contribution by Frankel and Romer and an unpublished version of the paper by Frankel and Rose, economists Francisco Rodriguez and Dani Rodrik raised several objections.[17] In the final, published version of their paper, Frankel and Rose successfully overcame every one of these objections. The authors note:

> Still, the key question concerns the implications of these perturbations [pointed out by Rodriguez and Rodrik] for the openness variable. *In every case,* regardless of whether the other controls are included or not, *the openness variable retains most of its magnitude and all of its statistical significance* in the presence of each of the three Rodriguez-Rodrik modifications. The t-statistics are 3 to 4.[18]

The only criticism with which Rodriguez and Rodrik are left is that the "implications of geography-induced differences in trade, on the one hand, and policy-induced variations in trade, on the other, can be in principle quite different." But even here, analytical arguments and evidence are against them. While trade-liberalization-induced trade and proximity-driven trade may in principle work differently from the viewpoint of static, resource allocation effects, there is a strong presumption that they would work similarly from the viewpoint of growth. Productivity increases resulting from pro-competitive effects of trade, improved access to high-quality inputs and technology, technological diffusion, and exploitation of scale economies are unlikely to differ dramatically according to the sources of trade expansion.

The empirical investigation of this hypothesis reveals as much. Frankel and Rose compare their estimates of the effects of openness on per capita income when openness is measured by all trade to estimates in which openness is measured only by distance- and size-induced trade. They are unable to reject the hypothesis that these estimates are equal. They conclude, "We see little evidence that our results are affected by reverse causality running from income to openness."[19]

A further point to note is that the criticism by Rodriguez and Rodrik is itself an assertion: they state that the impact of trade-policy-induced trade may be quite different from that of proximity-induced trade. But they do not substantiate this assertion empirically. The position they take is that unless the effect of trade-liberalization-induced trade on growth is explicitly shown to be similar to that of proximity-driven trade, the two sources must be presumed to have dramatically different, perhaps even qualitatively opposite, effects. But typically, trade barriers constitute a distortion, so the trade expansion induced by their removal is likely to be even more beneficial than the trade induced by proximity. Rodriguez and Rodrik assert that trade barriers may be correcting a preexisting distortion, so the removal of those barriers may turn out to be harmful. But they provide no evidence showing that this is the norm rather than the exception. The circumstances under which tariffs correct a preexisting distortion are rather limited, and therefore tariffs are likely to create distortion rather than correct it.

Finally, if we approach empirical evidence in the postmodern deconstructionist (or should we just say destructionist?) spirit, as Rodriguez and Rodrik do, we are unlikely to be persuaded by it no matter how overwhelming it may be. Unlike in physics, empirical evidence in economics can always be deemed unsatisfactory and incomplete. For example, suppose we could successfully link aggregate trade-liberalization-induced trade and per capita GDP. A skeptic could still reject such evidence, since it says nothing about how specific forms of liberalization impact per capita income. After all, the removal of import licenses, which allow bureaucrats to alter the precise import quantity from one year to another, is likely to impact incomes differently than the removal of strict import quotas. Likewise, the removal of restrictions on capital goods imports might impact GDP differently than the removal of restrictions on consumer goods. And, of course, the removal of tariff barriers might work still differently than the removal of non-tariff barriers. While one may want to undertake research to learn about the differential impacts of different instruments on per capita incomes, countries do not have the luxury to wait to decide upon their trade policies while this research is being conducted. The question we must then confront is whether the existing evidence points toward liberal or protectionist policies as being more suitable for growth.

I conclude this section by restating the asymmetry between the evidence provided by pro-free-trade economists and that offered by the advocates of protectionism. At the aggregate level, this chapter has marshaled very substantial evidence connecting growth and trade openness. Even econometric studies have come a long way toward establishing causation between trade and per capita GDP.[20] Free trade critics, on the other hand, have provided nothing that comes even close to this evidence in support of their case. Their argument that the experience during the 1960s and 1970s demonstrates the superiority of import substitution over outward orientation fails miserably: it is in fact the post-trade-liberalization era of the 1990s and 2000s that exhibits the highest growth rates in the developing countries taken together.

At a more disaggregated level, countries experiencing rapid (3 percent or more) growth in per capita incomes during 1961–75 accounted for only 16 percent of the population in the developing countries, compared with 44.4 percent during 1976–94 and 73.4 percent during 1995–13. Moreover, even during 1961–75, according to the evidence I have presented, the fast-growing countries relied on rapid expansion of trade rather than contraction.

When it comes to causation, free trade critics have offered absolutely nothing: they have conducted no econometric analysis worth its salt showing that high and rising barriers to trade lead to faster growth. In a paper, Rodrik does offers a graph showing a positive association between average tariff rates and growth rates, but it is far from clear whether this is to be taken seriously, for the author neither reports the statistical significance of his finding nor says anything about causation.[21]

Concluding Remarks

Our review of the available evidence allows us to minimally reach the following conclusions:

- *The assertion that 1960–73 constitutes the golden period of growth in the developing countries turns out to be a myth.* The Rodrik-Chang claim that the period 1960–73 (or the 1960s and 1970s more generally) represented the golden period of growth and therefore victory for import substitution industrialization fails to stand up to close scrutiny. The performance of developing countries as a whole during the last two and a half decades has been vastly superior to that during either the 1960s or 1970s. Compared with a growth rate of 2.9 percent during 1961–73, per capita income in the developing countries grew a hefty 4 percent during 1991–2013.
- *Growth miracles are rooted in trade openness.* Countries that have achieved sustained rapid growth in their per capita incomes have almost always done so while maintaining a high trade-to-GDP ratio, rapidly expanding it, or both. Our country case studies in later chapters show that sustained rapid growth has also involved low or declining barriers to trade.
- *Growth debacles are not linked to import surges.* Countries that have stagnated or declined in terms of per capita income over long periods of time have rarely experienced rapidly expanding imports at the same time.
- *We now have compelling evidence linking trade causally to per capita income.* A causal relationship exists between per capita income, on the one hand, and the volume of trade on the other, as shown by Frankel and Rose.

From a policy perspective, these conclusions establish a strong presumption in favor of liberal over protectionist policies. Indeed, once we accept the proposition that fast growth in per capita GDP positively correlates with fast growth in trade, rejection of a link between fast growth in per capita GDP and low or declining trade barriers is illogical. After all, one way to facilitate rapid growth in trade is to maintain low barriers or to bring them progressively down. True, fast growth in GDP itself helps expand trade, but so do low and declining trade barriers.

Where do the critics stand? They have not been able to counter the evidence provided by Frankel and Rose causally linking the volume of trade to per capita incomes. Nor have they provided *any* systematic evidence that high or increased protection or reduced volume of trade is beneficial for growth. Given this set of facts, any advice to the developing countries to opt for protectionist policies can only be viewed as purely ideological.

Notes

1. Rodrik 1999, ch. 4.
2. Chang 2007, 27.
3. This comparison does not change if we were to choose 1973 rather than 1975 as the cutoff point.
4. Khatkhate 2006.
5. Nayyer 2005.
6. Khatkhate 2006, 2204.
7. Chang 2007 cites "Chang (2002, table 4.2)" as the source of the 3 percent growth figure for the 1960s and 1970s. Chang 2002, table 4.2, in turn cites "World Bank 1980" as the source in a note below table 4.2, but the reference list at the end of the book makes no mention of World Bank 1980. A good guess is that World Bank 1980 refers to the *World Development Report 1980*. Growth rates in this source do match those in table 4.2 in Chang 2002.
8. Empirical work on which the estimates reported in this chapter are based was done in 2014. Therefore, it is based on the WDI database as accessed in October 2014. Subsequently, the World Bank has redefined the "East Asia and Pacific Region" in the WDI to include Japan, Australia, and New Zealand. As reported in this chapter and in the WDI database in 2014, "East Asia and Pacific Region" only includes the developing countries in the region.
9. Chang 2002, table 4.2.
10. Since Chang published his book in 2007, it may be reasonably asked how the comparison would work out till 2007. The growth rate even during 1981–2007, 3.2 percent, was higher than the 3 percent growth during the 1960s and 1970s. If we exclude the 1980s, the gap is significantly larger.
11. As noted earlier, I completed the work reported in this chapter in 2014. The World Bank regularly updates the World Development Indicators, and these were available through 2016 at the time of preparation of the final version of this chapter. Broad checks on the updated data confirm that updating of data does not impact any of the conclusions.
12. I originally provided this analysis in Panagariya 2004a.
13. To calculate this percentage, I have obtained the developing country population by adding the populations in East Asia and Pacific, South Asia, North Africa and Middle East, Sub-Saharan Africa, and Latin America.
14. See, e.g., Jeter 2009.
15. Many free trade advocates, myself included, view depreciation of the domestic currency as an essential part of a trade liberalization package that cuts across sectors (in contrast to liberalization in one or two sectors). Often protectionist policies are accompanied by an overvaluation of the domestic currency, which keeps exports expensive for foreign buyers

and imports cheap for domestic buyers and thus creates a bias in favor of the production of non-traded goods.

16. Frankel and Romer 1999; Frankel and Rose 2002.
17. Rodriguez and Rodrik 2000; Rodrik 2000.
18. Frankel and Rose 2002, 451.
19. Frankel and Rose 2002, 450.
20. Irwin 2015, 55–59, provides a more detailed and up-to-date account of the studies on trade openness and growth. In particular, see Wacziarg and Welch 2008; Billmeier and Nannicini 2013; and Estevadeordal and Taylor 2013.
21. Rodrik 2003.

7

Trade Openness and Poverty

The Empirical Evidence

At a conceptual level, the effects of openness on poverty can be divided into static and dynamic effects. Static effects principally refer to the changes in the earnings of the poor that trade liberalization brings about through reallocation of resources across sectors without taking into account the growth effects of liberalization. Within the industrial sector, liberalization in the poor countries increases the relative price of unskilled-labor-intensive goods. The resulting increase in the demand for unskilled labor leads to a rise in the unskilled wage via what trade economists call the Stolper-Samuelson effect, named after economists Wolfgang Stolper and Nobel laureate Paul Samuelson.[1] In addition, given that protection favors industry over the agricultural sector, its removal ends discrimination against the latter. This helps the vast majority of the poor who earn their living from agriculture. Finally, within a static context and in the absence of complementary tax reform, tariff liberalization is likely to result in a loss of revenue, thereby potentially adversely impacting redistributive payments to the poor. For this reason, economists usually advise complementing tariff liberalization with tax reform aimed at ensuring steady growth in tax revenue.

A qualification to the Stolper-Samuelson type of analysis is that it is possible to construct models in which this effect is reversed. For example, in a multiproduct setting, we can rank products according to skill intensity. Some developing countries may be exporters of products with intermediate skill intensity and importers of products with the lowest and highest skill intensities. In such a situation, trade liberalization that expands the exports may lead to a reduction in the relative wage of the unskilled. From a practical standpoint, however, this argument is not very compelling, since the countries with vast numbers of poor, such as India, Indonesia, and Bangladesh, are likely to have a comparative advantage in the most unskilled-labor-intensive products.

The dynamic effects of trade liberalization, which work through sustained rapid growth, help lower poverty through at least five channels:

- Holding income distribution constant, growth raises the incomes of the poor at the same rate as it raises incomes of other sections of the society. Even when we allow for income distribution effects, because this shift is gradual, sustained rapid growth overwhelms any adverse redistribution effects. Using the memorable terminology introduced by Bhagwati and later adopted by Bhagwati and Panagariya, rather than "trickle down," sustained rapid growth generates a powerful "pull-up" effect and helps bring ever-increasing numbers of the poor into gainful employment.[2]
- With the notable exception of India recently, growing output and employment shares of manufactures in general and of unskilled-labor-intensive manufactures such as apparel, toys, footwear, and other light consumer goods in particular have accompanied rapid growth in the developing countries. This growth pattern produces rapidly rising employment opportunities and rising real wages for the poor.
- Rapidly rising incomes also increase the demand for non-traded services supplied by unskilled or low-skilled workers. These may include construction services; tourism-related services; domestic household services; sales and repair services for various consumer durables including automobiles, refrigerators, washing machines, cooking ranges, and television sets; driving services; catering and related services; and a variety of low-end health- and education-related services. Because these services must be domestically supplied, they add to employment opportunities and rising real wages for the poor.
- While opening up the economy can and eventually will lead to a decline in tariff revenue, rapid growth can more than compensate for it through increased revenues from other sources, such as income tax and domestic indirect taxes. The increase in revenues, in turn, allows the government to achieve greater redistribution in favor of the poor through direct transfers as well as subsidized provision of social services in areas such as health and education.
- Growth that helps raise incomes of poor families also improves their ability to access public services in areas such as education and health. A common observation is that at very low levels of income, even if public schools and public health centers are provided, the poor fail to take advantage of them. Children of the poor often have to work rather than attend school to help their families make ends meet. Poor families also lack the means to travel to take advantage of health care facilities unless they happen to be located in their own village.

While the conceptual link between openness and poverty alleviation is strong, the question is ultimately an empirical one. Therefore, this chapter is devoted to the study of the empirical evidence on the subject. In doing so, I limit myself to the connection between openness and poverty directly as well as through growth. I do not explore some of the other channels, however, such as the impact through wages, increased revenue for redistribution, and increased demand for non-traded services.[3]

In the first section, I consider the early evidence linking growth and poverty, which relies on cross-country patterns and individual country episodes. In the second section, I report on a selected set of regression studies that estimate the impact of growth on poverty reduction. In the third section, I make five observations regarding the evidence. In the fourth section, I report the studies focusing on a direct link between trade openness and poverty alleviation. In the final section, I offer some concluding thoughts.

Growth and Poverty: Early Studies

I have noted that openness can reduce poverty indirectly through growth. Therefore, one avenue to studying the link between openness and poverty is to explore the link between growth and poverty. This latter relationship can be studied by examining the share of income of the bottom deciles of the population as per capita income rises. This is the question Bhagwati asked more than four decades ago when working for the Planning Commission in India. Using the crude income distribution data available to him at the time, he reached the conclusion that the share of the bottom three or four deciles moved little with changes in per capita income. That is to say, he concluded that the incomes of the poor rose more or less at the same rate as per capita income. To quote him:

> I can speak to the issue, as it happens, from the immediacy of personal experience. For I returned to India during 1961, to join the Indian Statistical Institute which had a small think tank attached to [Pitamber] Pant's Division in the Planning Commission. Having been brought in by Pant to work as his main economist, I turned immediately to the question of strategy for minimum incomes. I assembled such income distribution data as were then available for countries around the world, both functional and personal, to see if anything striking could be inferred about the relationship between the economic and political system and policies and the share of the bottom three or four deciles. You can imagine the quality of these data then, by looking at their quality now almost a quarter of a century later. . . .
>
> The scanning of, and reflection on, the income distribution data suggested that there was no dramatic alternative for raising the poor to minimum incomes except to increase the overall size of the pie. The inter-country differences in the share of the bottom deciles,

where poverty was manifestly rampant, just did not seem substantial enough to suggest any alternative path. The strategy of rapid growth was therefore decided upon, in consequence of these considerations, as providing the only reliable way of making a *sustained*, rather than a one-shot, impact on poverty.[4]

The fifteen-year plan, entitled "Perspective of Development 1961–76: Implications of Planning for a Minimum Level of Living," produced by Pant on behalf of the Planning Commission in August 1962, endorsed Bhagwati's conclusion. In consequence, it advocated growth as the key to alleviating poverty and recommended 7 percent annual growth. Additionally and significantly, it identified 20 percent of the population as consisting of groups that would be at best loosely integrated with the growing sectors of the economy. Recognizing that growth would fail to perceptibly improve the lot of these groups, the plan advocated the need for social safety nets and more targeted action for them.[5]

The emphasis on growth as the primary instrument of poverty alleviation early on by trade economists and policymakers was thus based on a careful analysis of the available evidence rather than any ideological predilection. Equally, these advocates of growth were well aware that there would be groups that lacked access to the mainstream of the economy and required targeted action. This is a far cry from allegations by free trade critics such as Chang:

> The poor *growth* record of neo-liberal globalization since the 1980s is particularly embarrassing. Accelerating growth—if necessary at the cost of increasing inequality and possibly some increase in poverty—was the proclaimed goal of neo-liberal reform. We have been repeatedly told that we first have to "create more wealth" before we can distribute it more widely and that neo-liberalism was the way to do that.[6]

We saw earlier that Chang is factually wrong about the developing countries performing poorly since the 1980s relative to the 1960s and 1970s.[7] But his assertion that the advocates of fast growth sought growth for its own sake is equally without foundation. Had Chang read the work of economists such as Jagdish Bhagwati and T. N. Srinivasan and the government of India's numerous policy documents written since the 1950s, he would not have made this mistaken claim. Instead, he relied on unspecified "neo-liberals" when claiming, "We have been repeatedly told . . ."

Returning to the evidence on growth and poverty: subsequent research has validated the hypothesis of the bottom deciles gaining in income as nationwide per capita income rises. In Parts III and IV, I will discuss this link in detail for specific countries that have experienced sustained rapid growth. Here I summarize the evidence on an aggregative basis without detailed discussion of any specific country. Due to limited data availability, earlier studies in this category relied solely on cross-country data. Gradually, however, data that permitted comparisons at two or more points in time within the same country became available. In more recent times researchers have been able to combine data across countries and over time within the same country. These studies also make extensive use of regressions to measure the quantitative impact of growth in per capita income on poverty.

In a study based on cross-sectional data for forty-four countries, economists Irma Adelman and Cynthia Morris dramatically concluded that "development is accompanied by an absolute as well as a relative decline in the average income of the very poor."[8] Other researchers quickly pointed out, however, that in reaching this conclusion, the authors had relied on a very indirect method with little scientific validity. William Cline, in particular, noted that in their stepwise variance analysis, these authors found that the share of the bottom three-fifths of the population in a set of countries with zero growth in per capita GDP exceeded that in the countries exhibiting 3 percent growth. They went on to argue that typical growth involves countries transitioning from the former set to the latter. It then followed that the share of income of the poor must decline before it rises as the growth process proceeds.[9] Cline went on to state, "This very indirect procedure appears misleading. A much more direct test of the hypothesis is to consider the regressions Adelman and Morris report. None of these shows a statistically significant decline in absolute income level for the poorest groups as per capita income level rises, in tests using the same cross-section data as that used in the step wise variance tests."

Soon after, using detailed cross-country data, Montek Singh Ahluwalia demonstrated that data did not support the "absolute impoverishment hypothesis" propounded by Adelman and Morris.[10] He estimated relationships in which average incomes of the poorest 20, 40, and 60 percent were successively hypothesized to depend on per capita gross national product, share of agriculture in GDP, share of urban population in total population, literacy rate, secondary school enrollment rate, population growth rate, and whether or not the country had a socialist government. He found the elasticity of average income of the poor with respect to national per capita income to be uniformly positive, though less than unity. This meant that, ceteris paribus, a 1 percent increase in nationwide per capita income raised rather than lowered the average income of the bottom 20, 40, and 60 percent of the population. Ahluwalia thus rejected the absolute impoverishment hypothesis.

Subsequent studies have consistently supported this essential finding. Gary Fields brought together evidence on all developing countries for which reliable income distribution data for two or more years were available at the time of his study.[11] He found thirteen such countries, of which ten had experienced a reduction in poverty and three an increase in it. Nine countries—Bangladesh, Brazil, Costa Rica, Pakistan, Puerto Rico, Singapore, Taiwan, Thailand, and Mexico—experienced "demonstrable improvements in the economic position of the poor" and also grew at a moderate to fast rate.[12] Only one country, Sri Lanka, achieved a substantial reduction in poverty in spite of slow growth, while two, Argentina and the Philippines, experienced increase in poverty despite fast growth. One country, India, neither grew nor achieved poverty reduction. This study demonstrated that while cases existed in which poverty alleviation and growth did not go hand in hand, they were exceptions rather than the rule.

Working independently of Fields but almost concurrently, Ahluwalia, Nicholas Carter, and Hollis Chenery studied twelve cases.[13] In each case, they found that real per capita income of the poorest 20 percent rose with growth. In a follow-up study, Fields compiled consistent data on poverty for eighteen countries.[14] Out of these, poverty fell in fourteen cases, rose in three, and did not change in one. In two of the cases in which poverty rose, economic growth had been negative. There was only one case in which economic growth had not brought poverty down.

Growth and Poverty: More Recent Studies

In a more recent comprehensive paper, economists Klaus Deininger and Lyn Squire have put together an extensive and high-quality data set on changes in poverty and income distribution in relation to growth.[15] They require that the measures of poverty and income distribution included in the data set be based on household surveys, comprehensive coverage of the population, and comprehensive coverage of income sources and household expenditures. They also require that two observations being compared be at least one decade apart. These qualifications are satisfied by eighty-eight cases of income growth and seven cases of income decline. They find that in the income growth group, income of the poor rises in seventy-seven cases and declines in eleven. In the income decline group, income of the poor falls in five cases and rises in two. Thus, out of a total of ninety-five episodes, thirteen fail to conform to the hypothesized positive correlation between growth and poverty reduction. Deininger and Squire further note that nonconformity in nine of these episodes disappears if longer periods are considered. In three of the remaining four cases, growth turns out to have been less than 2 percent. The overall message is clear: sustained rapid growth is almost always accompanied by reduced poverty. Only if growth itself is relatively low may poverty fail to register a decline.

Several regression studies reinforce these basic findings. In the following, I discuss the results of two of them in greater detail.[16] Martin Ravallion and

Shaohua Chen use survey data for sixty-seven countries, of which forty-two have at least two surveys.[17] The earliest survey relates to 1981 (Thailand) and the latest to 1993 (several countries). Selecting comparable pairs of surveys, the authors are able to construct 64 "spells" between 1981 and 1993. Each spell contains poverty ratios and per capita incomes at two different points in time for the same country. The authors use these spells to estimate the effect of rising average living standard on the poverty ratio. The response varies depending on the precise level of the poverty line, but it is uniformly negative: an increase in average living standard is consistently associated with a decline in the poverty ratio. Setting the poverty line at 50 percent of the average income or expenditure, they find that a 10 percent increase in average income or expenditure is associated with a 26 percent decline in the poverty ratio (for instance, if the poverty ratio is initially 50 percent, it drops to 37 percent in response to a 10 percent increase in the average income or expenditure). Raising the poverty line lowers the value of the estimated response. On the other hand, defining the poverty line at $1 a day at the purchasing parity exchange rate raises the magnitude of poverty reduction due to a 10 percent increase in the average income or expenditure to 31 percent.

In a subsequent and highly cited but controversial paper entitled "Growth Is Good for the Poor," David Dollar and Aart Kraay fully validate the conclusion tentatively reached in Pant's fifteen-year plan that "in countries at very different levels of development and with varying socio-political environments, the distribution of incomes follows a remarkably similar pattern, especially in respect of the proportion of incomes earned by the lowest three or four deciles of the population."[18] These authors compile a large data set consisting of eighty countries and spanning more than four decades and use it to study the quantitative impact of increased nationwide per capita income on the average income of the bottom 20 percent of the population. They conduct a number of different tests but never reject the null hypothesis that, on average, a 1 percent increase in nationwide per capita income raises the average income of the bottom 20 percent of the population by 1 percent. In other words, insofar as the bottom two deciles are concerned, on average the income distribution moves little with growth, so the average income of the poor moves proportionally with nationwide per capita income.

Each of the studies linking growth and poverty can be and has been subject to criticisms relating to data or econometric methodology. Specifically, economists Abhijit Banerjee, Angus Deaton, Nora Lustig, and Ken Rogoff have criticized the Dollar and Kraay study in the harshest terms in their evaluation of the World Bank research covering the period from 1998 to 2005.[19] Among other things, they contend that Dollar and Kraay measure the average income of the poor imprecisely, which biases the results toward their key finding of a 1 percent increase in the average income of the poor accompanying a 1 percent increase in nation-wide per capita income. To quote the evaluation report:

> Their [Dollar and Kraay's] measure of the incomes of the poor (the average per capita income in the bottom fifth of the population) is derived from aggregate national income using either estimates of the share of the bottom quintile from surveys, or from estimates of Gini coefficients of income inequality together with the assumption that incomes are distributed according to the lognormal distribution. The problem is that many of the estimates of the income shares and of the Gini coefficients are quite imprecisely measured and, when the data are uninformative about the true level of inequality, Dollar and Kraay's pro-cedure guarantees that, on average, the incomes of the poor will track average income. If the Gini coefficients were random numbers, the con-clusion would be guaranteed. So, in the end, we do not know how much of the result is genuine, and how much is driven by errors in the data.[20]

While the caution underlying this criticism regarding measurement error is well taken, in my judgment Banerjee and colleagues greatly overstate their case. It is unlikely that even they believe that the Gini coefficients used to estimate the average incomes of the bottom quintile are random numbers, else they them-selves would not use Gini coefficients in their own work, which some of them surely do. Admittedly, Gini coefficients and income shares of the poor for some of the countries for some of the years are subject to measurement errors, but that is a far cry from the view that they are random numbers.

Even more important to note is that Dollar and Kraay's results would be sus-pect if they greatly differed from those of other researchers. On the contrary, their results show remarkable consistency with virtually all other evidence on growth and poverty available from alternative sources. For example, contributions by Deininger and Squire and by Ravallion offer compelling evidence of near-zero correlation between growth in nationwide per capita income and change in the Gini coefficient. Ravallion puts this forcefully: "A common finding in the litera-ture is that changes over time in the extent of income inequality at the country level are uncorrelated with rates of economic growth. In other words, growth is distribution neutral on average."[21] The result in Dollar and Kraay's work that the average income of the bottom 20 percent of the population increases in propor-tion to the average nationwide per capita income is essentially a mirror image of this conclusion. Finally, a follow-up study by Kraay, which uses a more reliable database assembled by Ravallion and Chen at the World Bank, finds that growth effects on poverty dominate any distributional effects by a wide margin.[22]

Setting aside the specific value of the response of the average income of the bottom 20 percent of the population to the nationwide per capita income, the broader message that increases in the latter contribute significantly to poverty re-duction can be found in virtually every serious study, including those discussed here and others.[23] This same message also comes from the detailed country experiences (see Parts III and IV).

Growth and Poverty: Further Observations

Five further observations may be offered on the relationship between growth and poverty.

First, there is now considerable evidence that over time, income distribution moves very slowly relative to the change in per capita income. For example, the average annual percentage change in the Gini coefficients in the high-quality sample identified by Deininger and Squire turns out to be only 0.28 percentage points, compared with an average growth rate in per capita income of 2.16 per-cent.[24] Even in specific cases in which income inequality rises rapidly, growth overwhelms it. In the Deininger and Squire data set, the Gini coefficient moved from 41.3 percent in 1962 to 51.5 percent in 1991 in Thailand. But real incomes increased fourfold during the same period, leading to a vast decline in poverty. Therefore, even if one takes the view that growth is accompanied by deteriora-tion in the income distribution, the scope for poverty reduction through rapid expansion of per capita income is considerable.

Second, as illustrated by the experience of Thailand, in exceptional cases the Gini coefficient can shift substantially over a period of two to three decades. Therefore, the nature of growth does matter for how much poverty reduction a given amount of growth can deliver. In particular, growth that relies on rapid expansion of labor-intensive industries such as apparel, footwear, toys, light manufacturing, and consumer goods is likely to deliver a larger poverty reduc-tion for each percentage point of growth than one that is accompanied by rapid expansion of capital- and skilled-labor-intensive industries. South Korea in the 1960s and 1970s and India in the 1990s and 2000s offer contrasting experiences in this respect. While both were successful in bringing down poverty through rapid growth, the former did it more effectively because it saw the labor-intensive industries grow rapidly, which could "pull up" vast numbers of workers from agriculture into gainful manufacturing employment. In India, growth in the 1990s and 2000s relied more heavily on the capital- and skilled-labor-intensive industries, which has meant a slower decline in poverty for each percentage point of growth in per capita income.

Third, it bears emphasizing that the relationships derived from regression analyses are "on average" relationships. The experience of a given individual country will naturally differ from this "on average" relationship. Indeed, in exceptional cases, it may even be qualitatively different. Recall that when re-porting the individual country experiences over time compiled by Fields, we came across a few exceptional cases in which growth failed to reduce poverty and those in which poverty fell despite declining per capita incomes. The exist-ence of these variations across countries does not negate the fact that, at least ex ante, achieving sustained rapid growth remains by far the best strategy for reducing poverty within a country.

Fourth, the research described in the previous sections only tells us that growth is a powerful instrument of poverty reduction *in aggregate* and *over time*. It does not tell that growth improves the lot of *every* poor individual or house-hold and does so *immediately*. Both factors point to the need for anti-poverty programs. When poverty is widespread and intense, income transfers to the poor are essential to bring immediate relief to them. Likewise, groups outside the economic mainstream whom growth is expected to bypass must be aided for longer periods. This is not only a sensible economic policy on ethical grounds but also necessary to politically sustain the policies aimed at promoting rapid growth.

Finally, critics of the view that sustained growth is the most powerful instru-ment of poverty reduction cannot just get away with pointing to the groups not helped by growth or claiming that benefits of growth do not "trickle down" (i.e., accrue slowly) to the poor. Instead, they must provide positive and sys-tematic evidence demonstrating the superiority of *their* preferred instrument over growth. They must also show that the deployment of these redistributive policies at low levels of per-capita income is politically feasible even in the face of low or no growth. To date, all we have got from critics is flag-waving.

Directly Linking Openness to Poverty Alleviation

Up to this point, I have limited the discussion to the evidence linking trade openness and poverty indirectly through growth.[25] This is because the literature directly linking trade openness and poverty is sparse. Some suggestive evidence is provided by Dollar and Kraay, who rank a large number of countries according to three criteria: increased openness to trade as measured by the rise in trade-to-GDP ratio, GDP growth rate, and reduction in poverty.[26] It turns out that high-performance countries according to one criterion are also high-performance countries according to the other criteria. Thus, trade openness, growth, and pov-erty reduction go hand in hand.

There have been a number of studies attempting to establish a link between openness and growth using cross-country regressions, with some considering the effect of openness on poverty directly as well as indirectly through faster growth.[27] Dollar and Kraay find that openness impacts poverty entirely through growth.[28] Once the effect through growth has been taken into account, openness has no further direct effect on poverty. That is to say, the effect of trade on poverty works entirely through growth. Kraay explicitly decomposes the change in poverty due to trade into that working through growth and that directly impacting income distribution.[29] He finds that trade significantly lowers poverty through increased growth but has a small offsetting poverty-increasing effect through deterioration in the income distribution. The net effect is, of course, to reduce poverty. The difference between the findings of Dollar and Kraay and the findings of Kraay arises principally from the difference in the data sets they use.

Instead of measuring poverty by the average income of the bottom quintile, Emma Aisbett, Ann Harrison, and Alix Zwane measure it in terms of the headcount ratio.[30] They initially work with a large data set to determine the effect of trade openness on growth. Using a variety of measures of openness and control variables, they find this effect to be positive and robust to changes in specifications. They then go on to study the connection between growth and the headcount ratio measure of poverty using the World Bank database. Unsurprisingly, they find what other authors using this data set have found: growth lowers poverty in a major way. Putting these two results together, it would seem reasonable to conclude that trade openness helps bring poverty down.

Aisbett, Harrison, and Zwane offers some apparent consolation to anti-trade critics, however, when they study the relationship between trade openness and poverty ratio directly. For the restricted sample of countries and years for which they have data on poverty, they quantify the direct effect of openness on the poverty ratio, controlling for other relevant variables. While increased openness continues to be associated with reduced poverty in all specifications, the effect turns out to be weaker and not always statistically significant.

The fact that support for the link between openness and poverty alleviation is weaker when these are correlated directly than when the link is explored through growth is explained once we consider the fact that the former is based on a more restricted sample. Luckily, Aisbett and colleagues also estimate the effect of openness on growth within the restricted sample for which poverty measures are available. Within this sample, "the link between openness to trade and GDP per capita in levels or growth rates weakens significantly."[31] When one recognizes that the bulk of the effect of openness on poverty works through growth, this finding suggests that any hopes of finding a direct link between trade openness and poverty reduction within the restricted sample are likely to end up in disappointment.

Recently economist Devashish Mitra has redone the Aisbett, Harrison, and Zwane regressions using the updated poverty series from the World Development Indicators.[32] The new poverty headcount ratio in this series, based on the

$1.25-a-day poverty line, is much improved due to significant improvements in the International Comparisons Project as well as the availability of many more country-wide household surveys. Mitra finds that regressions that are otherwise similar to those in Aisbett, Harrison, and Zwane's study but deploy the updated poverty series yield strong evidence of a direct relationship between poverty reduction and trade liberalization.

Two additional recent studies rely on district- and state-level data from India to quantify the effects of trade liberalization on poverty between the late 1980s and the late 1990s. The idea these studies exploit is that different states (or districts) within the same country have different mixes of industries. Therefore, trade liberalization at the national level impacts the degree of protection in different states differently. This difference will typically impact poverty levels in different states differently as well.

Using district as the unit of analysis, economist Patia Topalova measures its openness by the weighted average of tariffs: the tariff in each sector is weighted by that sector's share in the total employment in the district.[33] The higher this weighted average tariff, the less open the district. Using the National Sample Survey data, Topalova then calculates the poverty ratio at the level of the district and quantifies the effect of the weighted average tariff on it. She finds that "rural districts where industries more exposed to trade liberalization were concentrated experienced a slower progress in poverty reduction." She further concludes that "compared to a rural district experiencing no change in tariffs, a district experiencing the mean level of tariff changes [reduction] saw a 2 percentage points increase in poverty incidence and a 0.6 percentage points increase in poverty depth. This setback represents about 15 percent of India's progress in poverty reduction over the 1990s."

A casual reader is almost sure to conclude from these statements that trade openness has had a detrimental effect on poverty reduction in India. But the "difference-in-difference" approach that Topalova uses does not allow us to infer anything about the effect of tariff reduction on overall poverty at the national level. At most Topalova shows that if one *assumes* that increased openness led to reduced poverty at the national level, the reduction was smaller in the districts where tariffs fell more. Alternatively, if one *assumes* that increased openness led to increased poverty overall, the increase was larger in the districts where tariffs fell more.

Interestingly, a follow-up study by economists Rana Hasan, Devashish Mitra, and Beyza Ural reverses the results of Topalova's work.[34] These authors begin by pointing out at least three important problems with her study. First, Topalova entirely ignores the fact that during the period of her analysis, consumer goods were subject to strict licensing. Therefore, tariff rates carried little information on the degree of protection enjoyed by these goods. To measure protection correctly, one must take the non-tariff barriers into account.

Second, Topalova's measure of weighted average tariff in a district suffers from a serious flaw: it assigns a tariff rate of zero to non-traded goods. This means that in calculating the average tariff in the district, Topalova multiplies the employment share of non-traded goods by zero. But goods may be non-traded precisely because tariffs and border barriers on their trade are prohibitively high. Ceteris paribus, this approach leads to a downward bias in measured protection in districts predominantly producing non-traded goods.

Finally, it turns out that according to the sampling strategy employed to collect the National Sample Survey data, samples at the level of the district, especially in the urban areas, are often not random. Sometimes district boundaries are redefined across surveys, making the analysis involving data over time problematic. Even more important, the sample size at the district level can sometimes be too small to give robust estimates of poverty. This fact is reflected in rather sharp fluctuations in the poverty estimates over time at the district level. Similar fluctuations are rare when poverty is estimated at the state or regional level.

Hasan and colleagues overcome these problems by including non-tariff barriers in their index of protection, avoiding the use of employment in non-traded sectors in the construction of the protection index, and conducting the analysis at the level of the state and regions. These and other corrections lead the authors to very different conclusions. To quote them:

> Our results are different from Topalova's. In no case do we find reductions in trade protection to have worsened poverty at the state or region level. Instead, we find that states whose workers are on average more exposed to foreign competition tend to have lower rural, urban and overall poverty rates (and poverty gaps), and this beneficial effect of greater trade openness is more pronounced in states that have more flexible labor market institutions.[35]

In terms of economic reasoning, the findings of Hasan and colleagues suggest that productivity gains from greater exposure to trade shield the workers against the adverse short-run employment effects that Topalova's results imply. Instead, increased efficiency allows the states with greater exposure to trade to offer better employment and wage prospects.

Before concluding this section, I wish to note an important limitation of studying the link between poverty and trade liberalization at the subnational level that applies to the studies done both by Topalova and by Hasan and colleagues. All states (or districts) within a country are subject to the same trade policy, yet this approach assigns different degrees of protection to different states based on the ex post employment structure. It is simply not clear why a given tariff reduction *on the margin* should be proportionately larger in a state in which the initial employment in that sector happens to be proportionately larger.[36]

On the Necessity of Complementary Reforms

Evidence presented so far makes a compelling case that sustained rapid growth is unlikely without low or declining barriers to trade. It also links sustained rapid growth intimately to sustained poverty reduction. Taken together, the two pieces of evidence establish a strong link between openness and poverty alleviation. Therefore, openness has to be an important element in any poverty alleviation strategy.

This being said, we can scarcely ignore the importance of complementary policies that help maximize the impact of growth on poverty alleviation and assist specific groups in taking advantage of the opportunities opened up by growth. Policies in the latter category are particularly pertinent to groups that may not be able to benefit from growth for one or the other reason. Several examples of such policies may be given.

First, how much openness and growth contribute to poverty alleviation crucially depends on what other policies the country puts in place. As the experience of India illustrates, the nature of growth has an important bearing on the extent of impact of growth on poverty. Declining barriers to trade have handsomely contributed to the growth of trade, incomes, and poverty alleviation in India during the last twenty-five years. But they have not achieved their true potential due to the absence of some key complementary policy reforms on the domestic front.

Until two decades ago, India exclusively reserved virtually all labor-intensive products for small-scale enterprises—enterprises that had a maximum of $200,000 in investment in plant and machinery and found it unprofitable to operate in export markets. As a result, growth in the formal sector has been concentrated heavily in the capital- and skilled-labor-intensive products. The result has been a much slower reduction in poverty in India than in China in recent years and in South Korea in the 1960s and early 1970s. Though the policy of reservation of products for exclusive production by small enterprises has now been eliminated, highly restrictive labor laws and other policy interventions that discourage large-scale production of labor-intensive products still hold back the growth of labor-intensive industry and therefore the strong "pull-up" effect that South Korea, Taiwan, and China experienced during their rapid growth phases.

Second, it is also important to design targeted polices to assist groups unable to access rapidly growing parts of the economy. For example, growth may be slow to reach the rural areas, where some settlements may be isolated from any modern centers of economic activity. Building roads that connect these settlements and villages to the centers of growth and bringing electricity to villages may help these sections of the population to translate their entrepreneurial talents into effective income and to better access well-paid jobs in the centers of growth.

Third, the lack of access to schooling may prevent the poor from fully sharing in the growth process, since even unskilled jobs in the organized sector often require some education so that the worker can follow directions to perform specific tasks in industrial processes. Those who live in extreme poverty and are cut off from the mainstream economy, such as the Scheduled Tribes in India, may be at a particular disadvantage. They are unable to access educational facilities due to locational and economic barriers. Targeted policy action is required under such circumstances.

Fourth, inadequate access to credit may further hamper the ability of the poor to take advantage of the profit opportunities opened up by rapid growth. The problem arises because they lack collateral. Because the government and financial institutions are ill equipped to monitor the vast numbers of small loans, absent collateral, default rates are extremely high, with loans used for consumption rather than invested in productive activities. There are two possible solutions to this problem. One, by granting formal titles to land and other property that poor people own, the government can turn the assets owned by the poor into effective collateral. And two, the government can facilitate the growth of institutions such as micro-credit that provide self-monitoring mechanisms for credit.

Finally, fiscal resources made available by rapid growth should also be used to fund cash transfers to the bottom deciles of the population. Governments often choose to give subsidies on the consumption of specific items such as food, fertilizer, electricity, water, and higher education. Often these subsidies are hijacked by the richer consumers, as has been the case in India over the last several decades. Cash transfers, by contrast, put money directly in the hands of the poor.

This list of complementary policies is not exhaustive. The specific circumstances of a given country would naturally require other policies to speed up poverty alleviation. The main principle to follow in selecting these policies is to ensure that they do not undermine the incentives for entrepreneurial activity.

Summary and Conclusions

The strong link between growth and poverty alleviation, when combined with the positive evidence on trade openness and growth, implies a strong link between openness and poverty alleviation. Studies that directly link trade openness and poverty alleviation are limited and less conclusive largely because the sample of countries for which high-quality evidence on poverty is available remains small. Some authors have tried to get at the direct link between trade openness and poverty alleviation using subnational jurisdictions as the unit of analysis, but these studies are plagued by conceptual problems.

In sum, while there is more than just casual evidence showing that trade openness is conducive to poverty alleviation on average, there is absolutely no evidence showing otherwise. I have not found a single study showing that openness has a statistically significant adverse effect on poverty alleviation, either directly or through growth. The country case studies greatly reinforce this conclusion. The only qualification to be added is that opening to trade may not always lower poverty, since it may not always lead to sustained rapid growth. But low or declining barriers to trade almost always serve as an important ingredient in sustained rapid growth and poverty alleviation.

Finally, it is important to remember that while openness and sustained rapid growth are the primary instruments of poverty alleviation, countries must put complementary policies in place to maximize the impact of growth on poverty and to assist groups that are not integrated into the growing sectors of the economy to take advantage of the opportunities opened up by growth. Barriers in the way of rapid growth of labor-intensive sectors must be removed. Policies to ensure access to elementary education must be put in place. Access to credit to the poor must be improved. Roads connecting villages and other hard-to-reach regions to the centers of rapid growth must be constructed, and rural electrification must be undertaken.

Notes

1. Stolper and Samuelson 1941.
2. Bhagwati 1988b; Bhagwati and Panagariya 2013.
3. Winters, McCulloch, and McKay (2004) provide some discussion of evidence along these lines.
4. Bhagwati 1988b, 541.
5. Planning Commission 1962.
6. Chang 2007, 28.
7. Once the reforms of the 1980s took root, the developing countries as a group could perform a lot better than in the 1960s and 1970s. Per capita income growth during 1991–2013, at 4.0 percent, has been vastly superior to the 2.9 percent growth achieved during 1961–80. Even if one insists on comparing the 1960s and 1970s with the entire post-1980 period, 1981–2013, the growth rate in the latter period, 3.2 percent, outperforms that in the former period (see Table 6.1).
8. Adelman and Morris 1973, 189.
9. Cline 1975, 377 n. 22.
10. Ahluwalia 1976.
11. Fields 1980.
12. Fields 1980 does not specify the cutoff points defining moderate and fast growth rates.

13. Ahluwalia, Carter, and Chenery 1979.
14. Fields 1989.
15. Deininger and Squire 1996.
16. Other studies include Roemer and Gugerty 1997; Timmer 1997; and Gallup, Radelet, and Warner 1998.
17. Ravallion and Chen 1997.
18. Dollar and Kraay 2002b. The quote relating to Pant is taken from Raj 1973, n. 21.
19. Banerjee et al. 2006.
20. Banerjee et al. 2006, 57. The Gini coefficient, defined later, is a measure of income inequality. It varies between 0 and 100. At 0, incomes are perfectly equal, with each household having the same income. At 100, incomes are the most unequal possible, with the entire income accruing to a single household.
21. Ravallion 2004, 3.
22. Kraay 2006, 205–6.
23. For example, see Roemer and Gugerty 1997; Timmer 1997; and Gallup, Radelet, and Warner 1998.
24. Also see Li, Squire, and Zou 1998.
25. In their comprehensive survey on trade openness and poverty, Winters, McCulloch, and McKay (2004) also discuss studies focusing on firms and specific sectors. I eschew these studies principally because we cannot infer from them the impact on overall poverty, which is what concerns us here. For instance, a study that considers the impact of the removal of restrictions on exports of rice on rice farmers alone does not inform us about the overall impact of the policy change on poverty. For instance, even if the change lowers poverty among rice farmers, it may increase overall poverty if it makes rice expensive for a vast number of poor people who consume but do not produce rice. The same applies to studies focusing on productivity effects of liberalization on firms in specific sectors.
26. Dollar and Kraay 2002c.
27. These include Dollar and Kraay 2002a; Kraay 2006; and Aisbett, Harrison, and Zwane 2008. The first two are the ones that consider the effect of openness on poverty directly as well as indirectly.
28. Dollar and Kraay 2002a.
29. Kraay 2006.
30. Aisbett, Harrison, and Zwane 2008.
31. Aisbett, Harrison, and Zwane 2008, 38.
32. Mitra 2016.
33. See Topalova 2007.
34. See Hasan, Mitra, and Ural 2007.
35. Hasan, Mitra and Ural 2007, 74.
36. To explain, suppose there is one exportable good and one importable good and that there are two states, A and B, within a country. The importable good is subject to a 20 percent tariff, and states A and B employ 20 and 40 percent of their workforces in the importable sector, respectively. All trade theoretic measures tell us that despite different employment patterns, the protection provided by the 20 percent tariff in the two states is identical. Yet the measure used by Topalova (2007) and by Hasan, Mitra, and Ural (2007) translates into a 4 percent tariff in state A and an 8 percent protection in state B. To make the problem further transparent, suppose the tariff rate is cut from 20 to 10 percent. From the trade theorist's perspective, this cut in the tariff rate amounts to equal liberalization for the two states. Under plausible assumptions—for example, assume the supply curve of the importable in state B is parallel to that in state A and lies horizontally twice as far from the vertical axis as the latter and that employment is proportional to the output—the tariff cut will lead to equal reduction in the output of the importable in the two states. But using the initial employment weights, the procedure employed by Topalova and by Hasan, Mitra, and Ural implies a cut of 2 percentage points in the tariff in state A and a 4 percentage point cut in state B and therefore different output reductions in the two states.

8

Trade Openness and Inequality

Beyond growth and poverty, inequality is the third battleground on which free trade critics wage their war. Therefore, if you manage to offer convincing evidence to connect trade openness to sustained rapid growth and poverty alleviation, you can be sure that critics will switch the subject to inequality. They would insist that the move to increased openness must still be resisted because it leads to increased inequality. Indeed, in the industrial countries, where the existence of high incomes has turned growth and abject poverty into less pressing issues, inequality has become the major battleground for critics of globalization. Nothing illustrates this better than the fierce debate that has raged in the United States and Europe around the treatise *Capital* by the French economist Thomas Piketty.

Though careful scholarly work to date has failed to produce compelling evidence linking openness and inequality causally, associating the two in any given situation is not especially difficult. Inequality can be measured along numerous dimensions: at the global, national, regional, or local level; in terms of distribution of income, expenditure, or wealth; in terms of human development indicators such as life expectancy, infant mortality, literacy rates, and nutrition; and across groups such as skilled versus unskilled workers, average rural versus average urban citizen, formal- versus informal-sector workers, and income or wealth of the richest relative to the poorest. It will be astonishing if evidence of openness accompanying increased inequality along one or more of these dimensions cannot be found.

The literature on inequality is vast and controversial, and it is not my intention to venture into a comprehensive discussion of it. Instead, I will introduce the commonly used measures of inequality; present some selective evidence and its connection to openness, if any; and argue that in the developing countries, wisdom lies in attacking inequality through poverty alleviation rather than by focusing directly on inequality, which comes in many forms. Excessive preoccupation with inequality risks the adoption of policies that undermine wealth creation and hence poverty alleviation.

Measures of Inequality

The commonest summary index of income distribution is the Gini coefficient. The index can be deployed to measure the distribution of income, expenditure, or wealth among the members of any given population. At one extreme, if the income (or expenditure or wealth) is perfectly equally distributed among the members of the population, the index takes the value of 0. At the other extreme, if it is perfectly unequal such that a single member of the population receives all of the income (or expenditure or wealth), the index takes the value of 1. Beginning with perfect equality, as we make income distribution more and more unequal, the value of the index rises. Some authors prefer to report the Gini coefficient in percentage terms and set its maximum value at 100. In this case, the Gini coefficient varies between 0 and 100.[1]

An important limitation of a summary measure such as the Gini coefficient is that any specific value of it is consistent with infinitely many distributions. For example, compare the distribution within two populations, A and B. Assume in each population the bottom half has one-half of the income and the top half the other half. Within population A, the distribution among the bottom half is uniform but among the top half unequal. Within population B, the distribution among the bottom half is unequal but uniform among the top half. It is then possible for the Gini coefficients associated with the two populations to have the exact same value. Overall, the two groups exhibit the same degree of inequality, but it is concentrated within different parts of the population in each of them.[2]

Given that the same value of the Gini coefficient can be associated with different income distributions, reading too much into the specific value of it can be misleading. For example, with the same value of the Gini coefficient, if inequality is the result of too little income at the bottom of the distribution, the situation is more offensive than if it is the result of too much income at the top. Increase in inequality is more tolerable when it comes with reduced poverty than when it is unaccompanied by the latter.

The Gini coefficient (or another similar index) is deployed to measure inequality across a variety of populations. The following is an illustrative list:

- *Global inequality across countries.* Measuring global inequality has occupied many analysts. One way this is done is by treating each country as the unit of observation and calculating the Gini coefficient of per capita incomes of the countries. In the hypothetical case in which all countries have the same per capita income, the Gini coefficient would be 0, and in the case in which all income is concentrated in one country, it would be 1. Perfect global equality, according to this measure, is consistent with vast inequalities within countries, since any given per capita income is consistent with an infinite number of distribution possibilities within the country.

- *Global inequality across households.* A very different measure of global inequality is obtained when we treat each household in the world as belonging to the same population and calculate the Gini coefficient for it. In this case, global inequality has a very different meaning than the previous one. Perfect equality now requires uniform income across all households, not just uniform per capita incomes across countries. Global inequality across countries as measured by the previous approach may rise even as global inequality across households declines. For instance, if the household income moderately declines in numerous sparsely populated poor countries such as those in sub-Saharan Africa, significantly rises in one or two highly populated poor countries such as India and China, and remains unchanged elsewhere, global inequality across countries would rise while that across households would decline.
- *Inequality within nations.* One way inequality is measured within a nation is by calculating the Gini coefficient across all households within a nation. Alternatively, analysts calculate the Gini coefficient for specific groups within a nation: rural population, urban population, and population within each state. In principle, it is possible for both rural and urban inequality to rise and yet national inequality to fall. This could happen, for instance, if rural incomes, which are on the average lower than urban incomes, rise faster than urban incomes and the rural population is substantially larger than the urban population. Inequality is also calculated within rural and urban populations of each state of a country.
- *Inequality across regions.* This inequality is measured by calculating the Gini coefficient across per capita incomes of various states or regions within a country and is analogous to global inequality across countries. It is possible for inequality across regions to be rising while inequality across households within the nation declines.

Many public policy debates also focus on "ratio" measures of inequality, which compare the average income of one group with that of another. An advantage of this type of measure is that it is easy to understand. But the disadvantage is that it fails to take into account the changes in income distribution relative to other units within the same population. I list here some commonly used ratio measures of inequality.

- *Urban-rural inequality.* The commonest measure of rural-urban inequality is the ratio of urban per capita income to rural per capita income. Because per capita income in urban regions typically exceeds that in the rural regions, an increase in this ratio is seen as representing increased inequality. Sometimes urban-rural inequality is also measured by the ratio of urban wages to rural wages.

- *Skilled-unskilled wage inequality.* Because skilled wages typically exceed unskilled wages, a rise in the ratio of skilled wages to unskilled wages is associated with increased wage inequality. This form of inequality has been a source of major controversies in the rich countries, where many analysts argue that increased openness is responsible for increased wage inequality there.

- *Formal-informal wage inequality.* The average wage in the formal or organized sector is typically higher than in the informal or unorganized sector. A rise in the ratio of the former to the latter is seen as representing increased wage inequality across the two sectors.

- *Rich-poor income ratio.* In the developed countries, inequality as measured by the share of the top 1 percent in income or wealth bracket has received much attention lately. Inequality in this context may be measured as the ratio of the top 1 percent to that of the rest of the population or to certain deciles at the bottom, such as the bottom 30 percent.

- *Rich-poor region inequality.* A simple measure of regional inequality that analysts sometimes deploy is the ratio of per capita income in the richest state to that in the poorest state. Faster growth in the richest state relative to that in the poorest state would produce rising regional inequality according to this measure.

In the context of the developing countries, poverty is defined in terms of the *absolute* level of income or expenditure necessary to achieve the minimum acceptable standard of living.[3] In contrast, the concepts of inequality are strictly *relative* in nature. They measure the degree of non-uniformity of distribution of a given total income or wealth among the members of the population. In view of this distinction, it is entirely possible for all members of a population to be rich according to some absolute standard and the distribution to be simultaneously highly unequal. Conversely, the distribution may be perfectly equal and yet the entire population may be poor. In an extreme situation, when the total income of a country is small, redistributing it to achieve perfect equality can make the entire population poor. This would have been the case, for example, in virtually all developing countries in existence in the 1950s. Per capita incomes in these countries at that time were below any reasonable poverty line, so an equal distribution would have raised the poverty ratio to 100 percent.

The distinction between absolute and relative levels must also be kept in mind when considering the ratio measures of inequality. With rising incomes, it is perfectly possible for per capita incomes of both rural and urban populations of a country to rise in absolute terms while urban-rural inequality rises. Likewise, rising skilled-unskilled wage inequality is consistent with rising absolute wages of both groups of workers.

Beyond Inequality Measures: The Social Context

There remains great fascination with measures of inequality among scholars and analysts on both sides of the free trade debate. Critics are particularly fond of marshaling these measures to establish that rising openness gives rise to rising inequality. Proponents of free trade, in turn, react by coming up with their own measures to counter the critics. Controversies abound not least because different indexes may exhibit different trends. A key controversy illustrating this point is the one relating to global inequality. As measured by the distribution of per capita incomes of nations, this inequality shows a rising trend in the 1990s, but as measured by the distribution of household incomes across the globe, it shows a declining trend. Free trade critics emphasize the former and proponents the latter.

But setting aside for now the issue of whether inequality has risen or fallen in recent years and what its relationship to openness is, we must ask a more fundamental question: does the measure of inequality at the center of a specific debate have a serious bearing on the welfare of the members of the population to which the measure relates? Put differently, do the members of the population over which inequality is calculated really care about where their income or wealth stands in relation to others in *that* population? For example, economists and policy analysts frequently express grave concern over even the tiniest increase in the Gini coefficient associated with a national income distribution. But in all likelihood, citizens of the country themselves are hardly exercised by what happens to their well-being relative to all other citizens of the country. Their welfare is much more likely to be impacted by changes in their position relative to others within the group with which they socially and professionally interact on a regular basis.

To put the matter dramatically, my welfare may be adversely impacted despite rising salary if simultaneously the salaries of other economists at Columbia University have gone up much more. But it makes little difference to my welfare if the gap between my income and that of billionaire Michael Bloomberg, who lives only a few miles away from my apartment, rises or drops by a factor of 100. New York City, where 17 percent of the population was dependent on food stamps in February 2009, twice voted Michael Bloomberg into the office of mayor. It mattered little that, with a net worth of $16 billion, Bloomberg was the eighth-richest American, according to the Forbes 400 list of richest Americans published in September 2008.

More than a decade ago, in January 2006, when I visited my native village in India, many in the village, recognizing that I was an economist, asked me why they had not experienced the same increase in prosperity as the people in the town next door during the preceding decade. I seriously doubt that any one of them had lost even a moment's sleep over why their incomes had fallen so dramatically relative to the residents of New Delhi, let alone billionaires Narayan Murthy of Infosys and Azim Premji of Wipro. More broadly, it is unlikely that any of them ever considered what had happened to their relative position in the national income distribution.

In India, Bihar is the poorest state and Kerala one of the richest. Going by the Gini coefficient, Bihar is among the states with the least inequality and Kerala among those with the highest inequality. If people truly cared about inequality as measured by the Gini coefficient, we should expect them to migrate from Kerala to Bihar. Of course, the reality is quite the opposite: much of the migration is from Bihar to Kerala.

This disconnect between inequality measures, something that researchers and analysts on both sides of free trade debate focus on, and the social context within which individuals evaluate their relative positions turns much more dramatic when it comes to the focus on global inequality. It is highly implausible that a farmer in Indonesia worries about what happens to his income relative to that of a U.S. farmer, let alone that of Bill Gates and Warren Buffett. It is this disconnect that has led Bhagwati to observe:

> In short, the preoccupation with inequality measures—and there are several—is somewhat ludicrous unless the economist has bothered to put them into social and political context. Cross-country comparisons, no matter what measure is deployed, are just so much irrelevant data mongering. . . .
>
> And this lunacy—how else can one describe it?—extends to what the World Bank has been doing in recent years, which is to put all the households of the world onto one chart to measure worldwide inequality of incomes. But what sense does it make to put a household in Mongolia alongside a household in Chile, one in Bangladesh, another in the United States, and still another in Congo? These households do not belong to a "society" in which they compare themselves with the others, and so a measure that includes all of them is practically a meaningless construct.[4]

It Matters How You Earn Your Billions and Spend Them

When inequality involves the accumulation of vast amounts of wealth by a few individuals, two factors, neither of which is captured by the conventional measures of inequality such as the Gini coefficient, condition public perceptions of it: how wealth is acquired and how it is disposed. If individuals acquire their wealth through wealth creation instead of rent seeking and recourse to bribery and corruption, the public is less likely to sanction them. For example, Indian billionaires Azim Premji of Wipro and Ajay Piramal of Piramal Group, who made their billions building India's information technology and pharmaceutical industries and exporting skilled services and medicines to highly competitive world markets, are revered rather than resented by their countrymen. On the other hand, Latin Americans view Mexican billionaire Carlos Slim with disapproval because his billions were partially earned via the exercise of monopoly power in the telecommunications industry.

In a similar vein, how the wealthy dispose of their wealth also influences public perception of inequality. Wealthy people who use their riches to help others within the community through philanthropy are likely to be socially more acceptable than those who indulge in conspicuous consumption. The rich among the Jains of India have had a long tradition of doing social good and have rarely been resented by the less well-off within the community. Billionaire Azim Premji, who maintains a modest living standard—driving a Toyota Corolla, flying economy class, and residing on the Wipro campus—is widely admired. As Bhagwati has written, one reason more inequality at the top may turn out to be paradoxically better than less inequality is that it may be accompanied by less conspicuous consumption.[5] As Premji once told the BBC, "At the end of the day there is only x-amount you can consume, frankly, so that itself becomes a limitation."[6]

The Evidence in Brief

The discussion in the previous section makes clear that if our concern is with inequality as it matters to people and the society, aggregate income distribution measures such as the Gini coefficient of per capita incomes, expenditure, or wealth are not likely to mean very much. Measures such as the skilled-unskilled wage ratio have had considerable salience in the developed countries largely because unskilled workers there represent the bottom deciles of the population and a decline in their relative position is seen as exacerbating poverty. This factor is sometimes reinforced by the implicit but incorrect assumption that the decline in relative wages also implies a decline in real wages. In the developing countries, the bulk of the poor are in the rural areas, but the skilled-unskilled wage ratio largely measures inequality among workers in the urban areas, so that measure does not have the same salience within the developing countries' socioeconomic context as it does in the developed countries.

For example, in the Indian parliamentary elections in 2009, virtually no political party or politician even mentioned skilled-unskilled wage inequality, which by all accounts has risen in recent years. Instead, the common theme of the ruling coalition, which won the election, was that the reforms pushed by its predecessor government had largely helped urban India and neglected the rural poor. Those commenting in the Indian press also rarely complain about the relative rise in the wages of the skilled. Instead, they reserve their concern for urban-rural and, especially, regional inequality. Even in authoritarian China, the concern is much more with these two forms of inequality than with either overall income distribution (as represented by the Gini coefficient of per capita incomes) or skilled-unskilled wage differences.

Much of the serious scholarly evidence attempting to relate inequality and trade openness relies on skilled-unskilled wage differences, however. Economists Pinelopi Goldberg and Nina Pavcnik, who provide the most comprehensive survey on the subject, base their findings largely on analyses of liberalization episodes in specific developing countries during relatively short periods. They choose not to rely on cross-country regressions to identify the effects of trade on inequality measures over longer time horizons due to data constraints. They note, "Inconsistencies in the measurement of inequality across countries, changes in the household survey response rates over time as incomes rise, and frequent changes in the design of household surveys within the same country make inference based on cross-country evidence, or comparisons of inequality measures over longer periods of time within a specific country, potentially less reliable compared to inference that relies on within-country evidence over shorter periods of time."[7]

The overall conclusion Goldberg and Pavcnik reach is that inequality as measured by the skilled-unskilled wage has risen in developing countries that liberalized trade in the 1980s and 1990s and for which data are available. The Gini coefficient of logarithm of wages also increases following trade liberalization in most of these episodes. A major exception to this latter finding is Brazil, where this measure of inequality exhibits remarkable stability during the 1980s and 1990s.

According to Goldberg and Pavcnik, while wage movements show rising inequality alongside trade liberalization, to date there is no evidence causally connecting it to the latter. There are at least three reasons for taking a skeptical view of such a connection. First, countries that liberalized trade in a major way in the 1980s and 1990s did so as part of an overall policy reform package. This fact makes it nearly impossible to isolate the effects of trade liberalization from those of other policy changes. For example, the 1991 trade liberalization in India was accompanied by a major liberalization of domestic and foreign investment regimes as well as macroeconomic stabilization that included fiscal consolidation. It was also followed in relatively quick succession by financial sector liberalization.

Second, the hypothesis of rising skilled-unskilled wage inequality in the face of liberalization in the developing countries is contrary to what is predicted by the key theory of international trade, the Heckscher-Ohlin theory. This theory predicts that trade liberalization in the developing countries, which happen to be abundant in unskilled labor relative to skilled labor when compared with their trading partners, would lower rather than raise skilled-unskilled wage inequality. This is because labor-abundant countries have a comparative advantage in goods using unskilled labor in large volumes relative to those using skilled labor in large volumes. Liberalization leads to the expansion of the former goods and contraction of the latter and thus shifts the demand away from skilled to unskilled labor and lowers skilled wages relative to unskilled wages.

Finally, a far more plausible explanation for the rising skilled-unskilled wage inequality around the world in the 1980s and 1990s is to be found in the nature of technical change during these decades. Technology has tended to become more intensive in the use of skilled labor, and technological improvement has been concentrated in sectors that use skilled labor more intensively. Both facts have led to a shift in labor demand away from unskilled toward skilled workers and hence increased wage inequality.

Two forms of inequality that can be seen to rise across the board in the fast-growing economies are urban-rural and regional inequalities. Even in South Korea during the 1960s and 1970s, which is frequently cited as a textbook example of rapid growth without increase in inequality, regional and urban-rural inequality rose.[8] More recently, rising urban-rural and regional inequalities alongside rapid growth have been widely documented in China and India.[9] The increase in these forms of inequality is not surprising, however, since rapid growth almost always accompanies the creation of agglomerations that concentrate in a small number of urban centers. This concentration almost always produces both urban-rural divide and regional disparities. In terms of causation, insofar as openness helps rapid growth and rapid growth is associated with urban-rural and regional disparities, an indirect link between trade openness and these two forms of inequality can be forged.

Finally, there is also some truth in the proposition that growth and therefore openness are accompanied by a widening gap between the wealth of those at the top and those at the bottom. Growth invariably requires wealth creation. In a fast-growing economy, if the creators of wealth keep even 5 percent of the wealth they create, with the rest spread among other citizens, incomes at the top can rise quickly. The experiences of both China and India testify to the validity of this proposition. Three decades ago, billionaires were unheard of in these countries. But rapid growth during the past three decades has already produced more than a hundred billionaires in each country. Thanks to these countries, Asia now has more billionaires than the United States.

Why Policy Action Specifically to Correct Inequality in a Poor Country Is Hazardous

The only forms of inequality that can be persuasively connected to trade openness are urban-rural and regional inequalities and inequality between those at the top and those at the bottom of the income pyramid. The variable linking trade openness and these forms of inequality is growth. If we accept the link, there are at least six reasons the case for fighting inequality except through poverty alleviation is weak.

First, it is important to verify whether the rising inequalities are the result of rich regions accelerating and poor regions decelerating or both regions accelerating but the rich region accelerating more. If it is the latter, as is often the case, attempts to arrest inequalities would also result in a slowdown in poverty alleviation. Even when in the early phase of rapid growth the poorer regions do not grow rapidly, there is a tendency for them to catch up in the later phases. This is true, for example, in China, where the interior provinces are now beginning to exhibit relatively rapid growth.

Second, even when inequality results from richer states accelerating growth and poorer states experiencing no change in their growth rates, the process will likely produce a beneficial demonstration effect. Often the examples of other countries experiencing rapid growth are not sufficient to persuade politicians to overcome inertia and change their policies. The arguments that those countries are subject to very different initial conditions, that their cultures and ethics are different, and that they have a very different political system are often invoked to justify continuation of bad policies. But when some states within the same country begin to grow rapidly, making similar arguments convincingly is far more difficult. For example, arguments such as "China is different" or "China is authoritarian" are sometimes used in India to defend bad policies. But such arguments do not have salience if Gujarat or Tamil Nadu becomes successful in achieving high growth rates and Uttar Pradesh does not. Indeed, the poorest states in India, Bihar and Orissa, have handed repeated electoral victories to state governments that have fostered pro-growth policies and successfully accelerated growth.

Third, to a large degree, urban-rural and regional inequalities provide an incentive for migration from rural to urban areas and from poorer to richer regions—an incentive that is necessary to achieve the eventual transformation from a primarily traditional rural economy to a modern urban economy. On the one hand, this migration contributes to maintaining growth momentum, and on the other, it helps reduce poverty. For example, workers from Bihar, the poorest state of India, can be found in significant numbers in the richer state of Punjab and the metropolitan cities of Delhi and Mumbai. In turn, these workers remit a part of their earnings to their families at home, thereby alleviating both urban-rural and regional inequality.

Fourth, insofar as direct action to address inequality is deemed necessary, it must be addressed through anti-poverty programs. The poor are typically concentrated in rural areas and in large states with low per capita incomes, as the experiences of both India and China demonstrate. Therefore, targeting the rural poor and the poor in the large states with low per capita incomes would often also work toward bringing down urban-rural and regional inequalities.

Fifth, insofar as inequality concerns relate to the wealthy at the top, it is important to remember the benefits of the inspiration effect. As long as wealth accumulation takes place in an open and competitive environment, the road to becoming a billionaire is open to all. Under such circumstances, the existence of a few self-made billionaires can serve to inspire others to emulate them. I often say that when Bill Gates initially visited India, the young in India were fascinated by his remarkable success but did not think any of them could accomplish the same. Less than ten years later, when they saw a large number of Indians themselves appearing on the Forbes list of billionaires, many of them changed their aspirations from wanting to become a millionaire within a few years to becoming a billionaire within a decade or two. Billionaire Azim Premji is reported to have told the BBC, "With the attention I got on my wealth, I thought I would have become a source of resentment, but it is just the other way around—it just generates that much more ambition in many people."[10]

Finally and most important, a government driven by equity (as opposed to poverty) considerations is almost sure to gravely undermine the incentives for wealth creation. It is not that policies that promote both growth and equity do not exist. Instead, the problem is that when equity becomes central to policymaking, governments are almost sure to go after policies that hit the creators of wealth hard and choke off the growth that is so essential to combat poverty. The policies introduced by Prime Minister Indira Gandhi in the late 1960s and the 1970s best illustrate this point. Gandhi adopted as a key objective combating what commonly came to be called the "concentration of wealth" in India. This led her to limit the entrepreneurial activity of the most successful firms to a handful of the most capital-intensive sectors, implement a virtual ban on foreign investment, reserve the manufacture of almost all labor-intensive products for enterprises with less than $100,000 in investment, and implement marginal income tax rates exceeding 95 percent. These policies gravely undermined incentives for wealth creation and resulted in a per capita income growth rate of approximately 1 percent. During these years, India saw little reduction in poverty.

A Cautionary Note on Redistributive Policies to Combat Poverty

Policies directly aimed at aiding the poor in improving their prospects fall into two categories: those that redistribute income and those that improve their ability to earn higher incomes. Each set of policies has its limitations, as any government deploying them must recognize. Redistribution done through indirect instruments—such as price supports on selected crops; subsidies on agricultural inputs such as fertilizer, electricity, and water; directed credit in favor of specific activities or enterprises; and public provision of health and education—may quickly turn regressive because those who are already well-to-do are better able to access them. For instance, the more land a farmer has, the larger the subsidies on fertilizer, electricity, and water she would absorb. Moreover, unless the government is highly capable, government-run programs result in vast amounts of leakages along the distribution chain, with the result that only a small part of the total expenditure reaches the intended beneficiaries. At the end of the day, the government may be better off making cash transfers to those living below the poverty line.

In the same vein, policies that help the poor profit from economic growth can also turn counterproductive. For instance, reserving the production of labor-intensive goods for small-scale enterprises in India, mentioned earlier, was aimed at assisting small entrepreneurs. But the policy stunted economic growth and therefore the creation of well-paid jobs for the poor. Likewise, the Indian constitution mandated reservation of a fixed proportion of the slots in public educational institutions and public sector jobs for the Scheduled Castes and Scheduled Tribes to correct for the past discrimination and to counter exclusionary attitudes by those in positions of power. As initially introduced, this was an eminently wise policy. Yet it has produced at best a limited payoff in terms of increased opportunity for the poor. Castes and tribes within the scheduled categories that happened to be initially better off managed to capture the lion's share of the reserved slots. For instance, in the early decades of the policy, the children of the poorest families among the Dalit had to work to help their parents earn a living. As a result, these children were unable to take advantage of reserved places in schools and, consequently, better-paid public sector jobs. Moreover, in due course, other caste groups with lesser claims to discrimination but greater political clout sought and got reservation. Arguably, this proliferation of reservation has served to undermine the spirit of competition and therefore undermined growth.

Concluding Remarks

Individuals care about equality within their immediate social context. What happens to their incomes or well-being relative to individuals outside this context has at best limited relevance to them. Indicators that measure inequality among members of much more widely defined groups that do not constitute a "society" in any meaningful way are of little relevance for evaluating the implications of inequality for the members of those groups. For instance, the measures of global inequality that have generated so much heated debate among scholars and policy analysts matters little to people themselves. A farmer in Mexico is not going to lose sleep over why his income is so much lower than that of a French farmer, let alone Bill Gates. The same also applies to aggregate national inequality measures: a farmer in Xinjiang, a poor western province of China, is likely to worry more about what happens to his income relative to that of a worker in the nearest urban center than about how his income compares to that of a top executive from Shanghai.

The available measures of inequality are not comparable across countries due to differences in sample design and other data limitations. Therefore, economists show a preference for judging the impact of openness on inequality by examining changes in the unskilled-skilled wage ratio as a result of trade liberalization within a single country. Much of the evidence based on this measure shows that inequality has risen alongside increased trade openness. This still turns out to be insufficient for identifying openness to trade as the cause of rising inequality because trade liberalization is typically part of a wider set of policy reforms, and because technology has been changing with openness as well. We cannot be sure whether the increase in inequality is to be attributed to trade openness, other policy changes, or shifting technology.

In any case, even inequality as measured by the skilled-unskilled wage ratio has had limited salience in the developing countries. The forms of inequality that attract much greater attention are urban-rural and regional inequality. These forms of inequality almost always rise with rapid growth, because rapid growth involves the creation of growth centers that are concentrated in a few agglomerations, which are usually urban. And even if the agglomerations begin in or near rural areas, they quickly turn into massive urban establishments. This concentration of growth necessarily brings with it urban-rural and regional divides. Insofar as sustained rapid growth itself requires trade openness, these indicators of inequality are indirectly related to the latter.

I have argued, however, that rising urban-rural and regional inequality does not warrant policy actions aimed at promoting equality beyond what is necessary to combat poverty. Poverty often concentrates in the rural areas and in low-per-capita-income regions. Therefore, directing anti-poverty programs to rural areas and regions with low per capita income will automatically work toward arresting the rise in urban-rural and regional inequality. An additional reason for avoiding direct action to combat inequality on top of anti-poverty programs is that undue focus on inequality is likely to result in the adoption of policies that undermine wealth creation. This was certainly the experience of India during the late 1960s and 1970s. The measures to arrest the concentration of wealth essentially stifled growth and deprived the government of fiscal resources necessary to combat poverty.

Notes

1. In effect, the Gini coefficient measures inequality as a fraction or percent of the maximum inequality possible. Therefore, by definition, the maximum inequality is 1 if measured as a fraction and 100 if measured in percent terms.
2. For the reader interested in understanding precisely what the Gini coefficient represents and how these subtle differences across distributions may exist despite the same value of the coefficient, I offer a graphical and intuitive explanation of it in Appendix 3.
3. In the context of the developed countries, poverty is defined in relative terms. For example, it may be defined as the proportion of population with income below per capita income by certain proportion. Under this definition, income level defining a person as poor rises as per capita income of the country rises.
4. Bhagwati 2004, 67.
5. To quote Bhagwati (2004, 66–67), "Indeed, the consequences of increased inequality, in any event, might be paradoxically benign, rather than malign. If a thousand people become millionaires, the inequality is less than if Bill Gates gets to make a billion all by himself. But the thousand millionaires, with only a million each, will likely buy expensive vacations, BMWs, houses in the Hamptons, and toys at FAO Schwarz. In contrast, Gates will not be able to spend his billion even if he were to buy a European castle a day, and the unconscionable wealth would likely propel him, as in fact it has, to spend the bulk of the money on social good. So extreme inequality would have turned out to be better than less acute inequality!"
6. Quoted in Schifferes 2007.
7. Goldberg and Pavcnik (2007, 40).
8. For example, Goldberg and Pavcnik (2007, 54) state, "The experience of the developing countries that globalized in the 1980s and 1990s contrasts with the experience of several Southeast Asian countries (South Korea, Taiwan and Singapore) that underwent trade reform in the 1960s and 1970s. The latter experienced a *decline* in inequality as they opened up their economies to foreign markets." Ho (1979) documents rising urban-rural and regional inequality in South Korea of the 1960s and 1970s, however.
9. For example, see Panagariya 2008 on India and Fan, Kanbur, and Zhang 2009 on China.
10. Quoted in Schifferes 2007.

PART III

MIRACLES OF YESTERYEAR

9

The Uncontroversial Cases of Hong Kong and Singapore

Hong Kong, Singapore, the Republic of Korea, and Taiwan, together known as newly industrialized economies (NIEs), were the first among developing countries to achieve double-digit or near-double-digit growth rates on a sustained basis. It was their early success in the post–Second World War era that led the vast majority of development economists to recognize that, contrary to their original view, inward-oriented, import-substitution policies were detrimental and outward-oriented policies essential to sustained rapid growth.

Economist Ian Little, who had once enthusiastically endorsed India's choice of import substitution over outward orientation, arguing that "risks of failure are much less" when entrepreneurs are guaranteed the domestic market, went on to produce the first comprehensive study challenging the efficacy of import substitution industrialization.[1] Jagdish Bhagwati, who had once expressed great disappointment at the love for foreign goods among his fellow citizens in his correspondence with the leading trade economist Harry Johnson, made a similar switch after he saw the contrast between the rising inefficiencies of the command-and-control regime in India and accelerated growth in outward-oriented NIEs.[2]

Institutions such as the World Bank, which had routinely encouraged planning and interventionist policies in the 1960s and 1970s, producing manuals on how to calculate shadow prices in the face of presumed widespread market failures, also switched their prescriptions as the 1970s came to a close. They now aggressively promoted greater openness and increased role for markets in the client developing countries. Unfortunately, however, the absence of local ownership of such liberalization programs and inadequate attention to complementary conditions such as macroeconomic stability, policy credibility, labor market flexibility, infrastructure, and political stability failed to produce any notable successes in the immediate aftermath.

This failure strengthened the hand of the revisionists who came to attribute even the successes achieved by the NIEs to calculated protection and selective promotion of infant industries rather than outward orientation. Beginning in the late 1980s, a revisionist view evolved in the influential works of political scientists Alice Amsden and Robert Wade and economist Dani Rodrik, who argued that the success of the NIEs was to be attributed not to outward orientation but to selective protection, infant industry promotion, and government coordination of private investments.[3] This view was less nuanced than the original analysis of economist Larry Westphal, who had also noted the positive role of infant industry promotion in the success of South Korea but saw outward orientation as among the most important elements in the country's development strategy.[4] Revisionists' emphasis on protection as the key element instead greatly strengthened the hand of many anti-free-trade politicians, analysts, and NGOs in the developing countries. It also renewed the debate among scholars about the role of free trade versus protectionism in development.

In this part of the book, I revisit the experiences of the NIEs during the 1960s and 1970s and discuss the key controversies surrounding them.[5] Two of the four NIEs, Hong Kong and Singapore, are more easily seen as success stories associated with outward orientation. But because they are city-states, critics often dismiss them as having at best limited relevance to other countries. Yet in my view they remain important and worthy of at least a brief look. Common sense suggests that the potential benefits of openness through specialization and exchange, access to foreign investment, and adaptation of foreign innovations are proportionately the largest for small economies. The experiences of Hong Kong and Singapore aptly illustrate this point.

The remaining two NIEs, Taiwan and the Republic of Korea, are larger and their experiences are more controversial. While there is no doubt that these countries liberalized trade prior to or just around the time they took off, they did not embrace liberal trade policies as fully as Singapore and Hong Kong, and they also intervened through domestic policy instruments more actively than the latter. This naturally makes it harder to establish a link between trade openness and sustained rapid growth, opening the door to diverse claims. Therefore, the experiences of Taiwan and Korea are discussed in Chapters 10 and 11 in substantial detail.

Hong Kong

Figure 9.1 shows the average annual growth rate of GDP in Hong Kong from 1961 to 2008 by decades. The economy grew at or near a 10 percent rate annually in the 1960s and 1970s. It then slowed down to 6.8 percent in the 1980s and approximately 4 percent subsequently. Thanks to this growth, per capita income in current U.S. dollars rose from $429.50 in 1960 to $30,863.30 in 2008. In

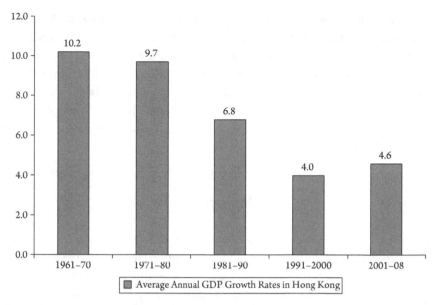

Figure 9.1 Average Annual Growth Rates by Decades in Hong Kong.
Source: World Bank WDI online (accessed May 15, 2010).

constant 2000 U.S. dollars, the change was from $3079.70 in 1960 to $34,587.10 in 2008. There is no longer any poverty in Hong Kong in the traditional sense of the term.

The rapid growth also brought rapidly declining levels of poverty. Economist Gary Fields reports that in constant 1966 prices, the proportion of the population living on less than HK$3,000 fell from 18 percent in 1966 to 7 percent in 1976. The principal source of the change was manufacturing wage increase, which amounted to 23.6 percent between 1965 and 1975. The Gini coefficient across households fell from 48.7 percent in 1966 to 43.5 percent in 1976.[6]

According to the 1994 Hong Kong Trade Policy Review by the General Agreement on Tariffs and Trade, Hong Kong has been free of all export and import duties since its British superintendent of trade adopted the policy in 1841.[7] The country is also free of all quantitative restrictions on exports and imports. While Hong Kong is perhaps among the most open developing countries in services trade as well, it does have restrictions in some services sectors. These result from non-conferral of the national treatment or bound market access in certain areas within the context of the World Trade Organization services trade negotiations.

Industrialization in Hong Kong took place under a wholly free trade regime, with trade playing a central role in it. According to economist Bela Balassa, Hong Kong offers the rare example of an economy with no history of import substitution industrialization in the post–Second World War era.[8] According to the World Bank's online World Development Indicators, trade in goods and services as a proportion of GDP between 1960 and 2008 achieved its minimum value of 141.5 percent in 1965 and its maximum value of 414.1 percent in 2008. As early as 1960, Hong Kong's exports and imports of goods and services as proportions of GDP were 83 and 92.7 percent, respectively. Therefore, the development of Hong Kong took place within an extremely open trade regime as measured by policies as well as outcomes.

Singapore

The history of Singapore in terms of trade and growth is not dramatically different from that of Hong Kong. It had a free trade regime in the 1950s but, unlike Hong Kong, it did go through a brief, mild period of import substitution in the 1960s. It also had very limited manufacturing in the 1950s relative to Hong Kong.

Figure 9.2 depicts the growth rates in Singapore by decades. Like Hong Kong, the country grew rapidly, though at rates slightly below those of the former during the 1960s and 1970s. But it outdid Hong Kong in the subsequent periods, maintaining growth rates above 7 percent during the 1980s and 1990s. The 2000s saw the growth rate fall significantly, to 4.9 percent.

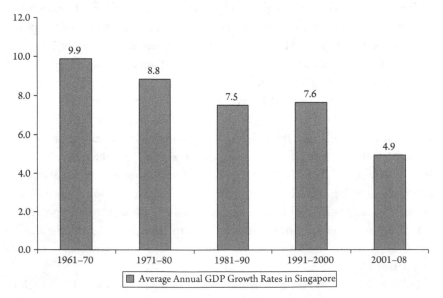

Figure 9.2 Average Annual Growth Rates by Decades in Singapore.
Source: World Bank WDI online (accessed May 15, 2010).

As in Hong Kong, declining poverty accompanied growth in Singapore. Fields estimates that in 1975 prices, the proportion of the population living on less than S$200 fell from 37 percent in 1966 to 29 percent in 1975 and 18 percent in 1980. Poverty was thus cut into half in just fourteen years. The Gini coefficient among individuals fell from 49.9 percent in 1966 to 45.5 percent in 1980. Overall, growth not only helped lower poverty but also produced greater equality of income.[9]

A Brief Political History

Singapore is located on a small island with a total land area of 720 square kilometers in 2018.[10] Other than a deep-water harbor, it has no natural resources. Sir Stamford Raffles founded the modern city of Singapore in 1819. In 1867, as part of the Straits Settlements, the city became a crown colony and remained so until 1959 except for the three years 1942–45, when Japan occupied it. As a Straits Settlement, Singapore was also a free port, which allowed entrepôt trade to flourish. The British used the port city as a base for managing and financing their investments in rubber estates, tin mines, and related activities in Malaya and Singapore. They adopted a largely non-interventionist policy, limiting their role principally to the maintenance of law and order and external defense. They even left the provision of some forms of infrastructure, such as telephone services and port management, to private companies.[11] On the one hand, this facilitated a strong tradition of reliance on the private sector, but on the other, it also deprived the country of the administrative, legal, and physical infrastructure necessary for the healthy growth of industry. Despite the near absence of agriculture, manufacturing accounted for only 13 percent of Singapore's GDP in 1960.[12] Services of various kind accounted for the bulk of GDP.

In June 1959, the People's Action Party (PAP) came to power with Lee Kuan Yew at the helm as the first prime minister. PAP, which has continued to rule till today, was keen on building up industry and saw a common market with the Federation of Malaya, which would bring duty-free access to the Malayan market, as an important means to that goal. Therefore, when Tunku Abdul Rahman, prime minister of the Malayan Federation, proposed the formation of a Federation of Malaysia that would include Singapore, Lee Kuan Yew supported it, despite opposition from some party members, and prevailed. In September 1963 Singapore became a part of the Federation of Malaysia.

The merger led to a confrontation with Indonesia, Singapore's second-largest trading partner, however. Singapore's entrepôt trade suffered as a result and the economy was set back.[13] During the period 1963–65, Singapore went through internal strife as well as confrontation with Malaysian leaders, which culminated in its separation from the federation on August 9, 1965.

Although the separation helped bring the Indonesian confrontation to an end in June 1966, Singapore now had to face Malaysian hostility. On top of that, in 1967, the British announced their intention to withdraw all military forces by March 31, 1971, which they later postponed to December 31, 1971. At US$550 million, the British military expenditure in Singapore was 12.7 percent of the country's GDP in 1967.[14] The prospect of withdrawal of this spending was sure to affect growth adversely.

These events had a profound impact on the making of economic policy in Singapore. Specifically, the failure to gain duty-free access to the Malayan market played an important role in nudging the country toward export-oriented development. The decision by the British to withdraw their military reinforced this decision.

Trade Policy and Trade Outcomes

Under the British, Singapore's economy was largely dependent on import and reexport trade. It imported primary products and raw materials from neighboring Southeast Asian countries and reexported them to the United States and Europe after processing and repackaging. Likewise, it imported finished products from the United States and Europe and reexported them to its Southeast Asian neighbors.

By 1959, when Singapore became independent, this entrepôt trade was in decline because its Southeast Asian neighbors were beginning to trade directly with their Western counterparts while also using raw materials domestically as they industrialized.[15] Therefore, in its election manifesto, PAP gave high priority to industrialization. After coming to power in 1961, it established the Economic Development Board (EDB), which provided investors with factory sites, finance in the form of long-term loans and equity, and technical assistance through feasibility studies, industrial research, and managerial training. Provision of these services did not target any specific sectors. This supportive role was necessary to stimulate and sustain growth. It fundamentally differed from the British-era regime of governmental indifference, which had resulted in the absence of any policies aimed at serving Singaporean interests.

Until 1960, Singapore had no protective tariffs or quantitative restrictions. The only customs tariff, applying to liquor, tobacco, and petroleum, was for revenue purposes. An equivalent excise duty was levied on domestic production of the same commodities.[16] Protective duties to promote industrialization were inaugurated, however, with tariffs on hard soap and detergents in 1960 and paints in 1962. In 1963, quantitative restrictions were also inaugurated, with import quotas imposed on flashlights, radio batteries, monosodium glutamate, and wheat flour. After merger with the Federation of Malaya, additional quotas were introduced. By May 1965, the number of commodities subject to import licensing had risen from their pre-Malaysian (i.e., September 1963) level of 8 to 230, with commodities defined relatively narrowly in terms of the six-digit Singapore Trade Classification.

Upon breaking away from the Malaysian Federation on August 9, 1965, Singapore abolished all but 88 import quotas. But it went on to replace quotas with tariffs on 68 out of the remaining 142 items. It also introduced protective tariffs on several previously unprotected items, with the result that the total number of dutiable items increased to 199 in 1966. This number kept climbing steadily in the subsequent years, reaching 229 in 1967, 295 in 1968, and 398 in 1969.

There is general agreement among economists with intimate knowledge of the Singapore economy that the level of protection in the 1965–69 period was extremely low.[17] At its peak, the average nominal protection rate was approximately 4 percent.[18] Tan and Ow carry out detailed calculations of nominal and effective protection for the year 1967. This exercise requires them to draw a correspondence between the Singapore Trade Classification and the Singapore Industrial Classification. As a result, they aggregate protected commodities into 104 products. Of these, 59 turn out to be subject to tariffs only, 25 to tariffs and quotas, and 20 to quotas only. Together, these products account for 21.6 percent of the total manufacturing output measured at world prices in 1967. The share of manufacturing in GDP was 16 percent in the same year.[19]

While this period is identified with import substitution, it is important to note that Singapore's government never lost sight of the basic rule for the success of such a policy: protection must be low and temporary, and within a reasonable time the industry should either be able to compete without protection or be allowed to liquidate. The annual report by the Singapore Department of Trade, quoted in Tan and Ow, describes the policy toward import quotas as follows:

> The need for this control on the import of each commodity was reviewed once in every six months from the date it was first enforced and decisions made in such reviews were announced quarterly. Where the particular industry had fairly found its feet but still needed some protection, the form of protection was modified by either changing the quota or replacing it by tariffs. In other cases, where the particular industry was found not making any serious effort to succeed in its ventures, import quota protection was withdrawn. Quotas were also

removed when industries were able to function without further protection from Government.[20]

Drawing on the same report, Balassa notes that tariffs too were gradually lowered and eventually eliminated.[21] This was truly an unusual experiment in import substitution. Protection was selective, relatively low, and eliminated according to a pre-announced schedule. In many other countries, especially in South Asia and Africa, protection was high and long-lasting.

Britain's 1967 announcement that it planned to withdraw its forces from Singapore in 1971 speeded up the switch to proactive, outward-oriented policies. The government expected the withdrawal to substantially cut local demand and therefore felt the urgency to look for external markets for Singaporean products. The government announced several incentives for exporters in 1967, partially offsetting the effect of import restrictions. The announcement also speeded up the removal of trade barriers.

Once the decision was made to reorient the economy toward exports, protection was reduced and eventually nearly eliminated. By 1974, Singapore had eliminated all import quotas and removed or lowered duties on a large number of products. For quite some time now, Singapore has had no duties in excess of 5 percent, and 90 percent of the tariff lines have been entirely free of duty.

A distinguishing feature of the transformation of Singapore has been the major role foreign firms have played in it. Oil refining, an important activity for the country, was based entirely on foreign capital. Hong Kong entrepreneurs established and developed the country's clothing and furniture industries, while American, Japanese, and European firms took the lead in the electronics industry. Wholly owned foreign firms were responsible for 65 percent of exports in 1972 and joint ventures for another 22 percent the same year.[22]

The output and exports of manufactures grew at impressive rates of 26 and 33 percent per annum, respectively, between 1965 and 1972.[23] More detailed trade data for Singapore for the early years are not readily available. The online WDI provides these data beginning in only 2001. The official statistics website of the Singaporean government also begins listing these data beginning in 1987. It is possible, however, to obtain some data beginning in 1976 from the World Development Reports of the World Bank, which began publication in 1978.

According to these reports, in 1976, merchandise exports and imports in Singapore stood at 106 and 146 percent of GDP, respectively. These ratios clearly show a highly open economy in terms of trade outcomes. For more recent years, the ratios are much higher. For example, the WDI reports goods and services exports and imports as a proportion of GDP to be 191.4 and 176.4 percent, respectively, in 2001. For 2008, these indicators stood at 234.3 and 215.3 percent, respectively.

The share of manufacturing also rose during the 1960s and 1970s. Tan and Ow report that manufacturing as a proportion of GDP rose from 13 percent in 1960 to 16 percent in 1967, 19.3 percent in 1970, and 21.9 percent in 1973. The share of agriculture was low at 4.1 percent in 1960 and fell further to just 1.9 percent in 1973. Entrepôt trade was the other major sector that lost share: it fell from 18 percent of GDP in 1960 to 11.6 percent in 1967 and 9.6 percent in 1973.

No Miracle?

Few development economists question the importance of trade to the success of Singapore. Even skeptics go only so far as to argue that import substitution played a role in the early years in the making of the miracle. Given its short phase, narrow coverage across products, and low level of protection, the importance of import substitution is debatable. The only other literature that questions the role of openness (and any other policies) in generating the high growth rates in Singapore and other NIEs is that on productivity. This literature contends that the entirety of Singapore's growth can be explained by the accumulation of physical and human capital and growth in labor, and none by productivity growth that is supposed to be helped by outward-oriented or other policies.[24] This literature gives no credit to policies at all, whether outward or inward oriented.

At the outset, one can question the entire approach underlying productivity analysis, which assumes a single, aggregate Cobb-Douglas production function with no scope for shifts in factor shares over a long period of time. Any effects resulting from the innovation of new processes and products are packed into a single exogenous parameter. With new products and production processes constantly replacing the old ones, these are rather heroic assumptions and must result in large measurement errors. At the most elementary level, with the composition of output shifting first in favor of unskilled-labor-intensive manufactures and then capital-intensive manufactures and skilled-labor-intensive services, the assumption of an unchanging technology (except for an exogenous productivity shift) simply cannot be true.

But even if we ignore this fundamental deficiency in the studies, Bhagwati points out other problems with the argument. He reminds that even if one accepts that all growth must be attributed to input growth and none to productivity, one must explain what led to the rapid accumulation of capital in the first place. Seen this way, "the East Asian miracle, in the sense of 'exceptionalism of outcomes' simply gets to be the miracle of East Asia's phenomenal increase in investment rates, i.e. it becomes an 'exceptionalism of the fundamentals of investment.'"[25] Bhagwati correctly points out that the sustained rise in investment rate in the NIEs took place in the private sector and was accompanied by sustained rapid growth. In contrast, a similar increase in the investment rate took place in the public sector in the former socialist economies in the postwar period, leading to blood, sweat, and tears but not growth.

Policies also matter for the very-long-run sustainability of growth. By boosting the savings and investment rates, the Soviet Union did manage to achieve sustained rapid growth for some years. But in the face of its inward-looking and command-and-control policies, its economy eventually collapsed. In contrast, East Asian economies rapidly recovered from the financial crisis that hit them in the late 1990s and returned to healthy growth.

Conclusion

Hong Kong and Singapore are both city-states with a long record of free trade. While Hong Kong remained a free trade country throughout the period of our analysis, Singapore briefly experimented with import substitution in the 1960s. The import substitution phase of Singapore was characterized by relatively low protection and a clear time-bound signal to firms that protection would be withdrawn if they did not show progress in adjustment. To be sure, the government was not a passive player in either case, though the degree of activism was far less pronounced in Hong Kong than in Singapore. Free trade had existed in both countries in the 1950s and before as well. But during those earlier years, government policies aimed at serving the national interest had been lacking. Instead, the policy was designed to serve the interests of the colonial power. In this sense, in the general spirit of this volume, the experiences of these countries illustrate the necessity, not the sufficiency, of pro-free-trade policies for sustained rapid growth even in small developing countries.

There is a view in the literature, emphatically advocated by Krugman, that the rapid growth in the Far Eastern economies was purely the result of rapid accumulation of capital and was no miracle at all. This view emanates from productivity calculations that show that virtually all growth can be explained by increased employment of the factors of production, with none left to be explained by policy-driven productivity growth. If we accept this view literally, no role for any kind of policy, whether outward oriented or protectionist, will be left.

Deeper analysis leads us to reject this view. For one thing, productivity analysis, which relies on an unchanging Cobb-Douglas technology except for an exogenous shift in productivity, is itself likely to be subject to large errors. More important, even if we accept the conclusion that no perceptible productivity increase took place during the miracle years, we must still explain the rapid capital accumulation itself, especially since it took place in the private sector and did lead to sustained rapid growth. This was in contrast to the experience in the former socialist countries, which successfully raised the investment rate in the public sector without a parallel increase in the growth rate.

Notes

1. Little, Scitovsky, and Scott 1970.
2. Bhagwati and Desai 1970; Bhagwati 1978; and Krueger 1978.
3. Amsden 1989; Wade 1990, 2004; Rodrik 1995.
4. Westphal (1990) provides the references to a number of his key contributions. It also summarizes his view on the Korean miracle and what other developing countries can learn from it.
5. I draw on Panagariya (2002b) in the second and third sections of this chapter and on Panagariya (2008, ch. 7) in the fourth section of this chapter.
6. Fields 1984, table 3.
7. General Agreement on Tariffs and Trade 1994.
8. Balassa 1982, 39.
9. Fields 1984, table 3.
10. In the 1960s, Singapore had a land area of 580 square kilometers. Over the years, the area has been increased through land reclamation.
11. Ow 1986, 228.
12. Tan and Ow 1982, table 9.7.
13. Ow 1986.
14. Ow 1986, 229.
15. Tan and Ow 1982, 280.
16. Lloyd and Sandilands 1986, 185.
17. Lloyd and Sandilands 1986, 185–86; Aw 1991, table 3.1.
18. Aw 1991.
19. Tan and Ow 1982, table 9.7.
20. Singapore Department of Trade 1968; Tan and Ow 1982, 281–82.
21. Balassa 1982.
22. Little 1979, 489.
23. Little 1979, 483.
24. Drawing on a number of studies on productivity growth, Krugman (1994b) makes this argument most emphatically.
25. Bhagwati 1999, 23.

10

Taiwan

An Early Triumph of Outward Orientation

Taiwan is one of the two countries—the Republic of Korea being the other—whose phenomenal growth in the 1960s and early 1970s led many development economists to embrace outward orientation over import substitution as the preferred trade policy for faster growth. During the 1950s, Taiwan had experienced rapid growth under import substitution. But as early as the mid-1950s, some influential policy analysts within the country began to notice that the policy was losing steam, and so they made a push for change in favor of export-oriented policies.[1] Some changes favoring exports were introduced in 1955, but they proved insufficient, and Taiwan saw growth rates decline in the second half of the 1950s. A second round of more substantial reforms during 1958–60 produced a more favorable outcome, reversing the slide in the growth rates. The policy change eventually led to a major transformation of the economy.

Leading scholars of development economics of the time have thoroughly analyzed the growth and structural shifts in agriculture, industry, foreign trade, and the labor market in Taiwan from the early 1950s to the early 1970s. Economist Walter Galenson brought together the contributions of these scholars in the important 1979 volume *Economic Growth and Structural Change in Taiwan*. My discussion below heavily draws on this rich volume.[2] With Ian Little synthesizing the policies responsible for the miracles in the NIEs and Japan, the volume broadly represents what is now considered the conventional wisdom on economic development. It places outward-oriented policies at the center of explanation of economic miracles. The contrary, revisionist view finds expression in the writings of Robert Wade and Dani Rodrik.

Although my discussion below begins with some historical background, it principally focuses on the approximately fifteen-year period from the late 1950s to the early 1970s. This is the key period during which the Taiwanese economy took off and grew on a sustained basis at near-double-digit rates and was transformed into an industrial powerhouse. I will argue that a switch to outward-oriented policies was the key to both catalyzing and sustaining the rapid growth that Taiwan achieved during this period. I will also discuss in detail why the contrary view, which gives credit for Taiwan's success to government interventions, lacks validity.[3]

The first section offers historical background and covers the period of the Japanese occupation. In the second section, I describe the transformation that took place in Taiwan between the late 1950s and early 1970s using data and charts. In the third section, I describe the trade and industrial policies Taiwan followed. In the fourth section, I connect these policies to the outcome. Here I also point out the important role of complementary domestic policies that helped outward-oriented policies turn from necessary to sufficient for rapid growth. In the fifth section, I offer a critique of the leading revisionist authors, Robert Wade and Dani Rodrik. The sixth and final section offers concluding thoughts.

From the Japanese Occupation to an Independent Taiwan

Taiwan was Japan's first overseas colony and was occupied by it from 1895 to 1945. During these years, Japan made a special effort to develop agriculture and build railways, ports, and power plants. By the late 1930s, Taiwan was far ahead of mainland China and most of the rest of Asia in agricultural techniques.[4] In the area of education, the Japanese concentrated nearly exclusively on primary education, offering the Taiwanese extremely limited opportunity to access secondary and college education. At the end of the Japanese occupation, three-fourths of the relevant age groups were enrolled in primary schools. But the enrollments in secondary schools and college were a measly 65,000 and 2,000, respectively.

The Japanese also denied Taiwanese any senior government or management positions. Therefore, a vacuum in administration was created when they left the country in 1945. This allowed mainlanders who moved to Taiwan during 1947–49 to fill the gap. The arrival of 1.5 million mainlanders, including 600,000 or more military personnel, increased the population of Taiwan by 25 percent over its 1945 level. In 1949, Taiwan's population stood at 7.4 million.[5]

Economically, Taiwan suffered major losses and decline in its income as a result of the Second World War. Its GDP did not recover to the level achieved in 1937 till 1950. Even so, per capita income remained below its 1937 level due to the increase in population following the arrivals from the mainland. It was only in 1953 that per capita income returned to its 1937 level.[6]

During the Japanese occupation, Taiwan had already emerged as a highly open economy. In the 1930s, merchandise exports as a proportion of the net national product amounted to 50 percent and merchandise imports 40 percent. Japan was the major trading partner, receiving 90 percent of Taiwan's exports and supplying an equal proportion of its imports. Much of the rest of the trade was with mainland China.

The Second World War resulted in a dramatic decline in trade. After the war ended and Taiwan was returned to China, an edict of the U.S. military government in Japan cut off all of Taiwan's trade with that country. During 1946–48, Taiwan reoriented its trade toward China, but by 1948 trade volume had reached only a quarter of its level in the 1930s. Moreover, hyperinflation accompanying the civil war in China spread to Taiwan.[7] During 1946–49, Taiwan suffered inflation rates of approximately 1,000 percent per year. The new Taiwanese dollar (NT$) was introduced in June 1949 backed by 100 percent reserves in gold, silver, foreign exchange, and export commodities. This helped bring down inflation, but the absolute rate still remained high. It fell to 500 percent in 1949–50, 80 to 100 percent in 1950–51, and 7 to 8 percent during 1952–60.[8]

During 1949–53, Taiwan also introduced land reform, which helped raise agricultural productivity. This involved redistribution of land taken from large farmers to landless or small farmers. Many of the large farmers in Taiwan had been Japanese who fled the country soon after the Second World War. The government was also able to use the Japanese commercial and industrial properties it seized after independence to compensate large Taiwanese farmers from whom land was taken for redistribution. Improved incentives following the land reform led to increased agricultural productivity via the adoption of multiple cropping, diversified farming, and use of new inputs.

The Economic Transformation

Taiwan's economic transformation involved accelerated growth and dramatic change in the structure of trade, output, and employment. Industrial products replaced the dominance of agricultural products in both output and trade. Industry also came to account for a larger and larger share of the workforce.

Growth

Figure 10.1 shows annual GDP growth rates in Taiwan from 1952 to 1980. Three main points may be noted. First, while the growth rates in the early 1950s were high, they exhibited a sharply declining trend in the second half of the decade.

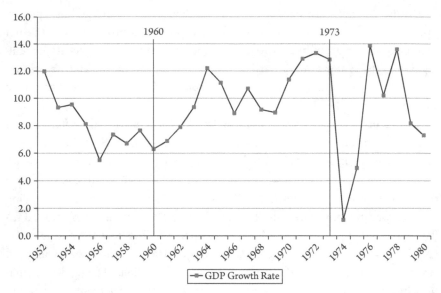

Figure 10.1 Annual GDP Growth Rates in Taiwan, 1953–80.
Source: Author's drawing based on data in Yu 1999, table 6-2.

The average growth rate during 1952–55 was 9.7 percent but fell by three percentage points to 6.7 percent during 1956–60. Second, beginning in the early
1960s, growth accelerated, peaking at the impressive figure of 13.2 percent in
1972. The turnaround began in 1961, with the growth rate rising to 6.9 percent
that year from the trough of 6.3 percent in 1960. But the growth rate did not
return to the average of 1952–55 until 1963. Finally, the oil price shock of 1973
hit Taiwan hard, with the growth rate dipping to 1.2 and 4.9 percent in 1974 and
1975, respectively. But Taiwan recovered astonishingly fast, achieving growth
rates between 10 and 14 percent in the subsequent three years.

Estimates strongly point to a break in the growth rate sometime in the early
1960s. For purposes of our discussion, I will choose this break point at the
border between 1962 and 1963, since this is when the high-growth path appears
firmly established. Taking the last year prior to the oil crisis, 1973, as the terminal
year of our analysis, the years 1952–73 can be divided into two halves, spanning
1952–62 and 1963–73, with growth rates of 7.9 and 11 percent, respectively.
There was, thus, a shift of 3 percentage points in the growth rate between the first
and second periods. Looked at slightly differently, the shift was much greater.
The trough at 6.3 percent in 1960 was almost 5 percentage points below the average of 1963–73 and a full 7 percent below the peak reached in 1972.

The higher growth rates during the second period were accompanied by a
rapid transformation of the economy. Trade became progressively more important, exports reoriented from agriculture to manufactures, the share of industry

in GDP rose rapidly, and the workforce substantially shifted out of agriculture into industry.

Rising Importance of Trade

Figure 10.2 depicts merchandise exports and total merchandise trade as proportions of GDP for each year from 1951 to 1976. From nearly 9 percent in the early 1950s, the exports-to-GDP ratio fell during 1954 and 1955 but recovered to the prior level during 1956–58. After 1958, the ratio began climbing and increased every single year until 1973 except 1960 and 1965. The decline in 1960 resulted from a sharp drop in agricultural exports. Non-agricultural exports consisting of mainly labor-intensive manufactures, which had taken off in 1959, experienced a sharp rise in 1960 as well. In view of the fact that Taiwan switched to outward-oriented policies during 1958–60, the export expansion beginning in 1959 is highly significant. Total exports as a proportion of GDP crossed the double-digit mark for the first time in 1959, rising to 15.1 percent in 1963, 26.1 percent in 1970, and 43.9 percent in 1973. The rise was especially rapid after 1967.

As a proportion of GDP, imports remained relatively stable around 12 percent until 1958 before jumping to 16.2 percent in 1959. Imports could exceed exports as a proportion of GDP by approximately 4 to 7 percentage points during this period principally because a large volume of aid from the United States was available

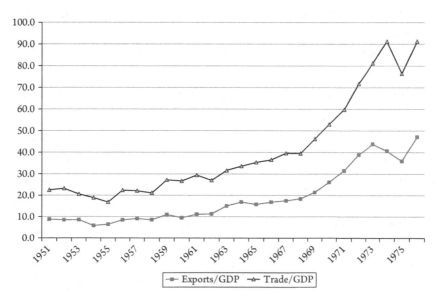

Figure 10.2 Merchandise Exports and Trade as Proportions of GDP, 1951–76.
Source: Author's construction based on Scott 1979, table 5.12.

to bridge the gap. Though aid had dramatically declined by 1963, imports could maintain their level and grow due to the pickup in exports. The end result was that the trade-to-GDP ratio rose from 20 percent in the early 1950s to 29.4 percent in 1961, 39.6 percent in 1967, 53 percent in 1970, and 91.3 percent in 1974.

A Sharp Rise in Labor-Intensive Exports

The expansion of exports in the 1960s and beyond was largely driven by a dramatic shift in the composition of exports toward labor-intensive products, as shown by Table 10.1. In 1952, food, beverage, and tobacco preparations accounted for 83.6 percent of Taiwan's total exports. Sugar alone accounted for 58.3 percent of exports, while rice accounted for another 19.5 percent.[9] Textiles, leather, wood, paper, and related products accounted for just 0.9 percent of the total exports. This structure remained unchanged in 1955. But by 1960, manufactures had emerged as a major item, with textiles, leather, wood, paper, and related products rising to 17.1 percent of the total exports and food, beverage, and tobacco preparations declining to 58.5 percent. This movement away

Table 10.1 **Composition of Taiwan's exports (percentage of total exports, in $ million)**

Item	1952	1955	1960	1965	1970	1975
Food, beverages, and tobacco preparations	83.6	84.6	58.5	39.1	9.4	7.3
Textiles, leather, wood, paper, and related products	0.9	2.4	17.1	26.2	30.3	24.4
Non-metallic mineral products	0.0	0.0	1.8	3.1	2.5	0.6
Chemical and pharmaceutical products	3.5	3.3	4.9	4.4	1.8	2.0
Basic metals	0.9	1.6	3.7	3.6	3.2	1.5
Metal products	0.0	0.0	0.6	1.1	1.4	1.6
Machinery	0.0	0.0	0.0	1.3	2.3	2.4
Electrical machinery and apparatus	0.0	0.0	0.6	2.7	8.8	9.6
Transportation equipment	0.0	0.0	0.0	0.4	0.6	1.4
Others	11.2	8.1	12.8	18.0	39.8	49.2
Total	100.0	100.0	100.0	100.0	100.0	100.0

Source: Excerpted from Ranis 1999, table 5.5, p. 122.

from primary products and into manufactures continued throughout the 1960s and 1970s. By 1970, food, beverage, and tobacco preparations had dropped to just 9.4 percent and sugar and rice to 3.2 percent of the total exports.[10] By 1970, clothing and footwear (included in the "others" category in Table 10.1) had emerged as major exports. Within twelve years, Taiwan had transformed itself from a largely primary product exporter to an exporter of labor-intensive manufactures.

The key reforms toward outward orientation took place during 1958–60. Against this backdrop, Table 10.2 reports the shares of agricultural and

Table 10.2 **Taiwan's agricultural and non-agricultural exports, 1952–71**

Year	Total ($ million)	Agricultural ($ million)	Non-agricultural ($ million)	Agricultural (as % of total)	Non-agricultural (as % of total)
1952	119.5	114.2	5.3	95.6	4.4
1953	129.8	121.2	8.6	93.4	6.6
1954	97.8	90.8	7.0	92.8	7.2
1955	133.4	124.4	9.0	93.3	6.7
1956	130.1	114.9	15.2	88.3	11.7
1957	168.5	155.4	13.1	92.2	7.8
1958	164.4	145.6	18.8	88.6	11.4
1959	160.5	128.4	32.1	80.0	20.0
1960	169.9	121.0	48.9	71.2	28.8
1961	214	131.9	82.1	61.6	38.4
1962	238.6	129.4	109.2	54.2	45.8
1963	357.5	218.2	139.3	61.0	39.0
1964	463.1	277.6	185.5	59.9	40.1
1965	487.9	286	201.9	58.6	41.4
1966	569.4	289	280.4	50.8	49.2
1967	649.9	296.9	353	45.7	54.3
1968	841.8	315.6	526.2	37.5	62.5
1969	1110.6	342.2	768.4	30.8	69.2
1970	1561.7	392.2	1169.5	25.1	74.9
1971	2135.5	480.1	1655.4	22.5	77.5

Source: Excerpted from Ranis 1999, table 5.2, p. 117.

non-agricultural exports along with the total value of exports on a continuous basis from 1952 to 1971. It can be seen that non-agricultural exports increased continuously, in both absolute and proportional terms. In 1959, total exports fell due to a sharp decline in agricultural exports, but non-agricultural exports, principal beneficiaries of the 1958–60 reform, showed a healthy growth. In dollar terms, they rose from $18.8 million in 1958 to $32.1 million in 1959.[11] The following year, agricultural exports fell again but the increase in non-agricultural exports more than made up for it. During 1959–63, non-agricultural exports grew at an average annual rate of 50.3 percent. In the process, the share of non-agricultural exports in total exports rose from 11.4 percent in 1958 to 39 percent in 1963. The process of structural transformation of trade continued in subsequent years, with this proportion rising to 77.5 percent in 1971.

Shift of Output and Employment into Industry

The structural transformation in exports was naturally accompanied by a transformation of the composition of output and employment across sectors. Table 10.3 reports the growth rates in agriculture, industry, and services. After declining during 1958–60, the average annual growth rate in industry began to accelerate. It rose from 8.9 percent during 1958–60 to 10.7 percent in 1961–63 and 14.6 percent during 1964–67. Taking the entire second period, 1961–63 to 1971–73, industry grew at the hefty annual rate of 15.26 percent.

With industry growing faster than either agriculture or services, the composition of output shifted in its favor. Between 1951–53 and 1958–60, the period

Table 10.3 **Growth rates (%) by major sectors in Taiwan**

Period	Agriculture	Industry	Services
1954–57	3.4	15.0	8.6
1958–60	6.3	8.9	5.9
1961–63	5.1	10.7	8.3
1964–67	8.0	14.6	10.3
1968–70	1.3	15.1	10.3
1971–73	3.8	16.3	10.2
1951–53 to 1961–63	4.93	11.52	7.56
1961–63 to 1971–73	4.37	15.26	10.28
1951–53 to 1971–73	4.66	13.38	8.91

Source: Excerpted from Kuznets 1979, table 1.11.

Table 10.4 **Composition of GDP in Taiwan**

Period	Agriculture	Industry	Manufacturing	Services
1951–53	33.2	26.2	15.5	40.6
1954–57	27.8	31.8	19.6	40.4
1958–60	27.2	33.8	21.4	39.0
1961–63	24.9	36.1	23.0	39.0
1964–67	22.4	39.9	26.7	37.7
1968–70	16.5	46.0	32.3	37.5
1971–73	13.1	51.3	37.9	35.6

Source: Excerpted from Kuznets 1979, Table 1.10.

frequently associated with import substitution, the share of industry in GDP rose from 26.2 to 33.8 percent (see Table 10.4). This shift accelerated during the outward-orientation phase, with industry claiming 51 percent of GDP by 1971–73. Within industry, the share of manufactures in GDP rose even more sharply, increasing to 37.9 percent in 1971–73 from just 15.5 percent in 1951–53. In parallel, the share of agriculture declined from 33.2 percent in 1951–53 to 13.1 percent in 1971–73.

The employment shares of various sectors shifted in parallel to output shares, though less rapidly. Figure 10.3 depicts the evolution of these shares.[12] In 1952, 60.5 percent of the labor force was employed in agriculture. This proportion fell to 52.7 percent in 1960, 36.8 percent in 1970, and 29.9 percent in 1975. Correspondingly, industry's share of employment rose from 18.4 percent in 1952 to 25.2 percent in 1960, 33.7 percent in 1970, and 41.2 percent in 1975. Services also saw their share in employment rise, though moderately and only until 1968.

Poverty and Inequality

There is unequivocal evidence that high growth in Taiwan was also accompanied by a sharp reduction in poverty. Economist Gary Fields reports the poverty rates for Taiwan in 1964 and 1972 at two different poverty lines.[13] In constant 1972 prices, the proportion of those having income below NT$20,000 was 35 percent in 1964 and 10 percent in 1972. At the higher poverty line of NT$40,000 in constant 1972 prices, poverty rates were 80 percent in 1964 and 35 percent in 1972. Alternatively, these improvements may be seen in terms of rising incomes of the bottom deciles. For example, in 1972 prices, per capita incomes between 1964

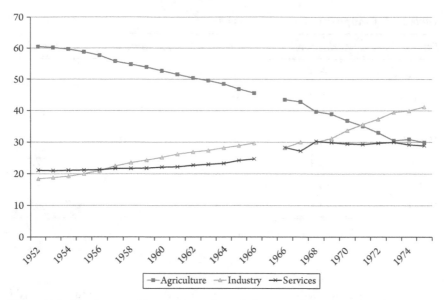

Figure 10.3 Employment Share of Agriculture, Industry, and Services, 1952–75.
Source: Author's construction based on Galenson 1979, table 6.2 for 1952–66 and table 6.3 for 1966–75.

and 1972 rose 109 percent, 98 percent, and 91 percent for the bottom, second, and third deciles, respectively. These increases compared with a 53 percent increase for the top decile of the population.

Growth in Taiwan between 1964 and 1972 thus produced larger gains at the bottom of the income distributions than at the top. This fact is reflected in a decline in the Gini coefficient from 32.8 percent in 1964 to 30.1 percent in 1972. Given that no major redistribution programs had existed during this period, this improvement in income distribution was largely the result of the pattern of specialization that accompanied growth. The expansion of labor-intensive sectors, which pulled many out of agriculture into gainful employment in industry and services, resulted in rapidly rising wages for the workers at the bottom of the income distribution ladder. This process was reinforced by rising productivity enforced by competition in world markets.

Trade and Industrial Policies

Japan returned Taiwan to China in October 1945. Around the same time, an edict of the U.S. military government in Japan cut off all of Taiwan's trade with Japan. This led to a reorientation of Taiwanese trade toward mainland China, but this too was short-lived. The fall of Shanghai in May 1949 handed the Chinese

Communist Party the final victory over the Nationalists, who fled to Taiwan. This event ended all economic ties between mainland China and Taiwan and, for the first time in its history, the latter was left entirely on its own. Two of Taiwan's immediate tasks were currency reform, to bring raging hyperinflation under control, and land reform, to effect greater equity in land ownership. Both these tasks were accomplished by 1952.

The Import Substitution Phase: 1951–60

Given that agriculture was already well advanced and land reform was the last important policy initiative to be taken in this area, the main task before the government was to set the country on the road to industrialization. Like other countries at the time, Taiwan chose the import substitution route to pursue this objective. Trade protection was the natural first step in this strategy. Accordingly, strict import controls were introduced in April 1951.[14] These controls came on the heels of a devaluation of the new Taiwanese dollar. At the time of its introduction in June 1949, the new Taiwanese dollar had been fixed at NT$5 per U.S. dollar. By 1953, it fell in value to NT$15.55 per U.S. dollar for most of the import and export transactions undertaken by private enterprises. Further devaluation took place in 1956, with the rate applicable to most transactions by private enterprises reaching approximately NT$25 per U.S. dollar.[15]

Analysts on both sides of the debate agree that the period 1951–57 was dominated by policies commonly associated with import substitution. Tariffs were high, strict import licensing was applied, and, despite several devaluations, the domestic currency remained overvalued throughout the period. Strict quantitative restrictions implemented through licensing generated large quota rents even after netting out the high tariffs. In 1953, quota premiums over landed import price plus custom duties equaled 48 percent on wheat flour, 33 percent on cotton yarn, 150 percent on cotton piece goods, 350 percent on soda ash, and 100 percent on ammonium sulfate.[16]

The ultra-high premiums made the production of these goods at home highly profitable. Scott, who otherwise attributes Taiwan's success to its subsequent turn to outward orientation, acknowledges that the increase in the profitability of import substitutes "must have been partly responsible for the doubling of manufacturing production between 1952 and 1958."[17] He further refers to the important role that K. Y. Yin, the vice chairman of the Taiwan Production Board from 1951 to 1954, played in promoting such industries as plastics, artificial fiber, glass, cement, fertilizer, plywood, and textiles through domestic policy measures over and above trade protection. The measures included loans on favorable terms, allocation of imported materials directly to manufacturers, and penalties on producers of poor-quality products.

An important feature of Taiwan's import substitution policy, missing from countries such as India and China during their phases of inward-looking policies, was the emphasis on quality. Scott mentions an interesting episode testifying to Yin's commitment to achieving high quality.[18] Dissatisfied by the low quality of Taiwanese-produced lightbulbs, in 1954 Yin ordered 20,000 bulbs destroyed in Taipei New Park and threatened to liberalize imports if the quality did not improve in three months. The threat worked, with quality improving within the stipulated time frame. This emphasis on quality was perhaps instrumental in generating quick export response once incentives shifted in that direction.

Apart from the usual efficiency costs that arise from vast differences in domestic costs of highly protected items and their import prices and from insulating domestic producers from the world's most competitive entrepreneurs, the scope for import substitution in any single item in a small economy is limited and can quickly be exhausted by domestic producers. Therefore, continued reliance on import substitution requires a progressive movement into newer items that are farther and farther away from the country's margin of comparative advantage. This limitation of import substitution in Taiwan's case interacted in an important way with foreign aid and trade balance.

From 1951 onward, exports of goods and services had financed no more than 65 percent of Taiwan's imports. The bulk of the remaining imports had been financed by aid from the United States. The government recognized, however, that it would not be able to count on U.S. aid indefinitely. This meant that Taiwan needed to either reduce its dependence on imports or increase its volume of exports. With respect to the former, import substitution into labor-intensive products and products of limited technological complexity such as textiles and clothing, footwear, plastics, paper, beverages, tobacco, and cement had been virtually completed by 1957. As for export expansion, exports of primary products offered little hope in view of rising population, limited land, peaking of productivity in agriculture, and the country's generally poor resource base. Therefore, the option was either to push import substitution into capital-intensive items such as chemicals, heavy industry, and machinery or to seek export markets for labor-intensive products.

Switching to Outward Orientation: Key Reforms of 1955 and 1958–60

Risks of progressive import substitution increasingly manifested themselves in the slowdown of economic activity in the second half of the 1950s. In an important book on industrialization in Taiwan, Ching-yuan Lin points out that some major manufacturing sectors such as textiles, wood products, and rubber goods had slowed down after the early 1950s as "easy" import substitution came to an end.[19] In turn, this led to a slowdown in the growth of the manufacturing sector as a whole. GDP grew significantly more slowly during 1955–58 than during 1952–55 (see Figure 10.1). After 1954, there was also a pronounced decline in the absolute level of gross private sector investment.[20]

In July 1955, the Executive Yuan passed a measure, the Regulation for Rebate of Taxes and Export Products, that provided for rebates of commodity tax, import duty, and defense tax paid on exports. In addition, for purposes of private sector exports, the domestic currency was devalued from NT$15.55 per U.S. dollar to NT$25 per U.S. dollar. Given the high rates of import duty and commodity taxes around this time, the rebates made some of the previously unprofitable exports profitable, while the devaluation boosted the value of the profits in the local currency. The measures led to a perceptible impact on non-agricultural exports, which grew 33 percent per annum during 1956–58 (Table 10.2). Indeed, the effect was strong enough to be reflected in a favorable movement in the total exports and a mildly rising trend in the exports-to-GDP ratio after bottoming out at 5.8 percent in 1954 (Figure 10.2).[21]

Several pieces of evidence ranging from a speech by the minister of economic affairs to articles by senior policymakers written in the second half of the 1950s point to wide recognition in policy circles that Taiwan needed to introduce additional measures that would make exports of manufactures profitable and stimulate private investment.[22] In addition, the politically powerful Commission on U.S. Aid (CUSA), consisting of officials of the Taiwan government and advisers from the United States Agency for International Development, played an active role in pushing for reforms.[23] In 1959, CUSA produced the Nineteen-Point Financial and Economic Improvement Plan. Among other measures, the plan recommended import liberalization, export promotion, and liberalization of foreign investment rules. The plan was implemented under the auspices of CUSA, which also controlled aid flows.

The key problem confronting many potential exporters of manufactures was that, given Taiwan's poor resource base, most of the potential export products required imported inputs accounting for two-thirds or more of the value of the product at world prices. But imported inputs were subject to strict licensing that produced very large rents. These rents exceeded the sum of the border price, custom tariff, domestic indirect taxes, and retailing costs by sufficiently large amounts that their processing for exports was unprofitable even taking into account the fact that the tariff and other indirect taxes were refundable under the 1955 reform. The only way to make exports profitable was to substantially eliminate quota premiums and provide inputs at world prices to exporters.[24] The reforms initiated in April 1958 and implemented over the following two years accomplished this task by the removal of quantitative restrictions on imports in many cases and streamlining the quota allocation in favor of exporters in others.

A further important reform, which complemented import liberalization, concerned the exchange rate. In November 1958, the domestic currency was devalued, with the result that the exchange rate applicable to the bulk of the import and export transactions by private enterprises changed from NT$25 to approximately NT$40 per U.S. dollar. This adjustment in the exchange rate greatly increased the profitability of processed exports achieved through the first reform.[25]

Additional reforms during this period included:

- The removal of export controls on more than two hundred items, simplification of procedures for tax rebates, waiver of the 2 percent harbor dues on exports, and the provision of easier credit terms for exporters
- The opening up of foreign investment, which brought multinational firms to the shores of Taiwan and helped expand the exports of electronic products
- Tax holidays, accelerated depreciation, a ceiling on corporate income tax rate, and other remissions to encourage investment

Policies During the 1960s and Early 1970s

Going by the formal level of restrictions applied to imports, the bulk of liberalization after 1958–60 reforms took place in the 1970s. Imports during the 1960s were divided into three categories: prohibited (not permitted under any circumstances), controlled (allowed only under extraordinary circumstances upon issuance of a permit), and permissible (freely allowed). Figure 10.4 shows the evolution of the number of items in each of these categories from 1968 to 1976. Until 1970, almost 42 percent of the items were in the controlled category. They fell to 18.4 percent in 1972 and 3 percent in 1974.

Unfortunately, these numbers by themselves do not tell us how restrictive the regime was, since the answer to that question depends on the classification of specific products across these categories as well as the severity with which the restrictions are enforced. For example, if the bulk of the products to be imported in large volumes in the absence of restrictions are included in the permissible category, the regime may be liberal even if the total number of products in the permissible category is small. Conversely, if these products are placed under the prohibited or controlled category, the effect may be highly restrictive even with a large number of products included in the permissible category.

In spite of this ambiguity, one thing is certain: the regulations ensured that throughout this period exporters enjoyed full free trade status in the sense

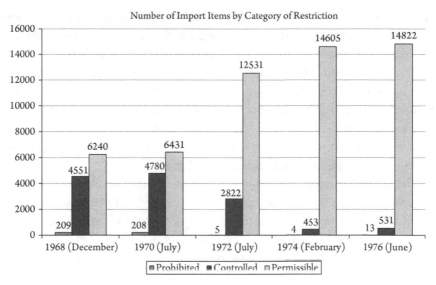

Figure 10.4 Import Restriction by Category, 1968–76.
Source: Author's construction based on Scott 1979, table 5.4.

that they were able to obtain all their inputs at world prices and sell their products at world prices. The effectiveness of this provision is reflected in the difference between gross and net customs revenues (the latter being gross revenue minus rebates) collected. Until fiscal year 1955–56 (beginning July 1, 1955), gross and net customs revenues, as proportions of total imports, were equal. A small difference of one percentage point between the two appeared in 1957–58 and 1958–59, and this difference grew in later years. From 1963–64 to the mid-1970s, the difference fluctuated between 5 and 8 percentage points.[26]

One further provision that added to the profitability of exports was the treatment of foreign exchange. Often exporters were given sufficiently generous foreign exchange allocations to allow them to legally sell a proportion of it on the open market. Because of the existence of exchange control, there remained a premium on foreign exchange in the open market.[27]

On average, import duties during the 1960s did not decline significantly. Gross tariff revenue as a proportion of imports was 25 percent in 1956–57. It fell to an average level of 19 percent during 1960–63 but rose back to 23–24 percent during the rest of the 1960s. It was only beginning in 1972–73 that the duties began to fall significantly, reaching 16 percent by 1975–76.

Two measures during the 1960s and early 1970s are worth mentioning on the export promotion side of the equation. First, a special law introduced in

January 1965 permitted the opening of export processing zones (EPZs). Taiwan pioneered the idea of combining within an EPZ a free trade zone, industrial parks, and all relevant government administrative offices. This allowed investors to cut the red tape involved in obtaining rebates of taxes on inputs and outputs. This was especially effective in attracting foreign investors, who are often less familiar with the local bureaucratic setup. Soon after the EPZs were introduced, Taiwan also began permitting bonded warehouses and factories, which could import raw materials duty free for export purposes. They had one important advantage over the EPZs: they could be located anywhere.

The second important incentive provided to exporters was the availability of low-interest credit. The Bank of Taiwan had introduced an Export Loan Program in July 1957 under which it extended short-term loans to exporting firms to finance the material and work in progress on export orders. In the initial years, the interest rate was fixed at 0.99 percent per month on loans payable in new Taiwanese dollars, compared with 1.65 percent per month on other secured loans. A similar margin existed on loans payable in U.S. dollars. This margin was preserved throughout the 1960s and narrowed only at the peak of the export boom in 1973–74.

The Real Effective Exchange Rate for Exports

I conclude this section on trade and industrial policy with a brief discussion of the real effective exchange rate for exports. Conceptually, the real effective exchange rate for exports tracks over time the total payment in constant-price domestic currency per dollar's worth of exports. Calculated by T. H. Lee and Kuo-shu Liang and shown in Figure 10.5, it represents the official exchange rate (NT$ per U.S. dollar) adjusted for export incentives per dollar's worth of exports, wholesale prices in Taiwan relative to abroad, and the Taiwanese exchange rate with respect to the major trading partners.[28]

Reflecting the switch to export-oriented policies during 1958–60, the new Taiwanese dollar substantially depreciated (while the U.S. dollar appreciated) in real terms in 1958 and 1959. Adding in the policy changes effected during those two years, the real effective exchange rate for exports moved from NT$27 per U.S. dollar in 1957 to NT$43.8 per U.S. dollar in 1959. The change represented a 62.22 percent appreciation of the U.S. dollar. It meant that when measured in constant-price local currency, each dollar's worth of exports fetched 62.22 percent more in revenues in 1959 than 1957. After 1959, the new Taiwanese dollar appreciated in real terms to some degree, but even at the peak, which occurred in 1963, the real effective exchange rate for exports remained NT$37.4. This rate meant that real revenues earned per dollar's worth of exports earned in 1963 still exceeded those earned in 1957 by 38.5 percent.

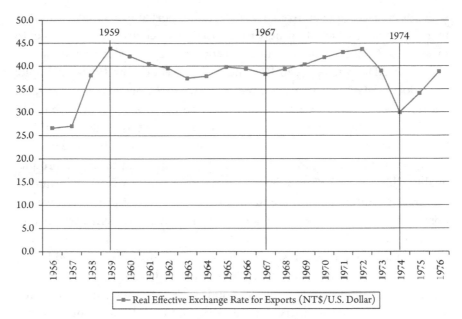

Figure 10.5 Real Effective Exchange Rate for Exports in Taiwan, 1956–76.
Source: Author's construction based on the calculations in Lee and Liang 1982, table 10.3.

Connecting the Outcomes to Policies

In linking outcomes to policies, I first look at the role of trade liberalization. I then turn to the complementary policies whose presence played a crucial role in ensuring that the benefits of openness were actually realized.

Link to Trade Policies

The importance of trade in the making of the Taiwanese miracle is difficult to ignore and it shows when critics try to do so. They avoid addressing the central policy question: could miracle-level growth have been sustained for as long as it was without outward-oriented policies? Instead, they divert attention to the presence of many interventions by the government. Alternatively, they offer superficial arguments to make the case that something other than openness catalyzed the initial growth.

Luckily, in the case of Taiwan, the centrality of trade can be established not only for sustaining high growth over the long term but also for catalyzing initial growth. Before I discuss this in detail, let me first note that trade was a key contributor to the growth of Taiwan even during the import substitution phase. During this phase, the country exported agricultural products in which it enjoyed comparative advantage and imported machinery and other manufactures in which its production costs were relatively high. Thanks to massive aid from the United States, the country was also able to maintain an import-to-GDP ratio between 10.5 and 17.2 percent during 1951–60 despite an exports-to-GDP ratio that ranged from 5.8 to 11 percent over the same period. Trade made imports of machinery and raw materials possible and helped sustain the 7.9 percent growth achieved during this period. The ability to import machinery and high-quality raw materials also allowed the import-substitution industrialization to proceed without compromising product quality. This was important if the products experiencing expansion during the import-substitution phase were to turn into major export products once the domestic market had been exhausted and the country switched to outward orientation.

The process of import substitution during the 1950s itself remained largely consistent with Taiwan's factor endowments. Industrialization progressed through rapid expansion of consumer goods such as textiles, apparel, bicycles, and wood and leather products. Between 1950 and 1957, the share of consumer goods in total imports steadily fell from 19.8 to 6.6 percent. By the late 1950s, the share of imports in the total expenditure on consumer goods dropped to 5 percent.[29] This essentially set the stage for turning the labor-intensive consumer goods into major exports. The major missing ingredient was the lack of profitability of exports, a problem that the reforms during 1958–60 effectively addressed, especially in the context of the real effective exchange rate for exporters.

Let me next turn to twin questions: what led to the initial acceleration in growth, and what allowed the accelerated growth to be sustained over a long period of time? In the Taiwanese case, an excellent prima facie case can be made that the initial spurt came from improved export performance. The reform of 1955 had begun to open the door to manufactures exports. It generated some response, with the share of non-agricultural exports rising from 6.7 percent in 1955 to 11.4 percent in 1958 (Table 10.2). The more substantial reforms of 1958–60, which led to a very large jump in the real effective exchange rate for exports (Figure 10.5), saw the share of non-agricultural exports rise to 20 percent in 1959, 28.8 percent in 1960, 38.4 percent in 1961, and 45.8 percent in 1962. The share temporarily fell during 1963–65, but this was due to the superior albeit short-lived performance of agricultural exports rather than poor performance of non-agricultural exports. Even during 1963–65, non-agricultural exports grew at an average annual rate of 23.2 percent. Their share too picked up in a major way beginning in 1966 and climbed to 77.5 percent of total exports in 1971. Total exports themselves had expanded from $18.8 million in 1958 to $1.7 billion in 1971.

The earliest year to which the spurt in the growth rate that was sustained can be traced is 1961, when the growth rate rose from 6.3 to 6.9 percent. Therefore, the spurt in non-agricultural exports preceded it by three years. From Table 10.3, we may also observe that during 1961–63, the annual average growth rate in industry had already jumped to 10.5 percent from 8.9 percent during 1958–60. Subsequently, this growth rate took another jump to 14.6 percent in 1963–67.

The main ingredient of the policy package implemented prior to the growth spurt was the introduction of export incentives, including the devaluation of the new Taiwanese dollar that led to a large jump in the real effective exchange rate for exports (Figure 10.5). Using numerical examples, Scott convincingly argues that the reforms in 1958–60 were crucial to making non-agricultural exports with a large content of imported inputs profitable.[30] He also shows that unit labor costs of manufactures measured in U.S. dollars dramatically fell in Taiwan following devaluation in 1959.[31] The real effective exchange rate for exports calculated by Lee and Liang, as shown in Figure 10.5, shows that the export incentives made exports highly profitable beginning in 1958 relative to 1957.

The next question relates to the role of outward orientation in sustaining the high growth. For starters, we may note that non-agricultural exports continued to grow at a rapid pace throughout the 1960s and early 1970s. Thanks to them, despite slow growth in agriculture, the total-exports-to-GDP ratio, which stood at 8.6 percent in 1958, rose to 21.4 percent in 1969 and then shot up to 43.9 percent in 1973. Non-agricultural exports grew at an average annual rate of 42.2 percent from 1958 to 1971, and their share in the total exports rose from 7.8 percent in 1957 to 77.5 percent in 1971.

Various interventions notwithstanding, outward-oriented policies also led Taiwan to specialize according to its comparative advantage and export labor-intensive products in exchange for capital- and skilled-labor-intensive ones. This observation is supported by more direct studies of the pattern of Taiwanese trade. For example, using data for 1966 and 1971, Kuo-shu Liang and Ching-ing Hou Liang show that export industries have "significantly lower ratios of fixed assets per worker than import industries, and their skill ratio is on average somewhat lower."[32] Studies by Ching-yuan Lin and Scott obtain similar results.[33] It was this pattern of specialization that paved the way for the rapid movement of the workforce out of agriculture into industry (see Figure 10.3) and thus helped sustain long-term growth while also transforming Taiwan from a primarily agricultural economy to a modern industrial one.

From the long-term sustainability viewpoint, one issue that may nevertheless seem puzzling is why capital accumulation continued at the rapid pace that it did. The Stolper-Samuelson theory tells us that the opening to trade, which progressively raises the price received by labor-intensive exports, would push the real wages up (as indeed happened in Taiwan in the 1960s and early 1970s) and the real return to capital down. The latter fact would diminish the incentive to accumulate capital and thus choke off growth. This is a standard theoretical problem one confronts in explaining super-high growth rates over prolonged periods.

A variety of endogenous growth models have been suggested to get around this problem.[34] My own view, however, is that the most plausible explanation of the Taiwanese experience is in terms of a model postulating technological differences between the advanced and poor economies. High rates of growth in the poor, labor-abundant economies can then be accompanied by technological catch-up, which counteracts the Stolper-Samuelson effect and allows both real wages and the return to capital to rise for some time. The incentive to accumulate capital is thus preserved until technological catch-up is complete.

The Role of Complementary Policies

An important question that must be addressed at this point is why the opening-up strategy was accompanied by sustained rapid growth in Taiwan while the same did not happen in many African and Latin American countries in the 1980s. The answer to this question lies in the presence of other complementary conditions and policies conducive to outward-oriented growth. In this section I outline some the more important of these conditions and policies.

First, with a firmly established one-party rule and no opposition, Taiwan was politically stable during this period. The government was highly capable and effective. At crucial points, as for example during 1958–60, when a change in course was warranted, it not only had the foresight to introduce that change but also the authority and capability to successfully implement it. This feature of the process made policies credible and the policy environment predictable for entrepreneurs.

Second, and perhaps most important from the viewpoint of industrialization through the expansion of labor-intensive products, Taiwan has had an extremely flexible labor market. Unions were weak, especially in manufacturing. Strikes were illegal. A minimum wage law existed but the level was set well below the market wage and was therefore redundant. Firms had full rights to hire and fire workers. The main social protection was in the form of a social insurance scheme, which was funded by a payroll tax of 8 percent covering all enterprises with ten or more workers. Additionally, there was mild protective legislation governing hours and conditions of work.[35] This regime was very different from the one prevailing in India, where the level of protection to workers in the organized sector was and remains extremely high and exceeds that in the developed countries along many dimensions. Labor market flexibility in

Taiwan ensured that as labor was drawn into manufacturing, real wages did not rise faster than productivity.

Third, the government also provided a stable macroeconomic environment. Once the hyperinflation following the Second World War had been brought under control, inflation remained low. This was especially true during the export orientation phase. The average annual increase in the consumer price index from 1961 to 1971 was just 3.4 percent.[36] This inflation was sufficient to allow the relative prices to adjust without creating undue uncertainty for investors. On the fiscal front, large amounts of aid in the 1950s had allowed the government to maintain a high share of expenditures in the GNP. But the share declined over time to 25 percent in 1974 from 38 percent in 1952.[37]

Fourth, as incomes rose, the savings rate rose as well. The average gross national savings as a proportion of GNP rose from 9 percent between 1952 and 1956 to 12.3 percent in 1962, jumped to 16.9 percent in 1963 and then grew steadily to 33 percent in 1973.[38] According to C. Sun and M. Y. Liang, during 1956–60, households and nonprofit institutions accounted for 37.6 percent of the total savings, private corporations for 10.4 percent, and government and public enterprises for 52 percent. During 1966–70, these shares changed to 57.5, 9.6, and 32.8 percent, respectively.[39] As in many other developing countries, in Taiwan the response of household savings to rising incomes was very substantial. The high interest rate policy pursued by the government perhaps played an important role in encouraging this saving.

Fifth, the government maintained and expanded infrastructure as needs arose. In the area of power, it not only made provision for industry at reasonable rates, it also brought electricity to rural areas. The country had inherited an excellent road and rail network from the Japanese. After independence, the government not only maintained this network but also expanded it. Of particular importance was the expansion of paved roads and linking of internal transport network to ports. The latter was especially crucial to facilitating the rapid expansion of trade that took place during the 1960s. Trade in processed products, which involves bringing raw materials into the country and sending out finished products, is particularly sensitive to the ability to rapidly move goods between factories and ports.

Sixth, the government played an important role in ensuring the availability of an educated labor force that could quickly adapt itself to industrial production processes. Recall that the Japanese had concentrated almost exclusively on primary education, ignoring secondary and college education. At the end of the 1960s, the government extended the length of compulsory education from six to nine years. By the mid-1960s, it further shifted the emphasis to secondary education, including vocational education. Overall expenditures on education rose from 2.1 percent of GNP in 1955 to 4.6 percent of GNP in 1970.

Vocational training increased sixfold between 1966 and 1974. The proportion of high school students in the vocational track rose from 40 percent in 1963 to 52 percent in 1972 and 70 percent in 1980. According to Ranis, "Most important to the success of the education system was the fact that vocational education was highly diversified, flexible and continuously responsive to changing market demands."[40]

Finally, liberal rules relating to foreign investment also made a modest contribution to the growth of manufacturing. The reforms during 1958–60 had opened the door to direct foreign investment with no cap on the share of foreign investors and full repatriation permitted. Foreign-owned enterprises enjoyed the same tax benefits as those locally owned and were not required to employ Chinese. They also enjoyed a guarantee against expropriation for at least twenty years. In 1976, 21 out of the 321 largest industrial corporations in Taiwan were foreign. These enterprises were heavily concentrated in electronics and were labor intensive and export oriented. They played an important role in giving Taiwan an early start in this sector, with happy results.[41] Data compiled by Ranis show that private foreign investment rose from approximately 4 percent of gross domestic capital formation in the early 1960s to 8 to 9 percent in the late 1960s and early 1970s. Ranis also points out that almost 13 percent of the total organized industrial labor force was employed in foreign enterprises.[42]

While acknowledging the importance of these complementary conditions, let me reiterate that it is difficult to imagine how Taiwan could have sustained its rapid growth without the ability to exploit world markets. To state the point more concretely, even if all the complementary policies mentioned above had been present, Taiwan could not have sustained rapid growth for long under a pure import substitution strategy. Indeed, that was precisely the experience in the 1950s, which led policymakers to rethink their strategy. Technological improvement, which was probably an important factor in maintaining high rates of return on capital, was itself tied to the country's ability to trade. But equally important, profitability and hence the incentive to accumulate capital would have been exhausted in a relatively short period of time if entrepreneurs had been confined to the small domestic market. India ran into this problem in the first four decades of its development even though it had a potentially much larger market.

Response to Critics

Major critiques of the view that outward orientation combined with flexible labor markets, sound fiscal management, and macroeconomic stability are the key to explaining the Taiwanese growth miracles have been offered by political scientist Robert Wade and economist Dani Rodrik. Because the writings of both have been influential, it is important to assess them in some detail.

Robert Wade

In his 1990 book, reprinted in 2004 with a new introduction, Wade argues that the view placing outward orientation at the center of Taiwan's growth, a view that Ian Little and other economists have espoused, cannot be right because the Taiwanese government extensively intervened in the making of the miracle. Characterizing the policy package Little credits for the success as neoclassical, he reasons:[43]

> In short, Taiwan seems to meet the neoclassical growth conditions un-usually well. Yet other evidence shows that the government has been intervening for decades, often quite aggressively, to alter the trade and industrial profile of the economy in ways that it judges to be desirable. We then face a formidable identification problem. How can we decide to what extent Taiwan's exceptional economic performance is due to the presence of many of the neo-classical growth conditions and to what extent the government's selective promotion policies? Ultimately, I cannot resolve the issue. But for my purpose it is enough to demon-strate that the government has indeed been guiding the market on a scale much greater than is consistent with neoclassical prescriptions or with the practice of Anglo-American economies. For the fact of such guidance has been almost completely overlooked by neoclassical economists. Recall Ian Little's claim that "apart from the creation of [these neo-classical conditions] . . . it is hard to find any good explana-tion for the sustained industrial boom." . . . In twenty thousand word essays on the mechanism of Taiwan's development, both Little and Gustav Ranis largely ignore the promotional role of government after the economic liberalization of 1958–62.

Let me first point out that the claim that Little missed or ignored the interventions by the Taiwanese government is patently false. Even a quick reading of Little's essay yields numerous instances of his acute awareness of the government interventions in various areas. Early in the essay, referring to the governments of the NIEs and Japan, he notes, "With the exception of Hong Kong, all these governments (including that of Japan) see a considerable role for themselves in *promoting and guiding* economic advance" (emphasis added).[44] Discussing the impact of the reforms of 1958–60, he says, "The effect of the new policies was not to create laissez-faire conditions for the whole industry, let alone the whole economy. They created a kind of dual economy in which exports, but only exports, could be manufactured under virtually free trade conditions."[45] He also discusses in some detail public ownership of banks, utilities, and industrial corporations and refers to the extensive quantitative restrictions on imports, high tariffs, and investment incentives including tax holidays, accelerated depreciation, and other remissions.

Later in the essay, Little devotes an entire section to the discussion of the role of planning. He refers to the important role played by the Joint Commission on Rural Construction in the promotion of agriculture.[46] He also notes the role of the government in the promotion of manufacturing: "The Ministry of Economic Affairs exercises considerable influence over industrialization for the home market, especially with respect to the promotion of mainly import-substitution manufacturing of capital-intensive intermediates—synthetic fibers, petroleum products and petrochemicals, steel, and nonferrous metals. In the earlier years, CIECD [Council of International Economic Cooperation and Development, which replaced the Council for U.S. Aid in the mid-1960s] performed the same function."[47]

It is clear that Little was fully aware of the interventions by the Taiwanese government that Wade catalogues in greater detail in his book. The same is also true of other contributors to the volume in which the essay by Little appeared. References to interventions by the Taiwanese government during the 1950s as well as 1960s can be found throughout the volume. Wade is thus factually incorrect in asserting that these authors "almost completely overlooked" government interventions. What they did not do was adopt the view that the interventions were central to the making of the Taiwanese miracle.

Turning to the more substantive weaknesses, as a critic, Wade had two burdens to discharge. First, he should have provided clear reasons that the precise explanation offered by the economists he criticizes was invalid. Second, he should have provided an alternative explanation that is more persuasive. He fails to deliver on both counts.

In trying to discharge the first burden, Wade argues that the neoclassical explanation could not have been at work since the Taiwanese government intervened extensively. But this is a non sequitur. There is no agreed-upon set of necessary conditions whose absence would render the neoclassical model inoperative. Nor is there a set of sufficient conditions whose presence in a country would guarantee that it is following this model. International capital mobility is often identified as a feature of the neoclassical model, but it was missing even from the European economies during their rapid growth in the post–Second World War reconstruction era. Taiwan permitted direct foreign investment in the 1960s and early 1970s, but Korea did not. There also remain wide differences among neoclassical economists on the role of the public sector versus the private sector in the provision of public goods. Traditionally, most neoclassicists thought that infrastructure and social services remain the responsibility of the government. But this too has changed today, with many economists taking the view that when governments are not capable, it is desirable to give a central role to the private sector in the provision of telecommunications, roads, ports, airports, education, and health. The bottom line is that significant interventions may exist in one part of the economy while another part gives entrepreneurs free play under neutral incentives and serves as the driver of rapid growth.

Therefore, the real issue is not whether the interventions Wade identifies render the neoclassical model invalid but whether they seriously undermine the interpretation offered by Ian Little and others. Additionally, we might ask whether the interventions identified by Wade dramatically altered the course of the economy relative to what it would have been in their absence. Could it not be that those interventions were ineffective, mutually canceling or simply reinforcing market forces? As a specific example, is it not possible that the import protection Wade identifies simply neutralized the export incentives, so on balance the regime was more or less what you would expect under free trade? This is not idle speculation; in the case of Korea, Larry Westphal and K. S. Kim find that when all trade interventions are aggregated, there remains only a small net bias in favor of exports relative to a free trade regime.[48]

Turning to Wade's second burden, he makes little effort to discharge it. He states at the outset that he cannot determine the extent to which the government's selective promotion policies contributed to Taiwan's exceptional performance. What follows in the book is a catalogue of the interventions, big and small, without articulation of a coherent explanation of how they added up to the miracle and whether these interventions would have led to the miracle even if the policies identified as important by Little and others had been absent. There are repeated references to the government acting strategically in specific contexts but no articulation of a "strategic action" model of economic development that he could recommend to other countries based on the Taiwanese experience. Ranis, who actively advocates import substitution in the early stages of development as necessary for the eventual success of outward-oriented growth policies, expresses his dissatisfaction with Wade's analysis: "Wade's [1990 book] *Governing the Market* describes government interventions on Taiwan *ex post*; but I could find no primer on just how to 'act strategically.' "[49]

The bottom line Wade offers is as follows:

> The fact of big leadership [meaning that the government leads private entrepreneurs through initiatives that significantly alter their investment and production patterns] or big followership [meaning that the government follows the lead of private entrepreneurs in designing its interventions] does not mean that government intervention has been

effective in promoting economic growth; it only means that government intervention cannot be dismissed as having made negligible
difference to outcomes. But the balance of presumption must be that
government industrial policies, including sectoral ones, helped more
than they hindered. To argue otherwise is to suggest that economic
performance would have been still more exceptional with less intervention, which is simply less plausible than the converse.[50]

This paragraph illustrates in sharp relief how revisionists drop the bar
when it comes to providing the proof of their own thesis. Recall that when
evaluating the thesis advanced by Ian Little and others, they demand that
the latter's policy package be shown to be a sufficient explanation of the
Taiwanese miracle and not merely a positive contribution to it on balance.
But for his own thesis, Wade wants to get away by simply demonstrating that
the government industrial policies "helped more than they hindered" the
process of development.

More importantly, in his response to Wade, Little goes further, questioning
the very logic underlying Wade's argument head-on:

> Since the less interventionist Hong Kong, Singapore, and Taiwan grew
> faster than Korea, it is unclear why Wade thinks it simply less plausible
> that less intervention would have been better, given also the widespread
> failure of government industrial policies elsewhere. I find it simply
> more plausible that Korea grew fast despite its industrial policies, than
> because of them.[51]

The final point concerns the direct involvement of the government in the
production activity. The absolute level of interventions discussed by Wade in
various sectors at various points in time notwithstanding, over time the government became less and less important to production activity. This is seen in
Figure 10.6, which shows the output shares of the public sector in industry as a
whole and in manufacturing. Both shares declined steadily between 1953 and
1972, with the decline accelerating in the 1960s.[52]

The large share of the public sector in the early years was due to the large
volume of assets that the government inherited from Japan when the latter left
the country. Four of the large inherited enterprises were returned to private
hands as part of the compensation to landlords under the land reform in the
late 1940s but the rest remained with the government. Remarkably, only one
new central government corporation was established between 1946 and 1969.
Because many more firms entered the private sector and private sector firms
grew faster than public sector firms, the contribution of the public sector to
output progressively declined in relative terms.[53]

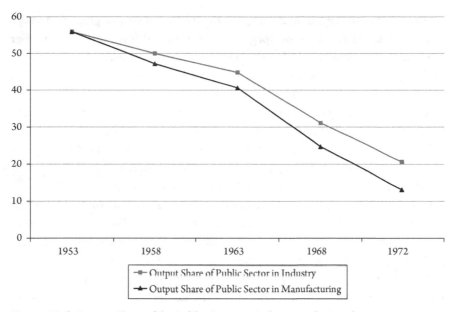

Figure 10.6 Output Share of the Public Sector in Industry and Manufacturing in Taiwan.
Source: Author's construction based on Ranis 1979, table 3.31.

Dani Rodrik

The critique by Rodrik can be divided into two broad parts.[54] In the first part, he offers arguments why the outward-orientation thesis explaining the Taiwanese and Korean miracles is wrong. In the second part, he offers his own alternative thesis based on a coordination failure model. I will consider each part of the critique in turn.

In discussing the role of openness in catalyzing and sustaining growth, Rodrik makes two key points. First, the timing of the introduction of incentives for exports and export response do not match. Specifically, exports follow rather than lead the spurt in growth. Second, at the time the growth spurt came, exports were too small to pull GDP ahead.

To make his first point, Rodrik compares the movements in two series: the ratio of total exports to GDP and a general measure of real exchange rate that begins in 1960. He notes that the former exhibited a spurt in 1963 and 1964, which coincided with an appreciation of the real exchange rate. Evidently, exports could not have been responding to incentives, which had risen in 1958–60 but fell during 1963 and 1964. The story of export incentives driving exports and exports driving growth simply does not work.

There are two problems with the data series Rodrik uses to drive home his point. First, unaware of the real effective exchange rate for exports calculated by

Lee and Liang, which I have depicted in Figure 10.5, he uses a general measure of the real exchange rate, which begins in 1960.[55] But this is a non sequitur. For one thing, with sufficiently large export-specific incentives, the real effective exchange rate *for exports* can show improved incentives even when a general measure of the real exchange rate does not do so.

Moreover, to gauge profitability in a post-reform period, one must compare the post-reform real effective exchange rate with the pre-reform rate. If the initial incentives to export granted by the reform are large, even a small subsequent reversal may leave exports highly profitable. This is not idle speculation. Once we consider the conceptually correct real effective exchange rate for exports calculated by Lee and Liang, which covers both pre- and post-reform years, it is seen that even during periods of appreciation in the 1960s, the revenue in constant-price local currency for each dollar's worth of exports remained minimally 38.2 percent above its level prior to the 1958–60 reform.

The second problem with Rodrik's critique arises with respect to the specific measure of export performance he uses. Whereas the reforms during 1958–60 were designed to stimulate manufacturing exports, he uses total exports (as a proportion of GDP) to measure export performance. But the total exports may behave quite differently than manufacturing exports, especially if they are heavily dominated by poorly performing agricultural exports, as indeed was the case around this time (see Table 10.2). As we have seen, agricultural exports did poorly during 1958–62 and masked the large positive response of manufacturing exports. And again, the improved performance of the total exports during 1963 and 1964 was due to a spurt in agricultural exports, which were less closely tied to the trade policy reforms.

More importantly, a major spurt in the growth of non-agricultural exports fully coincided with the 1958–60 reform. Both the reform and the surge in exports preceded the acceleration in the GDP growth rate. Rodrik's critique that total exports as a proportion of GDP did not respond until 1963 is an artifact of the poor performance of agricultural exports during 1958–62 and their stellar performance during 1963.

Rodrik criticizes some pro-free-trade authors for emphasizing the stability of the real effective exchange rate as being the key to Taiwan's excellent export performance during the times of mild appreciation in the 1960s. Here I partially agree with his criticism in the sense that the level of the exchange rate is far more important than its stability. If the exchange rate is significantly overvalued, stability can scarcely be a virtue. In the case of Taiwan, stability may have helped nevertheless, because its level was set at a figure that was profitable for exporters.

Rodrik's second criticism of the thesis that exports were the key to Taiwan's success is that the level of exports in Taiwan in the early 1960s was simply too small to pull up GDP at faster pace. There are two problems with his argument.

First, even if exports are small, the exportable sector is not. When the profitability of exports rises, investment increases in the entire export sector. Moreover, since the world markets are virtually limitless from the viewpoint of a small economy, demand does not constrain the investments in this sector. And as the exploitation of the economies of scale brings production costs down, domestic consumption of the products can also expand.

Second, as Bhagwati has argued, improved export incentives impact not just the existing export sectors but also those with potential to turn into export sectors in the future.[56] Sufficiently large export incentives may turn many non-traded but tradable and even imported products into export products. To give just one example from Taiwan, electrical machinery and appliances were not even among the country's export products in 1959. They appeared on the list for the first time in 1960 and came to account for 12.3 percent of Taiwan's vastly expanded total exports by 1970.[57] Clothing and footwear had expanded from 0.8 to just 2.6 percent of the total exports between 1952 and 1960. They rose to 4.9 percent in 1965 and shot up to 16.8 percent in 1970.[58]

It is also important to recognize that the acceleration of growth itself was cumulative in Taiwan. The GDP growth rate rose from 6.3 percent in 1960 to 6.9 percent in 1961, reaching the double-digit level for the first time only in 1964. By this time, total exports had already risen to 17 percent of GDP and non-agricultural exports had climbed to 40 percent of that. In current dollars, these exports grew at the astonishing annual rate of 47.5 percent from 1959 to 1964.

Both of the major criticisms of the conventional explanation of the Taiwanese miracle by Rodrik thus fail to stand up to close scrutiny. Let us next turn to his interpretation of the Taiwanese miracle. He argues that the government engineered a significant increase in the private return to capital by "subsidizing and coordinating investment decisions." In his story, there existed investments subject to substantial scale economies that would yield high rates of return if undertaken jointly but low rates of return if undertaken in isolation. But an individual investor could not be sure that investments that raised the return to a particular activity would be undertaken, and therefore the investor would either underinvest in that activity or not undertake the activity at all. If the government offered investment subsidies that made the activity attractive to the investor even when undertaken in isolation, all investment activities would in fact be undertaken and the country would reap the high social rates of return.

To clarify, consider an example. Suppose the return to investment in toothbrush production would be high if investment takes place simultaneously in toothpaste but not otherwise. If there are no scale economies, an individual investor can, of course, invest in both activities and reap the high return. If there are very substantial scale economies, however, capital constraints may allow the investor to invest in only one activity, say toothbrushes. But without assurance that someone will invest in toothpaste as well, the investor may find the investment unprofitable. Thus the coordination failure problem may arise. The government may break the logjam by underwriting the losses of both toothbrush and toothpaste manufacturers and thus help investors realize high rates of return. Since no losses will actually occur ex post, the government will not even have to pay the two manufacturers any subsidies. Rodrik argues that this is just what the government in Taiwan did, not by underwriting the losses but by giving explicit investment subsidies.

We know that trade expanded very rapidly in Taiwan during the growth process. So what is the link of this story to the rapid growth in trade? Here Rodrik argues that investments required machinery, which had to be imported. But beyond aid, which had been shrinking around this time, imports are not possible unless exports generate the necessary revenues. Rodrik concludes, "Thanks to appropriate macroeconomic and exchange rate policies, export supply was adequate to meet the increase in import demand, and rose alongside imports." In other words, Rodrik thinks exports were merely a passive response to the need for imports, which was itself a response to the investment boom that the government had engineered.

There are several problems with this story. First, when the avenue to trade is open, the coordination failure argument loses validity. In the toothpaste and toothbrush example, either the toothbrush manufacturer could export toothbrushes or the customers could import toothpaste. The higher return could be realized either way. To validate the argument, one must argue that there exist interdependent investment opportunities subject to scale economies in non-traded sectors. Rodrik is aware of this problem and argues that there indeed were such activities, but he offers few convincing examples. Private investment mostly grew in manufactures, which were by and large tradable and therefore not subject to the coordination failure problem.

Second, even if we ignore that problem, if Rodrik's story is correct, we must observe that the investment boom occurs first, followed by import expansion and growth acceleration and then export expansion. But as I have already argued, manufactures exports had begun to grow rapidly well before the growth spurt. As for the sequencing between exports and imports, using Rodrik's own data, economist Victor Norman points out that it was the reverse of what Rodrik predicts.[59]

Third, in view of the activist policies to boost exports in both Taiwan and Korea, the argument that export expansion was a passive outcome of the investment boom is problematic as well. Both Taiwan and Korea consciously went after exports by instituting a free trade regime for exporters. The governments made a significant effort to create the necessary administrative machinery to implement the exemptions of custom duties and indirect taxes on direct as well as indirect imports. Korea went even farther, setting export targets, which the government then carefully monitored on a regular basis. In his retrospective article in the *Journal of Economic Perspectives* entitled "Industrial Policy in an Export-Propelled Economy: Lessons from South Korea's Experience," Westphal describes the priority the Korean government assigned to exports in these terms: "If nothing else, policies toward exports have created an atmosphere—rare in the Third World—in which businessmen could be certain that the economic system would respond to and subsequently reward their efforts aimed at expanding and upgrading exports."[60]

In turn, the study by Westphal and Kim, on which Westphal draws, assigns a central role to activist trade policy in stimulating growth in Korea:

> The growth of manufactured exports over the fifteen years from 1960 to 1975 contributed to Korea's industrial development in various ways. Export expansion was directly responsible for more than one quarter of the growth of manufactured output and for an even larger fraction of the increase in manufactured employment. In turn, the manufacturing sector has accounted for almost 40 percent of the growth in both GNP and employment. These figures understate the contribution of export growth. They do not reflect the backward linkages to domestically produced intermediate inputs, the multiplier effect resulting from increased consumption and investment resulting from additional income earned, or the increase in economic efficiency that results from exporting in accordance with a country's comparative advantage.[61]

Westphal and Kim thus turn Rodrik's story on its head, partially attributing the growth in investment itself to export growth and the income increase stimulated by it.

Finally, even granting for the sake of argument that investment coordination catalyzed growth, we must ask whether this growth could have been sustained without the outward-oriented policies the countries pursued. India's experience points to an unequivocally negative answer to this question. India intervened far more heavily to boost investment. But unlike Korea and Taiwan, it did so in an autarkic environment and achieved far poorer results until it changed course. As far as trade openness is concerned, the prescription provided by Rodrik's story is no different from that offered by pro-free-trade advocates.

Concluding Remarks

The role of openness in the making and sustaining of the Taiwanese miracle has been seriously questioned by some analysts. The presence of interventions and protection during the high-growth period in this case is no more in question than it is in the cases of China and India. But it is also true that, as in China and India, the general movement of the economy was toward increased openness and a reduced role for the government, at least in manufacturing activities. There was a small surge in the government activity during 1973 to 1978 in Taiwan, but the country returned to more open and less interventionist policies soon after.

Taiwan undertook some important trade reforms during 1958–60, which gave exporters a free trade status. It also devalued the domestic currency, complementing it with export incentives, such that the revenue per dollar's worth of exports in terms of the domestic currency rose dramatically. Between 1958 and 1973, revenue per dollar's worth of exports in constant-price domestic currency was anywhere between 38.2 to 62 percent higher than in 1957. This level of improvement in the export incentives had a major impact on non-primary-product exports of Taiwan: they grew an astonishing 49.2 percent per annum during 1958–63. The share of non-primary products in total exports rose from 7.8 percent in 1957 to 39 percent in 1963. Some further liberalizing reforms were undertaken in the 1960s, and these helped sustain the growth in non-primary-product exports, which came to account for 77.5 percent of total exports by 1971. The proportion of merchandise exports in GDP also rose sharply, from 9.5 percent of GDP in 1957 to 31.5 percent in 1971. Evidence shows that Taiwan specialized in largely labor-intensive products during this period. Alongside these developments in the trade sector, the output and employment shares of manufacturing also expanded dramatically. With the share of industry in GDP rising from 31.8 percent during 1954–57 to 51.3 percent during 1971–73, Taiwan was transformed from an agriculture-dominated to industry-dominated economy.

Citing evidence, I have argued that although the government in Taiwan intervened heavily, at least until the early 1970s, that did not cause the outcome to deviate significantly from what a neutral policy regime would have produced. Sectors that showed the best performance on the export front were invariably labor intensive and were not subject to selective targeting. In Taiwan, the share of public sector in industrial and manufacturing outputs also fell over time.

I have offered reasons the criticisms by free-trade skeptics do not stand up to close scrutiny. Rodrik has argued that since incentives were introduced in the late 1950s and the exports-to-GDP ratio did not rise significantly in the early 1960s, outward-oriented policies could not have been behind the growth spurt. But Rodrik makes this argument on the basis of slow growth in the ratio of *total* exports to GDP. In fact, the export incentives had been aimed at manufacturing exports, and these responded splendidly in the late 1950s and early 1960s. Rodrik also argues that since exports as a proportion of GDP were tiny in the early 1960s, they could not have been behind the spurt in growth. I point out, however, that the effect of incentives must be measured not by the level of exports in the initial equilibrium but by the overall share of the exportable sectors in GDP and the impact the incentives have in terms of moving resources into existing and potential exportable products on the margin. The incentives may lead not only to a sizable expansion of the existing export products but also to many potentially exportable but not yet exported products.

I have also offered several criticisms of Rodrik's explanation of the Taiwanese miracle based on government-engineered investment coordination. For example, I argue that the investment coordination failure occurs only in non-traded goods, but it is the traded goods that were central to the success of manufacturing growth in Taiwan. I also note that rapid growth in exports and imports is an essential part of Rodrik's story, so from a policy perspective, there is no way for him to get away from outward orientation.

Finally, to address the critique by Wade, I have argued that while he offers a catalogue of interventions by the government, it is not clear how these interventions add up to a coherent growth strategy. Growth in Taiwan was driven by rapid growth in private sector investment and characterized by rapid expansion of exports by private entrepreneurs. The composition of output was also consistent with what we would expect under neutral policies. Therefore, a reasonable conclusion is that the government interventions more or less followed the lead of the private sector, reinforcing what the market equilibrium under neutral trade policies would have produced in the first place. To validate his thesis, Wade must convincingly argue that subtracting the "neoclassical" features of the Taiwanese economy but retaining the interventions he describes would still have left the miracle intact, and he does not come even close to successfully making this argument.

Notes

1. An influential article by K. S. Yin (1954), the vice chairman of the Taiwanese Production Board from 1951 to 1954, pointed out several problems associated with the process of industrialization and recommended remedies.
2. Galenson's 1979 volume has seven essays by authors specializing in their subject areas. In addition to his own substantial original work (Galenson 1979), each author draws on a wealth of writings by other authors, principally of Taiwanese origin. To avoid an excessively long list of references and the clutter that is likely to result, I cite the original references only when absolutely necessary. In a similar spirit, I do not cite the original sources of the data cited by the authors. The interested reader can find the original sources of the data in the respective chapters.
3. As discussed in Kuo 1999, the government's role did expand temporarily between 1973 and 1978, when it undertook the Ten Major Projects. These projects included six transportation projects, three heavy industry projects (steel, petrochemicals, and shipbuilding), and one nuclear power project. They absorbed 4.5 percent of the total investment in 1973 and 1974, 20 percent in 1975 and 1976, 13 percent in 1977, and 8 percent in 1978. Following the oil

crisis, growth in Taiwan had dipped, and these projects probably helped in the robust recovery beginning in 1976 (see Figure 10.1). I do not discuss this period in detail, since it is not subject to any major controversy.

4. Little 1979, 453–54.
5. Kuznets 1979, table 1.5.
6. Little 1979, 454.
7. This paragraph is based on Scott 1979, 301–11.
8. This and the following paragraph are based on Lee and Liang 1982, 311–13.
9. Ranis 1999, table 5.3, 118.
10. Ranis 1999, table 5.3, 118.
11. There is an apparent inconsistency between Figure 10.2 and Table 10.2. According to Figure 10.2 (based on data from Scott 1979, table 5.12), the exports-to-GDP ratio rose in 1959. But according to Table 10.2 (based on Ranis 1999, table 5.2), total exports fell. With the GDP growing, both of these observations could not be true. The explanation for the apparent discrepancy probably lies in the movement in the exchange rate. To calculate the exports-to-GDP ratio, the dollar value of exports must be converted into the domestic currency. With the domestic currency having depreciated in 1959, the slightly lower dollar value of exports in 1959 relative to 1958 could still translate into a significantly larger domestic currency value.
12. Because the employment data for 1952–66 and 1966–75 in Figure 10.5 come from two separate sources, they are not strictly comparable across these periods. This should be apparent from two different shares for each sector shown for the year 1966, which is common to the two series.
13. Fields 1980, table 6.19, 231.
14. According to Scott, although restrictions on import had existed since at least 1949, licenses were issued liberally until the introduction of the controls in April 1951. Scott quotes C. T. Chien as stating in a 1957 article that the period from June 1949 to April 1951 "may be considered as a period of free imports" (Scott 1979, 314 n. 9).
15. See Scott 1979, table 5.3, 326, for details. A lower price of the U.S. dollar was applied to imports and exports by government enterprises and imports of some basic raw materials and industrial products financed from U.S. aid. Two prominent items exported by government enterprises and subjected to the lower exchange rate were sugar and rice.
16. Scott (1979, 315) credits Ching-yuan Lin (1973) for these estimates of quota premiums. Quota premium is the excess of price an importer receives in the domestic market after subtracting the landed price plus custom duty.
17. Scott 1979, 315.
18. Scott 1979, 315 n. 14.
19. Lin 1973.
20. Scott 1979, 318.
21. I draw on Scott 1979, 324–25, for the discussion of the reforms described in this paragraph.
22. Scott 1979, 318–21.
23. Baldwin, Chen, and Nelson 1995.
24. Scott 1979, 321–24, provides empirical evidence supporting the argument in the text.
25. It is important to understand that the devaluation would not have helped without the first reform. This is because such a measure would have led to a proportional increase in the prices of exports and imported inputs in terms of the domestic currency. Therefore, if exports were unprofitable initially, they would have remained so after devaluation. But once the first reform created positive profits, their positive value rose in terms of the domestic currency with devaluation.
26. Scott 1979, table 5.6.
27. Lin 1973, 97–100.
28. Lee and Liang 1982.
29. Ranis 1979, 211.
30. Scott 1979, 321–30.
31. Scott 1979, figure 5.5.
32. Liang and Liang 1976. The quotation is taken from Scott 1979, 354.

33. Lin 1973, 131–37; Scott 1979, 355–57.
34. For example, Ventura 1997; Mulligan and Sala-i-Martin 1993.
35. This discussion of the labor market is based on Little 1979, 469.
36. I have calculated this average rate using the annual rates of change in the consumer price index in Lundberg 1979, table 4.4.
37. Lundberg 1979, 302. Little (1979, 478) provides an even lower share, stating that it fell from 19.6 percent in 1963 to 16 percent in 1973.
38. Little 1979, 476.
39. Sun and Liang 1982, 414.
40. This paragraph is based entirely on Ranis 1999, 121.
41. Little 1979, 478–79.
42. Ranis 1979, table 3.28, 251.
43. Wade 2004, 72
44. Little 1979, 467.
45. Little 1979, 475.
46. Little 1979, 485–90.
47. Little 1979, 489.
48. Westphal and Kim 1982. Similar calculations for Taiwan are not available.
49. Ranis 2003, 34.
50. Wade, 2004, 305–6.
51. Little 1996b, 12.
52. There was a small temporary reversal of this trend due to the initiation and completion of the Ten Major Projects between 1973 and 1978. Three of these projects were devoted to the development of heavy industry. For details, see Kuo 1999.
53. In the early 1970s, public enterprises produced sugar, heavy chemicals and fertilizers, machinery, non-ferrous metals and steel, petroleum products and petrochemicals (Little 1979, 467).
54. The key reference here is Rodrik 1995.
55. From the statement "Unlike in Korea, we do not have a synthetic measure of an effective exchange rate for exporters," I infer that Rodrik (1995, 65) was unaware of the work by Lee and Liang (1982). Curiously, he also makes no mention of the important paper by Scott (1979), who analyzes the implications of the 1955 and 1958–60 reforms for the profitability of exports in great detail.
56. Bhagwati 1999, 31.
57. Ranis 1979, table 3.22, 240.
58. Lee and Liang 1982, table 10.12, 333.
59. Norman 1995, 102.
60. Westphal 1990, 56.
61. Westphal and Kim 1982, 271.

11

South Korea

From Basket Case to Upper Middle Income

In the 1950s, South Korea was seen as a basket case, sustained only by massive doses of U.S. aid. Economic aid, exclusive of military aid, by the United States comfortably exceeded 10 percent of Korea's gross national product (GNP). With aid peaking in 1957, the prospects of Korea sustaining itself on a very low rate of domestic savings—and that on a very low level of income—seemed bleak. Yet by the mid-1960s, Korea had turned itself around and achieved an unprecedented near-double-digit growth rate. By the mid-1980s, it had acquired the status of an upper-middle-income country.[1] In 1996, it was even invited to join the OECD, a club consisting of mainly rich countries.

The story of Korea until the early 1970s closely resembles that of Taiwan. Beginning in 1973, some departures can be seen in terms of industrial targeting. From 1973 till the early 1980s, Korea targeted a set of capital-intensive industries. Setting aside this aberration, much of our analysis of Taiwan carries over to Korea.

Economists Charles Frank, Kwang Suk Kim, and Larry Westphal cover the period until 1972 in great detail in an excellent book-length study conducted as a part of the Bhagwati-Krueger NBER project.[2] In the historical narrative below, I liberally draw on this study. For the period from 1954 to 1972, I also make use of the rich data they provide. As in the case of Taiwan, I begin with some historical background leading up to the 1950s.

From the Japanese Occupation to the Korean War

Japan occupied the Korean peninsula from 1910 to 1945.[3] The end of Japanese rule in 1945 was accompanied by a de facto partition of the peninsula, with the United States administering the part south of the 38th parallel and the Soviet Union doing the same north of it. The arrangement came to an end in 1948 when the Republic of Korea was established in the south, with Synghman Rhee, a Princeton Ph.D. and longtime exile in the United States, becoming its president. In the north, the communists established the Democratic People's Republic of Korea the same year, with Kim Il-Sung as its head.

The Soviets left Korea in 1948 and the United States withdrew its armed forces from there in 1949. But the outbreak of the Korean War in June 1950 brought the U.S. military back to the region on behalf of South Korea, while China sent its military to fight on behalf of North Korea. The war proved very costly in economic as well as human terms, with casualties running in millions. An armistice eventually brought an end to the war in July 1953.

During the period of colonial rule, Japan dominated the Korean economy. In 1940, the Japanese owned 94 percent of the authorized capital of business establishments. In addition, 80 percent of the technical manpower was Japanese. Most Korean establishments were small, used simpler technology than the Japanese, and were often subsidiaries of Japanese companies. Therefore, the departure of Japan resulted in a significant decline in economic activity. Partition of the country compounded the problem. While machinery, textiles, and processed food industries had been located in the south, mineral resources and power generation were located in the north. Upon the country's partition, lack of electricity led to the closing down of many industrial establishments in the south. In 1948, manufacturing output was just 20 percent of what it had been in 1940. The country also faced severe food shortages.

An important accomplishment of the immediate post-independence period was land reform. The first step toward this reform was taken under the U.S. military government in 1947. The government redistributed the properties expropriated from the departed Japanese landlords. The second and more difficult step, involving expropriation of land from farms larger than three hectares and its redistribution to landless or small farmers, was completed under Rhee in 1949.

With the departure of the Japanese, the Korean yen was replaced at par by the won, the country's currency for centuries before the Japanese takeover. But this was followed by uncontrolled monetary expansion. Hyperinflation ensued. Between independence on August 15, 1945, and the end of 1949, currency in circulation expanded by fifteen times. As a consequence, the Seoul retail price index increased 123 times between June 1945 and June 1949. Internationally, the won depreciated at a rapid pace, dropping from 15 won per U.S. dollar in 1945 to 6,000 won per dollar in 1953. In February 1953, a new currency, the hwan, was introduced, with 1 hwan replacing 100 won. The new currency lasted till June 1962, when the won was reintroduced, with 10 hwan being equal to 1 new won. The new won was thus equal to 1,000 old won circulating from August 1945 to February 1953.

Overview of the Economy: 1954–2008

Economic development in Korea began in earnest after the end of the Korean War. Beginning in 1954 and ending in 2008, the year of the global financial crisis, the fifty-five-year economic history of the country can be divided into five separate periods. The first period, covering 1954–62, was one of reconstruction and recovery and broadly involved import substitution industrialization. The second period, 1963–73, is conventionally described as one of outward-oriented development under broadly neutral policies. The third period, 1974–82, was characterized by industrial targeting under an otherwise outward-oriented regime. The years 1983–95 saw the economy move away from targeting. During these years, Korea undertook concerted import liberalization and returned to a regime of neutral incentives. The period 1996–2008 began with the East Asian currency crisis and ended with the global financial crisis. This was the period of the slowest growth.

Columns 2 and 3 in Table 11.1 show the growth rates of the total and per capita incomes during the five periods. The key point to note is that while the economy got back on its feet during the import substitution period, it began to genuinely race ahead only under the outward-oriented period, 1963–73. The average annual growth rates of the total output during the two periods were 4.2 and 9.1 percent, respectively. The key controversies between the advocates of

Table 11.1 **Average annual growth rates in Korea**

Period	GDP	Per capita GDP	Exports of constant-price goods and services	Imports of constant-price goods and services
1954–62	4.2	1.3	13.9	5.2
1963–73	9.1	8.5	32.1	21.4
1974–82	6.9	5.1	14.0	12.2
1983–95	8.7	7.6	12.6	13.5
1996–2008	4.4	3.8	12.4	8.5

Note: All growth rates except those for 1954–62 are calculated using data reported in the World Bank's World Development Indicators Online (accessed May 1, 2010). Growth rates for the period 1954–62 in GDP and per capita GDP columns relate to GNP and per capita GNP, respectively, and have been calculated using the annual GNP and population growth rates reported in Frank, Kim, and Westphal 1975, ch. 2. These authors report GNP growth rates in table 2-4 and the population growth rate of 2.9 percent on page 12. Growth rates in constant-price exports and imports relating to 1954–62 are calculated using the export and import figures in Frank, Kim, and Westphal 1975, table 2-7, p. 15.

outward-oriented policies and their critics relate to the second, higher-growth phase.[4]

During the third phase, the growth rate fell to 6.9 percent. The period began with the introduction of industrial targeting and was subsequently characterized by macroeconomic problems resulting from the oil crisis as well as the large external debt incurred to finance investments in the targeted industries. By the end of the period, a stabilization package, which included more or less an end to the targeting, was introduced. The fourth phase, from 1983 to 1995, saw the economy move away from targeting, reinforced by concerted import liberalization. The economy grew 8.7 percent annually during this period. Then came the Asian financial crisis, which hit Korea especially hard. In all likelihood, by this time the country had considerably closed the technological gap with advanced countries, so the scope for continued miracle-level growth was nearly exhausted. Consequently, the years 1996–2008 saw the growth rate decline to 4.4 percent, a level much closer to the growth rates in industrial countries.

In the following, I will discuss in greater detail the first four periods, with the greatest attention paid to the second, since it is the most controversial.

Reconstruction and Recovery Under Import Substitution: 1954–62

Estimates by the Korean government place civilian war damages in South Korea at $3 billion, almost equal to the estimated GNP for 1952 and 1953 combined. In addition, a staggering one million civilians are reported to have lost their lives.[5] Relying on whatever limited data are available, Frank, Kim, and Westphal conclude that the total industrial production in Korea in 1953 was "probably not much more than one-third of the 1940 level."[6]

Once the Korean War ended, reconstruction and recovery got under way. During 1954–62, the economy grew at an average annual rate of 4.2 percent. But the average growth rate during the last four years of this period, 3.4 percent, was substantially below the 4.8 percent achieved in the first five years. Since the population grew by 2.9 percent per annum during this period, the rise in per capita income was relatively small.

Table 11.2 shows the growth rates of GNP and its major components on an annual basis from 1954 to 1972. With an average annual growth rate of 11.6 percent, mining and manufacturing constituted the fastest-growing sector of the economy during 1954–62. But this growth too was heavily concentrated in the earlier years, perhaps due to the post–Korean War recovery. Whereas the sector grew 16.3 percent per annum during 1954–56, it grew only 9.3 percent per annum

Table 11.2 **Average annual growth rates in Korea, 1954–72**

Year	GNP	Agriculture, forestry, and fisheries	Mining and manufacturing	Social overhead and services
1954	5.5	7.6	11.2	2.5
1955	5.4	2.6	21.6	5.7
1956	0.4	−5.9	16.2	4.0
1957	7.7	9.1	9.7	5.8
1958	5.2	6.2	8.2	3.5
1959	3.9	−1.2	9.7	7.5
1960	1.9	−1.3	10.4	2.8
1961	4.8	11.9	3.6	−1.1
1962	3.1	−5.8	14.1	8.9
1963	8.8	8.1	15.7	7.4
1964	8.6	15.5	6.9	3.0
1965	6.1	−1.9	18.7	9.9
1966	12.4	10.8	15.6	12.6
1967	7.8	−5.0	21.6	13.8
1968	12.6	2.4	24.8	15.4
1969	15.0	12.5	19.9	14.6
1970	7.9	−0.9	18.2	8.9
1971	9.2	3.3	16.9	8.9
1972	7.0	1.7	15.0	5.8
1954–62	4.2	2.6	11.6	4.4
1963–72	9.5	4.7	17.3	10.0

Source: Frank, Kim, and Westphal 1975, table 2–4, p. 11.

during 1957–62. The late fifties and early sixties were clearly characterized by a slowdown.

Exports of goods and services during this period were small, varying between 1.1 percent of GNP in 1954 to 3.5 percent in 1962.[7] In 1953, exports of goods and services were 2 percent of GNP. This proportion fell to 1.1 percent in 1954 and did not return to the 1953 level until as late as 1959. Exports largely consisted of mining, agricultural, and fisheries products. Imports of goods and services were much larger, ranging from 8.8 percent of GNP in 1954 to 14.3 percent in 1957. The gap between imports and exports as proportions of GNP in

1957 was a gigantic 12.8 percentage points. Virtually all the gap was covered by foreign aid, principally from the United States. Food grains and manufactured goods had the largest share in imports.

As in Taiwan, the 1950s were characterized by policies usually associated with import-substitution industrialization.[8] The domestic currency was highly overvalued. Given that the resident U.N. military establishment was the major buyer of the domestic currency, such overvaluation made practical sense. To provide incentives to exporters and deal with balance-of-payments deficits, multiple exchange rates were instituted, with the rate varying according to the type of transaction and the source of foreign exchange.

The government imposed high tariffs on goods that had domestic substitutes but lower ones on those without such substitutes. The former largely consisted of finished consumer goods. Other things being the same, lower tariffs were applied to raw materials than to finished goods. Food grain and non-competing equipment and raw materials entered duty free. Several major import-substituting industries were also exempted from tariffs on machinery and intermediate inputs.

As the domestic currency became more and more overvalued, the government progressively relied on quantitative import restrictions to hold the line on the balance of payments. The import-licensing program was revised twice a year to adjust to the pressures arising from the balance of payments. Domestic prices of imports typically exceeded the tariff-inclusive price.

Four main incentives were available to exporters at different times during this period. First, beginning in 1955, exporters were allowed to sell their foreign exchange deposits, held at the Bank of Korea, to importers at the market exchange rate. Second, between 1951 and 1955, they were allowed to use a small part of the foreign exchange earned to import certain popular items not permitted otherwise. Third, the government provided export subsidies and preferential credit on a limited scale. Finally and most important, beginning in 1959, imports of intermediate inputs used in exports were permitted duty free.

Growth and Development Under Neutral Incentives: 1963–73

A student-led revolution ousted President Rhee on April 26, 1960. It led to the establishment of the parliamentary form of government, and Chang Myon emerged at its head as prime minister on August 13, 1960. The Myon government survived less than a year, however. On May 6, 1961, Park Chung-hee staged a coup and installed a military government. The military government ruled for a little less than three years. Under U.S. pressure, elections were held in December 1963 and Korea returned to the presidential form of government. Park won the election and went on to head a nominally civilian government as president of Korea until his assassination on October 27, 1979. Much of the economic transformation of Korea took place during the eighteen years under Park. We first consider the period 1963 to 1973.

Economic Transformation

The years 1963–73 saw not only an acceleration of growth over what it had been during the period 1954–62 but also a structural transformation in the economy. Trade expanded rapidly, the shares of industry in output and employment grew significantly, poverty fell perceptibly, and investment and savings saw a major surge. We consider each of these subjects in turn.

Growth

Table 11.2 gives the annual growth rates of GNP and major sectors at 1970 constant prices from 1954 to 1972. The average annual GDP growth rate accelerated from 4.2 percent during 1954–62 to 9.5 percent during 1963–72. While growth rates of all sectors accelerated during the latter period, the numbers in the table suggest that growth was propelled by industry, a key target of the reforms. Industrial growth began picking up in 1962 and averaged an impressive 17.3 percent during 1963–72.

Trade

Figure 11.1 shows the evolution of exports and imports of goods and services as proportions of GNP beginning in 1953 and continuing until 1972. Starting at an extremely low level, exports as a proportion of GNP began rising in 1957. But this rise was initially very gradual. A discernible sign of acceleration in the ratio appears for the first time in 1965. That year exports rose 40.6 percent in real terms, and their growth slowed only a tiny bit in the subsequent seven years. The average growth rate of exports of goods and services in real terms during the eight years from 1965 to 1972 was a gigantic 35.7 percent. Despite a very rapid growth in GDP during these same years, the exports-to-GDP ratio more than quadrupled between 1965 and 1972, rising from 5.2 to 21.3 percent.[9]

The imports-to-GDP ratio showed a significantly different pattern than exports until about 1965. Initially aid and subsequently external borrowing allowed this ratio to be consistently higher than the exports-to-GDP ratio. Since exports were tiny until the early 1960s, imports largely fluctuated with aid during those years. It is not until 1966 that a clear rising trend in the imports-to-GDP ratio emerged. By this time, aid had declined considerably and exports

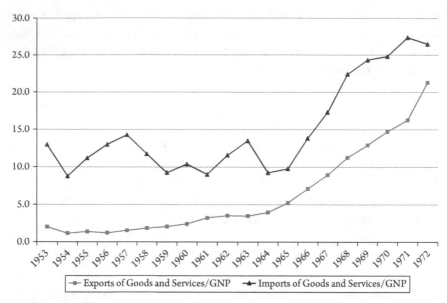

Figure 11.1 Exports and Imports of Goods and Services as Proportions of GNP.
Source: Author's construction using data in Frank, Kim, and Westphal 1975, table 2-7.

had begun to generate a significant and steady stream of revenues to finance the bulk of imports. In this sense, imports essentially followed aid in the early years and exports in the later ones, a point to which I will return in the context of the revisionist critique of Korea's growth experience.

The aggregate export data mask an important development during the early 1960s: while the definitive evidence of acceleration in the growth of exports at the aggregate level appears in 1965, the expansion in manufacturing exports, the key target of any outward-oriented strategy in the early stages of development, had been solidly under way even in 1961, the earliest year for which I am able to get data. Table 11.3, which shows the shares in total exports and the growth rates of exports of primary products and manufactures from 1961 to 1973, makes this point. Between 1961 and 1964, manufacturing exports grew at an average annual rate of 87.9 percent. This rate was higher than in any other subsequent four-year period. In 1961, the share of manufactures in total exports was 21.9 percent. It rose to 51.7 percent in 1963 and 62.3 percent in 1964. This transforming development remained hidden in the aggregate data until at least 1964 because agricultural exports, which accounted for 78.1 percent of total exports in 1961, grew at a slower average annual rate of 11.1 percent during 1962 and 1963. Only when agricultural exports grew 43.6 percent in 1964 did the total exports show a significant jump. Of course, by this time, manufactures had come to account for a large share in the total exports, so their rapid growth could be felt in the total exports. By 1972, the exports-to-GNP ratio had risen to 21.3 percent and manufactures came to account for 88.2 percent of total merchandise exports.

Table 11.3 **Shares of primary and manufacturing exports in total exports and their growth rates in Korea**

Year	Share of primary products	Share of manufactures	Growth in primary products	Growth in manufactures
1961	78.1	21.9	–	60.8
1962	73.0	27.0	23.6	62.8
1963	48.3	51.7	–1.4	185.0
1964	48.5	51.5	43.6	42.9
1965	37.7	62.3	16.2	80.4
1966	37.6	62.4	41.1	42.1
1967	29.9	70.1	11.8	57.3
1968	22.7	77.3	5.7	54.0
1969	21.0	79.0	30.1	43.5
1970	16.4	83.6	11.4	51.2
1971	14.0	86.0	15.0	38.5
1972	12.3	88.2	17.8	37.1
1973	11.7	88.3	71.2	80.2

Source: Excerpted from Frank, Kim, and Westphal 1975, table 6-2, p. 79.

Table 11.4 provides data on the evolution of some of the leading manufactured exports of Korea during the period under review. This table reveals two related facts. First, most of the products whose exports grew rapidly during the 1960s were labor intensive. These included plywood, woven cotton fabrics, clothing, footwear, and wigs. None of these items were subject to any kind of selective targeting. Second, exports of many of these products expanded rapidly. Between 1961 and 1963, plywood, woven cotton fabrics, and clothing together nearly quadrupled their share in the total exports. A revolution in the exports of labor-intensive products was thus already under way in the early 1960s. In the later years it only intensified, with new and unexpected items such as wigs and human hair emerging as major exports. It is remarkable that this item appeared on the list in 1964 for the first time and came to account for 10.1 percent of total exports by 1970.

Sectoral Outputs and Employment

The changes in the pattern of exports mirror those in output and employment. As in Taiwan, during the years of rapid growth the Korean economy underwent a dramatic structural transformation, with shares of agriculture

Table 11.4 **Shares of major manufactures in total exports, 1961–73**

Year	Total exports ($ million)	Plywood	Woven cotton fabrics	Plates and sheets of iron and steel	Electrical machinery and apparatus	Clothing	Footwear	Wigs and human hair
1961	42.9	2.8	2.1	1.2	0.0	0.0	0.0	0.0
1962	56.7	4.1	3.2	0.9	0.2	1.9	0.4	0.0
1963	84.4	7.5	5.1	9.8	1.1	5.5	0.8	0.0
1964	120.9	9.4	9.2	1.7	1.3	5.5	0.7	0.2
1965	180.5	10.0	5.8	5.7	1.8	11.5	2.3	1.3
1966	255.8	11.7	3.9	2.8	3.2	13.1	2.2	4.7
1967	358.6	10.2	3.5	0.3	2.6	16.5	2.3	6.3
1968	500.4	13.1	2.7	0.2	4.4	22.4	2.2	7.0
1969	702.8	11.3	2.6	0.5	6.0	22.9	1.5	8.6
1970	1,003.90	9.1	2.6	0.8	4.8	21.3	1.7	10.1
1971	1,352.00	9.2	2.3	1.5	5.5	22.5	2.8	5.2
1972	1,807.00	8.5	1.9	3.8	7.6	24.5	3.1	4.1
1973	3,254.20	8.3	1.7	4.0	10.6	23.0	3.3	2.5

Source: Excerpted from Frank, Kim, and Westphal 1975, table 6-3, p. 80.

in GDP and employment declining and those of manufacturing rising. Table 11.5 captures this transformation. The share of agriculture, forestry, and fisheries in Korea's GDP fell from 36.9 percent in 1960 to 24.9 percent in 1975. While the share of industry in general rose, the most dramatic gains were made by manufacturing, whose share rose from 13.6 percent in 1960 to 21 percent in 1970 and to 26.6 percent in 1975. In an economy that had been growing approximately 9 percent per year overall, the sharp rise in the share of manufacturing during 1960–75 implies a very rapid expansion of manufacturing in absolute terms.

Annual growth rates in mining and manufacturing are shown in Table 11.2. This sector had grown rapidly in the early 1950s as a part of the post–Korean War reconstruction but slowed down in the second half of the 1950s. A clear turnaround can be seen, however, beginning in 1962. With the sole exception of 1964, when it grew at just 6.9 percent, mining and manufacturing grew extremely rapidly in and after 1962, with the sector's average growth rate from 1962 to 1972 working out to be 17 percent.

These changes in sectoral output shares were also reflected in employment shares. According to Table 11.5, the employment share of manufacturing rose from

Table 11.5 **Sectoral shares in GDP and employment**

Year	Agriculture, forestry, and fisheries	Mining	Manufacturing	Other
A. GDP by sector (as percent of GDP)				
1960	36.9	2.1	13.6	47.4
1965	38.7	1.8	17.7	41.8
1970	25.8	1.3	21.0	51.9
1975	24.9	1.4	26.6	47.1
1980	15.1	1.4	30.6	52.9
1985	13.9	1.5	29.2	55.3
1990	9.1	0.5	29.2	61.2
B. Employment by sector (as percent of total employment)				
1960	68.3	0.3	1.5	29.9
1965	58.6	0.9	9.4	31.1
1970	50.4	1.1	13.1	35.4
1975	45.7	0.5	18.6	35.2
1980	34.0	0.9	21.6	43.5
1985	24.9	1.0	23.4	50.7
1990	18.3	0.4	26.9	54.4

Source: Yoo 1997, table 2.

1.5 percent in 1960 to 9.4 percent in 1965, 13.1 percent in 1970, and 18.6 percent in 1975. The share of agriculture, forestry, and fisheries declined from 68.3 percent in 1960 to 58.6 percent in 1965 and 45.7 percent in 1975. This shift in employment was accompanied by substantial increases in wages—approximately 7 to 8 percent annually during 1961–81. Thus, Korea was entirely transformed from a primarily agricultural nation to a primarily industrial one in a short period of time.

Poverty

Accelerated growth led to a rapid decline in poverty. At the poverty line of 121,000 won per month for a household of five at 1981 prices, the proportion of households living in poverty fell from 40.9 percent in 1965 to 14.8 percent in 1976. Poverty dropped in both rural and urban areas. In rural areas, the proportion declined from 35.8 percent to 11.7 percent between 1965 and 1976, and in urban areas, it fell from 54.9 percent to 18.1 percent.

The reduction in poverty was almost entirely the result of growth pulling the people at the bottom of the income ladder into gainful employment at ever-increasing wages. This is evidenced by the fact that Korea's most explicit anti-poverty program, the public assistance program, covered only 375,000 people at its peak in 1975. The program was introduced in 1961 and provided modest income support. As in Taiwan, growth in Korea had been driven by rapid expansion of labor-intensive manufacturing, which paved the way for workers to migrate from agriculture to manufacturing in large numbers. This process was also accompanied by rapidly rising wages in manufacturing.[10]

Savings and Investment

As in Taiwan, rising ratios of investment and savings to GDP accompanied the transformation of the economy (see Figure 11.2). In 1960, investment was 10.9 percent of GDP. With the domestic savings rate just 0.8 percent of GDP, foreign aid filled much of the gap. As foreign aid fell, however, the savings rate picked up, though it always remained below the investment rate, with rising foreign debt financing much of the gap in later years.

The key point, however, is that acceleration in the rate of investment went hand in hand with the acceleration in GDP growth. The first half of the 1960s saw an approximately 4 percentage point jump in the investment-to-GDP

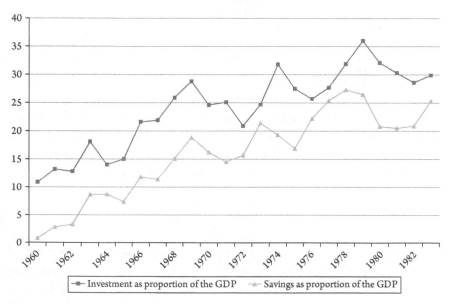

Figure 11.2 Savings and Investment as Proportions of GDP in Korea, 1960–85.
Source: Author's construction based on Bank of Korea data as reported in Harvie and Lee 2003, table 1.

ratio relative to 1960, with its value rising to 15 percent in 1965. Within the following five years, there was yet another jump, this time of approximately 10 percentage points. In 1970 and 1971, the investment rate stood at approximately 25 percent of GDP. Savings also rose, though they remained significantly below the investment rate, with the difference made up by foreign loans.

Policy Reforms

The export incentives put in place by 1959 had made considerable progress toward giving exporters free trade status. Two key problems remained. One, the quantitative restrictions and import licensing got in the way of entirely free access to imported inputs. And two, though the multiple exchange rate system allowed exporters to reap the benefits of the premium on foreign exchange in the open market, the system remained inefficient, with the official exchange rate highly overvalued.

Both the Myon civilian government and the Park military government were reformist.[11] The civilian government attempted to unify the exchange rate system and, as a part of that effort, devalued the hwan from 650 to 1000 hwan per dollar in January 1961 and to 1300 hwan per dollar in February 1961. In terms of the new won, which replaced the hwan in June 1962 at the rate of ten hwan per new won, the exchange rate moved from 65 won to 100 won per dollar in January 1961 and 130 won per dollar in February 1962. The reform remained partial under Myon, but the successor military government quickly completed it, fully unifying the exchange rates in June 1961.

Domestically, the military government also reformed the budget process, the taxation machinery, and the currency system. The currency reform, which involved replacing the hwan by the new won in 1962, was not entirely successful, however. Partially because of this but also because of the balance-of-payments pressures resulting from large food grain imports in the wake of a drought in 1962, the multiple exchange rate system was reintroduced in 1963 with import controls strengthened. The system of granting exporters foreign exchange certificates that could be sold for a premium to importers in the open market was reintroduced.

The civilian government, which came to the helm at the beginning of 1964, continued the reform process. In May 1964 it devalued the won by 50 percent, from 130 to 257 won per dollar. Initially the government continued to issue foreign exchange certificates, but in March 1965 those were discontinued and a single, floating exchange rate was adopted. After bouts of inflation in 1962 and 1963, Korea had achieved relative price stability by this time.[12] Moreover, it also secured a $9.3 million standby loan for a foreign exchange stabilization fund. Therefore, through intervention, the Bank of Korea was able to stabilize the nominal exchange rate around 270 won per dollar until 1967. In the subsequent years, the won depreciated steadily, averaging approximately 310.7 won per dollar in August 1970.[13]

In 1962, the business income tax rate on foreign exchange earnings was reduced to half the rate applicable to business income from other sources. As previously noted, a duty exemption on imported inputs had existed since 1959. In the early 1960s, exporters were also given full exemption from indirect tax on inputs and export sales. Finally, in 1965, all export incentives were extended to indirect exporters. Under this provision, producers of intermediate inputs used in exports could avail themselves of the whole set of export incentives available to direct exporters. In 1966, tariff exemptions on machinery and equipment imports were extended on both direct and indirect exports.

Other export incentives included assured availability of credit at preferential rates to cover working capital in proportion to the export activity; generous wastage allowances on imported inputs for export production; and, beginning in 1967, reduced prices of electricity and railway freight. The generous wastage allowance on imported inputs effectively allowed exporters to get the inputs duty free for a part of the output sold in the domestic market. It is estimated that these incentives amounted to 8.4 percent of the value of merchandise exports in 1968.[14]

Alongside these measures, in 1962, Korea also set up a firm-level export targeting system. Export targets were agreed upon between the government and the firms. A failure to meet the targets resulted in heavy administrative sanctions. But in the vast majority of the cases, exports exceeded the targets by a wide margin, so the targets turned out to be non-binding. Because large firms were at an advantage in meeting the quality and timely-delivery standards in the world markets, and because a small number of large firms is easier for the government to monitor than a large number of small firms, the emphasis on exports led to a greater expansion of large firms. The government reinforced this advantage by giving the larger firms greater preference in credit.[15]

Following the 1964 currency devaluation, the balance-of-payments situation improved considerably and cleared the path to import liberalization. The number of items eligible for unrestricted imports, which had dropped from 1,124 in the first half of 1964 to below 500 in the second half, steadily rose in the following years, reaching 3,082 by the first half of 1967. A major reform was then undertaken the same year and the positive-list approach to restrictions was replaced by a negative-list approach. Under the positive-list system, any item not listed as a permissible import was automatically presumed prohibited. Under the negative-list system, items prohibited were to be listed, with unlisted items automatically presumed as permitted. This reform considerably reduced the scope of import controls.[16]

Alongside the shift to the negative-list system, a tariff reform was attempted in 1967. But it led to very few changes in the end. With minor differences, the tariff structure put in place in January 1950 and marginally revised in 1957 remained operative during this period. Under the system instituted in 1950, no duties were imposed on food grains, non-competing equipment, and raw material imports required for industrial, educational, cultural, and sanitation facilities. A 10 percent duty was applied to essential goods for which domestic supply was a small proportion of the total demand. The same rate also applied to unfinished goods not produced in Korea. Unfinished goods produced in Korea were subject to a 20 percent duty. Finished goods were subject to a 30 percent duty if not produced in Korea and 40 percent if produced there. Finally, duties on semi-luxury items ranged from 50 to 90 percent and those on luxury items exceeded 100 percent. The adjustments in 1957 led to a 4.1 percent increase in the simple average of tariff rates.[17]

Neutrality of the Policy Regime

We may now ask two key questions: How did various incentives and disincentives add up relative to the free trade regime? And were the export incentives neutral or biased in favor of some sectors over others? Though the available evidence is based on detailed calculations relating to a single year, 1968, Westphal notes, "I am quite confident that they are representative of the central tendencies of Korean industrial policy since the reforms in the early 1960s. I do not, for example, find any fundamental differences—relative to the stylized facts being portrayed here—between them and the estimates for 1978."[18]

With respect to the first question, the calculations show that when the economy-wide implications of all interventions are considered, the policy regime exhibited a slight bias in favor of exports relative to what would have prevailed under free trade.[19] With respect to the second question, they show that the export incentives were more or less neutral except in the case of import-competing products, defined as items for which 10 percent or more of the domestic supply came from imports. With import-competing products accounting for only 10.6 percent of the total manufacturing value added in 1968, the overall bias was quite small.

Westphal offers the bottom line on the neutrality of export subsidies in these words: "Did these interventions do more than simply offset distortions arising from policies directed toward other objectives? Or to put the question another way, did these selectively administered interventions have a non-neutral impact? The available evidence indicates that with one possible exception, they generally did not. The possible exception arises in the case of infant industries being promoted by additional means of selective intervention."[20] Westphal goes on to note that selective infant industry promotion until 1972 was limited: it applied only to cement, fertilizer, and petroleum refining in the early 1960s and to steel and petrochemicals in the late 1960s and early 1970s. Contrary to the popular impression often conveyed by free trade critics, industrial targeting did not become important in Korea until 1973. Any shift toward capital-intensive exports prior to 1973 was largely driven by rising real wages.

The Real Effective Exchange Rate for Exporters

The real effective exchange rate for exports provides an overall measure of incentives available to exporters. The calculations spanning from 1955 to 1970 are depicted in Figure 11.3. The won depreciated (and the U.S. dollar appreciated) sufficiently in 1958 and 1959 that at constant prices a dollar's worth of exports brought 26.6 percent more revenue in 1959 than in 1957. Although the won regained some of its lost value through appreciation during 1961– 63, it depreciated again in 1964 such that a dollar's worth of exports fetched 18.5 percent higher revenue in constant-price won that year than in 1957. In the subsequent years for which the real effective exchange rate calculations

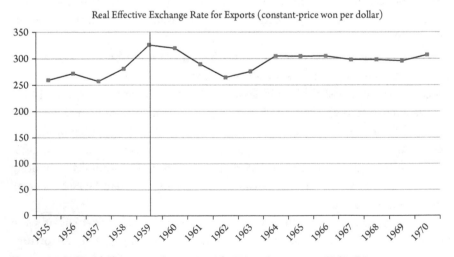

Real Effective Exchange Rate for Exports (constant-price won per dollar)

Figure 11.3 Real Effective Exchange Rate for Exports in Korea, 1962–75.
Source: Author's construction based on Frank, Kim, and Westphal 1975, table 6-5.

are available, export revenue per dollar's worth of exports remained minimally 15 percent above its 1957 level. Therefore, going by the real effective exchange rate calculations, it can be concluded that except during 1961–63, the real effective exchange rate offered 15 to 26.6 percent more revenue per dollar's worth of exports from 1959 to 1970 than in 1957.

Connecting Policies and Outcomes

The policies and outcomes in Korea closely resemble those in Taiwan. In this respect, much of the analysis of Taiwan applies to Korea. Regardless of the causation, the importance of rising trade openness (as measured by policy changes) and trade outcomes to sustaining high growth rates cannot be denied. From the early 1960s to the early 1970s, the policy regime moved progressively toward greater outward orientation. The trade-to-GDP ratio rose from 17 percent in 1963 to 47.8 percent in 1972. Therefore, by the time the government seriously got down to the targeted promotion of heavy and chemical industry (HCI), Korea was already a very open economy.

The success of outward-oriented policies in Korea had origins quite similar to those in Taiwan. Korea was politically stable and the government was committed, effective, and credible.[21] Entrepreneurs trusted the policy changes announced by the government and responded with investments in profitable sectors. Like Taiwan, Korea also had very flexible labor markets and a disciplined workforce. Education was accorded high priority, with many schools running multiple shifts to overcome space shortages. An important reform in 1965 raised deposit interest rates to encourage savings. This change plus rising incomes contributed to increased savings over time. By and large, the government also provided a stable macroeconomic environment, responding with appropriate stabilization measures whenever inflation showed signs of rising above normal rates.

In terms of market-driven development versus the success of interventionism, including selective targeting, at least for the period 1963–73, evidence strongly favors the former. As previously discussed, industrial targeting during this period was limited to a very small number of sectors. As for other policy interventions, careful calculations for 1968 led Westphal to conclude that when all interventions are considered, the policy regime's bias in favor of exports or import-competing products was minimal.

Based on the relative abundance of labor, we would predict that Korea would export relatively labor-intensive products. At a very crude level, this can be seen in Figure 11.4, which plots the evolution of the shares of the labor- and capital-intensive exports in total exports. The labor-intensive exports are defined as the sum of one-digit SITC-6 (manufactured goods classified chiefly by material) and SITC-8 (miscellaneous manufactured articles) exports, while the

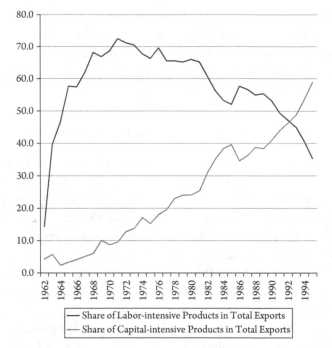

Figure 11.4 Shares of Labor- and Capital-Intensive Exports in the Total Exports of Korea, 1962–95. Source: United Nations Commodity Trade Statistics online (accessed June 5, 2010).

capital-intensive exports refer to SITC-7 (machinery and transport equipment) exports.[22] Consistent with other evidence, labor-intensive exports rose rapidly and came to account for 72.5 percent of Korea's merchandise exports by 1971. Of course, as Korea accumulated capital and its capital-to-labor endowment ratio rose, its capital-intensive exports expanded as well. Interestingly, the labor-intensive exports had peaked in 1971, which was at least a year before the HCI drive even began.

The factor-intensity calculations for exports and imports by Frank, Kim, and Westphal reinforce this pattern of specialization. Manufacturing exports exhibited a rising intensity of labor relative to capital between 1960 and 1968.[23] Based on direct factor usage, the labor-capital ratio (thousand person-years per billion won of capital at world prices) in manufacturing exports increased from 2.72 in 1960 to 3.55 in 1968. The total (direct plus indirect) labor-capital ratio exhibited this same pattern with much higher labor-capital ratios. The corresponding labor-capital ratios in manufactures imports were significantly lower.

The final piece of evidence along these lines is the large shift in the labor force from agriculture to industry. As in Taiwan, the manufacturing sector rapidly grew in Korea, absorbing increasing amounts of labor released by agriculture. As Table 11.5 shows, the employment share of manufacturing increased from 1.5 percent in 1960 to 13.1 percent in 1970 and 18.6 percent in 1975.

One further question concerns whether, in addition to helping sustain the high growth in the longer run, the switch to outward-oriented policies also provided the trigger for acceleration in growth. Once we focus on the exports of manufactures instead of total exports, we find that the case for export-oriented policies as the trigger turns out to be compelling. Rodrik's hypothesis that the government engineered an investment boom by solving the coordination failure problem with exports expanding passively to finance machinery imports fails to pass muster.

At the aggregate level, the break in GNP growth from low to high rate occurs in 1963 (see Table 11.2). But recall that with near-free-trade status granted to exporters by 1959, acceleration in the growth of manufacturing exports had begun as early as 1960. The voluminous growth in these exports during the first half of the 1960s could not have occurred without substantial investments moving into the sectors producing them. This is partially confirmed by the high rates of growth in the mining and manufacturing sector during 1960–63 (except in 1961). It is true that the 8.6 percent growth in 1964 was supported by 15.5 percent growth in agriculture, but by this time mining and manufacturing were already pulling the economy forward in a major way. Indeed, in the following year, 1965, growth in agriculture turned negative. Yet, thanks to the 18.7 percent growth in mining and manufacturing, GNP grew a solid 6.1 percent.

As in the case of Taiwan, critics point out that exports, especially those of manufactures, were too tiny to have such a major impact on growth. Once again, it must be remembered that it is the size of the exportable sectors (rather than exports) and the scope for the expansion of exports (rather than their initial level) that matter. Given the vast size of world markets, manufacturing exports were well placed to offer almost unlimited scope for expansion. It is unlikely that manufactures growth in the first half of the 1960s could have been as robust as it was without the export market being a major factor.

Outward Orientation with Industrial Targeting: 1974–82

In January 1973, Korea decided to formally launch a policy of selective targeting of HCI. The policy was initiated with a presidential announcement and remained in force until it was formally ended through the announcement of the Comprehensive Stabilization Program in April 1979. The HCI drive aimed to develop industries that were seen as strategic, including steel, non-ferrous metals, automobiles, ship-building, heavy machinery, and industrial electronics, among others.

At least three factors contributed to the switch in policy. First, in 1971, the U.S. military cut its forces in Korea by a third. The Korean government saw this move as the first phase of a full military withdrawal and felt the need to develop certain strategic industries for defense purposes. Second, throughout the 1960s and early 1970s, Korea had experienced large and rising absolute trade deficits. Though exports had grown faster than imports, since imports had grown from a much larger base, the trade deficit kept rising. One element in the HCI drive was to contain this trade deficit by slowing down the growth of imports. Finally, Korean policymakers also felt that rising competition from other East Asian countries in light manufacturing and a growing protectionist sentiment in the developed countries against labor-intensive exports necessitated a shift into other sectors.[24]

The most important instrument deployed to stimulate the targeted industries was directed bank credit at low and sometimes negative real interest rates. The government directed the commercial banks, which were largely state owned, to make loans to the favored industries and projects. Almost 60 percent of the bank loans and 75 percent of manufacturing investment went to targeted sectors over the course of the HCI drive. A substantial part of the investment was financed by external borrowing, which led to the expansion of foreign debt from 25 percent of GNP in 1970 to 49 percent in 1980.[25]

Other policy instruments deployed to promote targeted industries included tax and trade policy concessions.[26] The tax concessions included tax holidays, accelerated depreciation, and temporary tax credits for investment. The government also introduced a number of laws to accommodate these concessions. On the trade policy front, there was some reversal of the liberalization. In particular, some products were put back on the negative list and therefore subject to government approval for imports.

The GDP growth rate during 1974–82, 6.9 percent (see Table 11.1), was respectable but significantly below that achieved during the prior period. Growth in trade also slowed down considerably. Exports of goods and services grew 32.1 percent during 1963–73 but only 14 percent during 1974–82. Growth in manufacturing output and employment also saw some slowdown.

Return to Neutral Policies and Liberalization: 1983–95

The government announced the Comprehensive Stabilization Program on April 17, 1979. This effectively ended the HCI drive and provided for tighter fiscal and monetary management in the short run and liberalization in the long run. But President Park was assassinated on October 26, 1979, leaving the country in political turmoil. Prime Minister Choi Kyu-Hwa became acting president but was replaced by General Chun Doo Hwan under martial law in May 1980. Alongside this political turmoil, the second oil price crisis and a major crop failure resulting from a cold spell in the summer of 1980 added to the country's woes. The consumer price index rose 28.7 percent in 1980.

Chun was inaugurated as president in March 1981 and quickly embarked upon a program of economic stabilization and liberalization. A key element in the policy was to return the economy to a neutral regime, as had been the case until early 1970s. Having been held at 484 won to the dollar since 1974, the domestic currency had become overvalued. It was devalued to 660 won per dollar in 1980. In the following years, the government let the won depreciate in small increments, with the exchange rate successively changing to 701, 749, 796, 827, and 890 won per dollar over the following five years.[27] Alongside this, other stabilization measures were taken that helped bring inflation down to the levels experienced in the second half of the 1960s and early 1970s.

The 1980s also saw progress in trade and financial liberalization in Korea. While there had been some minimal trade liberalization in 1979, the process stalled due to the balance-of-payments difficulties in the early 1980s. But in 1983 the government set up the Tariff Reform Committee, which outlined a phased program of import liberalization. The recommendations of this committee resulted in a reduction in the average nominal tariff rate from 24 percent in 1983 to 19 percent in 1988 and 11 percent in 1990. Many of the tariff exemptions on imports by the strategic industries were also withdrawn in 1984. U.S. pressure played an important role in this round of import liberalization.

The promotion of strategic industries through preferential credit and tax treatment also came to an end in the early 1980s. Preferential interest rates that had been applicable to strategic industries and exporters were officially abolished in June 1982. The list of industries classified as strategic was trimmed and the concessions now took the form of tax breaks on technology development. The 1980s saw a major drive for upgrading of technology, principally through research and development by private firms. One policy instrument deployed for this purpose was the liberalization of foreign direct investment (FDI). In 1980, Korea liberalized regulations to facilitate FDI as a means of upgrading technology. In 1984, it also switched from a positive-list approach to a negative-list approach, meaning that sectors not specifically included on the negative list were now open to FDI.

Finally, starting in the early 1980s, Korea also undertook substantial financial sector liberalization. The measures included privatization of commercial banks, unrestricted entry of non-bank financial institutions, relaxation of directed credit, abolition of preferential interest rates for strategic or export industries, the introduction of new financial instruments, and the opening of the financial sector to FDI. While the government continued to exert controls over the sector in a variety of ways, there is no denying that the direction was toward liberalization and greater autonomy. The outcome was a rapid growth of the sector, with total credit rising from 68 percent of GNP in 1980 to 94 percent in 1984.

Overall growth in this immediate post-HCI era returned to the pre-HCI levels. GNP grew at a rate of 8.7 percent during 1983–95.

Responses to Critics

The responses to critics offered in the context of Taiwan in the previous chapter largely apply to Korea as well. Rather than repeat what has been said, in the following I will mainly attempt to answer questions directly connected to Korea. Rodrik argues that while the real effective exchange rate for exports was most favorable in 1959–60, the export spurt was observed in 1964, when the level of export incentives was "no more than 10 percent higher than in the preceding couple of years."[28] There are two problems with this argument. One, an analysis of manufacturing exports in general and labor-intensive exports in particular (see Tables 11.3 and 11.4, respectively) shows that exports of the products at which the reforms aimed grew at ultra-high rates in the early 1960s. The average annual growth rate of manufacturing exports during the four years from 1961 to 1964 was a gigantic 87.86 percent, with the result that the share of manufactures in total exports rose from 21.9 percent in 1961 to 62.3 percent in 1964. Two, Rodrik greatly understates the profitability of labor-intensive exports in 1964–65: revenue received in constant-price local currency for each dollar's worth of exports in each of these years was more than 18 percent higher than in 1957 and more than 15 percent higher than in 1962.

One additional issue with the Korea-specific context concerns industrial targeting during the HCI drive. There is no doubt that the HCI drive speeded up the development of a set of capital-intensive industries, thus producing a pattern of industrialization in the 1970s different from what a neutral set of policies would have produced. But it remains true that the growth rate of 6.9 percent during 1973–82, the period during which the policy was pursued, was significantly lower than in the preceding period as well as the following period, when more neutral policies were in place. Economists David Dollar and Kenneth Sokoloff provide more direct evidence of the relatively poor performance of the highly capital-intensive sectors supported by the HCI drive. They note, "It is interesting that, of the industries supported by the HCI program, it is the very capital-intensive ones that exhibit poor TFP [total factor productivity] growth, while those of medium and light intensity generally show high TFP growth."[29] These authors find strong evidence of a negative correlation between capital deepening and TFP growth.

Eventually, many of the industries promoted under the HCI drive came to thrive. This has led some pro-protection advocates to claim vindication of the HCI drive. For example, in a 2007 exchange on the Economists' Forum of the *Financial Times,* when I argued that the Korean growth rate had dropped during the heyday of the HCI drive, Ha-Joon Chang countered that this criticism could have held up in the early 1980s, when many of the HCI industries were in trouble and Ian Little first offered it. But this was no longer the case, since the industries promoted under the 1970s HCI drive—steel, shipbuilding, automobile, and electronics—were now a huge success.

This kind of defense of targeting once again gets back to the post hoc fallacy that I discussed in the context of the infant industry argument. One could equally argue that it is the return to the more neutral policies in the 1980s that forced the sectors targeted in the 1970s to shed their inefficient parts and become competitive. Furthermore, as capital became more abundant in Korea, these or similar industries would have successfully developed even absent the HCI drive. To convincingly argue the case for protection, Chang must show that the benefit-cost ratio was higher under promotion than would have been the case had the development of the same or similar industries been left to a more neutral set of policies. The success of an industry at some point in time can hardly qualify as scholarly evidence of the success of the policy promoting it twenty years earlier. Proper evidence must address the issue of whether the promotion plausibly led to an outcome superior to what would have been obtained in its absence.

Concluding Remarks

The role of openness in the making and sustaining of the Taiwanese and Korean miracles has been seriously questioned by some analysts. Therefore, I have discussed these two cases in detail. The presence of interventions and protection in these cases during the early decades of high growth are no more in dispute than in the cases of China and India. But, as in China and India, the general movement of the economies was toward increased openness and a reduced role for government, at least until the early 1970s. Korea had a short period of reversal beginning in 1973 when an aggressive effort at import substitution was made, but it was also accompanied by a decline in the growth rate.

Korea introduced several export incentives beginning in 1958, which led exports of manufactures to take off in the early 1960s. Frank, Kim, and Westphal provide data on manufactured exports beginning in 1961, which show that these exports grew at an annual average rate of 87.9 percent during 1961–64. The share of plywood in total exports tripled and that of woven cotton fabrics quadrupled during these four years. Clothing exports made their debut in 1962 and rose to 11.5 percent of total exports by 1965. This growth in exports continued with the result that manufacturing exports rose from 21.9 percent of total exports in 1961 to 62.3 percent in 1965 and 88.2 percent in 1972. The exports-to-GDP ratio rose from 3.2 percent in 1961 to 21.3 percent in 1972. Alongside that, output and employment shares of manufactures rose as well, with the former rising from 13.6 percent in 1960 to 26.6 percent in 1975 and the latter from 1.5 percent to 18.6 percent over the same period.

Citing evidence, I have argued that though the government in Korea intervened heavily, its interventions were broadly mutually cancelling, at least until the early 1970s. As Westphal notes, the outcome did not deviate significantly from what a neutral regime would have produced. Sectors that showed the best performance on the export front were invariably labor intensive and were not subject to selective targeting until 1973.

I have offered reasons the criticisms by free trade skeptics do not stand up to close scrutiny. Rodrik has argued that since incentives were introduced in the late 1950s and the exports-to-GDP ratio did not rise significantly in the early 1960s, outward-oriented policies could not have been behind the growth spurt. I point out, however, that Rodrik makes this argument on the basis of slow growth in the ratio of *total* exports to GDP. Once we look at manufacturing exports separately, we find that they grew handsomely during the early 1960s.

Rodrik has also argued that since exports as a proportion of GDP were tiny in the early 1960s, they could not have been behind the spurt in growth. I point out, however, that the effect of incentives must be measured not by the level of exports in the initial equilibrium but by the impact they have in terms of moving resources into existing and potential exportable sectors on the margin. In Korea, the incentives not only led to a sizable expansion of the existing export products but also turned some products not previously exported into exports. For example, neither clothing nor wigs and human hair were among Korea's exports in 1961. The first of these appeared on the list in 1962 and came to account for 23 percent of the total exports in 1973. The latter two appeared for the first time in 1964 and expanded to more than 10 percent of the total exports by 1970.

To conclude, once we look at the evidence carefully, Korea supports the case for outward orientation rather than protection, interventionism, and infant industry protection. When relying on the cases of Taiwan and Korea for their critique of free trade, the critics have looked at the evidence only superficially.

Notes

1. Under the World Bank classification, a country with per capita income between $3,125 and $9,655 at 1996 prices is classified as an upper-middle-income country. Korea's per capita income in 1987 had reached $3,248 at current prices (Harvie and Lee 2003). At 1996 prices, this figure would be significantly higer.
2. Frank, Kim, and Westphal 1975.
3. This section draws heavily on Frank, Kim, and Westphal 1975, ch. 2.
4. Additional controversies arise from industrial targeting, which was largely concentrated in the third period, but they are of lesser significance in my view.
5. Frank, Kim, and Westphal 1975, 11.
6. Frank, Kim, and Westphal 1975, 9.
7. These data are from Frank, Kim, and Westphal 1975, table 2-7, p. 15. Beginning from 1961, we have continuous up-to-date trade data available from the WDI. Trade-to-GDP ratios for the early 1960s in the WDI are higher than those in Frank, Kim, and Westphal 1975.
8. This discussion is solely based on Westphal and Kim 1982.
9. The series depicted in Figure 11.1 is taken from Frank, Kim, and Westphal 1975, table 2-7. These series show slightly different levels of the ratios than those reported by the WDI. But the trends in the two series are similar.
10. Poverty estimates and other information in this section can be found in Kwon and Yi 2008, tables 1 and 2.
11. Frank, Kim, and Westphal 1975, 42.
12. Very expansionary fiscal policy by the military government in 1961 and 1962 had led to high inflation in 1962 and 1963.
13. Frank, Kim, and Westphal 1975, ch. 4 and table 3-1.
14. Westphal and Kim 1982, table 8.2.
15. Harvie and Lee 2003, 269.
16. See Frank, Kim, and Westphal 1975, 48–49, for further details.
17. I have taken the information on tariff rates from Frank, Kim, and Westphal 1975, 36–37. The rest of the discussion in this section relies on Westphal and Kim 1982, 214–16.
18. Westphal 1990, 49–50. For the calculations reported in the text, Westphal draws on Westphal and Kim 1982. The estimates for 1978 mentioned in the quotation by Westphal are from Nam 1981.
19. See Westphal 1990, table 1.
20. See Westphal 1990, 46.
21. Westphal 1990, 58, notes that prior to the reforms, rent-seeking in relation to import licensing and tariff exemptions had provided an important source of revenue for businessmen and government officials. To convince them that he meant business, "President Park had a number of preeminent businessmen arrested shortly after he came to power, and then threatened them with the confiscation of their ill-gotten wealth." Park restored them to grace after they agreed to employ their wealth in development activities.
22. Korea's leading manufacturing exports during 1961–73, such as plywood, clothing, wigs, and cotton fabrics, all fall under one of the SITC-6 and SITC-8 categories.
23. Frank, Kim, and Westphal 1975, table 10-10.
24. This paragraph draws on Yoo 1997.
25. Harvie and Lee 2003, 271.
26. Yoo 1997, 6.
27. Harvie and Lee 2003, table 1.
28. Rodrik 1995, 62.
29. Dollar and Sokoloff 1990, 322.

PART IV

MIRACLES OF TODAY

12

India

From Near Autarky to Near Free Trade

India won its independence from the British on August 15, 1947, and adopted a democratic constitution on January 26, 1950. It launched the First Five-Year Plan to kick off its development program in earnest in the fiscal year 1951/52.[1] During the sixty years ending in fiscal 2011/12, the country has gone through extended periods of high and low protection and experienced both near-autarkic and near-free-trade regimes. It offers an excellent case study of the relationship between openness, on the one hand, and growth and poverty alleviation, on the other.

As in other countries, trade policy changes in India have not come about in isolation. Instead, they have taken place alongside policy changes in other areas. Therefore, trade policies cannot be shown to have a direct causal effect on growth and poverty alleviation at the aggregate level. Nevertheless, evidence in two forms can still be provided. First, at the aggregate level, there is a compelling case that autarkic policies are at the heart of any explanation of slow growth and stagnant poverty ratios in the first three decades. Symmetrically, a switch to sustained liberalization was essential to sustaining rapid growth and poverty alleviation in the subsequent decades. Second, some firm-level and state-level studies show a direct link between outward orientation and faster growth and poverty alleviation.

GDP growth estimates for India, calculated with a single year, 2004/5, as the base, span from 1951/52 to 2011/12. Beginning in 2012/13, official growth rates are based on a revised series, which switches the base year to 2011/12 while also making some methodological changes. Keeping this in view, I confine the analysis in this chapter to the years 1951/52 to 2011/12. I divide this sixty-year period into five distinct phases. The first two of these phases were broadly characterized by slow growth, stagnant poverty ratios, and near-autarkic trade policies. In contrast, the last three phases were characterized by declining trade barriers, rising growth rates, and significant poverty alleviation. The following sections summarize the evidence on growth and poverty during these phases and provide a detailed discussion of trade and related policies. I then turn to the link between performance and outcome at aggregate and micro levels, a critical examination of assertions by pro-protection critics, and concluding remarks.

Growth and Poverty

My discussion of growth and poverty in this section is brief principally because I have provided extensive details in an earlier book.[2] For example, I do not discuss in detail why I divide the sixty-year history into five phases in the way I do. Instead, I briefly present the comparative performance of the economy during the five phases in terms of growth and poverty alleviation.

The five phases span 1951–65, 1965–81, 1981–88, 1988–2003, and 2003–12.[3] Figure 12.1 shows the evolution of GDP from 1950/51 to 2011/12 with growth rates during the five phases noted in the top part of the figure.[4] From less than 1 percent per annum in the entire first half of the twentieth century, the GDP growth rate accelerated to 4.1 percent during 1951–65 (phase I) but dropped to 3.2 percent during 1965–81 (phase II). Growth recovered to 4.6 percent—half a percentage point above the level achieved in the first phase—during 1981–88 (phase III). The growth rate then steadily climbed up to 5.9 percent during 1988–2003 (phase IV) and to 8.3 percent during 2003–12

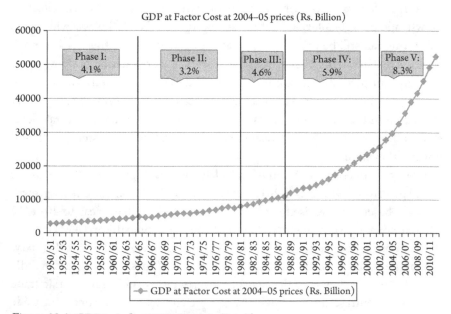

Figure 12.1 GDP in India, 1951–2012, in Five Phases.

(phase V). The global financial crisis brought down the growth rate in 2008/9 to 6.7 percent, but it rose back to 8.6 percent in 2009/10. Taking the last two phases together, the growth rate during 1988–2013 was 6.7 percent.

Growth rates in GDP per capita show similar variation during the five phases. The rate accelerated to 2 percent during phase I but decelerated to 0.9 percent during phase II. It then grew at ever-increasing rates: 2.4, 3.8, and 6.7 percent per year during 1981–88, 1988–2003, and 2003–13, respectively. Not only did GDP grow more rapidly during the later years, the rate of population growth also fell.

Changes in the poverty ratio—the proportion of the population living below the official poverty line—in the initial phases reflect both a low *initial* per capita income and meager growth in it *subsequently*. The country saw virtually no change in long-run poverty ratios until at least the mid-1970s. Figure 12.2 shows poverty ratios from 1951/52 to 1973/74. The poverty ratio during this period fluctuated with weather: good monsoons brought the ratio down and droughts took it back up with virtually no change in the trend ratio. The proportions of the poor in the 1950s and the first half of the 1970s hardly differed.

Major breaks in the poverty ratios appeared only during phases III–V. Because we lack poverty ratios at comparable poverty lines over the entire period, I concentrate below on the years 1993/94, 2004/5, and 2011/12. These

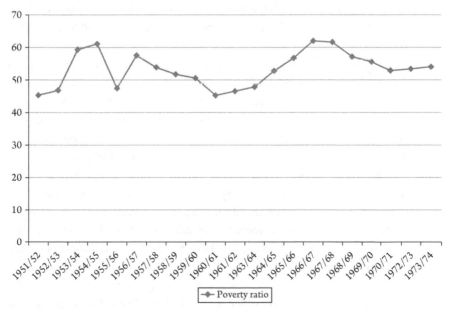

Figure 12.2 The Poverty Ratio, 1951/52 to 1973/74.
Source: Author's construction based on Datt 1998, table 1.

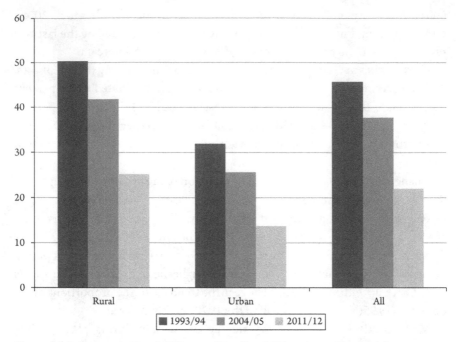

Figure 12.3 Poverty in Rural, Urban, and Rural and Urban Areas Combined.
Source: Author's construction based on estimates in Panagariya and More 2014.

are all post-reform years. We have extensive estimates for these years to illustrate some of the points made earlier in the context of the broader discussion
on poverty.

Figure 12.3 shows the poverty ratios in rural, urban, and rural and urban areas
combined in the years 1993/94, 2004/5, and 2011/12. Three points stand out.
First, poverty has steadily declined in both rural and urban areas and therefore
the country as a whole. Second, the decline in poverty from 1993/94 to 2004/5
is significantly smaller than that from 2004/5 to 2011/12. Taking into account
the fact that the former period spans eleven years and the latter only seven, the
annual decline in poverty is substantially higher in the second period. Recall
that this period is also characterized by a substantially higher rate of growth.
Therefore, faster growth is associated with an accelerated decline in poverty.
Finally, though rural poverty is higher than urban poverty, the decline in the
former has been sharper, and so the gap between the rural and urban poverty
ratios has shrunk.

Figure 12.4 separates out the socially disadvantaged groups known as the
Scheduled Castes (SC) and Scheduled Tribes (ST) in India. Once again, each
group has seen a steady decline in poverty during the period covered. Poverty
ratios are the highest among the ST, followed by the SC and the general

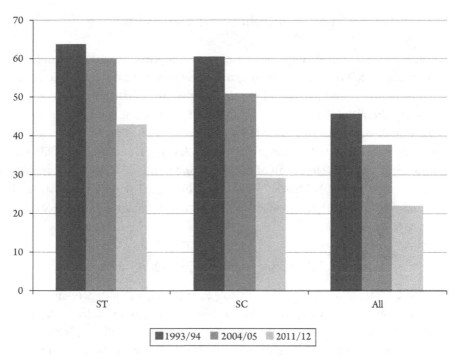

Figure 12.4 Poverty Ratios by Social Groups. Source: Author's construction based on estimates in Panagariya and More 2014.

population in that order. The fact that we see the highest poverty ratio among the ST is not surprising, since the tribes preponderantly live in rural areas and, more important, often outside of the mainstream society and economy. Yet what is remarkable is that rapid growth during the period 2004/5 to 2011/12 has been associated with a substantial decline in poverty within this group as well.

Indeed, the percentage point decline in ST poverty is larger than that in the general population during this period. As regards the SC, their spread between rural and urban areas is not dramatically different from the general population and they are embedded in the mainstream of the economy. As such, they are able to benefit more directly from growth and have experienced the greatest decline in poverty during the period. The SC poverty ratio has been rapidly converging toward the poverty ratio of the general population.

Detailed estimates show that poverty in India has seen a sharp decline along nearly all dimensions during the fast-growth phase of 2004/5 to 2011/12.[5] Whether we analyze by state, religion, or any other criterion, a perceptible decline in poverty can be seen. In view of the fact that India also saw a sharp expansion in social programs during this period, the evidence testifies to the power of growth, which helped increase revenues and thus made expanded social spending possible.

Economic Policy and Trade Flows

Because the purpose of the present case study is to investigate the role of trade policy and trade flows in explaining growth and poverty alleviation, I consider their evolution in some detail. My broad conclusion is that India began with a relatively liberal trade policy regime in phase I but became progressively more inward-looking beginning in the late 1950s. During the first ten years of phase II, the country became particularly protectionist. A very gradual process of liberalization began in the second half of the 1970s and continued, albeit at a gradual pace, through the 1980s. Phases IV and V saw the launch of more systematic and systemic reforms, with trade policy and foreign investment regimes becoming very open by the mid-2000s.

Phase I: A Liberal Beginning but Protectionist Ending

Jawaharlal Nehru, the first prime minister of India, viewed independence from the world markets as essential to preserving the country's political independence. While achieving this independence did not automatically imply a protectionist import policy, it did require realignment of the production basket to the consumption basket.[6] Full alignment of the two baskets required that the raw materials, components, and machinery necessary to produce the final consumption basket also be produced at home.

Nehru reasoned that since private entrepreneurs lacked resources to invest in machinery and other heavy industry, the public sector had to play an active role in their manufacture. This prescription translated into the public sector becoming an active player in manufacturing. Nehru also saw a need to direct the larger private-sector enterprises toward sectors of greater social value rather than those exhibiting greater private profitability. This prescription translated into investment licensing, whereby even modest levels of investments came to require a license specifying the product and its quantity to be produced.

Initially, during the 1950s, the policy regime remained relatively liberal. Private investors were given licenses relatively freely in areas identified as high priority by the government. Few entrepreneurs were heard complaining about complexity of procedures or delays in the issuance of licenses during this decade. Import licensing had also existed since the British introduced it in response to shortages induced by the Second World War, but these licenses were issued generously. The government issued import licenses for even consumer goods in significant quantities. Nehru also resisted the demands for nationalization of foreign companies by leftist parties and maintained a liberal foreign investment policy throughout his rule, which lasted until his death in 1964.

A major turning point came in 1958 when a balance-of-payments crisis struck India. The government seemed not to consider devaluation of the rupee as a possible solution—there are no records to be found of any discussions of the relative merits of different policy options—and chose a bureaucratic response to the crisis. It introduced a system of centralized foreign exchange budgeting whereby the Finance Ministry would estimate the available foreign exchange for each forthcoming six-month period and administratively allocate it among various claimants. This single policy change considerably tightened not only the import policy but also investment licensing: unless foreign exchange for the imports of machinery and raw material required for the manufacture of a product was available, an investment license for that product could not be issued. By the mid-1960s, the impact of tightening came to be widely recognized and found expression in a large number of government committees appointed to recommend ways to eliminate delays in the issuance of licenses.

The introduction of foreign exchange budgeting had an immediate detrimental impact on trade. This can be gleaned from Figure 12.5, which shows imports and total trade (sum of imports and exports) in goods and services as proportions of GDP from 1950/51 to 2011/12. Reflecting the relatively liberal trade policy regime in the 1950s, the trade-to-GDP ratio rose from 11.3 percent

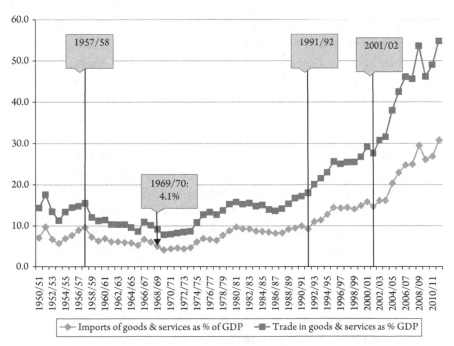

Figure 12.5 Trade in Goods and Services as Percentage of GDP, 1950/51 to 2011/12.
Source: Author's construction using Reserve Bank of India data.

in 1953/54 to 15.5 percent in 1957/58 alongside a growing economy. But once foreign exchange budgeting was put in place, trade declined steadily despite continued (albeit modest) increases in income. By 1964/65, the trade-to-GDP ratio had fallen to 9.5 percent. This declining trend continued well into the second phase, which turned out to be the most restrictive for both external and internal policies during the sixty-year history considered here.

Phase II: A Turn to Virtual Autarky

Nehru died in May 1964 and was succeeded as prime minister by Lal Bahadur Shastri. Shastri tried to move the economy away from heavy industry and gave priority to agriculture. He sowed the seeds of the Green Revolution and created the institutional infrastructure in agriculture that survives until today. The latter included the Agricultural Price Commission, the Food Corporation of India, and the National Dairy Development Board, all established in 1965. But Shastri died in January 1966. Nehru's daughter, Indira Gandhi, then took over as prime minister.

Political expediency almost always trumped other priorities under Gandhi. Early in her reign, she concluded that her political objectives would be best served by moving the country's economic policies farther and farther toward socialism. She went on to introduce numerous policy initiatives that placed the government at the center of economic activity and further tightened the command-and-control regime. Starting in the late 1960s, she nationalized the major banks, insurance companies, oil companies, and mines; reserved the most labor-intensive products exclusively for production by small-scale enterprises with a cap of approximately $100,000 on investment; banned large firms and business houses from investing outside the list of nineteen highly capital-intensive "core" industries; expanded price and distribution controls; imposed a virtual ban on the right of firms with three hundred (later revised to one hundred) or more workers to terminate employment under any circumstances; gave the government the right to acquire vacant urban plots exceeding 500 to 2,000 square meters in size (depending on the size of the city) for a pittance; placed a 40 percent ceiling on foreign investment in any firm with a small number of exceptions; and tightened controls of imports through extension of import licensing and other restrictions to all goods.

During this period, the government issued an import policy every six months in the form of the so-called Red Book. The main part of the policy was a long list of importable products with restrictions on who could import each, which varieties could be imported, and, sometimes, from which source imports had to come. Only actual users were permitted to import, and the importer had to provide satisfactory evidence that the product sought to be imported was not domestically available. This meant that the domestic producer of a product had automatic protection from imports. Domestic residents were not permitted to hold any foreign exchange. Importers needing foreign exchange had to obtain it from the central bank, and exporters had to surrender all foreign exchange to the central bank.

These restrictions on imports and foreign exchange reinforced the restrictions on domestic economic activity described earlier and turned the economy into virtual autarky. Imports of goods and services as a proportion of GDP, which had risen to 9.6 percent in 1957/58, fell to just 4.1 percent in 1969/70 (see Figure 12.5). Indeed, the ratio did not recover to the 1957/58 level until 1980/81. Foreign investment suffered an even worse fate, with some major companies such as IBM and Coca-Cola deciding to leave the country rather than bring their equity down to 40 percent or less. Even as late as 1990/91, foreign investment into India was a paltry $100 million.

The impact of various restrictions on the pattern of industrialization and efficiency was visible. Economist Garry Pursell vividly describes the costs the economy paid:

> During this period, import-substitution policies were followed with little or no regard to costs. They resulted in an extremely diverse industrial structure and high degree of self-sufficiency, but many industries had high production costs. In addition, there was a general problem of poor quality and technological backwardness, which beset even low-cost sectors with comparative advantage such as the textile, garment, leather goods, many light engineering industries, and primary industries such as cotton.[7]

The low quality of consumer goods was, in fact, evident to all who lived through this period in India, including myself. It was also a key reason why virtually no "Made in India" products could be seen in the supermarkets of the United States during the mid-1970s when I arrived there. Pursell reminds us of the detrimental effects import substitution had on the economy:

> Although import substitution reduced imports of substitute products, this was replaced by increased demand for imported capital equipment and technology and for raw materials not domestically produced or [produced] in insufficient quantities. During the 1960s and the first half of the 1970s, the former demand was suppressed by extensive import substitution in the capital goods industries and attempts to indigenize R&D. By about 1976, however, the resulting obsolescence of the capital stock and technology of many industries was becoming apparent, and a

steady liberalization of imports of capital equipment and of technology
started soon after.[8]

Phase III: Piecemeal Deregulation of Trade and Industry

As hinted at by Pursell, by the mid-1970s complaints from industrialists that the
command-and-control system was not working had begun to gain traction. At
least some of the bureaucrats involved in implementing the system also came
to appreciate its limits. But since the political will to admit that the controls had
gone too far was lacking, any changes had to be made bureaucratically within
the existing policy framework and justified as "rationalization" of the existing
system. At least four notable changes beginning in the late 1970s and continuing
into the 1980s resulted in some weakening of the import control regime. These
changes were not dramatic, but given how draconian the regime had turned by
the mid-1970s, even a small loosening had the potential to generate significant
benefits on the margin.

First, a committee was appointed under P. C. Alexander to recommend rationalization of import-licensing procedures. The committee issued its report
in 1978. Its most significant recommendation was that products not produced
domestically be freed from import licensing through their inclusion in the so-
called Open General Licensing (OGL) list that had been recently revived.[9] The
government implemented this and other recommendations of the committee in
1978/79. The OGL list proved an important instrument of piecemeal liberalization in the following decade. The inclusion of an item on the OGL list removed
several bureaucratic hurdles facing its import, though the importer still needed
approval for foreign exchange.

The number of capital goods items included in the OGL list expanded
steadily, from 79 in 1976 to 1,007 in April 1987, 1,170 in April 1988, and 1,329
in April 1990.[10] In parallel, intermediate inputs were also placed on the OGL
list, and their number expanded steadily over the years; based on the best available information, this number had reached 620 by April 1987 and increased to
949 in April 1988.[11] According to Pursell, "Imports that were neither canalized
nor subject to licensing (presumably mainly OGL imports) increased from
about 5 percent in 1980/81 to about 30 percent in 1987/88."[12] This observation is corroborated by a World Bank report, which states, "Most informed
commentaries on the trends in import policies agree that some loosening of raw
material controls has occurred in each year beginning with the 1977/78 policy,
except in 1980/81 when controls were tightened."[13]

Second, a substantial proportion of foreign exchange generated by exports
had come to be absorbed by canalized imports, that is, imports that were a

government monopoly. Several factors led to a decline in these imports and released foreign exchange for machinery and raw material imports. In effect, this release of foreign exchange helped facilitate the liberalization that was taking place through expansion of the OGL list. In addition to de-canalization of a small number of items, Pursell points to three factors as the key to a reduction in canalized imports: (1) increased domestic crude oil production and the decline in the world prices of crude oil and petroleum products in the 1980s led to a decline in imports of POL (petroleum, oil, and lubricants); (2) the success of the Green Revolution led to the disappearance of grain imports, while cotton imports fell for other reasons; and (3) a large decline occurred in the international prices of some of the other canalized imports, especially fertilizers, edible oils, non-ferrous metals, and iron and steel during the 1980s (until 1987). Between 1980/81 and 1986/87, the share of canalized imports in total imports fell from a hefty 67 percent to 27 percent. Over the same period, canalized non-POL imports as a proportion of total non-POL imports declined from 44 to 11 percent.

Third, several export incentives were introduced or expanded, which helped expand imports directly when imports were tied to exports and indirectly by relaxing the foreign exchange constraint. Specifically, exporters were given replenishment (REP) licenses in amounts that were approximately twice their import needs. They were allowed to sell unused REP licenses on the domestic market. A key distinguishing feature of the REP licenses was that they allowed the holder to import items outside of the OGL or canalized list. Typically, imports of these items were restricted and had domestic import-competing counterparts. The list of the items that could be imported under the REP licenses was expanded over time, increasing their liberalizing impact. As exports expanded, the volume of these imports expanded as well. This factor became particularly important during 1985–90, when exports expanded rapidly.[14]

Finally, during the second half of the 1980s, the central bank allowed the nominal exchange rate to depreciate significantly. The index of the nominal effective exchange rate dropped from its peak of 98.5 in 1985/86 to 67 in 1990/91. This was a little more than 30 percent effective depreciation in the nominal value of the rupee. Alongside, as shown in Figure 12.6, the real exchange rate fell from 98.5 to 75.6 over the same period. This very large real depreciation of the rupee played a significant role in the acceleration of growth of exports in the second half of the 1980s.

The depreciation of the rupee in the second half of the 1980s was preceded by its appreciation in the early 1980s, however. This may be seen in Figure 12.6. The index of the nominal effective exchange rate rose from 97 in 1978/79 to 105 in 1983/84 and that of the real effective exchange rate from 92 to 104 during the same period. This appreciation had a highly detrimental effect on export

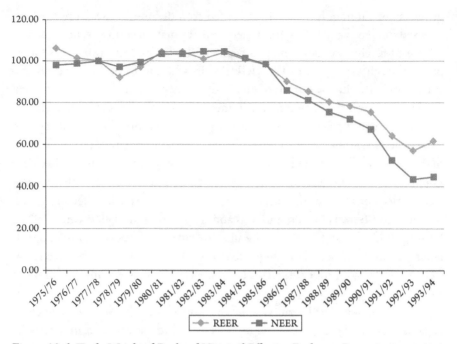

Figure 12.6 Trade-Weighted Real and Nominal Effective Exchange Rates. Source: Author's construction based on data in Reserve Bank of India 2008, table 153.

performance. The appreciation may have resulted from a belief in elasticity pessimism on the part of Reserve Bank of India governor I. G. Patel.[15]

The discussion of trade policy developments in the 1980s would be incomplete without a brief reference to the substantial escalation in tariff rates. An indicator of this escalation is the increase in tariff revenue as a percentage of imports from 27 percent in 1977/78 to 62 percent in 1987/88. Some analysts have concluded from this tariff increase that the period was characterized by increased protection. This inference is erroneous and unwarranted since the binding constraint on imports of products subject to tariff increases remained licensing. Virtually all tariff increases affected products outside of the OGL list and therefore those subject to strict licensing. As for the products on the OGL list, the government typically subjected them to the so-called tariff exemption, which amounted to a lower applied duty than the statutory one. The role of the tariff increases was to allow the government to skim off a larger proportion of the difference between the border and internal prices on goods subject to licensing in tariff revenues.

As Figure 12.5 shows, trade in goods and services as a proportion of GDP began at an extremely low level but started to rise in the second half of the 1970s. However, the appreciation of the real exchange rate beginning at the end of the

1970s led to stagnation in this ratio in the first half of the 1980s. It was only in the second half of the 1980s, when various liberalization measures began to take root, including especially the substantial favorable movement in the nominal and real effective exchange rates, that the trade-to-GDP ratio began to climb yet again. To some degree, the increase in the trade-to-GDP ratio from 13.6 percent in 1986/87 to 17.2 percent in 1990/91 understates the growth in trade. During this period, GDP growth itself had averaged an unprecedented 5.6 percent. Therefore, trade had to grow much faster to pull up the trade-to-GDP ratio.

Phases IV and V: Liberalization Triumphs

The shift in growth in phase III to a 4.6 percent rate can be attributed to the external liberalization just described, complemented by two domestic developments: limited deregulation of several domestic policies and expansionary fiscal policy. Domestic deregulation offered entrepreneurs greater flexibility in investment decisions through de-licensing of some sectors, liberal permission for the expansion of existing capacity, a hike in the threshold level of investment below which a license was not required, and expansion of the list of sectors open to large firms and big business houses. These measures were implemented in several steps over a period of more than ten years.[16]

The 1980s also saw the emergence of expansionary fiscal policy, substantially financed by borrowing abroad and reflected in rising current account deficits. One pair of influential authors, T. N. Srinivasan and Suresh Tendulkar, goes so far as to assign much of the credit for acceleration in growth during the 1980s to this demand-side factor.[17] Defense spending, interest payments, subsidies, and higher public-employee wages resulting from the implementation of the Fourth Pay Commission recommendations fueled these expenditures. Combined fiscal deficits at the central and state levels, which averaged 8 percent of GDP in the first half of the 1980s, went up to 10.1 percent in the second half.

While the fiscal expansion helped boost growth, it also sowed the seeds of a balance-of-payments crisis. From 1980/81 to 1984/85, the current account deficit ranged between 1.3 and 1.9 percent of GDP. It jumped to 2.4 percent in 1985–86, fell back to 2 percent in 1987–88, and then shot up to 3.1 percent in 1988–89 and 3.4 percent in 1990–91. Alongside this, the external-debt-to-GDP ratio rose from 17.7 percent in 1984/85 to 24.5 percent in 1989/90. The debt service ratio, which is the proportion of export revenues spent on servicing the external debt, rose from 18 to 27 percent.

All these factors undermined the credibility of the government as a borrower in the external markets and from the international financial institutions. Gradually, the small stock of foreign exchange reserves also became depleted. From an average of 4.6 months' worth of imports during the period 1984–87, the reserves fell to 3.9 months' worth in fiscal year 1987/88. The trend continued, with the reserves declining to 2.5 months' worth in 1988/89, 2 months in 1989/90, and just 1 month in 1990–91.[18] In June 1991, with confidence in the ability of the government to service its external debt completely lost, the crisis reached the doorstep of the country with the downgrading of its credit rating and complete loss of access to the world financial markets.

The crisis coincided with three developments that helped change the minds of some key political actors in favor of liberalization. First, the Soviet Union, on which India had patterned its system of planning and controls, collapsed. Second, China, a communist country that was more populous than India, decided to embrace liberalization beginning in the late 1970s, with excellent results. And finally, at least some key political figures and bureaucrats came to appreciate that India had lost out on growth and poverty alleviation under the command-and-control system and that even the modest liberalization of the 1980s had paid a dividend.

Therefore, the new government under Prime Minister Narasimha Rao that came to power in June 1991 was more sympathetic to putting an end to the command-and-control system, known as the license-permit raj. This willingness was reinforced by the IMF conditionality accompanying the loans India critically needed to replenish its foreign exchange reserves and unfreeze its access to the external financial markets. The result was a major set of reforms governing both external and internal transactions.

The Rao government issued the New Industrial Policy, which did away with investment licensing and the public sector monopoly on most industries. Within a matter of a few years, only five industries were left on the licensing list, all on health, safety, and environmental grounds. Likewise, the public sector monopoly came to be limited to railway transportation and atomic energy. The New Industrial Policy also abolished the concept of a 40 percent cap on foreign investment in any firm and immediately opened thirty-four industries to 51 percent foreign investment with no central government clearances required. Subsequently, most sectors were opened up, with 100 percent foreign investment permitted in the vast majority of the industries.

On the external front, the July 1991 reforms did away with import licensing on all but a handful of intermediate inputs and capital goods items. But de-licensing of consumer goods imports took another decade. In 1990/91, the highest tariff rate stood at 355 percent, the simple average of all tariff rates at 113 percent, and the import-weighted average of tariff rates at 87 percent.[19] With the removal of licensing, these tariff rates became effective restrictions on imports. Therefore, a major task of the reforms in the 1990s and beyond was bringing the tariffs down.

The reduction in industrial tariffs was accomplished through a gradual compression of the top tariff rate with a simultaneous rationalization through reduction in the number of tariff bands. The top rate fell to 150 percent in 1991/92, 110 percent in 1992/93, 85 percent in 1993/94, 65 percent in 1994/95, 50 percent in 1995/96, 40 percent in 1997/98, 35 percent in 2000/1, 30 percent in 2002/3, 25 percent in 2003/4, 20 percent in 2004/5, 15 percent in 2005/6, 12.5 percent in 2006/7, and 10 percent in 2007/8. There were some reversals along the way in the form of special duties and surcharges, but the peak rate since 2007/8 stands at 10 percent with some exceptions, such as automobiles and textiles. There exist no surcharges or special duties. The simple average of industrial tariff rates came down to 12 percent in 2007/8. Import duty collection as a proportion of total imports in 2005/6 fell to just 4.9 percent.

In agriculture, India, like the OECD countries, bound its tariffs at extra-high rates ranging from 100 to 300 percent when eliminating its non-tariff border measures under the Uruguay Round Agreement on Agriculture. India's average bound rate in agriculture is 115.2 percent.[20] This was well above the average applied tariff at 35.1 percent in 1997/98 and 41.7 percent in 2001/2. Liberalizing agriculture remains a contentious issue.

As a part of its liberalization policy, the government also lifted export controls over most products. Prior to the July 1991 announcement of reforms, exports of 439 items were subject to controls of varying types and degrees. The March 1992 Export-Import Policy reduced the number of items subject to controls to 296, and the process continued in subsequent years, with export prohibitions brought down to a small number of items on health, environmental, or moral grounds and export restrictions applying only to cattle, camels, fertilizers, cereals, groundnut oil, and pulses.

The lifting of exchange controls and elimination of overvaluation of the rupee that had discriminated against the traded goods sector formed an integral part of the reform in phase IV. The 1991 reform devalued the rupee by 17.8 percent against the dollar, from 21.2 rupees to 25.8 rupees per dollar. For a brief period the government maintained a dual exchange rate system, but it quickly unified it into a single rate and went on to accept the IMF Article VIII obligations of current account convertibility on August 20, 1994. In later years, bolstered by the accumulation of a large stock of foreign exchange reserves, India freed up many capital account transactions, though the rupee is still not fully convertible.[21]

Since 1991, India has also carried out a substantial liberalization of trade in services by opening the door wider to foreign investors. Traditionally, many services sectors had been either a government monopoly (telecommunications, airlines, insurance, and railways) or subject to heavy government presence (banking). All sectors except railways and atomic energy have now been opened to the private sector, including foreign investors. The current foreign investment regime in India operates on a negative-list philosophy, meaning that unless there are specific restrictions spelled out in the foreign investment policy, foreign investment without a cap is automatically permitted. Substantively, only atomic energy remains entirely off-limits to foreign investment. In some other cases such as banking, insurance, and telecommunications, sectoral caps below 100 percent apply.

The reforms in phases IV and V have gone far beyond the industrial de-licensing, trade, and foreign investment changes discussed above. For completeness, let me note that India has made remarkable progress in reforming the policy regime in areas such as taxation, the financial sector, telecommunications, the airline industry, and national highway construction. Some success was also achieved in the privatization of public sector enterprises under the National Democratic Alliance, which ruled from 1998 to 2004, but the process slowed down considerably under the successor United Progressive Alliance government. On the macroeconomic front, significant reforms have been introduced in the conduct of monetary policy, with most interest rates having been deregulated.

Role of Trade and Domestic Liberalization in the Transformation

India started off well in the 1950s, replacing policies that had served the interests of the colonizing power by those geared to national interest. Though many restrictive policies were introduced, at the implementation level the regime remained liberal in the 1950s. Investment and import licenses were liberally issued with no records of notable complaints of delay available. Though the regime began to tighten significantly in the late 1950s, it began damaging the economy seriously only in the mid-1960s. The result was a respectable annual growth of 4.1 percent during the period 1951–65. Of course, because the country started at an extremely low level of income, this growth proved too little to make a dent in India's widespread poverty.

The tightening of the import- and investment-licensing regime by the mid-1960s combined with the numerous controls in product and factor markets began taking a serious toll on India's growth. The years 1965–75 saw India's average GDP growth rate plummet to just 2.6 percent from 4.1 percent during 1951–65. With population growing at 2.3 percent per annum, this meant per capita income growth of just 0.3 percent—a virtual standstill in average living standard. Even the spiking of the growth rate in 1975/76 to 9.4 percent could pull GDP and per capita GDP growth rates in phase II (1965–81) to only 3.2 and 0.9 percent, respectively. Industrial growth fell from 6.7 percent in phase I to just 3.6 percent in phase II.

India was subject to several external shocks during phase II. These included two consecutive droughts during 1965/66 and 1966/67, two wars with Pakistan in 1965 and 1971, two more consecutive droughts in 1971/72 and 1972/73, and the oil price shock in October 1973. No doubt these shocks contributed to a slowdown in the Indian economy.

But these shocks are insufficient to explain the low growth rate India experienced during phase II. To begin with, while the average growth during phase I represented a significant improvement over that during the colonial era, at 4.1 percent it was modest. During this phase there had been no serious external shocks except the 1962 war with China.

Furthermore, the period from the early 1960s to the mid-1970s was also characterized by a much-improved external economic environment on account of the stellar performance of the developed countries. Growth in the developed countries during 1961–75 surpassed that in any other period. A large number of developing countries, which also faced many of the adverse shocks that afflicted India (except the wars with Pakistan), experienced accelerated growth in their economies.

South Korea, which decided to discard the import substitution policies of the 1950s and opted in favor of outward-oriented policies in the early 1960s, achieved growth rates in the range of 8 to 10 percent during these same years. Agriculture in Korea saw negative growth rates of 1.9 percent in 1965 and 5 percent in 1967, yet GNP expanded by 6.1 percent in 1965 and 7.5 percent in 1967. Had India too been more open to trade, the droughts would not have impacted its industrial growth as badly as they did. The near-exclusive dependence of the economy on local sources for raw materials meant that drought would have an immediate adverse impact not just on agriculture but also on industry.

By 1980, many observers saw the situation in India as being grim. In his 1980 book on poverty, economist Gary Fields described India as "a miserably poor country."[22] Yet a very different story began to unfold in the 1980s. The critical question we need to address is whether pro-market reforms in general and India's shift to an outward-oriented regime in particular have significantly contributed to accelerated growth and poverty alleviation beginning in the early 1980s. Prima facie, the timing of the reforms and acceleration in growth and poverty alleviation would seem to suggest a direct connection between policies and outcomes. But this is not without controversy.

Economists Bradford De Long, Dani Rodrik, and Arvind Subramanian have questioned the connection between the post-1970s growth acceleration and reforms arguing that the shift in the growth rate took place around 1980, while the reforms did not begin till 1991.[23] Though Subramanian seems to have parted company with Rodrik on this issue in his subsequent writings, the DeLong-Rodrik-Subramanian view has continued to find expression in the writings of many authors.[24] There are at least four reasons these authors are incorrect in voicing skepticism toward reforms, particularly those relating to the opening up of the economy to trade and foreign investment.

First, the shift in the growth rate in the early 1980s was only a tiny one. The average annual growth rate during phase III (1981–88) was 4.6 percent. While this represented a 1.4 percentage point increase over the growth rate in phase II (1965–81), it was just half a percentage point larger than what had been achieved during phase I (1951–65). And even this acceleration was not achieved without some deregulation of the economy, as detailed in my discussion of the policies during phase III.

Pointing to the increases in the tariff rates, Rodrik and Subramanian argue that the economy actually turned more, not less, protectionist during the 1980s. But as I have discussed in detail, measuring protection through tariff rate is erroneous when imports are actually being restrained by import licensing. The binding constraint on imports during the 1980s was import licensing rather than tariffs, and import licensing actually underwent some relaxation through the expansion of the OGL list and more relaxed issuance of import licenses on products not included in the OGL list. The key outcome variable, trade-to-GDP ratio, also points to some degree of relaxation of the trade regime. As one keen observer of trade policy in India, Pursell, puts it, "The available data on imports and import licensing are incomplete, out of date, and often inconsistent. Nevertheless, whichever way they are manipulated, they confirm the very substantial and steady import liberalization that occurred after 1977–78 and during the 1980s."[25]

Second, while growth did accelerate to 7.2 percent between 1988/89 and 1990/91, this acceleration was not sustainable without the reforms that took place in phase IV. In addition to the piecemeal external and internal liberalization, the acceleration in growth during the 1980s was also fueled by fiscal expansion financed by external borrowing. Fiscal deficit, current account deficit, and external debt had become significantly larger in the second half of the 1980s than in the first half. The ever-increasing interest payments on foreign debt were unsustainable in an economy characterized by a tiny stock of foreign exchange reserves, a relatively low exports-to-GDP ratio (7.2 percent in 1990/91), and the near absence of private capital inflows except bank deposits by non-resident Indians, which could not be counted on to continue in the face of serious weaknesses in the macroeconomic outlook. The balance-of-payments crisis in June 1991 amply proves this point.

Third, critics argue that although systematic reforms were launched in 1991, the growth rate during the 1990s was not much higher than in the 1980s. They conclude that these facts imply that reforms have failed to produce a superior outcome. But the acceleration of the growth rate to 8.3 percent during phase V falsifies such claims. Our comparison of growth rates in phases III, IV, and V testifies to acceleration in the growth rate accompanying systematic reforms in the 1980s, 1990s, and 2000s. But the difference becomes stark when we compare phase III with phase V. Even incorporating the super-high growth in the last three years of the 1980s into phase III, we get an average annual growth rate of 5.4 percent during 1981–91. In contrast, the growth rates during 1992–2003 and 2003–12 work out to 5.8 and 8.3 percent, respectively.[26] Thus, not only is the claim that the shift in the growth rate in the early 1980s happened without liberalization false, but the claim that the more systematic and far-reaching reforms of the 1990s and 2000s yielded no better outcome than what had been achieved in the 1980s is laughable.

Finally, it is inconceivable that the structural change that has accompanied the accelerated growth in phases IV and V could have taken place without the major reforms, including those relating to the external sector. It is worth mentioning just a few of the dramatic structural changes observed since the beginning of the 1990s:

- Trade in goods and services as a proportion of GDP rose from 17.2 percent in 1990/91 to a peak of 54.8 percent in 2011/12. Over the same period, exports of goods and services as a proportion of GDP rose from 7.2 percent to 24.1 percent.
- Foreign investment into the country rose from $100 million in 1990/91 to $46.6 billion in 2011/12.
- Remittances from abroad rose from $2.1 billion in 1990/91 to $66.1 billion in 2011/12.
- Software exports rose from $0.8 billion in 1995/96 to $62.2 billion in 2011/12.
- The number of phones in the country rose from 18.7 million at the end of March 1998 to 951 million at the end of March 2012. The number of phones per hundred individuals rose from 2.3 at the end of March 1999 to 78.7 at the end of March 2012. Even in rural areas, there were two phones per household on average by the end of March 2012.
- The total stock of passenger vehicles at the end of March 1990 was three million. In 2011/12, the annual *additions* to the number of passenger vehicles had reached 3.1 million.
- Investment as a proportion of GDP rose from 24.2 percent in 1990/91 to 36 percent in 2006/7 and remained above 30 percent till 2011/12.

There is no simple way to establish causation between policy change and these outcomes. Nevertheless, it would be a stretch to argue that the trade-to-GDP ratio could have tripled without massive trade liberalization, that foreign investment could have expanded this dramatically without the wide opening to foreign investment, that the automobile industry could have turned around without the end to strict investment licensing and opening the sector to foreign investment, and that the telecommunications revolution could have taken place without the implementation of the New Telecom Policy in 1999. Even the phenomenal increase in the investment-to-GDP ratio must be attributed in large measure to increased returns resulting from the reforms.

Further Criticisms and Responses

Critics have attacked India's reforms from a variety of angles to downplay their effectiveness and to bolster the case that protectionism and interventionism should get the credit for stimulating and sustaining growth and poverty alleviation in recent years. Not all of these arguments exclusively attack trade and foreign investment openness. But since trade and foreign investment openness have been important elements of India's reform strategy, these arguments require a response.

Protection and Interventionism Remain Pervasive in India

Some critics argue that India has done well because its reforms did not go as far as the advocates of liberalization advise. For instance, Ha-Joon Chang states, "The average growth rate of developing countries in this period [since the 1980s] would be even lower if we exclude China and India. These two countries, which accounted for 12 percent of total developing country income in 1980 and 30 percent in 2000, have so far refused to put on Thomas Friedman's 'Golden Straitjacket.' "[27] Rodrik expresses a similar sentiment, arguing that Indian liberalization remains a far cry from the "mainstream ideal."[28]

Frankly, this is a rather spurious explanation of India's success. For one thing, neither of these authors spells out precisely which policies India adopted or discarded to achieve the success it has seen. To say that the country succeeded because it did not adopt a set of policies that some consider ideal tells us nothing about the other policies whose adoption or abandonment was at the heart of the success. Without that, what positive lessons can we take from the success of one country and apply to other countries? In the end, we get back to Gustav Ranis's criticism of Robert Wade: that Wade describes at length government interventions in Taiwan but provides no primer on how to "act strategically."[29]

Furthermore, terms such as "straitjacket" and "mainstream ideal" mean different things to different analysts. For example, does a move from import licensing on all products reinforced by a simple average tariff of 113 percent to no licensing and a simple average tariff of 12 percent represent a move closer to the mainstream ideal with respect to trade openness? Likewise, does a move from a regime that permits foreign investment under only exceptional circumstances to one that restricts it in only handful of sectors qualify as the mainstream ideal with respect to foreign investment? How much tightening of a jacket is required before it qualifies as a straitjacket?

Even leaving these critical definitional issues aside, had India's liberalization in the 1990s been followed by deterioration in its performance, these same critics would have jumped to cite the experience as yet another example of liberalization leading to devastation. They would then have argued that the debacle was the result of India's having put on Thomas Friedman's "Golden Straitjacket" and that it would have been better off sticking to its inward-looking import substitution policies. This is not idle speculation: the authors have cited similar, even less far-reaching examples from Africa and Latin America to beef up the case against liberalization. But since the outcome in the Indian case was significant acceleration in growth and poverty alleviation, these authors are forced to hide behind the assertion that the policy shift itself has been minimal and therefore the credit must go to the protection and intervention policies that remain rather than those that have been withdrawn.

Few reform advocates expect countries operating within a democratic environment to turn into textbook cases of free trade and free enterprise economies, or what Rodrik calls mainstream ideals. They are aware that even developed countries are far from achieving that status. Therefore, what reform advocates are often seeking is a movement away from a near-autarkic and highly controlled regime to one that offers sufficient openness in trade and investment and sufficient freedom from domestic regulation. The idea is to give entrepreneurs the space to carry out their entrepreneurial activities while subjecting them to a certain degree of competition.

Economic theory tells us that when the initial distortion is large, even small policy changes can yield large benefits on the margin. Competition against the most efficient entrepreneurs in the world can make even public sector firms function more efficiently, as has been the case in India in such sectors as banking and telecommunications. Nevertheless, it bears noting that a one-time marginal opening up is unlikely to foster growth over long periods. India has been able to sustain and accelerate the process of growth and poverty alleviation precisely because it did not stop at the piecemeal process of liberalization it began in the late 1970s and early 1980s. India may not have turned into the mainstream ideal, as defined by Rodrik, but it has undertaken significant liberalization both externally and internally, and as a result India has a dramatically different policy regime today than it did twenty-five years ago, with the change being most surely in the direction of the mainstream ideal. Those of us who advocate reforms suggest further movement in this direction and can only wonder if Chang and Rodrik would advise the country to retreat.

The Indian Software Industry Owes Its Success to Infant Industry Protection

Some observers contend that India's software industry owes its success to infant industry protection. For example, Rafiq Dossani argues that "local entrepreneurship and a high level of infant industry protection enabled the Indian IT industry to reach a high growth path and allowed local skills to develop rapidly to keep pace with global changes."[30] But Dossani and other authors have not provided systematic evidence supporting this view. Dossani offers less than a paragraph in support of his hypothesis:

> Unlike the BPO [business process outsourcing] business in India, the software business began with an Indian firm, TCS [Tata Consultancy Services], in 1974. However, this was due to protection: in 1973 the Indian government required multinationals operating in India to reduce their shareholding to 40 percent. Many multinationals, including IBM (India's largest IT firm at the time) preferred to close shop rather than divest. This created an opportunity for Indian firms to provide software services. Multinationals were allowed to reenter beginning in 1985, although the playing field was not leveled for at least another decade.[31]

This reasoning amounts to no more than the post hoc fallacy to which Chang repeatedly resorts in his contributions on Japan and other developed countries. It is plausible that the departure of IBM created some rents for local firms with computer programming capacity and induced some innovation.[32] But this inference is hardly sufficient to link the ouster of IBM to the subsequent success of the IT industry. Even as late as 1995/96 the value of India's software exports remained below $1 billion. It was a whole slew of liberalizing steps—the relaxation of hardware and software imports in the mid-1980s under Rajiv Gandhi, the opening up of the foreign investment regime that brought foreign multinationals back into the country, the implementation of the New Telecom Policy in 1999—that helped the software industry grow. Indeed, Dossani recognizes the critical role of these measures and the harmful impact protectionist policies may have had:

> Indian software services are at the early stages of work. The relatively low value of their work may be due to the state's protectionist policies and the resulting absence of multinationals in the early years, though there is some indication that in recent years the presence of

multinationals has contributed to a rise in Indian value added. . . . The entry of multinationals (and the diaspora) was induced by sweeping reforms in foreign ownership rules, telecommunications policy, and venture capital policy since 2000.[33]

The bottom-line question we must ask is whether the Indian software industry would have failed to grow absent IBM's departure. While no one can tell with certainty, the more plausible answer is in the negative. While TCS would have found the industry less profitable in the short run had IBM chosen to stay, in the long run it would have benefited from interaction with IBM. It is also possible that some employees of IBM would have set up their own independent shops. And IBM's continued presence would have opened the door to outsourcing sooner.

Growth Is Due to Institutions, Entrepreneurship, and Technical Education and Training

Subramanian suggests that the poverty reduction and growth that resulted from the reforms in India—results that stand in sharp contrast to what happened after similar liberalizing reforms in Latin America—can be attributed to some key elements of India's development policy package in the early decades of development, especially under Nehru.[34] He points to three specific features of the package, labeling them as "fundamentals": (1) superior meta-institutions, including democracy, the rule of law, an independent judiciary, a free press, and a technocratic bureaucracy; (2) investment in the Indian Institutes of Technology (IITs) and Indian Institutes of Management (IIMs) and research institutes; and (3) creation of a large pool of entrepreneurs and managers, many of whom had their training in public sector enterprises.[35]

As stated, this argument does not challenge the desirability of the reforms India has undertaken. But at least an implicit message it conveys is that without this support for institutions, entrepreneurship, and education and training, the outcome of the reforms in the 1980s and subsequently would have been no more favorable than in Latin America. That is to say, India lost nothing and gained a lot from the policies it pursued in the first three decades of development. In fairness, I should emphatically note that Subramanian himself does not put the argument in this strong form. But readers favorably inclined toward command-and-control policies can be counted on to interpret it in this way. Several cautionary points must be made against uncritically accepting this message.

First, the experience of Latin America with liberalization has not been entirely uniform across the board. Moreover, the reform failures there have probably had more to do with macroeconomic instability and the lack of policy credibility resulting from frequent reversals of reforms. During the last three decades, Chile has steadily and credibly moved toward liberal trade and investment policies, with excellent growth and poverty outcomes. Regarding the large number of countries in which liberal reforms have not yielded similarly good outcomes, at least two points must be kept in mind. One, protectionist and interventionist policies had been delivering even worse outcomes in these countries, which is what led them to turn to more liberal policies in the first place. And two, the poor response to reforms was due to macroeconomic instability and lack of policy credibility. Argentina, Brazil, Peru, and Bolivia all went through extended episodes of hyperinflation in the 1980s. These episodes either coincided with or were quickly succeeded by debt crises. As debt crises were brought under control, many of the countries were engulfed in capital flow crises. In many countries, such as Argentina, Venezuela, Brazil, and Bolivia, reversals of reforms also contributed to the loss of credibility. In other countries, such as Colombia and Mexico, the presence of the drug trade and associated insecurity have contributed to investors' hesitation.

Second, it is important to appreciate that the creation of institutions such as a well-functioning democracy, an independent judiciary, a free press, and efficient bureaucracy and police does not require command-and-control and protectionist policies. On the contrary, a liberal economic policy regime is more compatible with the creation and preservation of democratic institutions. The command-and-control regime and protectionism created rents that politicians and bureaucrats could distribute as they saw fit, thus corrupting the entire political and bureaucratic system. Legal barriers in the way of privately profitable transactions in all walks of life—investment, trade, entry and exit of firms, and pricing and distribution of products and inputs— also created a vast number of disputes that overburdened the key institutions of judiciary and bureaucracy. Therefore, it can be argued that on balance the policies of external and internal controls weakened rather than strengthened the fundamental institutions.

In contrast, the recent move toward more liberal policies has led to institutional improvements and significantly improved service delivery. For instance, investors no longer have to line up at the Ministry of Commerce and Industry because the policy no longer requires them to obtain an investment or import license. Corruption at the border has dramatically declined because the level of protection is now very low. Any institutional change in the customs department and any change in the attitude of customs agents have also *followed* the shift in policy. Consumers no longer have to queue up at the Department of Telecommunication because its monopoly on telephones is long gone and telephones are freely available from multiple operators in the market. The same goes for automobiles and scooters, for which customers used to have to file applications and then wait years for delivery. Air travel and banking services today are likewise much improved because entry offered to private players has given rise to healthy competition. In the end, it is better *policies* that have led to the closing down of unproductive and counterproductive institutions such as the license-permit raj and paved the way for the emergence of high-productivity institutions such as reduced corruption among customs officials and a culture of service with a smile in banking, insurance, and the airline industry.

Third, the tradition of entrepreneurship in India has been a long-standing one. Entrepreneurs such as Jamsetji Tata, G. D. Birla, and Walchand Hirachand and industries as diverse as steel, textiles, jute, chemicals, railways, shipping, banking, and insurance had flourished even during the British period. History belies any claims, explicit or implicit, that protection and licensing helped create entrepreneurship. Indeed, it can be argued that the control system had the socially undesirable effect of channeling entrepreneurial talents into unproductive activities. Investors had to learn ways to obtain licenses for themselves while ensuring that their rivals did not get them, had to bribe officials to obtain allocations of critical inputs, and needed to work around the license-permit raj through both legal and illegal means. The outcome was the creation of a generation of entrepreneurs with poorer ethical and governance standards than the one preceding it. This class of entrepreneurs devoted its energies to rent-seeking activities rather than innovation and wealth creation. In contrast, the new generation of entrepreneurs, nurtured in the more open business environment in sectors such as communications, information technology, automobiles, and pharmaceuticals, have deployed their energies in innovation and wealth creation.[36]

Finally, it is tempting to conjecture that the promotion of heavy industry, which had been concentrated in the public sector by design, created greater demand for chemical, mechanical, and metallurgical engineers and management graduates and led the government to establish the IITs and IIMs. But a quick look at the history of IITs and the IIMs reveals that no such connection existed in reality.[37] Whereas the decision to promote heavy industry was made in the mid-1950s, the first IIT at Kharagpur in West Bengal had already come into existence in 1951. Contrary to the common impression, the idea of and initiative for the IITs did not originate with Nehru. Instead, it was Sir Ardeshire Dalal from the Viceroy's Executive Council who came up with the idea immediately after the Second World War and prior to India's independence. The idea was carried forward by the Sarkar Committee, appointed in 1946, with West Bengal Chief Minister B. C. Roy playing an important role in the setting up of the first IIT. In a similar vein, the IIM-Ahmedabad and IIM-Calcutta were established in

1961 with critical input and initiative coming from leading personalities in the respective host states.

Nevertheless, can one not argue that heavy industry served as useful training ground for engineering and management graduates of IITs, IIMs and other engineering and management institutions? While the answer to this question has to be in the affirmative ex post, the appropriate question to ask is whether a more liberal trade and investment regime would have ruled out the creation of the large skilled labor force India came to have by the 1980s. It stands to reason that this is not so, since in a more open trade and investment regime, India still would have needed engineering and management graduates to work in industries in which it had comparative advantage. It is not altogether clear that South Korea, which opted for a liberal trade and investment regime beginning in the early 1960s, suffered in the formation of engineering and management skills relative to India.

Concluding Remarks

In this chapter, I have presented a brief history of India's sixty years of experimentation with economic policies. I have divided the period into five phases. The first two of these phases, spanning 1951/52 to 1980/81, were characterized by low growth and virtually no poverty alleviation. Autarkic trade and foreign investment policies, heavy presence of the public sector in manufacturing, and a domestic command-and-control policy regime for the private sector dominated these phases. By 1980, India looked abysmally poor, with no real prospects for a turnaround.

Yet a gradual and ad hoc process of liberalization began in the second half of the 1970s, which gave way to more systematic and systemic reforms in the 1990s and 2000s. The last three phases of development, spanning 1981/82 to 2011/12, have seen India transform itself economically. I have argued in this chapter that, contrary to what some authors argue, opening up to foreign trade and investment and allowing market forces greater play have been the key to India's ongoing transformation. For example, the growth rate rose from 3.2 percent during 1965–81 to 8.3 percent during 2003–12. The proportion of the population living below the official poverty line fell from 45.7 percent in 1993/94 to 22 percent in 2011/12. Simultaneously, the economy saw a substantial opening up in terms of policies as well as outcomes. Trade in goods and services as a proportion of GDP rose from 15.8 percent in 1980/81 to 54.8 percent in 2011/12. Likewise, foreign investment rose from $100 million in 1990/91 to $46.6 billion in 2011/12. It is inconceivable that without a switch to outward-oriented policies, these changes in the openness indicators and accompanying growth and poverty alleviation would have been possible.

Notes

1. India's fiscal year begins on April 1 and ends on March 31. Therefore, 1951/52 refers to the period from April 1, 1951, to March 31, 1952.
2. In my book *India: The Emerging Giant* (2008) I offered an extensive analytic account of economic development in India until 2005. In the following, I draw upon this account with some updating. In the book, I divided the period into four phases and speculated that the fourth phase was likely to evolve into two distinct phases, with the latter years of the fourth phase defining a further accelerated period of growth.
3. Unless otherwise noted, a period such as 1951–65 in this chapter would refer to fiscal years ranging from 1951/52 to 1964/65 with the endpoint years included.
4. GDP growth rates reported throughout this chapter relate to GDP at factor cost. Until 2013/14, India reported this measure of GDP as its official GDP. Beginning in 2014/15, the country switched to GDP at market prices as its official GDP.
5. See Panagariya and More 2014.
6. To quote Nehru 1946, 403, "The objective for the country as a whole was the attainment, as far as possible, of national self-sufficiency. International trade was certainly not excluded, but we were anxious to avoid being drawn into the whirlpool of economic imperialism." In principle, output subsidy on products with positive imports and output tax on products with positive exports with no intervention in trade could deliver on this objective.
7. Pursell 1992, 429–34.
8. Pursell 1992, 434.
9. The OGL list had originally been introduced when the British first introduced licensing during the Second World War. But with the tightening of import licensing, the list was discontinued. It was reintroduced in 1976 with some seventy-nine capital goods items on it.
10. Pursell 1992.
11. World Bank 1988a, para. 2.59.
12. Pursell 1992, 441. Canalization of imports of an item meant that only the government could import it. Though the role of canalization has significantly declined in recent years, the government has always maintained monopoly over imports and exports of certain items in India.
13. World Bank 1987, 89, para. 4.25.
14. Several other export incentives that helped neutralize the import restrictions on a modest scale were offered in the second half of the 1980s. These are discussed in detail in Panagariya 2008, ch 4.
15. "Elasticity pessimism," which broadly states that depreciation of the domestic currency would worsen rather than improve the current-account balance, was pervasive among Indian bureaucrats and economists. In all likelihood, I. G. Patel, who served as Reserve Bank of India governor from December 1977 to September 1982, shared this view. His tenure as governor almost entirely coincides with the rising nominal effective exchange rate in Figure 12.6. The upward movement in the nominal effective exchange rate continued under his successor, Manmohan Singh, except during the last year of his tenure. True credit for the aggressive depreciation in the second half of the 1980s goes to R. N. Malhotra, who was at the helm at the Reserve Bank from February 1985 to December 1990.
16. See Panagariya 2008, ch. 4, for details.
17. Srinivasan and Tendulkar 2003.
18. Joshi and Little 1994, table 7.10.
19. World Trade Organization 1998.
20. World Trade Organization 2002, table III.1.
21. Capital account controls allowed India to substantially escape the fallout from the global financial crisis that originated in the United States in September 2008 and hit hard countries such as South Korea that were fully open to capital account flows.
22. Fields 1980, 204.
23. De Long 2003; Rodrik 2003; Rodrik and Subramanian 2005.
24. For example, Subramanian (2007) has stated, "In the Indian case, the triggers were clearly the policy reforms initiated in the early 1980s, and reinforced after 1991, which have

created a basic confidence in the private sector that the policy environment will be supportive rather than hostile." While Subramanian goes on to argue that the positive and significant response to liberalizing reforms in India compared to that in Latin America can be attributed to India's superior institutions and entrepreneurial talent, he clearly concedes the centrality of reforms to India's rise. This is contrary to the DeLong-Rodrik view, on which Rodrik and Subramanian (2005) elaborated. Indeed, as far as policy reform is concerned, Subramanian (2007) more or less agrees with the view put forth in Panagariya 2004b, which had been written partially in response to DeLong 2003 and Rodrik 2003. Other works written in a vein similar to Rodrik and Subramanian 2005 include Kohli 2006 and Nayyar 2006.

25. Pursell 1992, 441.
26. Because 1991/92 was a crisis year, I have excluded it from the periods considered in this paragraph: 1981–91, 1992–2003, and 2003–9.
27. Chang 2007, 27.
28. Chang 2007, 18–20.
29. Ranis 2003, 34.
30. Dossani 2006, 242.
31. Dossani 2006, 253.
32. Similar innovations had also taken place when in the early 1990s, the United States banned India from buying supercomputers. Having acquired access to enough hardware and software by then, Indian computer engineers managed to create their own supercomputer, Param, at a fraction of the cost India would have paid for the U.S. supercomputers. It then proceeded to export those computers to countries such as Canada.
33. Dossani 2006, 253–55.
34. Subramanian 2007.
35. Given the space constraints imposed by an op-ed, Subramanian (2007) could not be expected to give elaborate arguments and evidence in support of these hypotheses. But to my knowledge, he has not undertaken this task to date since writing the op-ed.
36. Though occasional corruption scandals have erupted in recent years, more often than not they have been the result of the government choosing to resort to non-transparent means of allocation of resources such as spectrum and coal mines.
37. See, for example, Wikipedia, "History of Indian Institutes of Technology," http://en.wikipedia.org/wiki/History_of_Indian_Institutes_of_Technology, and Wikipedia, "Indian Institute of Management Ahmedabad," http://en.wikipedia.org/wiki/Indian_Institute_of_Management_Ahmedabad.

13

China

From Isolation to Global Dominance

China has existed as a single nation for almost two thousand years, with only a few short-lived interruptions. Unlike India, it is largely homogeneous in language and culture. According to the 2010 national census, the Han people, with a common written language, account for 91.5 percent of the country's population.[1] Spread over the western half of China, various minorities account for the remaining 8.5 percent of the population. Geographically, almost 90 percent of the population is concentrated in the eastern half of the country. And within the eastern half, a substantial majority is in the southern half of the country.

The twentieth century began with the Qing dynasty ruling China, overthrown in 1911 and replaced by the Republic of China in 1912. Continuous civil war and a war of resistance against the Japanese followed during the subsequent four decades. Finally, the Chinese Communist Party of Mao Zedong successfully seized control of the country and established the People's Republic of China (PRC) on October 1, 1949.

The year 2013 was the last year of double-digit growth in China following the launch of its open-door policy in the late 1970s. Accordingly, for the purpose of this chapter, I treat this year as the terminal year. I divide the economic history of the country under the PRC into two broad periods: 1949–77 and 1978–2013.[2] From the viewpoint of both policy and performance, these periods constitute distinct phases. The former was characterized by tight central control and an inward orientation of the economy and the latter by a phased liberalization both externally and internally. The changes during the second period have culminated in the transformation of China into a highly open economy with significantly reduced domestic controls. They have also been accompanied by unprecedented growth, poverty alleviation, and the emergence of China as a dominant power in global trade.

The discussion of the two periods below is uneven. Whereas the discussion of the second period makes extensive use of data and charts, that of the first period largely relies on political-economic narrative. This is because the only available data on outputs of different sectors during the first period, which come from the official State Statistical Bureau of China (SSBC), suffer from such inconsistencies that they cannot be correct. In a nutshell, the high annual average growth rates of total income (6 percent) and per capita income (4.1 percent) between 1952 and 1979 recorded in these data are not consistent with the beginning and ending per capita incomes available from other, more reliable sources. Therefore, there is no option but to give up on a discussion of the economy using the SSBC data.

Instead, I rely on a detailed historical narrative to substantiate the point that in all likelihood, Chinese growth during this period was no different from that of India: below 4 percent in the aggregate and 2 percent in per capita terms. Because international trade is the subject of this volume, I also provide a discussion of the institutional arrangements governing the flow of exports and imports. Consistent with my suspicion of the available data, I do not offer a discussion of the measures of openness.

Growth Between 1949 and 1977: Rejecting the Official Statistics

Many analysts have criticized the official Chinese statistics for exaggerating GDP growth rates since 1980 and have gone on to offer alternative estimates that are lower. This criticism applies even more strongly to the statistics for the period between 1949 and 1979, though China scholars seem to accept them uncritically. To my knowledge, only T. N. Srinivasan, a longtime observer of both China and India, has frontally questioned the inconsistency of the statistics. He puts the matter thus: "Compared with data on India, data on the Chinese economy have always been and continue to be relatively sparse for the period before 1978. They are also of uncertain reliability, and their internal consistency has not been subject to rigorous examination."[3]

Indeed, the poor quality of the Chinese data casts serious doubts on the high growth rates during 1952–79 that international institutions and scholars of the Chinese economy frequently report without qualification.[4] This is because the per capita income growth during 1952–79 reported in the official Chinese data is inconsistent with the more reliable estimates of per capita incomes at the beginning and end of this period.

In its first major report on the Chinese economy, the World Bank noted that annual per capita GDP was $60 in 1950 in India and $50 in 1952 in China, measured in 1952 dollars.[5] These figures are consistent with the general agreement among scholars of India and China that per capita incomes in the two countries were low and approximately equal in the early 1950s. The World Bank report also states, however—on the authority of the SSBC—that per capita incomes in China grew at an average annual rate of 4.1 percent during 1952–79.[6] During 1950–79, per capita incomes in India grew at an average annual rate of 1.6 percent. Applying these growth rates over the relevant periods (twenty-seven years for China and twenty-nine years for India) to the corresponding beginning-year per capita incomes as per the World Bank report leads to the conclusion that per capita income in China in 1979 should have been 1.56 times that in India.[7]

But the World Development Indicators of the World Bank report that in 1979, per capita incomes in India and China in 2005 dollars were $280 and $207, respectively. That is to say, per capita income in China in 1979 was 0.74 times that in India instead of 1.56 times. If we accept these per capita income estimates for 1979 as well as those the World Bank report cites for the early 1950s, China could not have grown faster than India during 1952–79. In other words, we must reject the 4.1 percent per capita income growth reported in the official data.

As I noted, to my knowledge only Srinivasan has questioned the official Chinese rate of growth, with most other observers reporting it uncritically.[8] For example, in his brief overview of the Chinese economy in a paper that is otherwise devoted to agriculture, economist Justin Lin states that "real GNP per capita tripled between 1952 and 1978."[9] Annual per capita income growth implied by tripling of per capita GNP in twenty-seven years turns out to be 4.1 percent, the same as officially reported. In a similar vein, in his comprehensive book, economist Barry Naughton reports annual per capita income growth of 4.1 percent and GDP growth of 6 percent during 1952–78. While Naughton does discuss the problems afflicting post-liberalization data, he makes no comment on the reliability of pre-liberalization data.[10] Elsewhere in the book, he seems to accept as plausible the statistics reported in official data: "With planners pouring resources into industry, rapid industrial growth was not surprising: Between 1952 and 1978 industrial output grew at an average annual rate of 11.5 percent."[11]

There are only two alternatives to rejecting the official 4.1 percent growth rate of per capita income in China, and both are implausible. First, it may be that the Chinese income in 1952 was just $30 at 1952 prices, almost half that in India. This is not only an implausibly low per capita income at that time, it is also in conflict with the general acceptance of the fact that 1949–52 was a period of dramatic recovery that restored China's income to its prewar peak. Indeed, I have not come across a single author who argues that China's income in the early 1950s was just half that of India.

The second alternative is that the Chinese per capita income in 1979 was 1.56 times that of India. But this would imply either much higher per capita incomes today than those reported or significantly lower growth rates during the years since 1979. These possibilities are ruled out, however, on the grounds that the post-liberalization data have undergone much greater scrutiny by scholars;

pre-liberalization data are known to have been subject to falsification at various points in time; and serious statisticians, economists, and demographers were subject to various anti-rightist purges while Mao lived. Therefore, there is little escape from the conclusion reached by Srinivasan:

> The available data thus do not support any stronger conclusion than that India and China had roughly the same level of per capita income in the early 1950s. . . . If the World Bank figures of per capita GNP of the two countries in 1990 are taken at their face value, then their growth in the forty years following 1950 could not have been dissimilar either![12]

A Political-Economic History, 1949–77

Recognizing that the only available statistics on the evolution of the Chinese economy in the pre-liberalization era are wholly unreliable, I opt in favor of a qualitative historical account of political-economic developments. In broad terms, this account reinforces the conclusion that China could not have grown faster than India in per capita terms during this period.

Postwar Recovery, 1949–52

Having essentially committed to Soviet-style socialism soon after assuming power, the Chinese Communist Party (CCP) proceeded to put agriculture and industry back on their feet during the four years ending in 1952. In the countryside, its major initiative was a land reform whereby it confiscated all land from landlords and rich peasants without compensation and distributed it to poor and landless farmers. More than 40 percent of China's arable land was redistributed within a short period and land ownership was more or less equalized. During this period, the government allowed cultivators to privately own their land. The movement toward small cooperatives had begun but was still in its infancy, and in any case it allowed farmers to retain the rights to their land and its produce.

In urban areas, the government took over many factories, including those expropriated from the Japanese after the war and those left by Chinese capitalists who fled the mainland. The government welcomed non-communists who were willing to work with it, and many scientists and intellectuals joined the effort. Capitalists who stayed in China were also encouraged to expand their production. Relative to what was to follow, this period was characterized by a liberal approach to economic policy. By the end of 1952, the government had successfully rehabilitated agriculture and industry to their pre-revolution peaks.

The First Five-Year Plan, 1953–57

The recovery set the stage for the launch of China's long-term development strategy. Around this time, like India, China did not appreciate the importance of international trade and hence specialization according to comparative advantage. It too saw the production of everything at home as the only road available to industrialization. In view of the supposed success of the Soviet experience, it opted for the Soviet model. A trade embargo by Western nations, triggered by its support of North Korea in the Korean War, also led China to seek assistance from the Soviet Union. Therefore, the First Five-Year Plan, which spanned the years from 1953 to 1957, set China on a course toward Soviet-style development with significant Soviet involvement.

In the countryside, the government encouraged the formation of cooperatives. There were three forms of cooperatives.[13] First, there were "mutual aid team" cooperatives, in which four or five adjacent farm households pooled their farm tools and draft animals and exchanged labor on a temporary or permanent basis. Each household kept its land and harvest. This form of cooperative dominated in the early years until 1955.

The second form of cooperative, called "elementary" cooperatives, brought together twenty to thirty neighboring families that pooled not just their farm tools and draft animals but also land. The net output was then distributed according to ownership of land, tools, and draft animals, on the one hand, and the work performed, on the other. This form of cooperative also peaked in 1955, though it was never the dominant form.

The third form of cooperative, called "advanced" cooperatives or "collectives," imposed collective ownership of all farm tools, draft animals and land. Each household was paid according to work points earned. The size of the collectives varied from thirty to two hundred households. Until 1955, there were only five hundred collectives. But intervention by Mao led to their rapid expansion in the following two years. By the end of 1957, virtually all farms came under collectives, with their number rising to 753,000. The government also established its monopoly over grain purchases in the early part of the First Five-Year Plan. To extract surplus for investment in industry, it generally procured grain at "artificially low prices."[14]

It is in the area of industry that the Soviet involvement played a crucial role. It supplied massive economic assistance in the form of loans, turnkey projects, blueprints, and training of Chinese technicians. The Soviet Union and Eastern European countries were the principal suppliers for the 156 industrial projects China undertook during this period, locating them mainly in inland regions or in the northeast. Some six thousand Soviet advisors came to China, and ten thousand Chinese students went to the Soviet Union. The government also pushed through public ownership of shops and factories in the cities, converting them into cooperatives and "joint public-private" factories in which the state exercised considerable control.[15]

In 1956, Mao initiated the Hundred Flowers Campaign, whereby he invited all citizens, especially students and professors, to offer criticisms of the CCP's policies. Though initially slow to emerge, criticisms reached such heights that Mao eventually made a 180-degree turn and launched a repressive anti-rightist campaign. Most critics lost their jobs and were sentenced to either prison or manual labor in the countryside.

The detrimental effects of centralized control, which was progressively eliminating incentives for individual initiative, could be seen in both agriculture and industry even before the end of the First Five-Year Plan. In his comprehensive history of China, historian Jonathan Spence notes that in the fall of 1956, "things began to go poorly as the attempt to impose cooperative agriculture led to chaos and waste, compounded by bad management and contradictory orders."[16] In the urban pool of workers, which was rapidly enlarged, many were illiterate or otherwise unprepared for factory work. Simple mistakes such as failing to level installed equipment or running machines without oiling ruined them. Strict compliance with quantitative targets imposed by the state led to serious adverse impacts on product quality, even by domestic Chinese standards. Spence describes this effect as follows:

> The problem of quality control was aptly summarized by a Chinese newspaper article of 1955, which reported on a certain senior manager who ordered his inspector Li to certify substandard products, so that the company could meet its quota. When Li angrily refused, the manager promoted him to assistant manager. Li thereupon bullied his former fellow inspectors to pass substandard products, since now it was he who had to meet the quota.[17]

The Debacle Under the Great Leap Forward, 1958–60

The period 1958–60 saw the launch and massive failure of the Great Leap Forward.[18] Mao felt that the Soviet model of industrialization, based on the extraction of surplus from agriculture for investment in industry, would take a long time to work its way through China. He argued that China had to "walk on two legs"—that is, develop agriculture and industry simultaneously through mass mobilization. In agriculture, labor was to be mobilized to undertake large irrigation projects and expand the area under cultivation. In industry, labor was to contribute directly to production. Logistically, the mobilization was to be achieved through the creation of massive "people's communes." Under the commune system, decision-making was decentralized to local cadres and primacy was given to ideological purity over technical expertise. This gave local cadres decisive power over scientists and technicians, who were expected to become fully "Red and expert" through political guidance from the cadres.

By the end of 1958, China had converted 753,000 collective farms into 24,000 communes, each consisting of thirty collective farms of 150 households each. The communes came to cover 99 percent of all rural households in China. On the average, each commune included 5,000 households, 10,000 workers and 10,000 acres of cultivable land. Payment in the commune was made partly on the basis of subsistence and partly on the basis of work performed.[19]

Each commune included peasants from several villages who were to engage in local industrial production; giant irrigation, terracing, and construction projects; rural schooling; organization of local militia; and searches for petroleum and uranium. To mobilize women for work, common kitchens and childcare facilities were created. To free up land for commercial crops and other uses, untried methods of cultivation such as close cropping and deep plowing were encouraged. The former held that yield per acre could be enhanced dramatically by planting seeds densely, while the latter was based on the mistaken belief that deep planting would lead to extra-large roots. Factories were encouraged to move to the countryside so that peasants could gain work experience in them. Farmers were also encouraged to produce steel in backyard furnaces.

A bumper harvest in the summer of 1958, principally attributable to exceptionally good weather, led the top communist leadership to wrongly conclude that the Great Leap Forward was handsomely paying off.[20] The reality was quite the opposite. The years 1959, 1960, and 1961 were characterized by natural disasters including floods and droughts. This, accompanied by a diversion of peasants to non-agricultural activities, a resort to unscientific methods of cultivation, the breakdown of the traditional incentive system, and the diseconomies of excessively large communes, resulted in three back-to-back years of declining agricultural output. To add to the woes, crops in some areas could not be harvested due to labor shortages.

Matters were made worse by pressures from the top leadership on local cadres to report successes resulting from new innovative methods. The pressures led the cadres to file inflated reports of output to provincial and higher levels of administration. In turn, these reports became the basis for procurement of grain by the state to supply towns and cities and to export. With the anti-rightist campaign having driven any credible statistical system out of existence, there was no remaining source that could independently verify the outputs of various commodities. Determined to convince the outside world that his policies were succeeding, Mao also ensured that China continued to export significant quantities of grain in 1959 and 1960 to repay past loans and buy more machinery from the Soviet Union. The net effect of massive state procurements in the face of poor crop yields was unprecedented food shortage in the countryside and the greatest famine humanity has ever experienced. While precise numbers are still not known, demographic data suggest that 20 to 30 million deaths over and above normal levels took place during these years.

The Great Leap was a failure in the industrial arena as well. Mao had specifically campaigned to raise steel output, setting ever rising targets. To boost production, farmers set up backyard furnaces and even melted farm implements to meet their targets. Steel produced in backyard furnaces turned out to be of extremely poor quality, unsuitable for use in any worthwhile products. And melting of farm implements naturally had a detrimental effect on agriculture. By all accounts, industrial output significantly declined during the Great Leap.

No doubt, drought and flood contributed to the poor outcomes during these years. Soviet withdrawal of aid and technicians in July 1961 added to the woes. But the real problems were homegrown:

> Despite the importance of these difficulties, China's worst problem was bad policy. The people's communes were too large to be effective, they ignored age-old marketing patterns in the countryside, and they required administrative and transport resources that did not exist. Their structure and means of allocating resources removed almost all incentive to work, and the breakdown in the statistical system meant that the top leaders had grossly erroneous ideas about what was occurring. Thus, even after many rural areas were beset by massive starvation, the orders from above continued to demand large-scale procurement of foodstuffs. The rural cadres were so afraid of being branded rightist that they followed these unrealistic orders, thus deepening the famine.[21]

Retreat from the Great Leap and Revival of the Economy, 1961–65

By late 1960, the Great Leap strategy had been discredited and policy initiative passed into the hands of liberal-minded Liu Shaoqi, chairman of the PRC; Deng Xiaoping, secretary general of the CCP; and Zhou Enlai, premier of the State Council. While Mao, by his own description, "retired from the front line," this period also saw the rise of the People's Liberation Army (PLA) under Defense Minister Lin Biao. In turn, Lin promoted Mao's personality cult within the army.

Several steps were taken to reverse the Great Leap during 1961–65. Approximately 30 million peasants who had moved to the cities since 1957 and unemployed urban youths were sent to work in the countryside to assist agricultural recovery. Some 25,000 inefficient industrial enterprises were closed down.

Private cultivation was partially revived and private rural markets reopened. The state's grain procurement returned to normal levels, contributing to the revival of agriculture.

Policy changes giving greater play to individual initiative followed in almost all areas, with highly positive results. Individual farming was revived in preference to the collective system; older, pre-revolutionary art forms were revived; and rewards in industry were more closely aligned to the efforts of workers in industry. "In general, China during 1961–65 did a remarkable job of reviving the economy, at least regaining the level of output of 1957 in almost all sectors."[22]

Another important accomplishment of this period was the discovery of rich oil and gas deposits. Domestic oil production went up tenfold and gas production fortyfold relative to 1957. This rise in oil and gas production greatly reduced China's energy dependence on the Soviet Union.[23]

The Cultural Revolution, 1966–68

The years 1961–65 saw Mao sidelined. He eventually reasserted his authority through the so-called Great Proletarian Cultural Revolution, launched with the help of his wife and several other associates.[24] The principal agents of the Cultural Revolution were Red Guards, consisting of students from universities and high schools, some younger university professors, and urban youth who had been sent to the countryside in the aftermath of the Great Leap. Mao and his associates encouraged Red Guards to attack the "Four Olds": old customs, old habits, old culture, and old thinking. But they left it to the Red Guards to identify the objects and individuals associated with these old elements. While public humiliation was to be the commonest punishment for those identified as carriers of the "four olds," Red Guards often went far beyond it, engaging in destruction, physical abuse, and killings. Under the direction of a small group of Mao's confidants, purges reached higher and higher levels until even Liu Shaoqi and Deng Xiaoping were removed from their posts after being subjected to mass criticism and humiliation. Spence describes the destruction and violence in these graphic terms:

> With the euphoria, fear, excitement, and tension that gripped the country, violence grew apace. Thousands of intellectuals and others were beaten to death or died of injuries. Countless others committed suicide, among them Lao She, the author of the novel *Cat Country*, which had spoken so eloquently in 1932 against the Chinese who turned on each other. Many of the suicides killed themselves only after futile attempts to avoid Red Guard harassment by destroying their own libraries and art collections. Thousands more were imprisoned, often in

solitary confinement, for years. Millions were relocated to purify themselves through labor in the countryside.[25]

Although the Cultural Revolution formally ended in 1977, Mao ended
its active phase in 1968 and began rebuilding the CCP to establish order.
Unsurprisingly, the Cultural Revolution had a significant detrimental effect on
the economy: in 1968, industrial production dipped 12 percent below its 1966
level.[26] Even allowing for the possibility of significant error in reporting the extent of the decline, once we recognize that various sectors of the economy had
barely recovered to their 1957 levels of activity in 1965, a decline in 1968 relative
to 1966 would suggest that the entire decade following 1957 had been lost. This
observation reinforces the conclusion that the 6 percent annual growth between
1952 and 1979 reported in official data represents gross exaggeration.

An area that directly suffered long-term harm from the Cultural Revolution
was education. During the active phase of the revolution, schools and colleges
had been closed. When order was restored, several steps were taken to eliminate elitism from schools and universities. The time required to complete each
level of schooling was considerably compressed. Each student was required
to engage in several years of manual labor before gaining entry into a university. Recommendation by the applicant's work unit replaced the competitive examinations for university admissions. Collective study was encouraged
and formal examinations were discontinued. Study of politics and vocational
training replaced formal scholarship. Teachers no longer had the authority they
had traditionally held in the classroom.

The government heavily pushed for the youth to spend time in the countryside. Initially, only Red Guards were subjected to this requirement, but later it
was extended to most middle-school graduates. The youth were instructed to
learn from the poor and lower-middle-class peasants. Those of them sent to the
countryside during this period did not find their way back to the cities until
Mao's death in 1976.[27]

The Struggle for Succession, 1969–77

Lin Biao, who had been appointed defense minister in 1959, had consistently
strengthened the position of the military in domestic branches of the government and aligned himself closely with Mao. Lin emerged as the big winner of the
Cultural Revolution. The Ninth Party Congress, which met in April 1969, officially designated him as Mao's successor. The ambitious Lin quickly proceeded
to tighten the army's grip on power.

Mao soon realized that Lin was overly eager to succeed him and posed a direct threat to his own authority. Therefore, with the quiet help of Zhou Enlai,

he began to cut Lin down to size. According to official Chinese accounts, in the end, Lin Biao died in a plane crash in September 1971 while trying to escape to the Soviet Union following an abortive assassination plot against Mao. In the following weeks, Mao went on to purge almost the entire military command that had served under Lin.

The departure of Lin Biao from the scene strengthened the hand of Zhou Enlai, who tried to bring stability back to China. He attempted to revamp educational standards, began opening up the economy to the outside world, and facilitated the forward movement of the economy that had begun in 1969. He also brought back to office some of those who had been ousted during the Cultural Revolution. While Mao went along with these changes, he remained suspicious that they might reverse the gains of the Cultural Revolution and undermine his legacy.

Serious health problems led Mao and Zhou Enlai to bring Deng Xiaoping back to active duty in early 1973. Zhou intended to groom Deng as Mao's successor. But Mao's wife and her three closest associates, who together came to be called the "Gang of Four," saw Deng as a rival. Between mid-1973 and January 1976, Deng promoted the "Four Modernizations"—agriculture, industry, science and technology, and defense. But the Gang of Four continuously subjected him to radical attacks. By late 1975, the Gang of Four had convinced Mao that Deng's policies would lead to his eventual repudiation. As a result, Deng was purged yet again after Zhou died of cancer in January 1976.

Along with Deng, many of his followers in positions of power were purged as well. But as luck would have it, Mao died in September 1976 and a coalition of leaders from the government, military, and police purged the Gang of Four and brought Deng back. China finally had cohesive, pragmatic leadership at the helm, which paved the way for the systematic albeit gradual opening up of the economy externally as well as internally. The second half of this chapter will focus on the remarkable developments that followed.

International Trade Institutions, 1952–77

Before I turn to the second phase of Chinese development, spanning the period from 1978 to 2013, it is useful to briefly consider the Chinese international trade institutions as they existed during the first three decades following the establishment of the PRC in 1949. The trading system in China during this period was far more centralized and controlled than that in India. The prevailing philosophy was one of self-reliance, as in India, and every effort was made to isolate the domestic economy from world markets. Domestic needs were to be satisfied as much as possible by domestic production, with imports intended to fill critical gaps in areas such as food, essential raw materials, and capital goods. Special emphasis was placed on accessing technology, often embodied in machines.

Under the authority of the Ministry of Foreign Trade (MFT), the central government determined the annual physical quantities of imports and exports through a system of planning. The planning process determined which imports were required by identifying gaps between domestic needs and domestic production. Exports were then identified to finance the imports. The MFT established a limited number of centralized foreign trade corporations (FTCs)—twelve of them in 1978—and gave them monopoly of trade within their specified lines of business. The FTCs procured the goods for exports from the domestic market and signed contracts with foreign suppliers to import goods from abroad within their lines of business. Procurement of goods for exports and sales of imports were accomplished at domestic prices. Because the domestic currency, the renminbi, was overvalued, FTCs typically incurred losses on exports and made profits on imports. This was not an issue for FTCs, however, since the MFT absorbed any losses and skimmed off any profits. Because no entities other than the centrally controlled FTCs were permitted to engage in foreign trade, there was no need for any formal trade restrictions such as tariffs or import licenses, and none were imposed.[28]

In addition to the usual losses arising from the failure to specialize according to comparative advantage, exploit scale economies, and access the most productive technologies, this system imposed two other costs. First, given that the MFT absorbed losses and skimmed off profits, the FTCs had no incentive to minimize the costs of their operations. Second, the buyer and the seller of a traded product, whether it was an import or export, had no contact whatsoever with each other. Indeed, they did not even know each other. For imported products, this meant that the buyer had no way of remedying a situation in which the product received was not the one that had been sought. In the case of exports, a similar problem existed, so establishing reputation as an exporter was out of the question.

Growth and Poverty Outcomes, 1978–2013

Before I turn to the policy changes that took place beginning in the late 1970s, I summarize the evolution of the economy in terms of GDP, per capita GDP, and poverty profile. There remain issues of reliability of the Chinese data relating to the post-1978 period as well, but they are not so acute as to be discarded altogether. Differences across different sources are small enough to allow us to conclude with confidence that the 1980s and subsequent decades exhibited miracle-level growth. For example, China expert Nicholas Lardy notes that

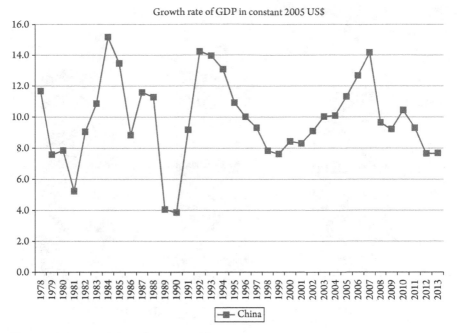

Figure 13.1 Annual Growth Rates in China, 1978–2013. Source: Author's construction based on data from World Bank WDI online (accessed April 30, 2015).

official Chinese sources place the growth rate during 1978–95 at 9.4 percent, while the World Bank places it at 8.2 percent.[29] The OECD offers the significantly lower estimate of 6 percent for the years spanning 1986–94, but even this rate represents an upward shift relative to what in all likelihood had been achieved during 1949–78.

Keeping this broad picture in mind, in the following I rely on the data reported by the World Bank in its online World Development Indicators database. Figure 13.1 plots the growth rates of GDP at market prices in constant local currency units from 1978 to 2013. Remarkably, in only three years out of three and a half decades did the growth rate fall below 6 percent. In four different years— 1984, 1992, 1993, and 2007—the growth rate breached the 14 percent mark. It is possible that these latter growth rates are subject to larger measurement error than others. Yet adjusting them downward by a few percentage points would not alter the overall impressive growth that the Chinese economy has exhibited.

Figure 13.2 shows the annual average growth rates of GDP and per capita GDP during the 1980s, 1990s, and 2001–13. Remembering that at a compound growth rate of 7 percent, any given amount doubles in ten years, China is more than doubling in per capita terms every ten years. This is a most remarkable growth. One way to appreciate this fact is to compare the evolution of per capita incomes of China and India during these decades, as done in Figure 13.3.

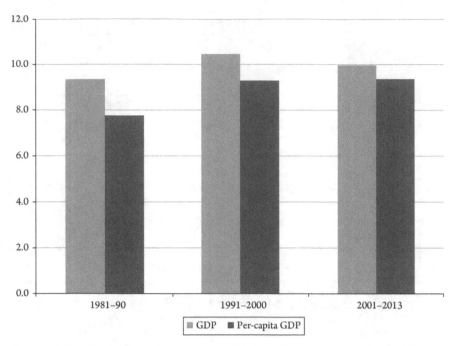

Figure 13.2 Annual Average Growth Rates of GDP and Per Capita GDP by Decades.
Source: Author's construction based on data from World Bank WDI online (accessed April 30, 2015).

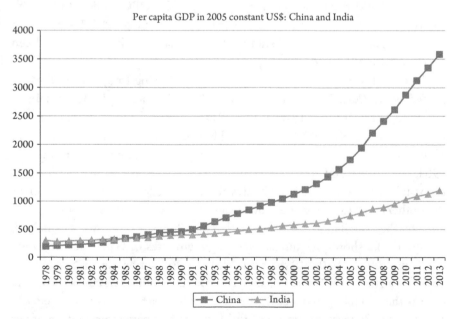

Figure 13.3 Evolution of Per Capita Incomes in China and India. Source: Author's
construction based on data from World Bank WDI online (accessed April 30, 2015).

In 1978, per capita incomes in 2005 dollars in India and China were $302 and $195, respectively. By 2013, they had risen to $1,190 and $3,583, respectively.

Turning to poverty, it must be acknowledged at the outset that the estimates for China are subject to larger errors than in many other countries. Economists Martin Ravallion and Shaohua Chen, whose estimates of poverty in China are widely reproduced including later in this chapter, note, "While NBS [National Bureau of Statistics] has selectively made the micro data (for some provinces and years) available to outside researchers, the complete data are not available to us for any year."[30] Therefore, Ravallion and Chen have to rely on grouped data that contain the number of individuals in specific income groups and the mean income in each group. In the early 1980s, even these grouped data are based on relatively small samples. For example, the 1980 rural household survey has 16,000 households and the 1981 urban household survey 9,000 households. It is only in 1985 that the sample size grows much larger, to 68,000 in rural areas and 30,000 to 40,000 in urban areas. Ravallion and Chen also note problems arising out of valuation of consumption of own-farm production at market versus procurement prices.

Given these problems, the levels of poverty even for a given poverty line must be taken with a grain of salt. Nevertheless, the change in the poverty ratio over time can be accepted with a greater degree of confidence as long as the under-lying methodology of collecting samples and calculations of estimates have not undergone dramatic change. Keeping this fact in view, Figure 13.4 and Figure 13.5 present the evolution of two poverty estimates. The lower estimate pegs the rural poverty line at 300 yuan at 1990 prices; the higher estimate is 850 yuan at 2002 prices. The urban poverty line is then adjusted based on price differences and is 1,200 yuan at 2002 prices.

At the official poverty line, rural poverty stood at approximately 41 percent in 1980 and fell to below 10 percent by 1984. The decline was even sharper if we go by the higher poverty line chosen by Ravallion and Chen: from approximately 76 percent in 1980 to 31 percent in 1984. As for urban poverty, it was approximately eliminated by the early 1990s. Indeed, going by its extremely low level in 1980, urban poverty does not appear to have been a serious problem in China and it has not been the subject of serious debate.

Rapid Growth in Exports and Imports, 1982–2013

I next turn to an account of the evolution of trade and foreign investment in China. In this section, I document the evidence showing rapid expansion of trade in aggregate. In the next section, I discuss the dramatic reorientation of the composition of trade in China according to its factor endowments. This is

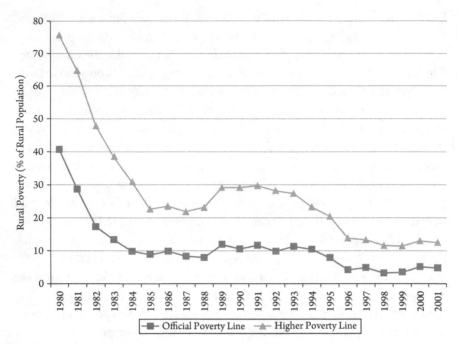

Figure 13.4 Rural Poverty, 1980–2001. Source: Author's construction using estimates in Ravallion and Chen 2007.

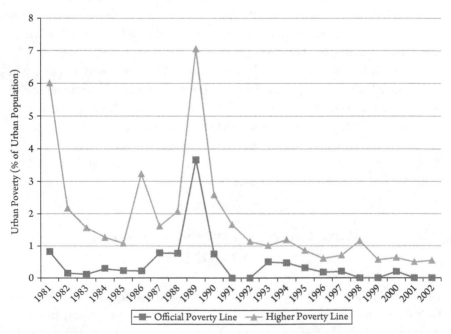

Figure 13.5 Urban Poverty, 1981–2002. Source: Author's construction using estimates in Ravallion and Chen 2007.

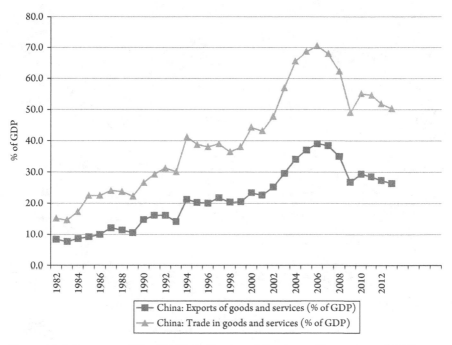

Figure 13.6 Exports and Total Trade in Goods and Services as Proportions of GDP.
Source: Author's construction based on data from World Bank WDI online (accessed April 30, 2015).

followed by a brief look at the expansion of foreign investment. I then discuss trade and foreign investment policies with the eventual objective of connecting them to performance in trade, growth, and poverty alleviation.

Figure 13.6 plots the exports of and total trade in goods and services as proportions of GDP from 1982 to 2013. Exports as a proportion of GDP rose from 8.4 percent in 1982 to the peak of 39.1 percent in 2006, though they fell steadily thereafter and stood at 26.4 percent in 2013. The ratio has risen steadily until 2006 except during a brief period beginning in 1995. Total trade as a proportion of GDP has risen from 15.1 percent in 1982 to the peak of 70.6 percent in 2006 but then exhibited a declining trend. In 2013, the ratio had fallen to 50.3 percent. The downward trend in the exports and trade as proportions of GDP notwithstanding, few analysts today would dispute that China is a highly open economy. Indeed, many argue that it is too open and has for a long time subsidized exports while taxing imports by undervaluing its currency.

Unlike the past examples of miracle growth countries, China also happens to be very large. This has meant that the rapid expansion of its exports and imports has led it to acquire a significantly large share in world exports and imports. This is particularly true of merchandise trade, since services account for only a small proportion of China's trade. Figure 13.7 shows the shares of China and the United States in world merchandise exports since 1980. From 0.9 percent in

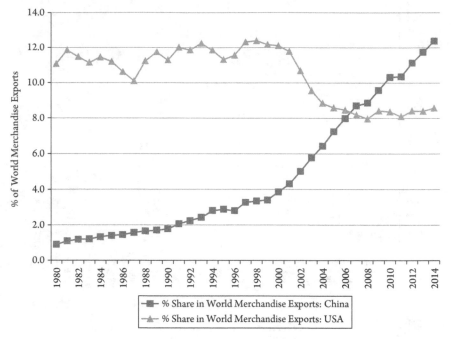

Figure 13.7 Shares in World Merchandise Exports, China and USA. Source: Author's construction using online data from World Trade Organization database (accessed April 30, 2015).

1980, China's share rose to 12.4 percent in 2014. Since 2007, its share has come to exceed that of the United States, with the gap in its favor becoming extremely large by 2014.[31]

Structural Transformation in International Trade, 1984–2008

As Lardy points out, the centrally controlled system of trade in China not only suppressed the overall volume of trade but also distorted the commodity composition of exports in the late 1970s and early 1980s: "In the late 1970s and first half of 1980s China's exports did not conform to the country's underlying comparative advantage in labor-intensive products. There was no significant correlation between labor-intensity in production, on the one hand, and the growth of exports on the other. Exports of some labor-intensive goods rose sharply; but so did exports of some capital-intensive products. Indeed, the single largest source of increased export earnings in the first half of the 1980s was from international sales of crude oil and refined petroleum products, among the most capital-intensive goods produced in China."[32]

But between the mid-1980s and the mid-2000s, the structure of exports from China underwent dramatic transformation. Initially, exports shifted toward light, labor-intensive manufactures. Over time, exports grew in sophistication, concentrating heavily on processing and assembly of various kinds of machinery and equipment. Table 13.1, which tracks the structure of Chinese exports in terms of one-digit Standard International Trade Classification (SITC) between 1984 and 2008, provides some preliminary insight into the changing structure. Before I describe it, let me note that in constructing Table 13.1, I have taken the current dollar values of annual exports of each one-digit commodity group in different years and calculated its average share in the total value of exports during 1984–90, 1990–2000, 2001–4, and 2005–8. Because the annual export value of each commodity aggregate is in current dollars, the aggregation over different years involves some error, but for our purpose of big-picture changes, the distortion is of no real consequence.

Table 13.1 **Changing composition of exports: percent share in total exports**

SITC Code	Item	1984–90	1991–2000	2001–4	2005–8
0	Food and live animals	12.4	6.7	3.9	2.5
1	Beverages and tobacco	0.5	0.6	0.3	0.1
2	Crude materials, inedible, except fuels	8.6	2.6	1.2	0.8
3	Mineral fuels, lubricants and related materials	13	3.6	2.6	2.0
4	Animal and vegetable oils, fats and waxes	0.3	0.2	0	0.0
5	Chemicals and related products, not elsewhere specified	5.8	5.4	4.5	4.9
6	Manufactured goods classified chiefly by material	21.1	18.9	16.6	18.0
7	Machinery and transport equipment	11.9	24.7	41.8	47.2
8	Miscellaneous manufactured articles	23.9	37.1	28.9	24.2
9	Transactions not classified elsewhere	2.5	0.3	0.2	0.2
	TOTAL	100	100	100	100

Source: Author's calculations using UN Commodity Trade data, Series Revision 2.

Three observations follow from Table 13.1. First, even during 1984–90, when some realignment of China's trade toward its factor endowments had already taken place, mineral fuels accounted for as much as 13 percent of its exports. Food and live animals accounted for another 12.4 percent. In contrast, SITC 6, 7, and 8, which largely consist of manufactures, accounted for only 57 percent of the merchandise exports.

Second, the joint share of the three manufacturing categories rose steadily to 80 percent during 1991–2000, 87 percent during 2001–4, and 89 percent during 2005–8. The twin facts that the total exports of China rose very rapidly and that the degree of concentration within SITC categories 6, 7, and 8 also rose rapidly suggest the presence of some very fast-growing export products in that country. I return to this point later.

Finally, shifts in the structure of Chinese exports *within manufactures* testify to their even greater dynamism. For instance, miscellaneous manufactures (SITC 8), which include products such as apparel and footwear, increased their share of total exports from 24 percent during 1984–90 to 37 percent during 1991–2000 and then fell to 29 percent during 2001–4 and 24 percent during 2005–8. The share of machinery and transport equipment (SITC 7) rose from 12 percent during 1984–90 to 25 percent during 1991–2000, 42 percent during 2001–4, and 47 percent during 2005–8. In later years, Chinese exports have clearly shifted from traditional light manufactures to more modern products.

The dynamism and shifting composition of exports is seen even more clearly in Table 13.2, which shows all SITC two-digit commodities that had 2 percent or higher share of total exports during 2005–8. The commodities are arranged in descending order of importance according to export volumes during 2005–8. The top three commodities together accounted for a whopping 36 percent of China's total merchandise exports during 2005–8. The most remarkable thing to note is that during 1984–90, these commodities accounted for a paltry 4.5 percent of the total exports, with the total exports being tiny. During this period, it was apparel and textiles that accounted for most exports: 14.3 and 13.8 percent, respectively. While apparel still accounted for 9.3 percent of the exports during 2005–8, textiles had declined to just 4.9 percent. Ultra-high rates of investment and large volumes of foreign direct investment have contributed to a shift in China's export structure toward somewhat more capital-intensive and technologically sophisticated products. While the available evidence points to specialization by China in the assembly and processing stages of production that are more labor intensive than prior stages of production, it is important to note that the top three of China's two-digit SITC exports during 2005–8—SITC 75, 76, and 77—were all classified under "machinery and transport equipment" within the SITC one-digit classification.

Table 13.2 **Two-digit SITC (Rev 2) commodities with 2 percent or higher share, 2005–8: percent share in total exports**

SITC Code	Commodity description	1984–90	1991–2000	2001–4	2005–8
S2-75	Office machines and automatic data processing equipment	0.4	4.8	12.9	13.4
S2-76	Telecommunications, sound recording and reproducing equipment	2.9	6.1	10.4	12.0
S2-77	Electric machinery, apparatus and appliances, nes,* and parts, nes	1.2	7.2	10.1	10.6
S2-84	Articles of apparel and clothing accessories	14.3	16.8	11.8	9.3
S2-89	Miscellaneous manufactured articles, nes	4.9	9.3	7.3	5.8
S2-65	Textile yarn, fabrics, made-up articles, nes, and related products	13.8	8.1	6.1	4.9
S2-67	Iron and steel	1.4	2.2	1.7	3.9
S2-69	Manufactures of metals, nes	2.0	3.1	3.4	3.7
S2-74	General industrial machinery and equipment, nes, and parts of, nes	0.6	1.4	2.7	3.6
S2-78	Road vehicles	4.0	2.1	2.6	3.1
S2-87	Professional, scientific, controlling instruments, apparatus, nes	0.2	0.7	1.4	2.4
S2-82	Furniture and parts thereof	0.5	1.4	2.1	2.2
S2-85	Footwear	2.0	4.4	2.9	2.1

* "nes" stands for "not elsewhere specified."

Source: Author's calculations using online United Nations Comtrade data.

It is instructive to plot the evolution of China's top four exports during 2005–8. This is done in Figure 13.8 using export values in current dollars. Remarkably, each of the top three items during 2005–8 accounted for less than $20 billion in exports until as late as 1999. Among the top four items during 2005–8, only apparel and clothing exports exceeded the $20 billion mark in 1999. But by 2005, exports of each of the three items had surpassed the exports of apparel and clothing. Moreover, by 2006, each of the top three items had registered exports in excess of $100 billion.

Before I conclude this section, it is important to note that while there is no doubt that Chinese exports have steadily risen in sophistication, one can easily overstate this fact. For example, in an interesting analysis of export data, Rodrik has reached the following conclusion: "China has somehow managed to latch on to advanced, high productivity products that one would not normally expect a poor, labor abundant country like China to produce, let alone export."[33] It turns out, however, that this conclusion is unwarranted because it is based exclusively on a comparison of China's export data with those of advanced economies. The problem arises because exports of the same product from different countries may contain very different domestically produced components.

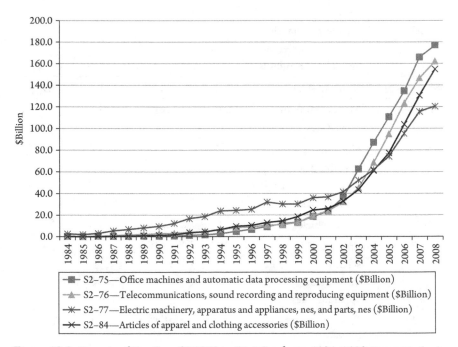

Figure 13.8 Exports of Top Four SITC Two-Digit Products, 1984–2008. Source: Author's construction using data from United Nations Commodity Trade Database.

When exports make use of tradable inputs, it is possible for two countries with identical export baskets to be specializing in very different production activities. A country that imports 90 percent components will have a very different pattern of specialization in production than one that produces all components domestically, even when the export baskets of the two countries are identical. Moreover, if processing trade, whereby a country imports the bulk of inputs and reexports them after adding a proportionally small amount of value, is concentrated in technically sophisticated products, the analysis of export data alone would lead to the erroneous conclusion that the country predominantly exports highly sophisticated products.

To account for this factor, economists Van Assche and Byron Gangnes analyze the *production* data for electronics products.[34] In contrast to Rodrik, they conclude, "Contrary to existing studies, we find no evidence that China's electronics production activities are more sophisticated than one would expect from its level of development. We also find little evidence that China is rapidly upgrading into more sophisticated production activities." In a similar vein, economists Robert Koopman, Zhi Wang, and Shang-Jin Wei find that China's technologically sophisticated export products such as computers, telecommunications equipment, and electronic devices have import content of nearly 80 percent.[35] This would mean that China's specialization is in activities quite different from those of countries exporting the same products with little import content.[36]

Foreign Direct Investment

Before I turn to a discussion of trade and foreign investment policy, let me briefly describe the trends in net inflows of foreign direct investment. Although China had begun to liberalize foreign investment in selective regions and selective industries in the late 1970s, FDI began to enter it in significant volumes only in the early 1990s. It exhibited two spurts: one beginning in 1992 and the other beginning in 2004 (Figure 13.9). In absolute terms, the second of these spurts was especially sharp.

In the first spurt, FDI rose from $4.4 billion in 1991 to $11.2 billion in 1992 and $27.5 billion in 1993, peaking at $44.2 billion in 1997. In 1993, FDI as a proportion of GDP peaked at 6.2 percent, a feat not repeated since that year despite considerable expansion of FDI in absolute terms. The second spurt began in 2004 and with the exception of two subsequent years (2009 and 2012), FDI rose steadily between 2003 and 2013. The absolute amount of FDI rose from $49.5 billion in 2003 to $347.8 billion in 2013. As a proportion of GDP, the latter volume stood at 3.8 percent.

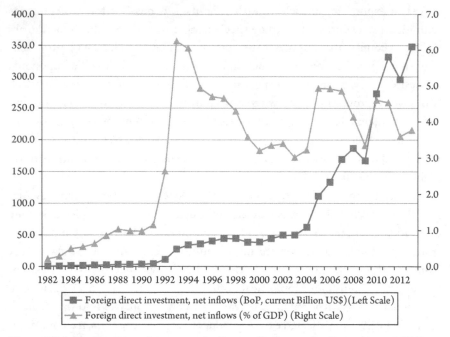

Figure 13.9 Foreign Direct Investment in Current Dollars and as Proportion of GDP.
Source: Author's construction based on data from World Bank WDI online (accessed April 30, 2015).

Trade Liberalization, 1978–2001

The phenomenal growth in and transformation of the structure of Chinese exports has not taken place without policy change. On the contrary, it is intimately linked to such change, the subject of this and the following section. Trade policy as it currently exists was firmly in place by 2007.[37] Therefore, the discussion ranges from 1978 to 2007. For clarity of exposition, it is divided into two parts: 1978–2001 and 2001–7. The changes in the second period are intimately linked to the conditions the country had to meet as a part of its entry into the World Trade Organization (WTO) in 2001.

Rights to Trade Abroad

Until at least the early 1990s, China had a highly complex and opaque trade policy regime even by Indian standards.[38] As already described, trade flows in the pre-liberalization era were controlled by centralized foreign trade corporations (FTCs) under the Ministry of Foreign Trade (MFT). The FTCs were organized along product lines such as iron/steel and textiles/clothing and had branch offices in the main provinces. In 1979, when China launched its "open-door" policy by enacting the Law of the PRC on Joint Ventures Using Chinese and Foreign Investment, twelve such FTCs existed.

Among other things, the new policy was accompanied by an expansion of entities with independent rights to conduct foreign trade. At the center, line ministries created their own FTCs that began to compete for exports and as suppliers of imports with their counterparts under the MFT. Branch offices of FTCs at the provincial and local levels became relatively independent: they still undertook trade on behalf of their central counterparts, but they also began to engage in international trade on their own. Provinces created their own FTCs for special needs as well. Trade conducted by FTCs directly under the Ministry of Foreign Economic Relations and Trade (MOFERT), which came to replace MFT, declined to 72 percent in 1984 from 89 percent in 1981.[39]

From the beginning, foreign-invested enterprises, whether joint ventures or wholly foreign owned, were given the right to conduct their own trade. This meant they could export what they produced and also import inputs they needed directly without having to go through FTCs. But they were not allowed to export goods produced by other enterprises or import inputs for other entities.

The second round of reforms was launched in September 1984 through the State Council's approval of the MOFERT Report on Reform of the Foreign Trade System. The general thrust of this report was to transfer power from the center to the lower levels of administration. The report recommended that FTCs be made independent of their administrative departments and be given full authority to carry out all day-to-day functions related to trade. Subject to the approval of MOFERT, large production enterprises could be allowed to handle foreign trade themselves. The report also recommended the adoption of an agency system under which FTCs were to become passive agents of enterprises and handle exports and imports for a service charge, leaving enterprises responsible for profits and losses. These changes considerably loosened MOFERT's hold over trade.

The third phase of reforms began in 1988 with the adoption of the Plan for Restructuring the Foreign Trade System. This round of reforms stressed increased regional autonomy and deepening of integration of production and trade activities. Among other things, this meant an enhanced role for enterprises, trading companies, and local governments in foreign trade decisions.

Under the reform, the government also began to confer trading rights on the large state-owned enterprises, which naturally helped bring the integration of production and trade activities. Provincial commissions of the MOFERT were also authorized to grant such rights for products not subject to export licensing. Qualifications for the direct rights included a minimum level of direct exports and qualified personnel to handle direct trade. The expansion of direct trading rights in the 1980s and early 1990s was limited, however.

Further reforms in the 1990s included the entry of foreign-invested joint venture FTCs and domestically owned private trading companies. The process of granting direct trading rights was streamlined and opened to private companies. Initially, qualification criteria were more stringent for private firms than for state-owned firms, but by the late 1990s they were harmonized across the two sets of firms.

The overall impact of these changes was a very substantial expansion of foreign trade companies. Recall that they had been limited to twelve, all of them at the center, in 1978. By 1985, this number had climbed to 800. It rose to more than 5,000 in 1988, 23,000 in 1998, and 35,000 in 2001. The number of manufacturing enterprises with trading rights also expanded, though it remained small in relation to the total number of such firms.[40]

Import Licensing

Under the pre-reform system, central FTCs had a monopoly on all external trade. Therefore, they could directly control exports and imports and there was no need for any export or import licensing. But once trading rights began to be decentralized and expanded, the government felt the need to introduce import licensing on selected products. During the 1980s, the scope of licensing expanded, particularly following the import surges in 1981 and 1984. At its peak in the late 1980s, licensing covered 46 percent of all imports.[41] Thus, the scope of licensing in China was never all-encompassing; indeed, it was narrower than in India.

Partially in response to external pressures, China began to reduce the scope of import licensing in the second half of the 1980s. By 1992, the share of imports subject to licensing had already fallen to 18 percent. In October 1992, as a part of its market access agreement with the United States, China committed to further reductions in the scope of import licensing over a period of several years. By mid-1997, only 5 percent of the tariff lines were still subject to import licensing. Toward the end of the decade, the proportion fell to 4 percent with the share of imports subject to licensing declining to 8.45 percent of all imports.[42]

Canalization and Exclusive Import Rights to "Designated" Companies

The policy of decentralization of trading rights did not result in an end to the state monopoly on trade in every product. Like India, China also continued to canalize the imports of handful commodities through one or more government companies. In 2001, seven products were still subject to this regulation: grain, vegetable oil, sugar, tobacco, crude oil and refined petroleum products, chemical fertilizers, and cotton. The annual quantity of imports of these products remained subject to approval by the State Council.

In addition, in 2001, China continued to limit the trading rights for six other products to "designated" trading companies. These products included natural rubber, timber, plywood, wool, acrylics, and steel and steel products. Lardy cites an example: 159 companies were authorized to import steel and steel products in 2000.[43] Products allowed exclusively through designated companies were not subject to monopolization of trade by the state, but access to them was somewhat limited since they had to be obtained through the designated companies. In 1998, the share of import goods not subject to either canalization or "designated" status was 89 percent.

Tariffs

Decentralization of trading rights was also accompanied by substantial increases in tariff rates. The average statutory tariff in 1982 had already gone from negligible levels in the pre-reform era to 56 percent.[44] There was a major overhaul of the tariff regime in 1985, which brought the average tariff down to 43 percent. The system remained intact until the government initiated a series of steps that brought the average tariff level down to 40 percent in 1993, 23 percent in 1996, and 15 percent in 2001. The combined effect of reduced import licensing and lowered tariffs meant that by 2001 China had a relatively open trade regime.

Export Licensing

China has also employed export restrictions during the last quarter century. These were more extensive during the 1980s and have now declined in importance. At least four reasons prompted these restrictions. First, in the 1980s and early 1990s, prices of products such as rice and pork were held well below world market prices. Export restrictions helped sustain these low prices. Second, for commodities such as raw silk and raw cotton, China felt it had monopoly power in world markets, so restrictions resulted in better terms of trade. Third, in some cases, China wanted to encourage high-value-added products, which could be accomplished by restricting the exports of raw materials. Finally, for many textiles and clothing products, China was subject to voluntary export quotas by the United States and European Union. Leaving aside textiles and clothing, at their peak in 1991 exports subject to licensing accounted for more than two-thirds of the total exports of China.[45] But by 1993, the proportion of export controls on goods other than textiles and clothing fell to 30 percent. By 1999, it fell further to 8 percent.

Foreign Exchange Retention Rights, Depreciation, and Tax Rebates

Prior to the initiation of the reforms, China had maintained an overvalued domestic currency, supporting it through strict foreign exchange control. Once the reform process got under way, however, China let the domestic currency depreciate while taking steps to make the exchange rate particularly attractive to exporters through a system of multiple exchange rates.

Starting in the early 1980s, the government operated an elaborate system of foreign exchange retention rights that allowed the central, provincial, and local governments and exporting FTCs and enterprises to share foreign exchange in varying proportions across different products. The center usually kept a higher proportion of foreign exchange for within-quota exports than for above-quota exports. It also kept a smaller share for light manufacturing products than for machinery and electronic goods. In 1991, shares were rationalized, with 60 percent of the foreign exchange going to the exporting FTC and 10 percent to the enterprise. Starting in 1988, the government allowed the retained foreign exchange to be traded at the Foreign Exchange Adjustment Centers operated by the State Administration of Exchange Control. The latter had the responsibility for the overall regulation of the sources and uses of foreign exchange.

Incentives for exports were also given through the exchange rate. Initially, in January 1981, the government introduced an internal settlement rate of RMB 2.8 per dollar for goods trade. The official rate of RMB 1.5 per dollar continued to apply to services transactions such as tourism. Over time the official rate was devalued, and in 1984 the two rates were unified at RMB 2.8 per dollar. The rate was further devalued to reach RMB 3.7 per dollar in July 1986. Three years later, in December 1989, the currency underwent another 21.2 percent devaluation, and then in January 1991 it fell to RMB 8.7 per dollar. A modest appreciation brought the rate to RMB 8.3 per dollar in mid-1995. Taking all changes together, the Chinese currency depreciated a little more than 80 percent between 1978 and 1995.[46]

Finally, China has had a system of rebating the value-added tax and customs duties paid on inputs used in exports. A partial rebate on the value-added tax was introduced in 1984. In 1994, the rebate was made 100 percent, though it was reduced again in 1995 and 1996 due to abuse—firms were claiming rebates on goods they never exported. After the Asian currency crisis, the rate was raised again. Duty drawback was introduced initially for foreign-invested enterprises but was extended subsequently to domestic enterprises as well.

Special Economic Zones (SEZs) and Open Cities

Special economic zones (SEZs) are designated areas within which economic activities—manufacturing, þanking, exporting and importing, and foreign investment—take place in a more liberal environment than is available in the rest of the economy. Four SEZs were created in 1979 in Shenzhen, Zhuhai, Shantou, and Xiamen. Of these, the first three were in Guangdong province, facing Hong Kong, and the last was in Fujian province, facing Taiwan.[47]

There were two important objectives behind the SEZs. First, the zones were to serve as focal points for investments from both domestic and foreign sources. Because of the location, authorities were particularly eyeing investments from Hong Kong and Taiwan. Second, in 1979 China was neither administratively equipped nor politically ready for liberalization throughout the country. Therefore, the SEZs were invented to serve as laboratories of economic reform for the rest of China. Policies that were successful in the zones were to be gradually extended to other parts of China. The experiment proved successful from both viewpoints. In 1979, all three SEZs in Guangdong were small fishing villages with small populations and virtually no industrial activity and infrastructure. Progress was initially slow, but starting in 1984 investment picked up pace, and by the end of the 1980s the SEZs had turned into modern cities. Xiamen in Fujian was also transformed economically.

Second, over time, many features of SEZs were extended to other cities. In 1984, fourteen coastal cities were designated "open cities." This process continued in the following years, increasing the number of open cities to 105 by 1991. In addition, 180 counties were also designated open.

Two features of SEZs especially distinguished them from the rest of the country. First, the SEZs enjoyed considerable administrative autonomy in the areas of investment, pricing, taxation, housing, and labor and land management policies. Most foreign investments could be approved locally. Second, the SEZs offered many economic incentives to investors not available in the inland provinces. The corporate income tax, normally 33 percent for foreign-funded enterprises and 55 percent for state-owned enterprises, was set at 15 percent for all enterprises in the SEZs. All imported inputs used in exports or sold within the zones were free of import duty and other indirect taxes. In addition, tax holidays available to foreign-funded enterprises were more generous in the SEZs than those available under the national tax legislation. Depending on the duration and amount of investment, nature of the technology, and duration of the project, tax holidays of up to five years were made available. Open cities also enjoy administrative autonomy but to a lesser degree than SEZs.

Foreign Direct Investment

China began to liberalize its foreign investment regime right at the beginning of the launch of the open-door policy in December 1978. The liberalization consisted of removal of the existing regulations as well as the provision of preferential treatment. Three sets of features were in place by 1990.

First, a 25 percent foreign investment gave an enterprise the status of a joint venture and qualified it for various tax incentives. At the same time, foreign equity investment could rise all the way up to 100 percent. Restrictions on the choice of sectors were minimal, and any preferences, sectoral or otherwise, took the form of incentives rather than barriers There was no lower or upper limit on the amount of foreign investment. Authorities in large open cities such as Shanghai could approve foreign investment projects up to $30 million locally. The limit in smaller open cities was $10 million and that in unopened cities $3 million. This autonomy greatly simplified the approval procedures.

Second, employment, wage, and pricing policies for joint ventures (including 100 percent foreign-invested enterprises) were flexible. Joint ventures were free to employ any required personnel on a contractual basis. Employees were subject to warnings, wage cuts, and dismissal. Except for a few product categories for which prices were set by the state, joint ventures were free to set their prices both at home and abroad.

Third, China also gave extra incentives to joint ventures (including 100 percent foreign-invested enterprises) and thus tilted the playing field in favor of foreign over domestic investment. These incentives were particularly generous in the SEZs and open cities. Additional preferential treatment was made available starting in 1986 to export-oriented or technologically advanced projects. To qualify as export oriented, joint ventures were required to export 50 percent or more of their output and generate at least as much foreign exchange as they used. To qualify as a technologically advanced project, the venture was to produce new products, upgrade domestic products, increase exports, or produce an import substitute.

This regime remained in place throughout the 1990s. Unlike India, China did not liberalize portfolio investment side by side with direct foreign investment. China's initial foreign investment was designed primarily to woo overseas Chinese entrepreneurs in Hong Kong and Taiwan who were facing rising wages in their respective domestic markets and were looking for a cheap source of labor. As previously noted, China also created the Special Economic Zones facing Hong Kong and Taiwan with a view to encouraging entrepreneurs there to relocate on the mainland. In the 1980s, foreign investment came principally from these two entities. But the sources became more diversified in the 1990s, with investors from Japan, the United States, and Europe entering the market.

Liberalization After Entry to the WTO, 2001–7

China entered the WTO on December 11, 2001, some fifteen years after its original application for membership in its predecessor institution, the General Agreement on Tariffs and Trade. As a part of its entry conditions, China undertook very substantial liberalization commitments. The vast majority of these obligations were to be implemented by the end of the fifth year from the accession date of December 11, 2001, which China did. In the following, I describe the trade policy regime as it existed in 2007.[48]

Agricultural and Non-agricultural Goods

All tariff lines in China are now bound at ad valorem rates, with applied most-favored-nation (MFN) rates approximately coinciding with them. The average bound rates for WTO agricultural, non-agricultural, and all products were 15.3, 9.0, and 9.9 percent, respectively, in 2007. Bound rates varied from zero to 65 percent for agricultural products and zero to 50 percent for non-agricultural products.

Between 2001 and 2007, the simple average of applied rates fell from 23.1 to 15.3 percent for agricultural products, from 14.4 to 8.8 percent for non-agricultural products, and from 15.6 to 9.7 percent for all products. International tariff peaks, defined as rates exceeding 15 percent, fell from 40.1 percent of the total tariff lines in 2001 to 15.4 percent in 2007. China applied the tariff rate quota to eight categories of imported goods spread over forty-five tariff lines at the eight-digit Harmonized System (HS) classification in 2007. The items were wheat, maize, rice, sugar, wool, wool tops, cotton, and chemical fertilizers. The purpose of the tariff rate quota was to meet minimum-access commitments under the WTO rules. China's in-quota tariff rates varied from 1 to 10 percent.

Under its WTO obligations, China eliminated quantitative restrictions on most though not all imports on January 1, 2005. It now maintains partial or complete prohibition on 6.5 percent of all eight-digit HS lines on grounds of, inter alia, public interest, environmental protection, and international commitments. Prohibited items include used clothes, secondhand precision instruments, games, and secondhand machinery and transport equipment.

China also maintains automatic and non-automatic import and export licensing on selected products. Automatic import licensing is applied to monitor import quantities for statistical purposes. Product lines subject to this form of licensing fell from 16 percent of all tariff lines in 2005 to 7.9 percent in 2007. Non-automatic import licenses are mostly issued in accordance with China's obligations under international conventions. The number of HS eight-digit tariff lines subject to this form of licensing fell to ten (0.1 percent) in 2007 from ninety (1.2 percent) in 2004. On the export front, tariff lines at the HS eight-digit level subject to export quotas and licensing administration rose from 319 in 2004 to 447 in 2007.

China also reduced the number of items subject to state monopoly (canalization) on foreign trade after it entered the WTO. In 2007, principal import items still subject to state trading consisted of grain (including wheat, maize, and rice), sugar, tobacco, crude oil and processed oil, chemical fertilizer, and cotton. The Ministry of Commerce issues and adjusts annually the list of goods subject to state trading and the list of authorized state trading enterprises. China permits some products that are otherwise subject to state trading to be imported by other enterprises, provided they meet certain specified criteria. A handful of export items are also subject to canalization. In 2007, these included rice, maize, cotton, coal, crude oil, processed oil, tungsten ore and products, antimony ore and products, silver, tobacco, tea, silk, cotton products, and fossil fuels.

For items not subject to state trading, China has now extended the rights to export and import to all firms operating in China, whether domestic or foreign. This does not automatically confer distribution rights in the domestic market, but it does abolish the old system under which only designated companies had the right to export and import.

Services

WTO entry also led to significant liberalization in a number of China's services sectors. The country agreed to grant access through transparent and automatic licensing procedures in banking, insurance, legal and other professional services, tourism, telecommunications, and construction. It also opened the retail distribution sector to foreign entry. In the following, I discuss details of entry provisions as they existed in 2007.

In banking, foreign financial institutions were permitted to provide services without client restrictions for foreign currency business effective from the accession date. The major barriers faced by foreign banks operating in China in the 1990s were related to their domestic currency operations. Under the entry conditions, China agreed to lift all geographical limits and numerical limits on foreign banks providing domestic currency services by January 2005. China agreed to license all foreign applicants that met the prudential criteria and to allow them to conduct domestic currency business with Chinese firms and individuals within two and three years of the entry, respectively. China further agreed to grant full national treatment to foreign banks five years after accession.

Under the provisions existing in 2007, foreign commercial banks that have had a representative office in China for at least two years and have total assets of $10 billion or more are eligible for the establishment of a wholly foreign-funded subsidiary bank. A Chinese-foreign joint venture bank is subject to the same asset requirement. A foreign bank wishing to establish a branch is required to have total assets of $20 billion or more and must have maintained a representative office in China for at least two years in the area where it applies to establish its first branch.

China has also permitted limited foreign equity participation in Chinese banks. A limit of 20 percent is imposed on equity investment by a single foreign financial institution in a Chinese financial institution. If the combined foreign equity in an unlisted Chinese financial institution exceeds 25 percent, the latter is regulated as a foreign-funded financial institution. This provision does not apply to listed Chinese financial institutions. Penetration by foreign banks in China has been limited. The share of foreign banks in total banking assets rose from 1.4 percent in 2003 to 2.1 percent in 2007. State-owned commercial banks remain dominant, with their share in the total banking assets declining from 58.1 percent in 2003 to 55.2 percent in 2007.

In insurance, China has been gradually expanding the scope of business of foreign companies. The latter have been allowed to offer property and casualty insurance on a nationwide basis. China agreed to lift all geographic restrictions on the operation of foreign insurance companies within five years of accession. Foreign insurance companies are allowed to enter the market as 100 percent foreign-owned subsidiaries for non-life insurance and up to 50 percent foreign-owned for life insurance. They must, however, satisfy a set of conditions in terms of years of operation at home, solvency, a minimum level of assets, record of no illegal behavior, and so forth.

In terms of insurance premiums, foreign companies accounted for approximately 5 percent of the national market share in 2006. The share of foreign insurance companies in total assets of the sector rose from 1.96 percent in 2001 to 4.38 percent in 2005. If the foreign-invested share in Chinese insurance companies is taken into consideration, foreign insurance companies would account for 27.4 percent of total income.

Prior to its WTO entry, China did not allow foreign companies in the provision of any telecommunications services, including the Internet. Following the entry, foreign participation is allowed up to 49 percent for basic telecom services and up to 50 percent for value-added telecom services. Under China's General Agreement on Trade in Services (GATS) commitments, foreign equity participation is limited to 49 percent in fixed line and mobile services. In practice, foreign equity investment in fixed-line and mobile services has remained below these limits.

China has also gradually opened its distribution sector to foreign suppliers. The liberalization process started in 1992 when joint ventures in the sector were first permitted. But substantive reforms in the sector resulted from China's GATS commitments. These commitments have led to a step-by-step increase in access to foreign suppliers, especially through the commercial presence of providers. For a number of products, China introduced foreign participation through joint ventures and then introduced foreign majority ownership followed by wholly foreign-owned enterprises. Over time, the country has also expanded the range of products that foreign enterprises are allowed to sell, along with the geographical scope of their operations. One restriction that continues to apply is that suppliers with thirty or more outlets are not permitted to sell certain products.

Finally, China has also opened the door to foreign investors in the transportation sector. Since 2002, China has permitted foreign investors to hold up to 49 percent of the capital in all-cargo, all-passenger, or combined airlines provided that the holding of a single foreign investor and its affiliates is 25 percent or less. Foreign investors are also allowed to invest in civil airports, public air transport enterprises, general aviation enterprises, and air transport projects relating to aviation fuel, airplane maintenance, freight transport, storage facilities, ground services, airline food, and parking lots. In maritime transport, in most cases, foreign entry is permitted through majority-owned equity joint ventures. Wholly foreign-owned enterprises are only allowed for maritime cargo storage and warehousing services. Foreign investment is also permitted in port services. State-owned harbor companies, foreign-invested enterprises, or private enterprises may operate a port's harbors.

Relating Policies to Outcomes

At one level, the coincidence of acceleration in the growth rate and poverty alleviation, liberalization of trade and direct foreign investment, and the phenomenal expansion of trade and foreign investment documented above speaks for itself. It is inconceivable that without sustained liberalization, trade and foreign investment could have grown at the rapid pace they did; without this growth in trade and investment, economic growth and poverty alleviation could never have become what they did. True, there was much else happening in terms of relaxation of diverse domestic policy restraints, restructuring of public sector enterprises, and provision of infrastructure and social services by the government. Yet none of these could have succeeded in bringing about the phenomenal transformation of China if the country's leaders had chosen an inward-oriented trade and foreign-investment regime. Openness may not have been sufficient, but it surely was necessary to achieve the transformation China has seen since the early 1980s.

It is a reasonable inference that China has benefited from all forms of openness. The country has specialized according to its comparative advantage, which has helped it exploit the usual static gains from trade. It has gained from access to world-class technology through imported machines and direct foreign investment. High-quality intermediate input imports have allowed it to improve the quality of its products. Foreign investors have brought much-needed links to world markets as well as state-of-the-art management practices. Above all, the pressure to compete against the best in the world has led entrepreneurs to adopt management practices and technologies necessary to improve productive efficiency. Even in the public sector, the effort to restructure state-owned manufacturing enterprises, which led to a dramatic decline in employment and rise in profitability, was partially motivated by pressures brought about by foreign competition.

Because growth outcomes and policy changes are interactive—liberalizing measures that give rise to improved growth outcomes induce the authorities to liberalize further—establishing a formal causal relationship between the two and precisely measuring the contribution of openness to growth is fraught with technical difficulties. Nevertheless, even skeptics often recognize the positive contribution of openness to trade and foreign investment to growth in China. Nowhere is this better illustrated than in the context of the debate on currency undervaluation by China and global imbalances. Even a skeptic such as Dani Rodrik, who otherwise downplays the importance of openness and free markets in China's success, has written that as much as 2.15 percentage points of China's growth is to be attributed to undervalued domestic currency.[49] Surely, if one accepts the positive growth effects of currency undervaluation, one can scarcely deny a similar impact of trade liberalization!

Before I turn to the arguments that skeptics use to question the contribution of openness, it is useful to explain why the response of trade, growth, and poverty alleviation to openness in China has been much more pronounced than in India. Until fiscal year 2003/4, the growth rate in India had remained below 6 percent compared to near 10 percent in China in the 1980s, 1990s, and 2000s. Trade expansion during the last two and a half decades has also been much less in India than in China. Admittedly, a partial explanation for the difference lies in India's delayed liberalization. Liberalization in India in the 1980s was minimal. Significant liberalization took place in the 1990s but even then strict import licensing on consumer goods was not abolished until April 1, 2001. The peak tariff rate on non-agricultural products, at 35 percent, was still quite high. But that rate came down to 12.5 percent in 2006–7 and currently stands at 10 percent. Today, India is almost as liberal as China in the areas of trade in non-agricultural products, services, and foreign investment, though it remains significantly more protected in agriculture.

The bigger part of the explanation for the more muted response in India lies in its domestic policies. Reservation of virtually all labor-intensive products for exclusive production by small-scale enterprises (which were subject to an investment cap of less than $100,000), draconian labor laws that deprived firms with a hundred workers or more the right to lay off workers under any circumstances, and the absence of a modern bankruptcy code hampered the growth of industry in general and large-scale manufacturing in labor-intensive sectors in particular. The shares of manufacturing and industry in GDP have remained low and unchanged in India since 1991. Although the small-scale-industries reservation was gradually phased out beginning in 1998, inflexible labor markets still hamper the growth of industry, especially in the labor-intensive sectors. Successful sectors in India have been either capital intensive (petroleum refining, automobiles, and auto parts) or skilled-labor intensive (software and pharmaceuticals). Decades of exclusion of large firms and big business houses from labor-intensive sectors have also hard-wired Indian entrepreneurs to keep away from these sectors.

In contrast, the domestic policy regime in China has been friendly to large-scale enterprises, giving them full freedom to hire, fire, and set wages. Predictably, China successfully reoriented the production basket according to its comparative advantage, specializing in labor-intensive industries such as apparel, footwear, and toys during the 1980s and 1990s. Toward the late 1990s, as its skill level improved, it moved into processing activities tied to more technologically advanced products such as office machines, electrical machinery, and telecommunications. With such flexible labor markets, large-scale firms flourished in China and allowed very rapid expansion of manufacturing.

Questioning the Skeptics

Despite such significant evidence to the contrary, skeptics continue to challenge the positive contribution of openness to China's successful transformation. Because China liberalized gradually, did not go all the way to free trade, only partially dismantled the public sector, and maintained significant deviations from a fully free-market regime, skeptics have found the ground fertile for disputing the positive contribution of liberal policies. The technical difficulties of establishing a causal link between openness and growth, resulting from two-way causation, have given them an added edge.

The key argument that skeptics offer is that China did not liberalize in textbook fashion. Ha-Joon Chang is fond of saying that China (and India) succeeded because they "have so far refused to put on Thomas Friedman's Golden Straitjacket."[50] Rodrik is more sophisticated and couches the argument in terms of a lack of correspondence between policies that pro-free-trade and pro-market economists recommend and those observed in China (and other successful East Asian economies) at any point in time.[51] He argues that if an intelligent Martian were given a list of policies that pro-market and pro-free-trade economists recommend for sustained rapid growth, he would be led astray by the boom China has exhibited since the late 1970s: he would find no resemblance between the policies on the list and those pursued by China.

Both these critics exploit the fact that absent a major political and economic upheaval such as that in the former Soviet Union in the late 1980s, politics almost always dictates gradualism in policy reform. Under democracy, the opposition, bureaucracy, NGOs, a free press, and, most importantly, interest groups expecting to lose from the reform throw a lot of sand into the process. The leadership may also anticipate such opposition and choose to move in small steps on its own. An authoritarian regime may sometimes be in a position to introduce big-bang changes, but more often than not it too is forced to opt for the gradual path due to internal differences among the ruling elite and the fear of a revolt in case the big bang ends up administering a shock to the economy.

To this political factor, we may add the economic argument that a gradual approach would minimize the adjustment costs and risk of reversal. For instance, big-bang import liberalization is almost certain to massively even if temporarily throw many in the import-competing sectors into unemployment. In contrast, gradual liberalization would allow resources to move into expanding export sectors. As liberalization proceeds and gains credibility, entrepreneurs also begin to anticipate change and move resources into sectors likely to expand, thereby smoothing out adjustment.

Because the political-economic case for the gradual approach is so compelling, it is no surprise that lately recommendations for big-bang changes are hard to find even in the IMF and World Bank loan conditions. For instance, loan conditions imposed on India by the IMF and World Bank in 1991 were sufficiently mild that even after significant *additional* unilateral liberalization of trade and foreign investment by India during the first half of the 1990s, Rodrik could state that India's "trade policy regime remained heavily restricted late into the 1990s."[52]

In the specific case of China, ideological barriers against *any* move toward a regime that enhanced individual freedom of action in the late 1970s were very

substantial. Not only did those advocating change have to overcome opposition from the followers of Mao, they also had to balance the benefits of economic opening up against the risk of demands for political opening up that the
former was likely to engender. The Tiananmen Square tragedy subsequently
demonstrated that political risk was truly significant.

Once we recognize that policy change must be gradual, it is not surprising
that even a steadily reforming economy would look highly distorted at various
points. The more distorted it is initially, the more distorted it would look at any
point in time for a given pace of liberalization. Once this fact is recognized, the
criticism offered by Chang and Rodrik is dramatically weakened. In terms of
Chang's metaphor, the question no longer remains whether the country has put
on "Thomas Friedman's Golden Straitjacket" but whether it has taken off the
protectionist straitjacket and put on a new, more flexible jacket whose protectionist wrinkles can be ironed out over time. Or, in terms of Rodrik's metaphor,
we must give the Martian a chance to study the history of policy rather than
restrict his observation to an instant. We must ask him to verify not whether
the snapshot at a point in time resembles the policy package recommended by
pro-market economists but whether a video or multiple snapshots taken at various points in time show the country shifting toward the package recommended
by the latter. If the answer to this question is in the affirmative, the country's
success represents the triumph of the pro-market model (even when the regime
looks highly distorted at a given point in time), not the efficacy of "many recipes"
advocated by Rodrik.

When the policy regime is initially highly distorted, even a substantially deep
reform can leave the regime still very distorted. For example, between the late
1970s and late 1980s, China went from a complete central monopoly over international trade to a highly decentralized regime with competition among
thousands of FTCs replacing the monopoly of twelve centrally controlled FTCs.
Yet the snapshot of the trade policy regime in the late 1980s looked highly distorted and far from what one would call an open economy.

Nevertheless, suppose we grant Rodrik his point that catalyzing near-double-
digit growth in 1980s China required only modest liberalization.[53] The question we must then confront is whether the country could have accelerated per
capita GDP growth from 7.7 percent in the 1980s to 9.3 percent in the 1990s
and 9.4 percent in the 2000s without additional liberalization. To be sure, cumulative trade and foreign investment liberalization during the 1980s, 1990s,
and 2000s has placed China among the most open economies today, especially
within the developing world. Would Chang and Rodrik argue that the additional
opening up during the 1990s and 2000s was entirely orthogonal to the performance of the Chinese economy during those decades? If so, they are likely to

find few takers among policy analysts and virtually none among the Chinese policymakers.

The experience of India offers considerable additional positive evidence of the need for continued movement toward an incentives-based regime to sustain rapid growth over a long period. Small bits of liberalization by India in the late 1970s and early 1980s yielded small but positive gains in growth, with the annual average growth rate rising from 3.2 percent during 1965–81 to 4.6 percent during 1981–88. More significant liberalization during the second half of the 1980s and especially during the early 1990s had the growth rate shifting to 6.5 percent during 1992–97. But with liberalization stalling beginning in the mid-1990s, the economy began to lose steam and the growth rate dipped back to 5.2 percent during 1997–2003. It was only additional significant liberalizing reforms in the late 1990s and early 2000s that finally launched the economy into its 8-percent-plus growth trajectory during 2003–12. Going by this experience, it is most likely that if China had chosen either a standstill or reversal of course in the 1990s and 2000s, its performance would have deteriorated.

A related but alternative argument that skeptics often make is that China succeeded through the deployment of industrial policy favoring the growth of high-tech products. I briefly touched on this issue in the context of the pattern of China's exports, but we may elaborate on it further in the present context. Economists Lee Branstetter and Nicholas Lardy, who express strong disagreement with the claim that China has managed to specialize in products similar to those exported by rich countries and that its pattern of exports does not reflect its factor endowments, have argued that a closer look at data reveals that products exported by China in large volumes are not high-tech products at all.[54] To quote the authors, "The single biggest US import product from China in the consumer electronics, office equipment and computers, and communications equipment categories, respectively, is DVD players, notebook computers, and mobile telephones. Each of these is a high volume, commodity product sold primarily by mass merchandisers of electronic products. For example, in 2003 the United States imported more than 31 million DVD players from China with an average unit cost of under $80, more than 7.5 million notebook computers with an average unit cost of $550, and more than 20 million mobile telephones with an average unit cost of less than $100."

Three final points may be noted. First, advocates of protectionism have provided no compelling evidence that interventions ubiquitous in the 1980s or 1990s were essential to sustaining the double-digit growth that China experienced. On the contrary, progressive liberalization allowed China to sustain and even accelerate growth in per capita incomes. If the view that the interventions in the 1980s were required for double-digit growth is to be defended, one needs to explain why the removal of some of those interventions later on did not lead to adverse growth outcomes.

Second, even if the claim of industrial policy contributing to China's growth is validated, it does not diminish the importance of openness to rapid growth. Insofar as the argument relies on specialization in high-tech products, it must rely on an open economy, for the bulk of the market for these products existed abroad and not at home. This point brings us back to the argument made early in this book: efficacy of industrial policy and openness are separate issues.

Finally, none of what has been said should be interpreted as suggesting that the government in China has been a barrier to growth. Compared to India, the government in China has been far more effective in the provision of infrastructure and education, which played important complementary roles in the rapid transformation of China. Effective provision of infrastructure by the government has been critical in ensuring that goods could move in and out of the country smoothly as production locations gradually moved away from the coast. It was also pivotal to facilitating the movement of workers from the countryside to the cities and, indeed, conversion of rural or semi-urban areas into vibrant cities. In a similar vein, in expanding education at a rapid pace at all levels, China has been successful in replicating the performance of its East Asian neighbors to a substantial degree.[55] This investment in human capital, centrally driven by the Chinese government, has been important to creating necessary skills at various levels.

Concluding Remarks

The World Development Indicators report that per capita incomes in China and India in 2005 dollars were $195 and $302, respectively, in 1978. In addition, there is agreement among scholars that per capita incomes in the two countries in the early 1950s were not wildly different. Given these facts, China could not have grown faster than India in per capita terms during 1952–79. Reliable data for India are available and place its growth at 1.6 percent per annum in per capita terms, so a reasonable estimate of Chinese growth will also be around 1.6 percent per annum in per capita terms. This argument leads to a clear rejection of the estimate of 4.1 percent provided by official Chinese sources and commonly cited. The implication is that the command-and-control and autarkic policies under Mao delivered annual per capita growth of approximately 1.6 percent.

The period following 1979 offers a sharp contrast to this outcome. During the 1980s, 1990s, and 2000s, China gradually but steadily liberalized its economy both externally and internally. The detailed description of the changes in trade policy in this chapter shows China transforming from a strict central monopoly over all trade, with trade flows determined as residual in a planning exercise, to near free trade by 2007. China abolished virtually all non-tariff barriers and cut the simple average of tariff rates down to 8.8 percent in non-agricultural products and 15.3 percent in agricultural products. China has also opened virtually all services sectors to foreign suppliers, though sectoral caps on foreign investment and domestic regulation in some sectors place some restraint on the entry of foreign suppliers.

In terms of outcome, trade as a proportion of GDP has risen steadily. Exports of goods and services as a proportion of GDP rose from 8.4 percent in 1982 to 14.7 percent in 1990 and 23.3 percent in 2000, peaking at 39.1 percent in 2006. The country's share of world merchandise exports rose from 0.9 percent in 1980 to 12.4 percent in 2014. This is well above the U.S. share of 8.6 percent.

China's growth and poverty alleviation have seen progress that matches the country's performance in international trade. Based on official figures, which probably overstate incomes by small margins, GDP in China grew at rates of 9.3, 10.5, and 10 percent during the 1980s, 1990s, and 2001–13, respectively. With its population growth barely 0.6 percent, the country grew 9.4 percent in per capita terms during 2001–13. With this dramatic growth, poverty rates have come crashing down. Based on the official poverty line, the rural poverty ratio fell from 10 percent in 1984 to 4.75 percent in 2001. Urban poverty has been all but eliminated.

This description suggests a very strong relationship between trade liberalization, on the one hand, and growth and poverty alleviation, on the other. But this is not an uncontested view. The argument critics make is that China was able to boost its growth rate to 10 percent with limited liberalization in the 1980s and that it continues to intervene in the market in a variety of ways including through a significant presence of the public sector in production activity. I have argued, however, that this argument hardly lends support to the position held by free trade critics. The shift to 10 percent growth required *freer*, not more *restricted*, trade. More importantly, the double-digit growth was sustained through a continued liberalization that brought the economy to near-free-trade equilibrium by 2007.

As regards interventions that continue, free-trade critics have provided no compelling evidence that their maintenance was necessary to the double-digit growth. The fact that continued liberalization was accompanied by some acceleration in per capita income growth suggests that the interventions were a hindrance rather than aid to growth. The explanation for the gradual liberalization is to be found not in a grand growth strategy through industrial policy but in political economy, which often permits only small changes at a time in policy.

Notes

1. While there is considerable diversity among the Han people, they are much more homogeneous than the various religious, ethnic, caste, and cultural groups in India.
2. In this chapter, years refer to the calendar year and periods such as 1949–77 indicate all years from the beginning of 1949 to the end of 1977.
3. Srinivasan 1994, 4.
4. World Bank 1983; Lin 1994; Naughton 2007.
5. World Bank 1983, 1:43, table 1.2. The report in turn relies on Eckstein 1975, 214, table 7.
6. World Bank 1983, 1:76, table 3.8. The 4.1 percent annual growth relates to per capita net material product (NMP). The NMP approximately equals GDP excluding services not contributing to goods production, meaning services directly consumed. These latter include personal and public services. A comparison of the calculations by the World Bank for the growth rates of the NMP and GDP during the 1970s (World Bank 1983, 1:76, table 3.8, and 1:213, table 6.10) shows that the growth rates of the two income measures are nearly identical.
7. Eckstein 1975.
8. See Srinivasan 1994.
9. Lin 1994, 28.
10. Naughton 2007, 140–2.
11. Naughton 2007, 56.
12. Srinivasan 1994, 5–6.
13. Lin 1994.
14. Spence 1990, 547.
15. Naughton 2007, 66–67.
16. Spence 1990, 568.
17. Spence 1990, 546.
18. I draw on Encyclopaedia Britannica 2010a, 2010b, in the rest of this paragraph.
19. Lin 1994, 35.
20. Spence 1990, 579, reproduces the following assessment by the Central Committee of the CCP at an August 1958 meeting:

> The people have taken to organizing themselves along military lines, working with militancy, and leading a collective life, and this has raised the political consciousness of 500 million peasants still further. Community dining rooms, kindergartens, nurseries, sewing groups, barber shops, public baths, happy homes for the aged, agricultural middle schools, "red and expert" schools, are leading the peasants toward a happier collective life and further fostering ideas of collectivism among the peasant masses.... In the present circumstances, the establishment of the people's communes with all-around management of agriculture, forestry, animal husbandry, side occupations, and fishery, where industry (the worker), agriculture (the peasant), exchange (the trader), culture and education (the student) and military affairs (the militiaman) merge into one, is the fundamental policy to guide the peasant to accelerate socialist construction, complete building of socialism ahead of time, and carry out the gradual transition to communism.

21. Encyclopaedia Britannica 2010b.
22. Encyclopaedia Britannica 2010b.
23. Spence 1990, 596.
24. The discussion in this paragraph is based on Spence 1990, 605–6.
25. Spence 1990, 606.
26. Encyclopaedia Britannica 2010b.
27. The discussion in this and the previous paragraph relies heavily on Encyclopaedia Britannica 2010b.
28. This discussion is based on World Bank 1983, 1988b.
29. Lardy 2002, 12, table 1-2.
30. Ravallion and Chen 2007, 4.

31. To keep perspective, it is important to remember that services exports form a significantly larger proportion of the United States' total exports than those of China.
32. Lardy 2002, 31–32.
33. Rodrik 2006.
34. Assche and Gangnes 2010.
35. Koopman, Wang, and Wei 2008.
36. Dean, Fung, and Wang (2011) subject Rodrik's hypothesis to an econometric test and reject it.
37. A reasonably comprehensive account of trade policy changes in China is also available in Branstetter and Lardy 2006, which draws heavily on Lardy 2002.
38. This is best illustrated by the title I used for my 1993 paper in *World Economy*: "Unraveling the Mysteries of China's Foreign Trade Regime."
39. MOFERT was created in March 1982 by merging the MFT, the Ministry of Economic Relations with Foreign Countries, the Import Export Commission, and the Foreign Investment Control Commission.
40. Lardy 2002, 40–45, table 2-3.
41. Lardy 2002, 39.
42. Lardy 2002, 39.
43. Lardy 2002, 42.
44. Lardy 2002, table 2-1.
45. Lardy 2002, 47. The two-thirds figure may seem high, but it resulted substantially from the voluntary export quotas by the United States and the EU. By 1991, textiles and clothing were among China's largest exports.
46. This paragraph relies entirely on Lardy 2002, 49.
47. In 1988, Hainan Island was also declared an SEZ.
48. This description is based on the 2008 WTO Trade Policy Review of China.
49. See his blog entitled "Making Room for China in the World Economy," December 17, 2009, at http://www.voxeu.org/index.php?q=node/4399 (accessed March 7, 2010).
50. Chang 2007, 27.
51. Rodrik 2007, 16–21.
52. Rodrik 2007, 20.
53. As I have noted elsewhere in the book, when the initial distortion is large, as was surely true of late 1970s China, at least in terms of static theory, the gains from even a small reduction in the distortion are large. This result will likely extend to endogenous growth models, in which case small policy reforms yielding large gains in the growth rate when the initial distortion is large would be quite consistent with theoretical expectation.
54. Branstetter and Lardy 2006.
55. See, for example, Hanushek and Woessmann 2011.

14

Other Success Stories in Asia, Africa, and Latin America

In the last several chapters, I have presented detailed case studies of countries whose experiences have shaped the thinking of and debate on the importance of trade openness among scholars. More such case studies could be presented, but perhaps the ratio of additional insight to additional space would not justify it. Nevertheless, an intermediate approach involving brief profiles of several other countries from different parts of the world will help demonstrate one important fact: the prominent cases discussed so far—all of them from Asia—say something about commonality of policy rather than where they are located. When successes emerge, no matter in which part of the world, they are systematically accompanied by low or declining barriers to trade and a high or rising role of international trade in the economy.

To economize on space, in this chapter I limit myself to a presentation of growth performance and evidence on trade openness in a number of other countries. In each case, the full story is more complex and involves a variety of other liberalizing reforms, along with the important role of the government in areas such as infrastructure, education, and skill development. But I omit these details, making the limited point that growth successes require outward-oriented trade policies. To avoid spurious cases that may arise purely from large favorable shifts in the terms of trade, I exclude oil-rich economies. Some of the included countries may rely on some oil or mineral exports, but these exports are not the key to their success. I begin with a few additional cases from Asia. The discussion takes 2013 as the terminal year.

Asia

Table 14.1 identifies fifteen countries in Asia (excluding Central Asia) that have experienced growth rates equaling or exceeding 5 percent during the decade

Table 14.1 **Growth rates of GDP at constant 2005 prices in fast-growing Asian economies, 1994–2013**

Country	1994–2013	1994–2003	2004–13
Bangladesh	5.6	5.0	6.2
Bhutan	7.3	7.0	7.6
Cambodia	7.7	7.5	7.9
China	9.8	9.5	10.2
India	6.8	6.1	7.5
Indonesia	4.6	3.4	5.8
Lao PDR	7.1	6.4	7.8
Malaysia	5.3	5.6	5.0
Maldives	6.8	10.1	6.1
Mongolia	6.5	3.7	9.2
Myanmar	9.8	9.4	13.6
Philippines	4.6	3.9	5.4
Singapore	5.9	5.4	6.4
Sri Lanka	5.5	4.5	6.5
Vietnam	6.8	7.3	6.4

Source: Author's calcuations using the WDI online data (accessed January 17, 2015).

2004–13. The table also shows growth rates in these countries during 1994–2003. Remarkably, with the exception of Indonesia, Mongolia, the Philippines, and Sri Lanka, countries that experienced 5 percent or higher growth during 2004–13 also grew 5 percent or more annually during the prior decade, 1994–2003. Taking the two decades together, only Indonesia and the Philippines fell short of the 5 percent benchmark.

I have already discussed the role that trade liberalization played in the rapid growth of China and India in the earlier chapters. The other countries in Table 14.1 are not very different in terms of trade liberalization being a part of their success stories. Trade liberalization was the centerpiece, for example, of the process of "economic renovation" or *doi moi* that Vietnam launched in 1986. Economists Yoko Niimi, Puja Vasudeva-Dutta, and Alan Winters, who study in detail the connection between the country's liberalization program and poverty alleviation, write, "The core principles of this gradualist reform process were the provision of a legal and institutional framework for and encouragement of the private sector, movement towards an outward-oriented external policy, the replacement of administrative controls with economic incentives, and the promotion of agriculture through de-collectivization and land reform." They add, "An important facet of the renovation process was the complete turnaround of external sector policy from inward-oriented import substitution to outward-orientation."[1]

The authors go on to describe in detail various measures liberalizing both trade and foreign direct investment. Trade as a proportion of GDP rose rapidly from 52 percent in 1992 to 71 percent in 1998. The composition of exports shifted away from agriculture and petroleum to handicraft and light manufactures. Apparel and clothing accessories performed especially impressively, rising from just $1.4 billion in 1997 to $17.1 billion in 2013. Niimi and colleagues study the link between trade liberalization and poverty alleviation and conclude, "Despite its incompleteness and hesitancy, trade reform in Vietnam over the 1990s reduced poverty. Exports and imports boomed and the prices of some tradable goods increased strongly. We find signs of these effects in the household data, with the real incomes of the poor tending to increase via their engagement in the rice, coffee and light manufactures sectors."[2]

Cambodia exhibits a pattern similar to that of Vietnam. According to Chap Sortharith and Chheang Vannarith, the country eliminated all quantitative restrictions on trade in 1994.[3] In 2001, it reduced the number of tariff rates from twelve to four, bringing the top tariff rate down from 120 percent to 35 percent. Subsequently, the country also undertook a program of trade facilitation to cut the time required to move goods into and out of the country. Trade responded handsomely to liberalization, with exports expanding from $1.4 billion in 2000 to $9.2 billion in 2013. Once again, apparel and clothing accessories account for a large part of these exports. They rose from $1 billion in 2000 to $5 billion in 2013. Given the highly labor-intensive nature of these exports, a direct link between them and poverty alleviation can be drawn.

The critical role of trade liberalization in stimulating growth in Bangladesh is also well documented. According to a study by the World Bank, the number of trade-related items subject to physical import controls fell from seventy-nine during 1991–93 to twenty-four during 2003–6.[4] As a proportion of all tariff lines, these items fell from 6.4 percent to 1.9 percent over the same period. Tariffs fell as well, with the simple average of all tariffs declining from 70.6 percent in 1991/92 to 16.3 percent in 2004/5. Export response to liberalization has been significant, with total exports rising from $1.3 billion in 1989 to $24.3 billion in 2011. As in the cases of Vietnam and Cambodia, apparel and clothing accessories have been the major exports, rising from just $450 million in 1989 to $19.2 billion in 2011 and $26.7 billion in 2015. In contrast, India, a country nearly eight times as populous as Bangladesh, exported apparel worth just $18.2 billion in 2015. These exports of a highly labor-intensive product have created a large number of well-paid jobs and helped raise the general level of wages and lower poverty.

Minimally, this discussion illustrates that trade openness has been an important part of the growth process in the three countries. A closer look at other successful cases in Asia would point to the presence of the same association. When
growth happens, low and declining barriers to trade invariably accompany it.

Africa

Perhaps the single most remarkable feature of the development experience
during the last two decades is the emergence of several success stories in Africa.
Table 14.2 identifies as many as twelve non-oil-exporting countries from Africa
that have seen GDP grow at 5 percent or more during the decade spanning
2004–13. The only exception included in the table is Botswana, which grew at
4.5 percent during the decade. The reason for the inclusion of this country despite its failure to meet the 5 percent threshold is that it not only grew at a similar
pace of 4.8 percent during 1994–2003 but also had clocked a growth rate of over
7 percent during the 1980s. Arguably, overall Botswana has been the biggest success story of Africa.

Table 14.2 **Growth rates of GDP at constant 2005 prices in fast-growing
African economies, 1994–2013**

Country	1994–2013	1994–2003	2004–13
Botswana	4.6	4.8	4.5
Burkina Faso	6.0	6.0	6.0
Cabo Verde	7.9	10.6	5.3
Ethiopia	7.5	4.0	11.0
Ghana	5.9	4.3	7.6
Kenya	3.9	2.5	5.3
Malawi	4.1	2.8	5.4
Mozambique	7.3	7.4	7.2
Namibia	4.3	3.3	5.3
Rwanda	6.8	6.0	7.7
Sierra Leone	3.8	2.1	5.5
Tanzania	5.8	4.7	7.0
Uganda	6.9	6.9	7.0

Source: Author's calcuations using the WDI online data (accessed January 17, 2015).

At independence, in 1966, Botswana was one of the poorest countries in the world. By 2007, its per capita income had reached $6,100, making it an upper-middle-income country. As economist Michael Lewin points out, this success is to be attributed partially to good luck in the form of discovery of diamonds and other valuable minerals and partially to able leadership, which provided good governance. The latter included liberal trade policies. To quote Lewin, "Two things Botswana did not do are also significant. Unlike many African countries, it did not adopt a policy of import substitution, and it did not expand the extent of state-owned productive entities, which employ only about 5 percent of the workforce in Botswana."[5] The country has been a member of the South African Customs Union, which required a low common external tariff regime. Of course, insofar as discoveries of diamonds and other minerals translated into revenues and wealth through exports, there was also a direct connection between increased prosperity and trade.

Uganda offers a more recent success story. It has grown at average annual rates of 7 percent during 2004–13 and 6.9 percent during 1994–2003. According to economists Sarah Ssewanyana, John Mary Matovu, and Evarist Twimukye, the proportion of the population living below the poverty line fell from 56.4 percent in 1992/93 to 31.1 percent in 2005/6 and 24.5 percent in 2009/10. The country has also made good progress in terms of social indicators. While the success has many policy dimensions, trade liberalization and outward-oriented policies are prominent among them. The Economic Recovery Program implemented during the 1990s "focused on ensuring macroeconomic stability; liberalizing the foreign exchange system, trade, prices and marketing systems; improving the incentive structure and business climate to promote savings mobilization and investment; and rehabilitating the economic, social, and institutional structure."[6] The effect of these liberalizing measures is reflected in the rise in the exports-to-GDP ratio from 7.1 percent in 1993 to 11.4 percent in 2003 and 20.2 percent in 2013.

Mozambique offers another recent success story from Africa. Economists Jorge Braga Macedo and Luís Brites Pereira point out that soon after its independence in 1975 the country was engulfed in a civil war that lasted till 1992 and claimed nearly one million lives.[7] The civil war, combined with the Marxist-socialist ideology of the governments in the immediate post-independence era, stunted economic development. In the 1980s, the country began to move away from central planning and started giving a greater role to market forces. For example, it removed price controls on vegetables and fruits. In 1987, it enacted the Economic Rehabilitation Program. Referring to that program's structural reforms, Macedo and Pereira note, "These included the stabilization of the exchange rate, trade liberalization, extensive privatizations and tariff and financial

sector reforms. However, it was only after the consolidation of peace that any significant improvements had the opportunity to occur."[8] The authors go on to note
that after the 1992 Rome Treaty was signed and a new constitution allowing
for democratic elections and progress toward a market economy was adopted,
Mozambique was able to match the best performers in the subregion, such as
Mauritius and South Africa.

Once again, trade liberalization and expanding trade are an integral part of
the Mozambican story. The country grew at impressive 7.4 and 7.2 percent annual rates during 1994–2003 and 2004–13, respectively. In turn, exports as a
proportion of GDP grew from 12.9 percent in 1993 to 28.9 percent in 2003 and
30.2 percent in 2013. This expansion in trade has occurred against the backdrop
of a decline in the highest tariff from 35 percent in 1999 to 30 percent in 2002
and 20 percent in 2007. The simple average of applied tariffs fell from 13.8 percent in 2001 to 10.2 percent in 2008.[9]

One further success story from Africa worth brief attention is Tanzania. At independence in 1961, the country adopted a socialist model of development that
involved the nationalization of businesses and industries and the collectiviza-
tion of agriculture. The strategy proved a failure, with the economy performing
extremely poorly, especially between the mid-1970s and 1990. Economist
Sebastian Edwards notes that Tanzania was the second-poorest country in the
world in 1991, with Mozambique being the poorest. Only fifteen years earlier,
in 1976, twenty-four countries had been poorer than Tanzania. Nominal per
capita GNP dropped by 45 percent, from $180 to $100, between 1976 and
1991. Edwards states, "The collapse of the Tanzanian economy between the
mid-1970s and the early 1990s represents one of the most spectacular economic
disintegrations ever experienced in a country not affected by a major war or natural disaster."[10]

But Tanzania has had a major comeback during the past two decades.
According to the World Bank per capita income ranking in nominal dollars, in
2014 as many as nineteen countries were below Tanzania. The country grew at
annual rates of 4.7 percent during 1994–2003 and 7 percent during 2004–13. In
2013 its per capita income in nominal dollars stood at $695.

As in other countries, this growth has taken place against the background
of considerable liberalization and rationalization of the external trade regime
in terms of both the treatment of the exchange rate and trade policy. This is
best stated in the summary observations of the WTO Trade Policy Review for
Tanzania, released in February 2000. It notes, "The reforms that Tanzania has
undertaken since 1985—and at a more accelerated pace in the past few years—
have resulted in a trade policy framework that has been significantly liberalized
and that is essentially based on tariffs. Export restrictions have been eliminated,
as have foreign exchange controls. Tanzania has been making a concerted effort

to create an environment that is conducive both to domestic and foreign invest-ment. In keeping with the Government's desire to promote Tanzanian exports, particularly agricultural products, it has placed emphasis on open markets abroad." The summary adds, "The recent reform of Tanzania's customs duties has resulted in a simplified five-tier structure with tariff rates of 0 percent, 5 per-cent, 10 percent, 20 percent, and 25 percent. . . . The simple average of applied import duties is 16.2 percent."[11]

The response of exports to liberalization in Tanzania has been more muted than in other countries and somewhat erratic as well. In nominal dollars, they have risen from $0.5 billion in 1991 to $2.2 billion in 2003 and $7.8 billion in 2013. As a proportion of GDP, they rose from 10.3 percent in 1991 to 24.1 per-cent in 1995 but fell back to 12.5 percent in 1999. They then rose more steadily, peaking at 21.3 percent in 2012 and dropping yet again to 17.9 percent in 2013.

Latin America

Of all the developing country regions, it is Latin America that seems to fail to fit the pattern of liberal trade policies being associated with faster growth that is observed in most countries. Therefore, it is no surprise that free trade skeptics draw their inspiration disproportionately from this region. What these critics forget is that nothing else seems to have worked in Latin America either. After all, this is the region that pioneered the import substitution industrialization model and eventually abandoned it because it failed to deliver. Latin America has simply not produced the kind of rapid growth that many Asian countries and recently some African countries have been able to produce.

But even in this region, we have been able to observe a few moderate successes in recent decades. And sure enough, when these successes have materialized, even in this region, an open trade regime has turned out to be an integral part of the story. Latin America does not defy gravity after all!

Table 14.3 lists four countries that have annually grown above 5 percent during 2004–13 and two that have grown slightly below this threshold. The latter two, Chile and Costa Rica, have been included in the table despite failing to meet the 5 percent threshold because they have sustained 4 to 5 percent growth over a substantial period of time and are among the best-performing countries in Latin America over a longer time period. Among the six countries listed in the table, only two, Peru and the Dominican Republic, crossed the 5 percent threshold over the full two-decade period spanning 1994–2013. Only the Dominican Republic reached the 5 percent threshold in each period taken on its own.

In recent years, Peru has been the best-performing Latin American country, growing at an annual rate of 6.4 percent during 2004–13. This growth was

Table 14.3 **Growth rates of GDP at constant 2005 prices in fast-growing Latin American economies, 1994–2013**

Country	1994–2013	1994–2003	2004–13
Chile	4.6	4.7	4.4
Costa Rica	4.5	4.4	4.7
Cuba	4.5	3.4	5.9
Dominican Republic	5.1	5.0	5.2
Peru	5.4	4.3	6.4
Uruguay	3.3	1.0	5.6

Source: Author's calcuations using the WDI online data (accessed January 17, 2015).

preceded and accompanied by steady trade liberalization. According to the WTO Trade Policy Reviews, conducted in 2000, 2007, and 2013, Peru maintains no protective quantitative restrictions and the simple average of tariff rates fell from 16 percent in 1993 to 13.6 percent in 1999, 8.2 percent in 2007, and 3.2 percent in 2013. The country now has one of the lowest average tariffs in Latin America. It reduced its highest tariff from 20 percent in 2007 to 11 percent in 2013. It also increased the percentage of its tariff-free lines from 43.6 to 55.9 percent between 2007 and 2013. During this same period, fourteen regional trade agreements signed by Peru came into force. These agreements, particularly the one with the United States, led Peru to issue new laws on customs, government procurement, and intellectual property rights.

These liberalizing measures have handsomely translated into growing exports. In nominal dollars, they rose from $4.3 billion in 1993 to $7.6 billion in 1999, $31.2 billion in 2007, and $48 billion in 2013. The ratio of exports (of both goods and services) to GDP rose from 12.7 percent in 1993 to 15.5 percent in 1999 and 30.5 percent in 2007 before dropping to 23.7 percent in 2013. Peru's exports partially consist of minerals and commodities, which exhibit large price fluctuations from year to year, accounting for an occasional dip in the exports-to-GDP ratio. Even so, the trend in both absolute levels of exports and the exports-to-GDP ratio is in the upward direction.

Like Peru, the Dominican Republic has been a country with low protection. It maintains no protective quantitative restrictions and its tariff protection is low. According to the WTO Trade Policy Reviews conducted in 2002 and 2008, the average applied tariff was 8.6 percent in 2002 and 7.5 percent in 2008. During the same period, the Dominican Republic also abolished two separate surcharges, of 10 percent and 2 percent, both levied exclusively on imports. The share of duty-free lines increased from 13 to 55 percent during the same period. Exports as a proportion of GDP have been high, though they have not shown a linear movement, falling from 32.5 percent in 2002 to 24 percent in 2008 and rising marginally to 25.5 percent in 2013. In absolute terms, exports have risen steadily, however, from $8.6 billion in 2002 to $11.5 billion in 2008 and 15.6 billion in 2013.

No account of growth and openness in Latin America can be complete without a brief reference to Chile. This country was a pioneer in breaking away from the popular import substitution industrialization model early in its history and embarking upon the path of unilateral trade liberalization. Economists Sebastian Edwards and Daniel Lederman offer a careful, detailed account of this liberalization. As they show, in 1973 the maximum tariff was 220 percent and average tariff 94 percent.[12] In addition, the country maintained a large number of quantitative restrictions and a system of multiple exchange rates. But from that year onward, protection was steadily lowered, with the result that quantitative restrictions and multiple exchange rates were eliminated. With a uniform tariff rate established across different commodities, the maximum and average tariff fell to 15 percent in 1988 and 6 percent in 2003. This trade regime, complemented by a vast network of free trade agreements, remains in force today.

The liberalization has been accompanied by both an expansion of trade and steady growth in incomes. In nominal dollars, exports rose from $2.2 billion in 1973 to $5.4 billion in 1981, $12.7 billion in 1993, $26.4 billion in 2003, and $32.6 billion in 2013. While exports as a proportion of GDP stood at 13.7 percent in 1973, they peaked at 43.8 percent in 2007 before declining to 32.6 percent in 2013. During periods when most other Latin American countries were reeling under high inflation or debt crises, Chile performed spectacularly. It grew 6.9 percent during 1976–81, 5.2 percent during 1982–93, 4.7 percent during 1994–2003, and 4.4 percent during 2004–13. In 2005 constant dollars, its per capita income rose from $2,590 in 1976 to $5,060 in 1993, $6,948 in 2003, and $9,728 in 2013. Unlike most of its neighbors, who have shown a tendency to get stuck in the middle-income trap, Chile has continued to grow steadily.

The Curious Case of Mexico

An important omission from the list of countries from Latin America up to this point is Mexico, a favorite of free trade critics, who commonly cite it as the ultimate example of a country that opened to trade and failed to sustain high growth.

The twin facts that Mexico has opened its economy over the past three decades and has performed poorly economically are not in question. During the 1980s, the country undertook substantial liberalization. Subsequently, after it entered the negotiations for the North American Free Trade Agreement (NAFTA), it opened up the economy selectively via a series of free trade area (FTA) agreements. Today, it is among the countries with the largest number of FTA agreements.

Economist Ernesto Lopez-Cordova provides a lucid summary of Mexican trade policy from 1982 to 2009.[13] In the early to mid-1980s, when it began liberalizing trade, the country had already tried the import substitution strategy for four decades. Between 1982 and 1985, it cut the coverage of imports subject to licensing from 100 percent to 37.5 percent and reduced the average tariff from 27 to 25.5 percent. By 1987, goods subject to licensing dropped to 27.5 percent and the average tariff to 10 percent. In 1986, Mexico also became a signatory to the General Agreement on Tariffs and Trade and bound its tariffs at 50 percent.

This process of liberalization came to a temporary end in 1987, with tariffs inching up to an average level of 14.5 percent by 1994. According to the 2002 WTO Trade Policy Review of Mexico, the average tariff rose further to 16.5 percent in 2001 but fell to 11.2 percent in 2007. Beginning in 2009, Mexico undertook additional measures to liberalize trade. According to the 2013 Trade Policy Review, the country brought the average tariff down to 6.2 percent by 2012. The average tariff on manufactures declined from 9.9 percent in 2007 to 4.6 percent in 2012 and the proportion of tariff-free lines rose to 58.3 percent. Mexico also reduced the number of tariff lines from eighty-eight to twenty-eight between 2009 and 2012, but dispersion remained high, with positive tariff rates ranging from 3 to 254 percent.

Between 1988 and 2005, Mexico turned to forging FTA agreements. First came NAFTA with the United States and Canada, concluded after prolonged negotiations in 1994. NAFTA was followed by another dozen FTA agreements involving more than forty partner countries by 2005. With tariff rates in Mexico on countries without an FTA agreement rising during most of this period, partner countries in the FTA agreements came to enjoy higher margins of tariff preference.

This description shows that despite some reversals along the way, Mexico undertook significant liberalization between 1982 and 2012. From all goods being subject to licensing in 1982, it has moved to no import licensing. It has also liberalized tariffs by significant margins. Yet, the economy has not exhibited growth acceleration. It grew at annual rates of 1.9, 3.6, and 2.1 percent during 1981–90, 1991–2000, and 2001–13. Critics point to this performance as the failure of trade liberalization.

When trade liberalization fails to produce predicted gains in growth, often the failure occurs at the level of trade volume. An absence of complementary factors such as infrastructure, flexible factor markets, availability of credit, and political stability subverts trade liberalization and prevents its translation into trade expansion. What makes the Mexican case more puzzling is that its trade did expand rapidly in the wake of liberalization. In nominal dollars, its exports rose from $26.6 billion in 1982 to $179.6 billion in 2000 and $400.3 billion in 2013. The exports-to-GDP ratio rose from 15.3 percent in 1982 to 26.3 percent in 2000 and 31.7 percent in 2013. Even the structure of exports shifted, from the dominance of oil to dominance of manufactures, between the early 1980s to the mid-2000s.[14] This response is broadly comparable to that in most of the countries that have achieved high growth rates on a sustained basis.

Different factors at different points in time explain why Mexico's opening up failed to translate into robust growth. During the 1980s, Mexico faced severe macroeconomic instabilities. It had ended the 1970s with a heavy external debt. Three-fourths of interest payments on this debt were tied to variable interest rates. In the early 1980s, interest rates in the United States skyrocketed, raising debt payments. This was made worse by a large depreciation of the peso caused by high inflation at home. Debt service came to absorb 142 percent of the total current account earnings and 24 percent of GDP in 1982.[15] Mexico was unable to service its debt and had to approach the International Monetary Fund, the United States, and other Western economies for intervention. It was as a part of the conditionality associated with this intervention that trade liberalization of the 1980s was undertaken. While the IMF and Western economies came together to restore Mexico's access to capital markets, they did not provide any debt relief. Consequently, capital outflows went up, inflation remained high, and investment fell during 1982–88. While liberalization and devaluation of the peso gave a boost to exports and a shift in them toward non-oil items, the growth response was muted.

Eventually, debt relief came through the 1989 "Brady Plan," which led to a more manageable macroeconomic situation for Mexico. By the end of 1993, the United States Congress also gave approval to NAFTA. As such, the outlook for Mexico appeared optimistic. Unfortunately, however, a crisis was once again brewing. With Mexican inflation still exceeding U.S. inflation and the Mexican authorities allowing the nominal exchange rate to depreciate only in small amounts under the crawling peg system, the peso had been appreciating in real terms through the 1990s. This appreciation manifested itself in a rising and large current account deficit.

Then a series of political shocks in 1994, including the assassination of the ruling party's presidential candidate in the elections due that year, shook investor confidence and led to capital flight. That made it difficult for the authorities to defend the exchange rate along the crawling peg, and the peso had to be devalued by a wide margin in December 1994. This devaluation, known as the peso crisis, once again dimmed the chances of rapid growth, at least in the immediate future.

Following the peso crisis, there has been no major macroeconomic shock to the Mexican economy. Yet while trade grew handsomely in the following years, the economy performed at average levels at best. How do we explain this limited growth response in the face of rapid expansion of trade?

To answer this key question, first note that manufacturing exports as a proportion of total exports have been extremely high during the 1990s and 2000s. This proportion was 71 percent in 1991, rose to a peak of 85.2 percent in 1998, and fell back to 74.3 percent in 2011. Given this dominant role of manufactures in the merchandise export basket, any impact of exports must appear in the total output of manufactures.[16] But the share of manufactures in GDP has been relatively low and has exhibited a mildly declining trend. In most years during the 1990s, this share was approximately 20 percent, and it fell to the 17–18 percent range in the following decade.

Nearly four-fifths of Mexican merchandise exports during the 1990s and 2000s have gone to the United States. These exports mostly originate in maquiladoras, located along the U.S.-Mexico border, which import semi-processed inputs and export them back out, mainly to the United States. These maquiladoras function as enclaves with minimal links to the rest of the Mexican economy. They have direct access to foreign capital, inputs, and technology and draw only small volumes of labor from the rest of Mexico. Because the bulk of the activity involves processing imported inputs using foreign capital, domestic value added is limited despite the high value of the exported products. This explains the limited contribution exports have made to domestic manufacturing output.

Once the reason for the limited contribution of exports to growth is understood, the remaining puzzle is why the rest of the economy has failed to perform well despite the significant reforms that have been undertaken. Several authors have analyzed this question, and the essence of their findings is threefold. First, some key input sectors in the formal economy are dominated by inefficient oligopolies that supply inputs at very high prices, thereby undermining the competitiveness of the user industries. Second, regulation has encouraged firms to remain small and operate in the informal sector.[17] These firms are characterized by low productivity and are unable to take advantage of productivity-enhancing technologies. Finally, poor access to credit has played a particularly detrimental role in Mexico.

In the first category, we have sectors such as telecommunications and electricity. In telecommunications, Carlos Slim, the richest man in the world, owns Telmex, which has had near monopoly over markets for landline phone service, mobile telephony, and Internet. According to economist Gordon Hanson, Telmex controlled 90 percent of landline phones and 70 percent of mobile phones in 2006–8.[18] Mexico is also known to be among the countries with the highest tariffs on both landline and mobile telephony and lags behind most comparable countries in Internet subscribers per capita. In a similar vein, despite being a net oil exporter, Mexico exhibits very high electricity tariffs. According to Hanson, electricity rates in Mexico are 1.1 to 1.7 times those in the United States. Two state-owned companies with strong labor unions, low productivity, and high wages produce all electricity in Mexico. Poor service and high tariffs can place low-productivity small firms at a great disadvantage.

Growth in Mexico has also been hampered by regulations and incentives that encourage firms to stay small and operate in the informal sector. A heavy burden of inspections, tax incentives, and stringent labor laws combine to encourage this phenomenon. This, in turn, has had a detrimental effect on productivity. To quote Hanson, "Informality keeps firms in existence that would be forced to exit, either because of poor management or outdated technology, if they had to compete for inputs with formal sector firms on a level playing field. One consequence of informality is, therefore, the survival of small, unproductive enterprises. The dispersion in productivity across plants in Mexico is much higher than in the United States. In 2004, 36 percent of manufacturing employment in Mexico was in establishments with fewer than 50 workers and 22 percent was in establishments with fewer than 10 workers. Enterprises with less than 10 employees tend to have very low TFP . . . with 91 percent of these plants having productivity levels below their industry average. The majority of these micro-enterprises are informal."[19] To some degree, the problem of small and informal firms is alleviated in the manufacturing sector because it includes the vibrant maquiladoras, which are generally large and operate in the formal sector. In the services sector, the problem is far more acute: we have either oligopolies such as those in telecommunications and electricity or a preponderance of small, informal firms.

Economists Aaron Tornell, Frank Westermann, and Lorenza Martinez point to poor access to capital as having a particularly major adverse impact on growth prospects in Mexico.[20] They analyze the economy during the period 1994 to 2002 in terms of traded and non-traded sectors and show that real credit nosedived between 1994 and 2002, with the credit-to-GDP ratio declining from 49 to 17 percent. Because the traded-goods sector had access to foreign markets, it was hit less hard. Consequently, the largest effect of the credit crunch was felt in non-traded goods. Growth during this period was significantly higher in the traded sector than in the non-traded sector.

While the reforms undertaken by Mexico in the wake of the peso crisis have had a favorable impact on the recovery of loans that are easily collateralized, such as those for autos and homes, recovery for most other commercial loans can be far more of a problem. To quote Hanson, "As a result, the difficulty lenders have in seizing assets from borrowers continues to hinder credit provision. In the 2004 World Bank Doing Business Indicators, Mexico scored a 0 out of 4 in protections provided to creditors, putting it among just 11 countries (out of 132) in the lowest category.... [O]ne sees that despite Mexico's reforms domestic credit to the private sector actually declined from the 1990s to the 2000s, with its performance relative to comparison countries showing no improvement."[21]

Concluding Remarks

Success stories among developing countries are not limited to Asia. They can also be found in Africa and Latin America. In this chapter, I have provided brief profiles of several countries in the three continents that have experienced 5 percent or higher growth during 2004–13. I have shown that in each case, trade liberalization and expanding trade are integral parts of the success story.

The case of Mexico turns out to be rather curious. Though it has witnessed rapid expansion of trade in the wake of trade liberalization, it has failed to achieve rapid growth in incomes. Usually when trade liberalization fails to generate growth, it is because it has not generated a significant trade response. The case of Mexico is different, however, and more complex. Drawing on a rich body of the literature that exists on this question, I have noted that the failure in Mexico is attributable to poor access to credit, regulations that encourage firms to remain small and operate informally, and continued oligopolies in certain critical input sectors.

Notes

1. Niimi, Vasudeva-Dutta, and Winters 2003, 3–4.
2. Niimi, Vasudeva-Dutta, and Winters 2003, 42.
3. Sortharith and Vannarith 2010.
4. World Bank 2004, Table 2.1.
5. Lewin 2011, 86.
6. Ssewanyana, Matovu, and Twimukye 2011, 56.
7. Macedo and Pereira 2010, 23.
8. Macedo and Pereira 2010, 23–24.
9. Tariff rates are drawn from the WTO Trade Policy Review of Mozambique, 2009, and Macedo and Pereira 2010, 43.
10. Edwards 2012, 2.
11. World Trade Organization 2000.
12. Edwards and Lederman 2002, table 10.3.
13. Lopez-Cordova 2012.
14. Lopez-Cordova 2012, table 3.
15. Buffie 1989.
16. Services exports are less than 5 percent of the total exports in Mexico.
17. See Hanson 2010 and the studies he cites in n. 1.
18. Hanson 2010, 14.
19. Hanson 2010, 9–10.
20. Tornell et al. 2004; Hanson 2010.
21. Hanson 2010, 6.

15

In Conclusion

In this volume, I have endeavored to marshal analytic arguments, cross-country empirical evidence, and individual country experiences over time to persuade the reader of the superiority of pro-free-trade policies over protection. The challenge to critics of free trade is to produce similar arguments and evidence in favor of protection. They must subject themselves to the same high standards of proof that they demand of their opponents. Without either a logically tight argument or credible empirical evidence, simply pointing to this or that damage that freeing up trade might do and asserting how protection could help build infant industries will simply not do.

The late 1980s and the 1990s offered an opportune time for the views of free trade critics to flourish. Trade liberalization forced on many countries by the World Bank and International Monetary Fund conditionality during the 1980s had produced no significant positive results.[1] At the same time, the 1960s and the first half of the 1970s, when protection had been generally high, had seen healthy growth in many developing countries. This allowed the critics to claim that the import substitution era of the 1960s and the first half of the 1970s represented the "golden age" of development, while the turn to liberal policies had been a disaster. It did not matter that the miracle economies of Singapore, Hong Kong, South Korea, and Taiwan had built their successes on outward-oriented policies during these years. Because all these economies except Hong Kong had activist governments, enough elbow room remained to argue that clever activist policies rather than outward-oriented policies had delivered the high growth in these countries. Critics also neglected to give due credit to the fact that the 1960s and the first half of the 1970s saw industrialized countries open up their economies wider and grow at unprecedented rates. In doing so, these countries not only provided examples of the success of outward-oriented policies, they also became an important engine of growth for the developing countries.

The world is different today, however. Country after country in the developing world has come to accept that it cannot afford to miss out on the opportunities offered by world markets, with the result that most governments today own the liberal policies of their countries. The resulting policy credibility and the adoption of complementary policies have come together to produce splendid results in many countries. The two largest developing countries, China and India, with a combined population of more than 2.5 billion, have achieved massive gains in per capita incomes and poverty reduction. Several other smaller countries in Asia, Africa, and Latin America have also experienced growth and poverty reduction not witnessed before. The performance of the developing countries as a whole since the early 1990s has been decisively superior to that during any other period. And this has happened during a time when the advanced economies of the world have done rather poorly, with a major crisis in 2008 rocking the global economy.

This broad picture can, of course, serve as only the beginning of a defense of the case for free trade. Just as the French economist Frederic Bastiat said 170 years ago in his brilliant book *Economic Sophisms*, proponents of free trade have to work a lot harder to defend their case than their opponents. They must expose the falsehood of the conclusions derived from half-truths by the latter while also producing positive evidence in support of their case. This has been the task of and reason for this volume, with developing countries at its center.

A favorite theme of the opponents of free trade in the context of developing countries has been the infant industry argument for protection. It is remarkable that a logically tight case for infant industry protection has not been produced to date and yet the argument continues to have currency in many respectable quarters. Free trade opponents have provided loosely constructed arguments and invoked misleading analogies. In this volume, I have systematically exposed the flaws in their arguments and their analogies. In a nutshell, once the mechanism through which the externality travels from incumbent firms to new entrants is explicitly specified, a logical case for infant industry protection cannot be made.

The cross-country evidence gathered in this volume reveals a strong association between trade openness and growth. Rapidly expanding trade almost always accompanies sustained rapid growth. Even if this evidence is contaminated by two-way causation, it points to liberal trade over protection as the correct policy choice. If the two variables move together, growth will be helped by policy actions that expand rather than contract trade. Luckily, the best available evidence even points to the causation flowing from trade to growth. By separating out geographically determined trade using the gravity model, economists have been able to provide compelling evidence that expanding trade leads to higher per capita incomes.

Country case studies point in the same direction. I have reviewed several major cases of sustained rapid growth and found that in every case, low or declining barriers to trade were an integral part of the growth strategy. The case studies reveal that in no country was a growth strategy pursued in isolation. Instead, several complementary policies accompanied the opening up of the economy. That being said, I do not find a single case in which high or rising protection has accompanied sustained rapid growth.

A common argument made by critics is that if we take a snapshot of a rapidly growing economy such as Taiwan in the 1960s or China in the 1980s, we would observe continuing high levels of protection. This raises the question of why protection rather than liberalization might not be the source of the rapid growth. The answer to this misleading critique has two parts. First, in both cases, liberalization preceded or accompanied growth acceleration. If the countries still looked highly protected, it is because they began too far away from the free trade position and too close to autarky. Second, if protection was indeed the source of rapid growth in these cases, its reduction during the following years should have led to a decline in the growth rate. But the opposite was observed when Taiwan in the 1970s and China in the 1990s and 2000s opened their economies further.

A common criticism by free trade critics derives from a lack of growth following trade liberalization in many cases. This criticism gained substantial currency when trade liberalization in the 1980s and early 1990, induced by the International Monetary Fund and World Bank through loan conditionality, failed to produce growth. The view I have taken in this context is that low or declining barriers to trade are necessary but not sufficient for sustained rapid growth. Liberalization will fail to generate the predicted trade response if, for example, country governments do not own the policy and therefore it is not credible. It will also fail if external or internal transport barriers are high. This can be especially a problem in Africa due to poor connectivity on the continent and a lack of easy access to the sea for many countries. Given that trade liberalization is likely to influence growth through trade expansion, the failure of trade to respond to growth is also likely to result in a failure to generate growth.

A more intriguing case is provided by Mexico, which liberalized in the 1980s and 1990s, experienced substantial trade expansion in the 1990s and 2000s, and yet did not witness significant growth acceleration. I considered this case at some length. The explanation for the failure of trade liberalization to accelerate growth in a major way despite the expansion of trade is twofold. First, much of the trade expansion took place within enclaves located near the border with the United States. These enclaves receive the bulk of their capital via foreign direct investment, import semi-processed components, process them, and reexport the final products. Even though this translates into a substantial value of final goods exports, the domestic value added in those exports is small. As a result, trade expansion has not been accompanied by any significant rise in the share of manufactures in GDP. The direct contribution of exports to the GDP has been small as well.

Second, with the export sector being an enclave, positive spillover from it to the rest of the economy has been limited. The question then is why the rest of the economy has not shown dynamism on its own. Here monopolies in some major product markets (for example, telecom and oil) and highly distorted land and labor markets and regulations, which discourage firms from growing larger, have kept Mexico trapped in low-productivity equilibrium. The answer to its problems is more, not less, competition.

In sum, if the devotees of protection want to persuade scholars to adopt their viewpoint and not mislead unsuspecting and innocent policymakers, they need to offer much more evidence in favor of their case. It will not suffice to offer half-baked arguments for infant industry protection, often relying on the post hoc fallacy, and point fingers at cases in which liberalization failed to deliver. If they insist that free trade advocates produce iron-clad evidence of a causal link between trade and growth, they must subject themselves to the same standard of proof. Or at least they must produce evidence that matches what free trade advocates have produced. To date they have not even come close to doing so.

At one level, the failure to bring the Doha Round to a genuine completion and the spread of regional trade blocs point to a trading system that is unable to move forward. While this pessimistic view may seem justified from the short-run perspective, the long-term perspective offers a far more optimistic picture. Indeed, the post–Second World War era represents a huge triumph for free trade and therefore for free trade advocates.

The decades immediately following the Second World War brought a massive opening of markets in the advanced industrial economies in the West. The 1960s and 1970s additionally saw significant opening in a few developing countries as well. The vast majority of the developing and Eastern Bloc countries remained hesitant during these decades. But nearly all have come to embrace liberal policies in the subsequent years.

In most cases, liberalization during the 1980s was done tentatively and under pressure from the international financial institutions. But the conversion to liberal trade has been more genuine in the last two decades. With the exception of Chile, which had begun liberalizing its trade in the mid-1970s, many countries in Latin America began switching to outward-oriented policies in the 1980s. China, a communist country, suddenly turned liberal in its trade and foreign investment policy in the late 1970s and has stayed the course to date. India, which refused to recognize the critical importance of world markets until the 1980s, also became a genuine liberalizer beginning in 1991. Today, even most of the African countries are highly open. Free trade has largely triumphed in the developing world. Nevertheless, now that imports account for a significantly larger proportion of domestic consumption in most of the developing countries, the temptation for shortsighted policymakers to return to import substitution is that much stronger. Free trade advocates can scarcely afford to let their guard down.

Note

1. There are at least two reasons this happened. First, when national governments do not own the policy changes and resent their external imposition, they either reverse them once the loan money has been received or simply subvert them at the implementation level. Second, there is often a lag between policy change and response in terms of accelerated growth. In part, the lag is related to the reform's initial lack of credibility. It is only when investors see the policy remain in place for a few years that they feel convinced that there will not be a reversal.

Appendix 1

COMPARATIVE ADVANTAGE AND THE GAINS FROM TRADE UNDER SCALE ECONOMIES

In this technical appendix, I present a more complete discussion of the principle of comparative advantage and the large gains from trade that arise from removing even small tariffs in the presence of scale economies.

The Principle of Comparative Advantage

Assume, as in the text, that a representative worker in India working for a year can produce 1 bushel of wheat or 1 shirt. Call the rest of the world USA and assume one worker there produces either 6 bushels of wheat or 2 shirts per year. I deliberately assume that USA enjoys a higher productivity than India in the production of each commodity. I now demonstrate that despite this fact, both USA and India stand to benefit from trade.

The key point to note is that the productivity advantage of the American worker over his Indian counterpart is *proportionately* greater in wheat than in shirts: he is six times as productive in wheat but only twice as productive in shirts. In the trade economist's jargon, USA has an *absolute* advantage in the production of both goods but *comparative* advantage in wheat. Symmetrically, India has an absolute disadvantage in the production of both goods but comparative advantage in the production of shirts: an Indian worker's productivity is one-sixth that of his U.S. counterpart in wheat but half as much in shirts.

According to the principle of comparative advantage, both the United States and India can benefit if they specialize in the good of their comparative advantage—USA in wheat and India in shirts—and obtain the other good from the other country through international trade. To illustrate this proposition, imagine that USA specializes in the production of wheat, India in shirts, and they trade these products at the price of 1 shirt for 2 bushels of wheat. Recall that given its technology, USA must sacrifice 3 bushels of wheat to produce 1 shirt domestically. But through international trade, it has to part with only 2 bushels of wheat for 1 shirt. Therefore, it stands to benefit from selling 2 bushels of wheat to India for 1 shirt. The remaining question is whether India will agree to sell 1 shirt for 2 bushels of wheat to USA. Since India can domestically obtain only 1 bushel of wheat for each shirt it sacrifices, it will readily sell 1 shirt to USA in return for 2 bushels of wheat.

It is easy to verify that as long as USA and India exchange the two products at a price between their internal rates of transformation, they can both benefit. The internal rate of transformation is 1 shirt for 1 bushel of wheat in India and 1 shirt for 3 bushels of wheat in USA. As long as the international price is 1 shirt for more than 1 but less than 3 bushels of wheat, both countries gain from specialization and trade. The price I chose above, 1 shirt for 2 bushels of wheat, satisfies this condition. In effect, trade provides each country with a superior technology (compared to domestically available technology) for converting its good of comparative advantage into the good of comparative disadvantage.

The essential idea underlying the principle of comparative advantage has a simple parallel in everyday life. Suppose the most skillful surgeon in the town is also the most efficient nurse. Should she specialize in surgeries, specialize in nursing services, or do a little bit of both? The answer is specialization in surgery, leaving nursing services to nurses. Specialization allows the surgeon to perform more surgeries and the nurses to earn a decent living as well. The theory of comparative advantage applies this same principle to the nations: like the surgeon in this example, USA has an absolute advantage in both activities, but its advantage is proportionately greater in wheat.

Though the gains from trade arise solely from differences in *relative* productivity differences, the absolute levels of productivity are not irrelevant. They have important implications for real wages and therefore living standards. In the USA-India example, the higher productivity in USA translates into higher real wages and therefore higher living standards.

The India-USA example shows that free trade benefits both countries relative to their autarky equilibriums. A different question concerns whether free trade maximizes the gains from trade. While the answer to this question from the *global* welfare perspective is positive, it is negative from an individual country's viewpoint if that country is large enough to influence the world prices. To see this, suppose the free trade price at which India and USA exchange the two goods is 1 shirt for 2 bushels of wheat and that India sells 50 shirts for 100 bushels of wheat. Suppose further that by restricting its sales to 40 shirts, India is able to raise the world price of shirts to 2.5 bushels of wheat. It can then obtain the same amount of wheat (100 bushels) for fewer shirts, making it unambiguously better off. This benefit, of course, comes at the cost of USA, which now ends up with fewer shirts for the same amount of wheat exports. USA would recognize that it can turn the terms of trade back in its favor by restricting its own trade and would resort to tit-for-tat protection. The net result may be no change in the world price and reduced trade that leaves both India and USA worse off. One key reason for the existence of the World Trade Organization is to discourage countries from imposing these tit-for-tat import restrictions.

Several additional conclusions follow from more formal treatments of the Ricardian theory. Most of them can be found in the standard textbooks on international trade.[1] The most important ones are:

- Assuming perfect competition in all markets, countries specialize in the products of their comparative advantage.
- Trade normally raises real wages in both countries. In the worst-case scenario, it raises the real wage in one country and leaves it unchanged in the other.
- These conclusions remain valid in the presence of transport costs and non-traded goods.
- These conclusions also remain valid in the presence of many goods and many countries.
- The principle of comparative advantage also remains valid in the presence of international factor mobility.[2] In the case when one country is absolutely more productive than the other in all goods, free mobility would lead all labor to move to that country, thus eliminating the need for international trade in goods.

Scale Economies and Larger Gains from Trade

Paul Romer has shown that the cost of protection—or, conversely, the gains from trade liberalization—can be much larger in the presence of scale economies resulting from fixed selling cost in the import market than in the traditional models of constant returns to scale.[3] In the traditional analysis, we use simple demand and supply curves to measure the cost of protection. In Figure A1.1, let DD be the demand curve for a product that is not domestically produced. Suppose first that the product is produced at a fixed marginal cost MC and supplied competitively by foreign producers. In this case, the supply curve coincides with the marginal cost curve. Under free trade, the price paid equals MC and the gains from trade equal the area under the demand curve and above line MC.

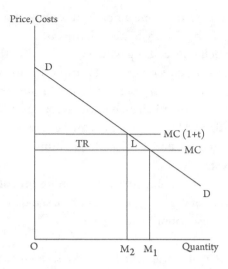

Figure A1.1 Traditional Analysis: The Cost of Protection Is Triangle L

The introduction of a tariff at ad valorem rate t shifts up the price facing the buyers to MC $(1 + t)$. This leads to a shrinking of imports from M_1 to M_2. The rectangle denoted TR represents the tariff revenue, and triangle L represents the loss due to the tariff. For small values of the tariff such as 10 percent, this triangle is small in relation to the total expenditure on the good.

Suppose, however, that the product under consideration is differentiated and has many different varieties. Varieties are symmetric such that the demand curve for each of them is the same. Each variety is produced and sold by a different firm. There is a constant marginal cost of production, MC, of each variety. In addition, a fixed cost must be incurred on each variety before any sales occur. This latter cost, which may represent a marketing cost, varies across firms. Only those firms able to recover their total costs enter the market. Figure A1.2 depicts the equilibrium for the marginal import variety that just breaks even. Varieties with higher fixed costs of marketing do not enter the market since they incur losses. Varieties with lower fixed costs make pure economic profits.

The equilibrium is now very different from that under perfect competition. With fixed costs of marketing and constant marginal cost of production, the average cost of production is downward-sloped, as shown by the curve marked AC. In equilibrium, each firm enters with a variety not supplied by any other firm. Given the same demand for each variety, if two or more firms produced a common variety, they would have to share the market, with each producing on a lower scale and higher cost than would be the case if each produced a unique variety. Therefore, profit maximization dicates each firm to enter with a unique variety.

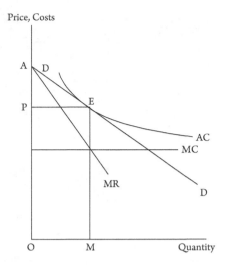

Figure A1.2 Large Losses from Small Protection

With only one firm supplying each variety, the equilibrium is characterized by monopoly. The producer now equates the marginal revenue to marginal cost and sets the price at P. By assumption, the variety under consideration is the last one supplied and just breaks even. This is the reason the price exactly coincides with the average cost. The consumers' surplus shown by triangle APE represents the gains from trade.

The introduction of even a tiny tariff now shifts up the average cost curve above that shown by AC. This has the immediate implication that the monopolist can no longer recover the full costs of production and will exit the industry altogether. This is dramatically different from the competitive case in which a small tariff only reduces the imports of the product by a small amount at the margin. The exit of the producer in the present case in turn leads to a loss of the entire gains from trade represented by triangle APE. This is in contrast to the loss of the small triangle marked L in the previous, perfectly competitive case.

Notes

1. For an example, see Bhagwati, Panagariya, and Srinivasan 1998, ch. 4.
2. In an influential op-ed in the *New York Times*, Charles Schumer and Paul Craig Roberts (2004) argued that allowing international factor mobility invalidates the principle of comparative advantage and trade may actually hurt one or more countries. This is a false assertion reflecting the authors' poor understanding of trade theory. Opening to trade in goods with or without factor mobility leads to at least as good an outcome as that under autarky for each country.
3. Romer 1994.

Appendix 2

THERE IS NO LOGICAL CASE FOR INFANT INDUSTRY PROTECTION

In this appendix, I employ a simple model to demonstrate three propositions related to infant industry protection in the presence of spillover effects. The propositions are:

(I)   Consider an infant industry, which faces an import price that is lower than its initial per unit cost. Suppose that the act of production costlessly leads to learning for unspecified reasons, which lowers the future cost of production for incumbent firms as well as new entrants sufficiently that it is socially beneficial to establish the industry. In such circumstances, production activity would fail to emerge on its own but temporary protection at an appropriate level during the learning phase would ensure the establishment of the industry.

(II)   In the above industry, if we explicitly identify the source of costless learning (such as improved worker skills) rather than arbitrarily attribute it to the act of production, an efficient solution would emerge without any government intervention, even with the prospects of spillover. No infant industry protection is required.

(III)   If the source of learning is costly innovation or costly worker training and learning spills over to future potential entrants, on its own the production activity would once again fail to emerge. But in this case temporary protection would fail to lead to investment in socially beneficial innovation or worker training. Instead, it would lead the incumbent firm to undertake production activity at the pre-learning higher social cost behind the wall of protection.

Let us consider each of these propositions in succession.

Learning Results from the Act of Production

Let there be two periods, 1 and 2. Learning takes place in period 1. Domestic demand is fixed at 1 unit in each period and exports are ruled out because of high transport costs. The following notation is used:

P = world price in each period
C = per unit cost of production in period 1
Z = per unit cost of production in period 2

The social rate of discount is set at zero. By assumption:

(1) $$Z < P < C$$

(2) $$P - Z \geq C - P > 0$$

The cost in period 1 exceeds the price at which established foreign suppliers sell. The production cost in period 2 falls because of the learning in period 1. Inequality (2) says that production cost falls sufficiently in period 2 that profits in period 2 offset the losses in period 1. Therefore, overall, the production activity is socially beneficial.

Because the cost in period 2 falls for all including new entrants, competition among them would force the price in that period to Z. This means that profits in period 2 will be zero, with all benefits of learning passing to consumers. But this will result in the incumbent firm failing to recover the losses in period 1. Therefore, it will choose not to enter the production activity in the first place.

Suppose the government introduces a temporary tariff in period 1 at rate t such that

(3) $$P + t = C$$

This will allow the incumbent firm to recover its costs in period 1. The price will still fall to Z in period 2, but this will not be a problem since the incumbent firm has no losses from period 1 to recover. A temporary tariff will allow the socially beneficial infant to emerge.

Though this example appears to support the case for infant industry protection, being based on an entirely implausible assumption, it cannot be taken seriously. The assumption that production activity by the incumbent firm by itself lowers the production cost for the other future entrants as well is wholly unreal. The mechanism by which such transmission of learning takes place to other firms must be specified. We see in the example immediately below that specifying such a mechanism leads to a breakdown of the case for protection.

Making Explicit the Source of Costless Learning: Improved Worker Productivity

Suppose that the reduction in cost in period 2 results from an increase in worker productivity. Therefore, both the firm and workers know that engagement in production activity gives workers an asset, which has value. The value of this asset is exactly equal to $P - Z$, the potential profit in period 2. Therefore, the incumbent firm can induce the workers to accept a wage in period 1 that would cut its costs by $P - Z$. That is to say, it can cut its cost in period 1 to

$$(4) \qquad \alpha = C - (P - Z)$$

Note that workers accept the wage cut because it is exactly offset by the asset they acquire in terms of higher future productivity, which promises to fetch them a higher future wage in equal amount. The critical question is whether this cost is sufficiently low to allow the firm to operate profitably in period 1. That is to say, is

$$C - (P - Z) \leq P$$

or, equivalently, is

$$P - Z \geq C - P?$$

This inequality is, of course, the same as (2), which is required to ensure that the production activity is socially beneficial. The remaining question is whether the higher wage cost in period 2 will allow production activity to continue in that period. That production activity is indeed feasible in period 2 follows from the fact that the cost in period 2 rises from Z to $Z + (P - Z) = P$, the import price.

Therefore, this case requires no intervention by the government. The incumbent firm can reduce the wages in period 1 exactly by the value of increase in worker productivity in period 2 to avoid any losses. The increased wage the workers would demand in period 2 as a result would still allow firms in period 2 to break even.

Specifying the Source of Learning: Costly Innovation

Let us now assume that the fall in the cost in period 2 from C to Z is the result of a costly innovation. Let I = cost of innovation incurred in period 1. With innovation cost added, the production activity is socially beneficial provided the loss in period 1 is offset by profit in period 2. That is to say,

(5) $$P - Z \geq C + I - P$$

No Intervention Equilibrium

If the firm invests in innovation, it incurs a loss in period 1 equaling

(6) $$L = C + I - P$$

In period 2, it needs to recover this loss. Given (5), it can recover the loss if it can sell the product at P in period 2. But due to the spillover of the innovation, potential entrants, who did not incur the cost of innovation, can all produce the product at Z. Therefore, competition among them would force the price down to Z. In that case, the incumbent firm will fail to make any profit in period 2 and it would not be able to recover the loss from period 1. Without intervention, innovation and production will fail to emerge.

Import Protection Equilibrium

Recognizing that competition in period 2 drives profits in that period to zero and prevents the investment in a socially beneficial innovation from taking place, suppose the government introduces a tariff in period 1 that allows the incumbent firm to fully recover its production cost plus the cost of innovation in period 1 itself. That is, with t the per unit tariff, we have

(7) $$P + t = C + I$$

Now the incumbent firm knows that a potential entrant will still force period 2 profits down to zero by forcing the price down to Z in that period. So it knows that it will make no profit in period 2. Therefore, if it chooses to invest in the innovation, its total profits over the two periods would be zero. The loss to the consumer in period 1 due to higher price is recovered by the government in the form of tariff revenue.

But given the positive cost of innovation, the firm would realize that if it chooses not to invest in the innovation and produces the product using the old technology, given the tariff, it can earn strictly positive profits in period 1:

$$(8) \qquad \pi = (P + t) - C = (C + I) - C > 0$$

So we will end up with no innovation and the firm will stay in business in period 2 only if the government decides to extend protection to that period as well. Temporary protection fails to encourage the infant industry to learn. Instead, it takes advantage of the tariff to profit by staying with the old technology, which, given $P < C$, imposes a net social cost on the economy.

Appendix 3

MEASURING INEQUALITY: THE GINI
COEFFICIENT

Figure A3.1 helps explain the construction of the Gini coefficient in precise terms using income distribution across households within a country as the example; it also helps demonstrate the limitations of the index. Begin by lining up all households in the country along OO′ in order of rising per capita household income, with the poorest household at O and the richest one at O′. Dividing OO′ into 100 equal parts, the poorest 20 percent of households are between 0 and 20, the next poorest 20 percent are between 20 and 40, and so on.

Next, measure the cumulative share of households in the total income along the vertical axis. This means that for each household located on OO′, we measure the combined income share of all households up to that household on the vertical axis. For example, for the household located at 20, we measure the combined income share of the bottom 20 percent of households along the vertical axis. If the national income is distributed entirely equally across households, the cumulative shares would all lie along chord ON. This is because equal distribution implies that the first 20 percent of households have a 20 percent share of the total income, the first 40 percent of households have a 40 percent share of the total income, and so on. Of course, 100 percent of the households must always account for 100 percent of the national income.

In general, income distribution is not entirely equal and is likely to lie along a curve such as OMN. This curve shows that the bottom 20 percent of the population has less than 20 percent of the share, the bottom 40 percent of households have less than 40 percent of the share, and so on. But as we move toward richer and richer households, the cumulative share rises along a steeper path. This signifies the fact that the households near the top of the distribution have a larger share of income than other groups in the population.

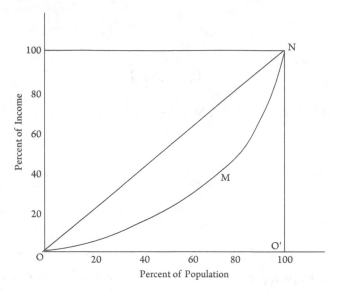

Figure A3.1 The Gini Coefficient

The Gini coefficient is the ratio of the area trapped between diagonal ON and curve OMN to the area of triangle OO'N. The closer OMN is to the diagonal ON, the smaller this ratio and the more equal the income distribution. To see why, observe that as we increase the share of the households at the bottom of the distribution (i.e., near point O), curve OMN moves inside and closer to the diagonal near origin O and the ratio measuring the Gini coefficient declines. Likewise, lowering the share of the households near the top of the distribution involves making OMN flatter near point N, which also moves OMN inside and toward the diagonal. Alternatively, recall that the diagonal ON represents the most equal distribution. Therefore, it is intuitively plausible that the closer OMN is to the diagonal, the more equal the income distribution. In the limit, if OMN coincides with the diagonal, the ratio defining the Gini coefficient drops to zero, its minimum possible value. At the other extreme, if the entire income is concentrated in the last household, OMN coincides with triangle OO'N and the ratio defining the Gini coefficient rises to 1, its maximum possible value.

An important point to observe is that the Gini coefficient is a very aggregative measure. While convenient due to its simplicity, it can also mask important differences between income distributions. For example, think of one distribution for which curve OMN moves along the diagonal for the bottom 20 percent of households but lies below the diagonal for the remaining population, and another distribution for which curve OMN moves along the diagonal for the top 20 percent of households but lies below the diagonal for the remaining households. Assume further that other than this difference, the two distributions are entirely symmetric relative to diagonal ON. They will then be associated with the same value of the Gini coefficient despite being quite different. A society that values equality at the bottom and is willing to tolerate inequality at the top would prefer the first of these distributions to the second.

REFERENCES

Adelman, Irma, and Cynthia Taft Morris. 1973. *Economic Growth and Social Equity in Developing Countries*. Stanford, CA: Stanford University Press.

Ahluwalia, Montek Singh. 1976. "Inequality, Poverty and Development." *Journal of Development Economics* 3: 307–42.

Ahluwalia, M. S., N. G. Carter, and H. B. Chenery. 1979. "Growth and Poverty in Developing Countries." *Journal of Development Economics* 6: 299–341.

Aisbett, Emma, Ann Harrison, and Alix Peterson Zwane. 2008. "Globalization and Poverty: What Is the Evidence?" In *Trade, Growth and Poverty*, edited by Elias Dinopoulos, Pravin Krishna, Arvind Panagariya, and Kar-yiu Wong, 2:33–61. New York: Routledge.

Amiti, Mary, and Josef Konings. 2007. "Trade Liberalization, Intermediate Inputs, and Productivity: Evidence from Indonesia." *American Economic Review* 97: 1611–38.

Amsden, Alice. 1989. *Asia's Next Giant: South Korea and Late Industrialization*. New York: Oxford University Press.

Aw, Bee-Yan. 1991. "Singapore." In *Liberalizing Foreign Trade: Lessons of Experience in the Developing World*, edited by Demetris Papageorgiou, Armeane Choksi, and Michael Michaely, 2: 309–428. Cambridge, MA: Basil Blackwell.

Aw, Bee-Yan, Sukkyun Chung, and Mark J. Roberts. 2000. "Productivity and Turnover in the Export Market: Micro-Level Evidence from the Republic of Korea and Taiwan (China)." *World Bank Economic Review* 14, no. 1: 65–90.

Balassa, B. 1982. "Development Strategies and Economic Performance: A Comparative Analysis of Eleven Semi-industrialized Economies." In *Development Strategies in Semi-industrialized Economies*, edited by B. Balassa, 38–62. Baltimore: Johns Hopkins University Press.

Baldwin, R. F. 1969. "The Case Against Infant-Industry Tariff Protection." *Journal of Political Economy* 77, nos. 5–6: 295–305.

Baldwin, R., T. J. Chen, and D. Nelson. 1995. *Political Economy of U.S.-Taiwan Trade*. Ann Arbor: University of Michigan Press.

Banerjee, Abhijit, Angus Deaton, Nora Lustig, and Ken Rogoff. 2006. "An Evaluation of World Bank Research, 1998-2005." Washington, DC: World Bank. https://openknowledge .worldbank.org/handle/10986/17896

Bardhan, Pranab K. 1971. "On Optimum Subsidy to a Learning Industry: An Aspect of the Theory of Infant-Industry Protection." *International Economic Review* 12, no. 1: 54–70.

Bastable, Charles, F. 1887. *The Theory of International Trade*. Dublin: Hodges, Figgis.

Bastiat, Frederic. 1845 (1996). *Economic Sophisms*, edited and translated by Arthur Goddard. Irvington-on-Hudson, NY: Foundation for Economic Education.

Beason, Richard, and David E. Weinstein. 1996. "Growth, Economies of Scale, and Targeting in Japan (1955–1990)." *Review of Economics and Statistics* 78, no. 2: 286–95.

Bhagwati, Jagdish. 1978. *Foreign Trade Regimes and Economic Development: Anatomy and Consequences of Exchange Rate Regimes*. New York: National Bureau of Economic Research.

Bhagwati, Jagdish. 1988a. "Export-Promoting Trade Strategy: Issues and Evidence." *World Bank Research Observer* 3: 27–58.

Bhagwati, Jagdish. 1988b. "Poverty and Public Policy." *World Development* 16, no. 5: 539–55.

Bhagwati, Jagdish. 1999. "The 'Miracle' That Did Happen." In *Taiwan's Development Experience: Lessons on Roles of Government and Market*, edited by Erik Thorbecke and Henry Wan, 21–39. Boston: Kluwer Academic Publishers.

Bhagwati, Jagdish. 2002. *Going Alone: The Case for Relaxed Reciprocity in Freeing Trade.* Cambridge, MA: MIT Press.

Bhagwati, Jagdish. 2004. *In Defense of Globalization.* New York: Oxford University Press.

Bhagwati Jagdish, and Padma Desai. 1970. *India: Planning for Industrialization.* London: Oxford University Press.

Bhagwati, Jagdish, and Arvind Panagariya. 2013. *Why Growth Matters.* New York: Public Affairs.

Bhagwati, Jagdish, Arvind Panagariya, and T. N. Srinivasan. 1998. *Lectures on International Trade.* Cambridge, MA: MIT Press.

Bhagwati, Jagdish, and V. K. Ramaswami. 1963. "Domestic Distortions, Tariffs, and the Theory of Optimum Subsidy." *Journal of Political Economy* 71: 44–50.

Bhagwati, Jagdish, and T. N. Srinivasan. 1975. *Foreign Trade Regimes and Economic Development: India.* New York: National Bureau of Economic Research.

Bhalla, Surjit, and Tirthatanmoy Das. 2006. "Pre- and Post-Reform India: A Revised Look at Employment, Wages and Inequality." *India Policy Forum* 2: 182–253.

Billmeier, Andreas, and Tommaso Nannicini. 2013. "Assessing Economic Liberalization Episodes: A Synthetic Control Approach." *Review of Economics and Statistics* 95: 983–1001.

Branstetter, Lee, and Nicholas Lardy. 2006. "China's Embrace of Globalization." NBER Working Paper no. 12373, National Bureau of Economic Research.

Brecher, Richard. 1974a. "Minimum Wage Rates and the Pure Theory of International Trade." *Quarterly Journal of Economics* 88: 98–116.

Brecher, Richard. 1974b. "Optimal Commercial Policy for a Minimum Wage Economy." *Journal of International Economics* 4: 139–49.

Buffie, E. F. 1989. "Mexico 1985–86: From Stabilizing Development to the Debt Crisis." In *Developing Country Debt and Economic Performance*, edited by Jeffrey D. Sachs, 141–68. Chicago: University of Chicago Press.

Chang, Ha-Joon. 2002. *Kicking Away the Ladder: Development Strategy in Historical Perspective.* London: Anthem World Economics.

Chang, Ha-Joon. 2007. *Bad Samaritans: Rich Nations, Poor Policies and the Threat to the Developing World.* London: Random House Business Books.

Chen, Shaohua, and Martin Ravallion. 2004. "How Have the World's Poorest Fared Since the Early 1980s?" *World Bank Research Observer* 19, no 2: 141–70.

Clerides, Sofronis K., Saul Lach, and James R. Tybout. 1998. "Is Learning By Exporting Important? Micro-Dynamic Evidence from Colombia, Mexico, and Morocco." *Quarterly Journal of Economics* 113, no. 3: 903–47.

Cline, William R. 1975. "Distribution and Development: A Survey of Literature." *Journal of Development Economics* 1, no. 4: 359–400.

Corbo, V., Anne Krueger, and Fernando Ossa. 1985. "Introduction." In *Export-Oriented Development Strategies: The Success of Five Newly Industrializing Countries*, edited by V. Corbo, Anne Krueger, and Fernando Ossa. Boulder, CO: Westview Press.

Coe, David, Elhanan Helpman, and Alexander Hoffmaister. 1997. "North-South Spillovers." *Economic Journal* 107: 134–49.

Corden, Max. 1974 (1997). *Trade Policy and Economic Welfare.* Oxford: Clarendon Press.

Corden, W. M., and R. Findlay. 1975. "Urban Unemployment Inter-Sectoral Capital Mobility and Development Policy." *Economica* 42: 59–78.

Dean, Judith M., K. C. Fung, and Zhi Wang. 2011. "Measuring Vertical Specialization: The Case of China." *Review of International Economics* 19, no. 4: 609–25.

Deininger, Klaus, and Lyn Squire. 1996. "A New Data Set Measuring Income Inequality." *World Bank Economic Review* 10, no. 3: 565–91.

DeLong, J. Bradford. 2003. "India Since Independence: An Analytic Growth Narrative." In *In Search of Prosperity: Analytic Narratives of Economic Growth*, edited by Dani Rodrik. Princeton, NJ: Princeton University Press.

Dollar, David, and Aart Kraay. 2002a. "Trade, Growth and Poverty." *Economic Journal* 114, no. 493: F22–F49.

Dollar, David, and Aart Kraay. 2002b. "Growth Is Good for the Poor." *Journal of Economic Growth* 7, no. 3: 195–225.

Dollar, David, and Aart Kraay. 2002c. "Spreading the Wealth." *Foreign Affairs*, January/February, 120–33.

Dollar, David, and Kenneth Sokoloff. 1990. "Patterns of Productivity Growth in South Korean Manufacturing Industries, 1963–1979." *Journal of Development Economics* 33: 309–27.

Dossani, Rafiq. 2006. "Globalization and the Offshoring of Services." In *Brookings Trade Forum 2005: Offshoring White-Collar Work*, edited by Lael Brainard and Susan Collins, 241–67. Washington, DC: Brookings Institution.

Easterly, William. 2002. *The Elusive Quest for Growth: Economists' Adventures and Misadventures in the Tropics.* Cambridge, MA: MIT Press.

Eckstein, Alexander. 1975. *China's Economic Development: The Interplay of Scarcity and Ideology.* Ann Arbor: University of Michigan Press.

Edwards, Sebastian. 2012. "Is Tanzania a Success Story? A Long Term Analysis." NBER Working Paper no. 17764, National Bureau of Economic Research.

Edwards, Sebastian, and Daniel Lederman. 2002. "The Political Economy of Unilateral Liberalization: The Case of Chile." In *Going Alone: The Case of Relaxed Reciprocity in Freeing Trade*, edited by Jagdish Bhagwati. Cambridge, MA: MIT Press.

Encyclopaedia Britannica. 2010a. "Great Leap Forward." *Encyclopedia Britannica Online.* Jan. 14, 2010. http://search.eb.com.ezproxy.cul.columbia.edu/eb/article-9037865.

Encyclopaedia Britannica. 2010b. "China." *Encyclopedia Britannica Online.* Jan. 14, 2010 http://search.eb.com.ezproxy.cul.columbia.edu/eb/article-71850.

Estevadeordal, Antoni, and Alan Taylor. 2013. "Is the Washington Consensus Dead? Growth, Openness, and the Great Liberalization, 1970s–2000s." *Review of Economics and Statistics* 95: 1669–90.

Fan, Shenggen, Ravi Kanbur, and Xiaobo Zhang. 2009. *Regional Inequality in China.* London: Routledge.

Fields, Gary. 1980. *Poverty, Inequality and Development.* Cambridge: Cambridge University Press.

Fields, Gary. 1984. "Employment, Income Distribution and Economic Growth in Seven Small Open Economies." *Economic Journal* 94, no. 373: 74–83.

Fields, Gary. 1989. "Changes in Poverty and Inequality in Developing Countries." *World Bank Research Observer* 4, no. 2: 167–85.

Findlay, Ronald, and Kevin H. O'Rourke. 2007. *Power and Plenty: Trade, War, and the World Economy in the Second Millennium.* Princeton, NJ: Princeton University Press.

Frank, Charles R. Jr., Kwang Suk Kim, and Larry E. Westphal. 1975. *Foreign Trade Regimes and Economic Development: South Korea.* New York: National Bureau of Economic Research.

Frankel, Jeffrey, and David Romer. 1999. "Does Trade Cause Growth?" *American Economic Review* 89, no. 3: 379–99.

Frankel, Jeffrey, and Andrew Rose. 2002. "An Estimate of the Effect of Common Currencies on Trade and Income." *Quarterly Journal of Economics* 117, no. 2: 437–66.

Galenson, Walter. 1977. Economic Growth, Income and Employment." Paper presented at the conference on Poverty and Development in Latin America, Yale University, April.

Galenson, Walter. 1979. "The Labor Force, Wages, and Living Standard." In *Economic Growth and Structural Change in Taiwan: The Postwar Experience of the Republic of China*, edited by Walter Galenson, 384–47. Ithaca, NY: Cornell University Press.

Gallup, John L., Steven Radelet, and Andrew Warner. 1998. "Economic Growth and the Income of the Poor." Harvard Institute for International Development, November.

General Agreement on Tariffs and Trade. 1994. *Trade Policy Review: Hong Kong*, vol. 1. Geneva: GATT.

George, Henry. 1886 (1949). *Protection or Free Trade: An Examination of the Tariff Question, with Special Reference to the Interests of Labor.* New York: Robert Schalkenbach Foundation.

Goldberg, Pinelopi Koujianou and Nina Pavcnik, 2007. "Distributional Effects of Globalization in Developing Countries." *Journal of Economic Literature* 45, no 1: 39–82.

Greenwald, Bruce, and Joseph E. Stiglitz. 2006. "Helping Infant Economies Grow: Foundations of Trade Policies for Developing Countries." *American Economic Review* 96, no. 2: 141–46.

Grossman, Gene, and Henrik Horn. 1988. "Infant-Industry Protection Reconsidered: The Case of Informational Barriers to Entry." *Quarterly Journal of Economics* 103, no. 4: 767–87.

Grubel, H. G. 1966. "The Anatomy of Classical and Modern Infant Industry Arguments." *Weltwirtschaftliches Archiv* 97, no. 2: 325–44.

Haltiwanger, John. 2012. "Job Creation and Firm Dynamics in the United States." In *Innovation and the Economy*, edited by Josh Lerner and Scott Stern, 12:17–38. Chicago: University of Chicago Press.

Hamilton, Alexander. 1913. *Report on Manufactures [1791]*. Presented by Mr. Smoot. August 30. 63rd Congress, 1st Session, Document no. 172.

Hanson, Gordon. 2010. "Why Isn't Mexico Rich?" NBER Working Paper no. 16470, National Bureau of Economic Research.

Hanushek, Eric A., and Ludger Woessmann. 2011. "The Economics of International Differences in Educational Achievement." In *Handbook of the Economics of Education*, edited by Eric A. Hanushek, Stephen Machin, and Ludger Woessmann, 3:89–200. Amsterdam: North Holland.

Harris, J. R., and M. P. Todaro. 1970. "Migration, Unemployment and Development: A Two-Sector Analysis." *American Economic Review* 60: 126–42.

Harvie, Charles, and Hyun-Hoon Lee. 2003. "Export Led Industrialization and Growth: Korea's Economic Miracle 1962–1989." *Australian Economic History Review* 43, no. 3: 256–86.

Hasan, Rana, Devashish Mitra, and Beyza Ural. 2007. "Trade Liberalization, Labor Market Institutions and Poverty Reduction: Evidence from Indian States." *India Policy Forum* 3: 71–122.

Hausmann, Ricardo, and Dani Rodrik. 2003. "Economic Development as Self-Discovery." *Journal of Development Economics* 72, no. 2: 603–33.

Ho, Samuel P. S. 1979. "Rural-Urban Imbalances in South Korea in the 1970s." *Asian Survey* 19, no. 7: 645–59.

Imbs, Jean, and Romain Wacziarg. 2003. "Stages of Diversification." *American Economic Review* 93, no. 1: 63–86.

Irwin, Douglas. 1996. *Against the Tide*. Princeton, NJ: Princeton University Press.

Irwin, Douglas. 2004a. "The Aftermath of Hamilton's 'Report on Manufactures.'" *Journal of Economic History* 64, no. 3: 800–21.

Irwin, Douglas. 2004b. "Review of *Kicking Away the Ladder: Development Strategy in Perspective*." https://eh.net/book_reviews/kicking-away-the-ladder-development-strategy-in-historical-perspective (Accessed December 16, 2017).

Irwin, Douglas. 2005. *Free Trade Under Fire*. Princeton, NJ: Princeton University Press.

Jeter, Jon. 2009. *Flat Broke in the Free Market*. New York: W. W. Norton.

Johnson, Harry G. 1965. "Optimal Trade Intervention in the Presence of Domestic Distortions." In *Trade, Growth and Balance of Payments*, edited by R. Caves, H. Johnson, and P. Kenen, 3–34. Chicago: Rand McNally .

Joshi, Vijay, and I. M. D. Little. 1994. *India: Macroeconomics and Political Economy: 1961–91*. Washington, DC: World Bank.

Kanbur, Ravi. 2001. "Economic Policy, Distribution and Poverty: The Nature of the Disagreements." *World Development* 29, no. 6: 1083–94.

Keller, Wolfgang. 2004. "International Technology Diffusion." *Journal of Economic Literature* 42: 752–82.

Kemp, M. C. 1960. "The Mill-Bastable Infant Industry Dogma." *Journal of Political Economy* 68: 65–67.

Khatkhate, Deena. 2006. "Indian Economic Reform: A Philosopher's Stone." *Economic and Political Weekly* 41, no. 22: 2203–05.

Kraay, Aart. 2006. "When Is Growth Pro-Poor? Evidence from a Panel of Countries." *Journal of Development Economics* 80, no. 1: 198–227.

Kohli, A. 2006. "Politics of Economic Growth in India, 1980–2005. Part I: The 1980s." *Economic and Political Weekly*, April 1, 1251–59.

Koopman, Robert, Zhi Wang, and Shang-Jin Wei. 2008. "How Much of Chinese Exports Is Really Made In China? Assessing Domestic Value-Added When Processing Trade Is Pervasive." NBER Working Paper 14109, National Bureau of Economic Research.

Krueger, Anne. 1978. *Foreign Trade Regime and Economic Development: Liberalization Attempts and Consequences*. New York: National Bureau of Economic Research.

Krueger, Anne. 1997. "Trade Policy and Economic Development: How We Learn." *American Economic Review* 81, no. 1: 1–22.

Krueger, Anne. 2004. "Opening Remarks." Speech delivered to the African Governors of the International Monetary Fund, October 4. http://www.imf.org/external/np/speeches/2004/100404.htm.

Krugman, Paul. 1979. "Increasing Returns, Monopolistic Competition, and International Trade." *Journal of International Economics* 9: 469–79.

Krugman, Paul. 1994a. "Proving My Point." *Foreign Affairs* 73, no. 4: 198–202.

Krugman, Paul. 1994b. "The Myth of Asia's Miracle." *Foreign Affairs* 73, no. 6: 62–78.

Kuo, Shirley W. Y. 1999. "Government Policy in the Taiwanese Development Process: The Past 50 Years." In *Taiwan's Development Experience: Lessons on Roles of Government and Market*, edited by Erik Thorbecke and Henry Wan, 43–93. Boston: Kluwer Academic Publishers.

Kuznets, Simon. 1979. "Growth and Structural Shifts." In *Economic Growth and Structural Change in Taiwan: The Postwar Experience of the Republic of China*, edited by Walter Galenson, 15–131. Ithaca, NY: Cornell University Press.

Kwon, Huck-Ju, and Ilcheong Yi. 2008. "Economic Development and Poverty Reduction in Korea: Governing Multifunctional Institutions." *Development and Change* 40, no. 4: 769–92.

Lal, Deepak, and Sarath Rajapatirana. 1987. "Foreign Trade Regimes and Economic Growth in Developing Countries." *World Bank Research Observer* 2, no. 2: 189–217.

Lall, Sanjay. 2003. "Roberts on Infant Industries: Another Comment." *Oxford Development Studies* 31, no. 1: 14–17.

Lardy, N. 2002. *Integrating China into the Global Economy*. Washington, DC: Brookings Institution.

Lee, T. H., and Kuo-Shu Liang. 1982. "Taiwan." In *Development Strategies in Semi-industrialized Economies*, edited by Bela Balassa, 310–50. Baltimore: Johns Hopkins University Press.

Lewin, Michael. 2011. "Botswana's Success: Good Governance, Good Policies and Good Luck." In *Yes Africa Can: Success Stories from a Dynamic Continent*, edited by Pum Chuhan-Pole and Manka Angwafo. Washington, DC: World Bank.

Li, Hongyi, Lyn Squire, and Heng-Fu Zou. 1998. "Explaining International and Intertemporal Variations in Income Inequality." *Economic Journal* 108, no. 446: 26–43.

Liang, Kuo-shu, and Ching-ing Hou Liang. 1976. "Exports and Employment in Taiwan." In *Conference on Population and Economic Development in Taiwan*. Taipei: Institute of Economics, Academia Sinica.

Lin, Ching-Yuan. 1973. *Industrialization in Taiwan: 1946–72*. New York: Praeger.

Lin, Justin. 1994. "Chinese Agriculture: Institutional Changes and Performance." In *Agriculture and Trade in China and India*, edited by T. N. Srinivasan. San Francisco: International Center for Economic Growth.

List, Frederick. 1856. *National System of Political Economy*. Translated by E. A. Matile. Philadelphia: J. B. Lippincott.

Little, I. M. D. 1960. "The Strategy of Indian Development." *National Institute Economic Review* 9, no. 1: 20–29.

Little, I. M. D. 1979. "An Economic Reconnaissance." In *Economic Growth and Structural Change in Taiwan: The Postwar Experience of the Republic of China*, edited by Walter Galenson. Ithaca, NY: Cornell University Press.

Little, I. M. D. 1996a. "India's Economic Reforms 1991–96." *Journal of Asian Economics* 7, no. 2: 161–76.

Little, I. M. D. 1996b. "Picking Winners: East Asian Experience." Social Market Foundation occasional paper, February 1.

Little, Ian, Tibor Scitovsky, and Maurice Scott. 1970. *Industry and Trade in Some Developing Countries*. London: Oxford University Press.

Lloyd, P. J., and R. J. Sandilands. 1986. "The Trade Sector in a Very Open Re-export Economy." In *Singapore: Resources and Growth*, edited by Chong-Yah Lim and P. J. Lloyd, 183–219. Singapore: Oxford University Press.

Lopez-Cordova, Ernesto. 2012. "Mexican Unilateral Liberalization in the Middle of the Economic Crisis." GTA Analytical Paper no. 2. CEPR and Global Trade Alert.

Lucas, Robert. 1988. "On the Mechanics of Economic Development." *Journal of Monetary Economics* 22, no. 1: 3–42.

Lundberg, Erik. 1979. "Fiscal and Monetary Policies." In *Economic Growth and Structural Change in Taiwan: The Postwar Experience of the Republic of China*, edited by Walter Galenson, 263–307. Ithaca, NY: Cornell University Press.

Macedo, Jorge Braga de, and Luís Brites Pereira, 2010. "Cape Verde and Mozambique as Development Successes in West and Southern Africa." NBER Working Paper 16552, National Bureau of Economic Research.

Mayer, Wolfgang. 1984. "The Infant-Export Industry Argument." *Canadian Journal of Economics* 17: 249–69.

McKinnon, Ronald. 1971. "On Misunderstanding the Capital Constraint in LDCs: The Implications for Foreign Trade Policy." In *Trade, Balance of Payments, and Growth: Essays in Honor of C. P. Kindleberger*, edited by J. Bhagwati et al. Amsterdam: North Holland Press.

McKinnon, Ronald. 1973. *Money and Capital in Economic Development*. Washington, DC: Brookings Institution.

Meade, James. 1955. *Trade and Welfare*. London: Oxford University Press.

Melitz, Marc. 2003. "The Impact of Trade on Intra-Industry Reallocations and Aggregate Industry Productivity." *Econometrica* 71: 1695–725.

Melitz, Marc. 2005. "When and How Should Infant Industries Be Protected?" *Journal of International Economics* 66: 177–96.

Mill, James. 1821. *Elements of Political Economy*. London: Baldwin, Cradock & Joy.

Mill, John Stuart. 1848 (1909). *Principles of Political Economy*. London: Longmans, Green.

Mitra, Devashish. 2016. "Trade Liberalization and Poverty Reduction." *IZA World of Labor*, June, http://wol.iza.org/articles/trade-liberalization-and-poverty-reduction-1.pdf.

Mulligan, C., and X. Sala-i-Martin. 1993. "Transitional Dynamics in Two-Sector Models of Endogenous Growth." *Quarterly Journal of Economics* 108, no. 3: 739–73.

Murphy, K., A. Shleifer, and R. Vishny. 1989. "Industrialization and the Big Push." *Journal of Political Economy* 97: 1003–26.

Myint, Hla. 1958. "The 'Classical Theory' of International Trade and the Underdeveloped Countries." *Economic Journal* 68, no. 270: 317–37.

Nam, Chong Hyun. 1981. "Trade and Industrial Policies, and the Structure of Protection in Korea." In *Trade and Growth of the Advanced Developing Countries in the Pacific Basin*, edited by Wontack Hong and Lawrence B. Krause, 187–211. Seoul: Korea Development Institute Press.

Naughton, Barry. 2007. *The Chinese Economy: Transitions and Growth*. Cambridge, MA: MIT Press.

Nayyar, D. 2006. "Economic Growth in Independent India: Lumbering Elephant or Running Tiger?" *Economic and Political Weekly*, April 15, 1451–58.

Nehru, Jawaharlal. 1946. *The Discovery of India*. New York: John Day.

Niimi, Yoko, Puja Vasudeva-Dutta, and Alan Winters. 2003. "Trade Liberalization and Poverty Dynamics in Vietnam." Prus Working Paper no. 17. University of Sussex, Brighton, UK.

Norman, Victor. 1995. "Discussion." *Economic Policy* 20: 101–3.

Ow, Chin-Hock. 1986. "The Role of Government in Economic Development: The Singapore Experience." In *Singapore: Resources and Growth*, edited by Chong-Yah Lim and P. J. Lloyd, 221–67. Singapore: Oxford University Press.

Panagariya, Arvind. 1980. "Variable Returns to Scale in Production and Patterns of Specialization." *American Economic Review* 71, no. 1: 221–30.

Panagariya, Arvind. 1993. "Unravelling the Mysteries of China's Foreign Trade Regime." *World Economy* 16, no. 1: 51–68.

Panagariya, Arvind. 1994. "Why and Why-Not of Uniform Tariffs." *Economic Studies Quarterly* 45, no. 3: 303–21.

Panagariya, Arvind. 2002a. "Cost of Protection: Where Do We Stand?" *American Economic Review: Papers and Proceedings*, May, 175–79.

Panagariya, Arvind. 2002b. "Trade Liberalization in Asia." In *Going Alone*, edited by Jagdish Bhagwati, 219–301. Cambridge, MA: MIT Press.

Panagariya, Arvind. 2004a. "Miracles and Debacles: In Defense of Trade Openness." *World Economy* 27, no. 8: 1149–71.

Panagariya, Arvind. 2004b. "Growth and Reforms During 1980s and 1990s." *Economic and Political Weekly*, June 19, 2581–94.

Panagariya, Arvind. 2008. *India: The Emerging Giant*. New York: Oxford University Press.

Panagariya, Arvind. 2018. "Return of Protectionism: Panagariya Sounds Alarm Bells over Modi's New Trade Template for India." *Economic Times*, February 12, https://economictimes .indiatimes.com/news/economy/policy/budget-2018-has-ensured-the-return-of-protectionism/articleshow/62876012.cms (accessed March 28, 2018).

Panagariya, Arvind, and Vishal More. 2014. "Poverty by Social, Religious and Economic Groups in India and Its Largest States: 1993–94 to 2011–12." *Indian Growth and Development Review* 7, no. 2: 202–30.

Planning Commission. 1962. *Perspectives of Development 1961–76: Implications of Planning for a Minimum Level of Living*. New Delhi: Planning Commission.

Pursell, Garry. 1992. "Trade Policy in India." In *National Trade Policies*, edited by Dominick Salvatore, 123 58. New York: Greenwood Press.

Raj, K. N. 1973. "The Politics and Economics of 'Intermediate Regimes.'" *Economic and Political Weekly*, July 7.

Ranis, Gustav. 1979. "Industrial Development." In *Economic Growth and Structural Change in Taiwan: The Postwar Experience of the Republic of China*, edited by Walter Galenson, 206–62. Ithaca, NY: Cornell University Press.

Ranis, Gustav. 1999. "The Trade-Growth Nexus in Taiwan's Development." In *Taiwan's Development Experience: Lessons on Roles of Government and Market*, edited by Erik Thorbecke and Henry Wan, 113–40. Boston: Kluwer Academic Publishers.

Ranis, Gustav. 2003. "Symposium on Infant Industries: A Comment." *Oxford Development Studies* 31, no. 1: 33–35.

Ravallion, Martin. 2003. "The Debate on Globalization, Poverty and Inequality: Why Measurement Matters." World Bank Development Research Group Working Paper 3038.

Ravallion, Martin. 2004. "Globalization and Inequality." In *Brookings Trade Forum 2004*, edited by S. Collins and C. Graham, 1–23. Washington, DC: Brookings Institution.

Ravallion, Martin, and Shaohua Chen. 1997. "What Can New Survey Data Tell Us About Recent Changes in Distribution and Poverty?" *World Bank Economic Review* 11, no. 2: 357–82.

Ravallion, Martin, and Shaohua Chen. 2007. "China's (Uneven) Progress Against Poverty." *Journal of Development Economics* 82, no. 1: 1–42.

Reinert, Erik. 2007. *How Rich Countries Got Rich and Why Poor Countries Stay Poor*. London: Constable and Robinson.

Ricardo, David. 1817. *On the Principles of Political Economy and Taxation*. London: John Murray.

Rodriguez, Francisco, and Dani Rodrik. 2000. "Trade Policy and Economic Growth: A Skeptic's Guide to the Cross-National Evidence." In *NBER Macroeconomics Annual 2000*, edited by Ben S. Bernanke and Kenneth Rogoff. Cambridge, MA: MIT Press.

Rodrik, Dani. 1995. "Getting Interventions Right: How South Korea and Taiwan Grew Rich." *Economic Policy* 20: 55–107.

Rodrik, Dani. 1996. "Coordination Failures and Government Policy: A model with Applications to East Asia and Eastern Europe." *Journal of International Economics* 40: 1–22.

Rodrik, Dani. 1999. *The New Global Economy and Developing Countries: Making Openness Work*. Washington, DC: Overseas Development Council.

Rodrik, Dani. 2000. "Comment on Frankel and Rose." Kennedy School of Government, Harvard University.

Rodrik, Dani. 2003. "Institutions, Integration, and Geography: In Search of the Deep Determinants of Economic Growth." In *In Search of Prosperity: Analytic Narratives of Economic Growth*, edited by Dani Rodrik. Princeton, NJ: Princeton University Press.

Rodrik, Dani. 2006. "Industrial Development: Stylized Facts and Policies." In *Industrial Development for the 21st Century: Sustainable Development Perspectives*, edited by David O'Connor, 7–28. New York: UN-DESA.

Rodrik, Dani. 2007. *One Economics, Many Recipes: Globalization, Institutions, and Economic Growth*. Princeton, NJ: Princeton University Press.

Rodrik, Dani, and Arvind Subramanian. 2005. "From 'Hindu Growth' to Productivity Surge: The Mystery of the Indian Growth Transition." IMF Staff Papers, 52/2.

Roemer, Michael, and Mary K. Gugerty. 1997. "Does Economic Growth Reduce Poverty?" Harvard Institute of International Development, March.

Romer, Paul. 1986. "Increasing Returns and Long-Run Growth." *Journal of Political Economy* 94, no. 5: 1002–37.

Romer, Paul, 1994. "New Goods, Old Theory, and the Welfare Costs of Trade Restrictions." *Journal of Development Economics* 43: 5–38.

Rosenstein-Rodan, P. 1943. "Problems of Industrialization of Eastern and South-Eastern Europe." *Economic Journal* 53: 202–11.

Rosenstein-Rodan, P. 1961. "Notes on the Theory of the 'Big Push.'" In *Economic Development for Latin America*, edited by H. S. Ellis and H. C. Wallich. New York: St. Martin's.

Ruffin, Roy. 2002. "David Ricardo's Discovery of Comparative Advantage." *History of Political Economy* 34, no. 4: 727–48.

Samuelson, P. A. 1969. "The Way of an Economist." In *International Economic Relations: Proceedings of the Third Congress of the International Economic Association*, edited by P. A. Samuelson, 1–11. London: Macmillan.

Schifferes, Steve. 2007. "India's Reluctant Billionaire." BBC News, February 7.

Schumer, Charles, and Paul Craig Roberts. 2004. "Second Thoughts on Free Trade." *New York Times*, January 6.

Scott, Maurice. 1979. "Foreign Trade." In *Economic Growth and Structural Change in Taiwan: The Postwar Experience of the Republic of China*, edited by Walter Galenson, 308–83. Ithaca, NY: Cornell University Press.

Singapore Department of Trade. 1968. *Annual Report*. Singapore: Ministry of Finance.

Smith, Adam. 1776. *The Wealth of Nations*. London: J. M. Dent & Sons.

Solomon, Richard H., and Nigel Quinney. 2010. *American Negotiating Behavior: Wheeler-Dealers, Legal Eagles, Bullies, and Preachers*. Washington, DC: United States Institute of Peace.

Sortharith, Chap, and Chheang Vannarith. 2010. *Asean Free Trade Area and Cambodian Industries*. CICP e-book no. 6. Phnom Penh: Cambodian Institute for Cooperation and Peace.

Spence, Jonathan. 1990. *The Search for Modern China*. New York: W. W. Norton.

Srinivasan, T. N. 1994. "Overview." In *Agriculture and Trade in China and India*, edited by T. N. Srinivasan. San Francisco: International Center for Economic Growth.

Srinivasan, T. N. 2008. "Globalization and Poverty." In *Trade, Growth and Poverty*, edited by Elias Dinopoulos, Pravin Krishna, Arvind Panagariya, and Kar-yiu Wong. New York: Routledge.

Srinivasan, T. N., and S. Tendulkar. 2003. *Reintegrating India with the World Economy*. Washington, DC: Institute for International Economics.

Srinivasan, T. N., and Jagdish Bhagwati. 2001. "Outward-Orientation and Development: Are Revisionists Right?" In *Trade, Development and Political Economy: Essays in Honor of Anne Krueger*, edited by Deepak K. Lal and Richard Snape, 3–26. London: Palgrave.

Ssewanyana, Sarah, John Mary Matovu, and Evarist Twimukye. 2011. "Building on Growth in Uganda." In *Yes Africa Can: Success Stories from a Dynamic Continent*, edited by Pum Chuhan-Pole and Manka Angwafo. Washington, DC: World Bank.

Stiglitz, Joseph. 2002. *Globalization and Its Discontents*. New York: W. W. Norton.

Stiglitz, Joseph, and Andre Charlton. 2005. *Fair Trade For All—How Trade Can Promote Development*. Oxford: Oxford University Press.

Stolper, Wolfgang F., and Paul A. Samuelson. 1941. "Protection and Real Wages." *Review of Economic Studies* 9, no. 1: 58–73.

Subramanian, Arvind. 2007. "India Is Converging, but Why?" *Business Standard*, November 23.

Succar, Patricia. 1987. "The Need for Industrial Policy in LDC's-A Re-Statement of the Infant Industry Argument." *International Economic Review* 28, no. 2: 521–534.

Sun, C., and M. Y. Liang. 1982. "Savings in Taiwan in 1953–80." In *Experiences and Lessons of Economic Development in Taiwan*, ed. Guoding Li. Taipei: Institute of Economics, Academia Sinica.

Tan, Augustine H. H., and Chin Hock Ow. 1982. "Singapore." In *Development Strategies in Semi-industrialized Economies*, edited by Bela Balassa, 280–309. Baltimore: Johns Hopkins University Press.

Timmer, Peter. 1997. "How Well Do the Poor Connect to the Growth Process?" Harvard Institute for International Development, CAER II Discussion Paper #17, December.

Topalova, Petia. 2007. "Trade Liberalization, Poverty and Inequality: Evidence from Indian Districts." In *Globalization and Poverty*, edited by Ann Harrison. Chicago: University of Chicago Press.

Tornell, Aaron, Frank Westermann, and Lorenza Martinez. 2004. "NAFTA and Mexico's Less-than-Stellar Performance." NBER Working Paper 10289, National Bureau of Economic Research.

Torrens, Robert. 1815. *Essays on the External Corn Trade*. London: J. Hatchard.

Van Assche, Ari, and Byron Gangnes. 2010. "Electronic Process Upgrading: Is China Exceptional?" *Applied Economics Letters* 17, no. 5: 477–82.

Ventura, J. 1997. "Growth and Interdependence." *Quarterly Journal of Economics* 112: 57–84.

Wacziarg, Romain, and Karen Horn Welch. 2008. "Trade Liberalization and Growth: New Evidence." *World Bank Economic Review* 22: 187–231.

Wade, Robert. 1990. *Governing the Market: Economic Theory and the Role of the Government in East Asian Industrialization*. Princeton, NJ: Princeton University Press, 1990.

Wade, Robert. 2002. "Globalization, Poverty and Income Distribution: Does the Liberal Argument Hold?" Working Paper 02-33. London School of Economics.

Wade, Robert. 2003. "Reply to John Roberts on Infant Industry Protection." *Oxford Development Studies* 31, no. 1: 8–14.

Wade, Robert. 2004. Governing the Market: Economic Theory and the Role of the Government in East Asian Industrialization. 2nd ed. Princeton, NJ: Princeton University Press.

Warner, Andrew. 2003. "Once More into the Breach: Economic Growth and Integration." Working Papers 34, Center for Global Development, Washington DC.

Westphal, Larry E. 1978. "The Republic of Korea's Experience with Export-Led Industrial Development." *World Development* 6: 347–82.

Westphal, Larry E. 1982. "Fostering Technological Mastery by Means of Selective Infant-Industry Protection." In *Trade, Stability, Technology and Equity in Latin America*, edited by Moshe Syrquin and Simon Teitel, 255–79. New York: Academic Press.

Westphal, Larry E. 1990. "Industrial Policy in an Export-Propelled Economy: Lessons from South Korea's Experience." *Journal of Economic Perspectives* 4, no. 3: 41–59.

Westphal, Larry E., and K. S. Kim. 1982. "Korea: Incentive Policies for Exports and Import Substitution." In *Development Strategies in Semi-industrialized Economies*, edited by B. Balassa, 212–79. Baltimore: Johns Hopkins University Press.

Winters, Alan, Neil McCulloch, and Andrew McKay. 2004. "Trade Liberalization and Poverty So Far." *Journal of Economic Literature* 42, no. 1: 72–115.

Wolf, Martin. 2004. *Why Globalization Works*. New Haven, CT: Yale University Press.

World Bank. 1983. *China: Socialist Economic Development*. 3 vols. PUB-3391. Washington, DC: World Bank.

World Bank. 1987. *India: An Industrializing Economy in Transition*. Report no. 6633-IN. Washington, DC: World Bank.

World Bank. 1988a. *India: Recent Developments and Medium Term Issues*. Report no. 7185-IN. Washington, DC: World Bank.

World Bank. 1988b. *China: External Trade and Capital*. PUB-6680. Washington, DC: World Bank.

World Bank. 1993. *The East Asian Miracle, Economic Growth, and Public Policy*. New York: Oxford University Press.

World Bank. 1999. *1999 Annual Review of Development Effectiveness*. Washington, DC: World Bank.

World Bank. 2000. *World Development Report 2000: Consultation Draft*. January. Washington, DC: World Bank.

World Bank. 2004. *Trade Policies in South Asia: An Overview*. Poverty Reduction and Economic Management Sector Unit, South Asia Region, Report no. 29949, September 7. Washington, DC: World Bank.

World Bank. 2014. *World Development Indicators Online*. Accessed October 2014.

World Trade Organization. 1998. *Trade Policy Review: India*. Geneva: WTO Secretariat.

World Trade Organization. 2000. *Trade Policy Review: Tanzania*. Geneva: WTO Secretariat.

World Trade Organization. 2002. *Trade Policy Review: India*. Geneva: WTO Secretariat.

Xu, Bin, and Jianmao Wang. 1999. "Capital Goods Trade and R&D Spillovers in the OECD." *Canadian Journal of Economics* 32, no. 5: 1258–74.

Yatawara, Ravindra. 2000. "Timing Is Everything: On the Determinants of Commercial Policy Changes." In *Essays on the Reform of Trade and Exchange*, 1–57. PhD dissertation, Columbia University, New York.

Yin, K. Y. 1954. "Adverse Trends in Taiwan's Industrial Development." *Industry of Free China*, August.

Yoo, Jungho. 1997. "Neoclassical Versus Revisionist View of Korean Economic Growth." Development Discussion Paper No. 588, Harvard Institute for International Development, Harvard University, Cambridge, MA.

Yu, Tzong-Shian. 1999. "A Balanced Budget, Stable Prices and Full Employment: The Macroeconomic Environment for Taiwan's Growth." In *Taiwan's Development Experience: Lessons on Roles of Government and Market*, edited by Erik Thorbecke and Henry Wan, 141–55. Boston: Kluwer Academic Publishers.

INDEX

The letter *f* following a page number denotes a figure. The letter *t* following a page number denotes a table.